AI-Driven Business Model Innovation

Maryam Khokhar
Tongji University, China

IGI Global
Scientific Publishing
Publishing Tomorrow's Research Today

Vice President of Editorial Melissa Wagner
Managing Editor of Acquisitions Mikaela Felty
Managing Editor of Book Development Jocelynn Hessler
Production Manager Mike Brehm
Cover Design Phillip Shickler

Published in the United States of America by
IGI Global Scientific Publishing
701 East Chocolate Avenue
Hershey, PA, 17033, USA
Tel: 717-533-8845
Fax: 717-533-8661
Website: https://www.igi-global.com E-mail: cust@igi-global.com

Library of Congress Cataloging-in-Publication Data

Names: Khokhar, Maryam, 1989- editor.
Title: AI-driven business model innovation / edited by: Maryam Khokhar.
Other titles: Artificial intelligence driven business model
Description: Hershey, PA : IGI Global Scientific Publishing, [2025] | Includes bibliographical references and index. | Summary: "This book aims to provide a comprehensive systematic literature review that delves into how AI can drive innovative business models that enhance profitability and contribute to environmental sustainability"-- Provided by publisher.
Identifiers: LCCN 2024054440 (print) | LCCN 2024054441 (ebook) | ISBN 9798369395714 (hardcover) | ISBN 9798369395721 (paperback) | ISBN 9798369395738 (ebook)
Subjects: LCSH: Business--Data processing. | Artificial intelligence--Industrial applications. | Sustainable development--Data processing.
Classification: LCC HF5548.2 .A53 2025 (print) | LCC HF5548.2 (ebook) | DDC 658/.0563--dc23/eng/20241002
LC record available at https://lccn.loc.gov/2024054440
LC ebook record available at https://lccn.loc.gov/2024054441

British Cataloguing in Publication Data
A Cataloguing in Publication record for this book is available from the British Library.

Table of Contents

Detailed Table of Contents

The rapid advancement of Artificial Intelligence (AI) in organisational training is revolutionizing learning and development. This research paper delves into the essential role of Human Resources (HR) in managing change during the shift to AI-enhanced learning systems. Utilizing a review method, this study examines the strategies HR departments employ to facilitate this transition. The research underscores the crucial role of clear communication, continuous training, and active employee participation in the change process. It highlights HR's responsibility in fostering a culture of adaptability and resilience, along with the importance of strategic planning and stakeholder engagement. Additionally, the study identifies common barriers to successful implementation, such as resistance to change and the necessity for HR professionals to develop AI competencies. This paper contributes valuable knowledge on best practices and potential challenges, offering guidance on how HR can effectively manage change amidst technological advancements.

The digital age has seen an unparalleled evolution in technology, particularly with immersive technologies like augmented reality (AR), virtual reality (VR), and mixed reality (MR), leading us toward a metaverse-defined future. This chapter explores their transformative impact on various industries as we stand on the brink of a convergence between digital and physical realms. Tracing the historical trajectory and pivotal milestones of AR and VR development, it examines their current state and convergence with domains like AI and IoT. Examining their applications across sectors such as healthcare, education, and retail, the chapter unveils innovative business models emerging within the metaverse. From redefining consumer behavior in e-commerce to revolutionizing traditional learning methods, immersive technologies are reshaping industries and necessitate understanding for individuals, businesses, and policymakers navigating this transformative landscape.

Artificial Intelligence (AI) is transforming the way businesses work, driving a fundamental instability in traditional business paradigms. This chapter addresses the role of AI in driving business model innovation, investigating how companies employ AI technologies to enhance decision-making, optimize processes, and generate new value propositions. By integrating AI into fundamental business processes, companies may change from static, linear models to dynamic, data-driven strategies, allowing for better scalability and agility. Through a series of case studies and examples, the chapter illustrates significant sectors and industries where AI-driven business models have arisen. It also covers the barriers to AI adoption, including technological, ethical, and organizational hurdles, and offers insights into future trends and the developing landscape of AI-powered business transformations.

AI is thus emerging as the progressive tool in the new business models given the efficiency it creates in the processes of decision making and operations. The application of business analytics especially through the use of AI can assist firms in arriving at better decisions since the make their decision based on a large amount of data. AI makes man's work simple, fast, efficient and close to perfect—thus fewer errors are likely to occur. The application of the analytical tools relates to the formulation of the plan based on the insight in order to attain strategic results. Moreover, AI chatbots and virtual assistants enhance the system of more advanced customer communication as well as customer experience. By analysing the market tendencies AI helps predict the future tendencies as well as enhancing the innovative aspect of business development such as providing new business models in terms of services, business, and data-as-service business. AI might improve delivery of service to the customers of the company, hence improving its competitiveness.

Businesses are fundamentally changing because of AI, allowing for a greater focus on creativity. The chapter introduces advancements in AI like machine learning, predictive analytics, and natural language processing that help boost customer service, operational efficiencies and asset monetization opportunities. Key considerations will include personalized customer engagements, process efficiencies, optimizing resources and planning to set up new business models—subscription-based services/platform economies, etc. Emerging technologies like artificial intelligence have broader implications in e-commerce, finance, manufacturing—showing how firms use AI strategies to gain competitive advantage and foster business growth. In addition, the chapter addresses ethical considerations like bias, privacy as well as workforce implications and their role in ensuring responsible AI practices. AI can improve flexibility, realizing the highest level of value and maintaining competitive advantage.

Preface

Artificial intelligence (AI) has emerged as a transformative force across industries, reshaping traditional business models and redefining value creation in unprecedented ways. As editors of this volume, we aim to provide a comprehensive exploration of how AI is driving business model innovation, addressing the challenges and opportunities it presents. From enhancing operational efficiency to fostering sustainability, AI is revolutionizing the core strategies that businesses employ to stay competitive in a rapidly evolving global economy.

This book serves as a bridge between theory and practice, offering insights from leading academics, industry practitioners, and innovators. It covers a broad spectrum of topics, including knowledge management, immersive technologies, customer value creation, and sustainable business practices. Each chapter contributes to a nuanced understanding of AI's role in fostering agility, scalability, and innovation. By presenting diverse perspectives, this collection equips readers with the knowledge to navigate and leverage AI-driven transformations effectively.

We are delighted to present this work to a wide audience, including researchers, policymakers, business leaders, and academicians. Whether you are exploring the potential of AI for strategic decision-making or understanding its societal implications, this book provides a foundation to engage with the complex interplay between technology and business innovation. As the world embraces a digital future, we hope this volume will inspire new ideas and contribute to meaningful discourse on AI's transformative potential.

The chapters in this book provide a comprehensive examination of how artificial intelligence (AI) is driving business model innovation across diverse industries and organizational practices. Each chapter offers a unique perspective on AI's role in shaping business strategies, enhancing operational efficiency, and fostering sustainable development. Through theoretical analysis, case studies, and practical recommendations, the contributors explore how AI is redefining core business functions such as customer service, human resources, and product development.

This section is designed to guide readers through the key themes and insights presented in each chapter. From understanding the role of human resources in AI-driven transitions to exploring the possibilities of immersive technologies and sustainability, each chapter addresses the essential components of AI-driven innovation. Readers will gain knowledge on both the challenges and opportunities posed by AI, as well as the ethical considerations that accompany its widespread adoption.

The following chapter summaries offer a clear roadmap of the book's content, enabling readers to identify areas of interest and relevance. Whether you are a business leader, researcher, or policymaker, these chapters provide essential insights to help you navigate the transformative impact of AI on business models, operational strategies, and value creation.

CHAPTER OVERVIEW

Chapter 1

This chapter investigates the critical role of human resources (HR) in facilitating the transition to AI-driven learning systems. Through strategic planning, continuous training, and stakeholder engagement, HR professionals foster adaptability and resilience, enabling organizations to navigate technological advancements effectively.

Chapter 2

Immersive technologies such as augmented reality (AR), virtual reality (VR), and mixed reality (MR) are transforming industries. This chapter explores their integration with AI and IoT, highlighting their applications in sectors like healthcare, education, and retail. It also examines innovative business models emerging within the metaverse.

Chapter 3

This chapter delves into how AI drives business model innovation, enabling companies to adopt data-driven strategies. Through case studies, it identifies key sectors where AI has enhanced decision-making, optimized processes, and fostered scalability, while addressing barriers to adoption and ethical considerations.

Chapter 4

Focusing on the Horn of Africa, this chapter examines how AI enhances customer value through innovation models. Employing advanced analytical techniques, it highlights AI's impact on business strategies and the importance of creative approaches in maximizing its benefits.

Chapter 5

Sustainability and innovation converge in this chapter, which offers theoretical and practical frameworks for embedding sustainable practices in business processes. It provides strategies for organizations aiming to achieve financial performance while addressing environmental and social challenges.

Chapter 6

This chapter explores AI's role in streamlining decision-making and improving operational efficiency. It discusses the application of AI analytics, chatbots, and market trend predictions to drive innovation and competitiveness in modern business models.

Chapter 7

AI advancements like machine learning and natural language processing are examined in this chapter. It emphasizes their impact on customer engagement, operational efficiency, and asset monetization while addressing ethical considerations to ensure responsible AI use.

Chapter 8

This chapter outlines the potential of AI in promoting sustainability through innovations in product design, supply chain transparency, and industry-wide collaboration. It underscores AI's role in creating environmentally friendly and economically viable business solutions.

Chapter 9

This concluding chapter highlights the synergy between business model innovation and AI. It offers insights into how these elements redefine enterprise capabilities, enabling organizations to adapt to evolving consumer needs and create new value streams.

Chapter 10

This study explores the transformative impact of Artificial Intelligence (AI) on business structures and employment in India, utilizing Structural Equation Modelling (SEM) to assess its effects on operational efficiency, innovation, and workforce dynamics. Findings indicate that AI significantly enhances corporate efficiency and innovation while necessitating workforce reskilling.

CONCLUSION

The rapid evolution of AI is not just a technological phenomenon but a profound reshaping of business landscapes. By integrating AI into organizational practices, companies can unlock new opportunities for innovation, sustainability, and competitiveness. The chapters in this book provide a roadmap for understanding and leveraging these opportunities, with actionable insights for diverse stakeholders.

As AI continues to advance, the necessity for collaboration between industries, governments, and academia becomes ever more critical. This volume emphasizes the importance of ethical considerations and strategic foresight to ensure that AI-driven transformations align with societal and environmental goals. By fostering interdisciplinary dialogue, we can collectively navigate the complexities of this digital era.

We thank the contributing authors and collaborators for their invaluable insights and efforts in creating this volume. It is our hope that this book will inspire readers to embrace AI as a catalyst for positive change and innovation, paving the way for a future defined by sustainable growth and shared prosperity.

Maryam Khokhar
Tongji University, China

Chapter 1
A Study of HR's Role in Managing the Shift to AI-Enhanced Knowledge Management Systems:
The Expedition From Resistance to Resilience

D. Baisakhi
https://orcid.org/0000-0002-3413-3405
Center for Management Studies, Jain University, Bengaluru, India

Harold A. Patrick
https://orcid.org/0009-0004-5349-6799
Center for Management Studies, Jain University, Bengaluru, India

Shilpa Sandhu
Center for Management Studies, Jain University, Bengaluru, India

Divya A. Reddy
https://orcid.org/0000-0003-4028-2981
Center for Management Studies, Jain University, Bengaluru, India

Richa Tiwari
https://orcid.org/0000-0002-4857-2580
Center for Management Studies, Jain University, Bengaluru, India

Manjit Kour
https://orcid.org/0000-0003-1043-3187
Chandigarh University, India

Manisha Tripathi
Center for Management Studies, Jain University, Bengaluru, India

ABSTRACT

The rapid advancement of Artificial Intelligence (AI) in organisational training is revolutionizing learning and development. This research paper delves into the

DOI: 10.4018/979-8-3693-9571-4.ch001

essential role of Human Resources (HR) in managing change during the shift to AI-enhanced learning systems. Utilizing a review method, this study examines the strategies HR departments employ to facilitate this transition. The research underscores the crucial role of clear communication, continuous training, and active employee participation in the change process. It highlights HR's responsibility in fostering a culture of adaptability and resilience, along with the importance of strategic planning and stakeholder engagement. Additionally, the study identifies common barriers to successful implementation, such as resistance to change and the necessity for HR professionals to develop AI competencies. This paper contributes valuable knowledge on best practices and potential challenges, offering guidance on how HR can effectively manage change amidst technological advancements.

1.0 INTRODUCTION

Industry 4.0 brought change in the production system of value chain system where the production value is organized centrally and digitized, automated, and self-synchronized via technology (Veza et al., 2015; Prifti et al., 2017). These innovations have created new forms of inter-organization relationships that are aimed at achieving strategic goals of efficient cost and resource management (Sivathanu et al., 2018). While I4.0 offers great potential for value co-creation in a broad range of industries (Leone et al., 2020), it poses multifaceted challenges to socio-technical systems. This evolution entails the need for new forms of meaning making regarding both longstanding and new entrant business, most notably in fields concerning the changing workforce dynamics which involve altered career jobs and new professional contingencies. In other words, for the sake of managing this change the creation of new types of skills in the workforce is required, especially for handling the implementation of automation and labor substitution (Devezas and Sarygulov, 2017; Lu, 2017; Ustundag and Cevikcan, 2018). One peculiar feature of this process is the growing integration of artificial intelligence (AI) into work domains, which complement human cognition skills by solving previously cognitive tasks (Tambe et al., 2019; Iaia et al., 2023). Therefore, the human-AI co-working calls for a right mix of social and technical and psychomotor skills in the workforce. Raising such a need for a more profound interlocution between humans and AI agents, this issue aims to focus on the lack of research in the area of collaboration concerning the effects of such partnership on employee Human Resource Management (HRM) related to their motivation and job satisfaction (Glickson and Woolley, 2020). Perhaps in a group of employees who are unmotivated or lack adequate skills, AI integration can lead to a creation of what is referred to as "Luddite anxiety" and therefore related technology suspicions that may slow the acceptance of AI as a reasonable addition to a workplace (Ferrario et al., 2020; Ostmeier and Strobel, 2022). Both managers and employees, therefore, must keep adjusting as AI progresses in the future. In this dynamic environment, human agents can achieve a state of balance if contributing to AI development and at the same reinforcing and developing our unique and valuable human endowment like instincts, integrative ability, and societal competency (Jarrahi, 2018). While such intuitive skills are critical, it is critical to go through a process to build the essential analytical skills and the ability to apply high-end technologies to organizational practices (Davenport and Kirby, 2016). It is becoming increasingly important to know who is able to manage this human-AI cooperation effectively (Pranciulyte-Bagdziūniene and Petraite, 2019; Del Giudice et al., 2023); it is crucial to determine who will work with AI systems further (Jarrahi, 2018; Herrmann and Pfeiffer, 2023). Still, this crucial problem is poorly researched, and thus, there is another gap in the literature (Sundaresan and Zhang, 2022). The present chapter intends

- To explore how HR assesses and counteracts employee resistance to AI Augmented Learning Systems.
- To assess the strategies which can be implemented by HR to foster adaptability and resilience among employees during the transition AI enabled learning systems.
- To examine the future consequence of integrating the AI-enhanced learning systems in the development of the employees and overall performance of the organization.

1.1 The Fourth Industrial Revolution and Transformation of Automation to Augmentation

The substantial and far-reaching impact of Industry 4.0 (I4.0) is evident, with new opportunities emerging for business models, jobs, organizational structures, and workflows (Maresova et al., 2018; Vrontis et al., 2022). This transformative revolution is reshaping society on a global scale by altering the incentives, rules, and norms that govern economic life. It has a profound effect on communication, learning, relationships, and the structures of firms (Deguchi et al., 2020). Conventional manufacturing firms are also gradually stepping into the I4.0 technologies for improving organizational performance, cost control, and quality-productivity convergence (Chiarini, 2021). Although integration, connectivity, automated decision-making, and adjustability are some benefits of I4.0 (Kusiak, 2018) or new technologies like IoT, CPS, Big Data, and AI require more professional workers (Mourtzis,2020). This presents a paradox for human resources: on one hand, automation and IoT are disrupting conventional manufacturing paradigms, and technologies like blockchain and AI are blurring the lines between the digital and physical realms (Kusiak, 2018; Mourtzis, 2020). At the same time, these technologies are in a way enlarging human capacities: increasing productivity and throughput/speed in a range of industries and sectors, and changing technical work processes. (Mourtzis, 2020). Amidst these developments, it is crucial to anticipate the impact of such technological changes on workers, particularly in terms of job security and working conditions. Digital technologies are enabling the breakdown of jobs into smaller, more task-oriented components (Holm & Lorenz, 2022), while servitization is leading to a more fragmented workforce (Brynjolfsson, 2022). Tasks that are difficult to automate, namely problem-solving, intuition, creativity, and persuasion remain reliant on human involvement, and there is a growing emphasis on soft skills like self-organization, emotional intelligence, and communication. These skills, coupled with the need for lifelong learning and digital proficiency, are increasingly important in the modern workforce (Spence, 2022).

Ensuring that human resources remain resilient, adaptable, and engaged is not only about addressing skill gaps but is also essential for developing new methods of human-machine interaction (Arslan et al., 2021; Ardito et al., 2022). However, the impact of the fourth industrial revolution on human resources has been uneven (Rana & Sharma, 2019). Two primary evolutionary paths can be identified through the lens of human-machine interaction (Spence, 2022): first, the IoT-based phase (or era of automation), which focuses on labor substitution (Weber, 2016; Del Giudice, 2016; Coupe, 2019); and second, the AI-based phase (or era of augmentation), characterized by the integration of human labor with machine capabilities (Sorko et al., 2016; Szabo-Szentgróti et al., 2021). As Spence (2022, p. 244) explains, "Automation involves replacing people with machines to perform certain repetitive tasks without human intervention or guidance. Augmentation, on the other hand, refers to adding machines into a work environment to increase human productivity."

1.2 "Augmentation"-The AI Enabled Phase

McAfee and Brynjolfsson (2017) emphasized that the automation phase has the potential to significantly disrupt labor markets. As automation replaces human labor, it may widen the gap between returns on capital and labor, leading to a net displacement of workers without prospects for reintegration (Brynjolfsson, 2022; Vrontis et al., 2022). This concern is backed by evidences as empirical studies that court affects employment negatively. At the same time, a rather rich literature has examined how AI might bring value propositions to human resources management, especially as a response to threats like job automation (Coupe, 2019; Ivanov & Webster, 2019; Arslan et al., 2021), evolving job requirements (Hmoud & Laszlo, 2019; Vrontis et al., 2022), and the need for new skill development (Arslan et al., 2021).

Up to now, the HR function has had a very utilitarian view of technology because its main concern has been to deliver skills support to threatened employees. However, a new wave of literature that has emerged more recently paints AI in a positive and transformative lens as it undertakes a new focus on how it will revolutionize HR to close the competency gaps arising from IoT developments. (Cooke et al., 2020).

Based on sexing research, it is seen that Industry 4.0 technologies could accentuate more interactive combination between personnel and machine (Jöhnk et al., 2021). One disintegration process is the incorporation of social robots and AI agents in industrial systems. These technologies assist humans in executing some roles such as the assembly line and offer plain or individualised recommendations together with learning procedures executed through the digital algorithms (Ivanov & Webster, 2019; Evjemo et al., 2020). Such a development indicates that work's automatization is no longer just limited to using artificial tools but entails the employees' coworkers, colleagues, or even friends, in a way, (Seeber et al., 2020).

Wilson and Daugherty (2018) also showed that both humans and robots could complement each other in order to enhance organizational output in a harmonized working relationship. However, the integration of AI agents for interaction with the human workers, even for simple procedural tasks has not yet been extensively studied with respect to the HR perspective (Libert et al., 2020). One obvious objection is that such interactions can distort perception of meaningfulness of work of human beings. Preconceptions, attitudes, beliefs, and perceptions all have a part to play in defining the effectiveness of humans and AI cooperation (Driskell et al., 2018).

A similar problem consists of "technology apprehension," which suggests the uneasy sensation which people could experience if they stand before utilizing new technologies (Okumus et al., 2017). Yet again, such anxiety may remain temporary but still exacerbate the effects on people's willingness to accept the AI agents in their working environment as being equal participants (Novak & Wisdom., 2018). Consequently, writers have stressed clarifying expectation, changes in job tasks, training (Sampson et al., 2020) and giving sufficient time to adapt (Arthanat et al., 2019). Further, integrity issues related to human-AI communication have been discussed because such problems can affect AI implementation in organizational settings to a large extent. (Gillath et al., 2021; Eubanks, 2022).

However, if human-AI integration will be done inappropriately or if there is a negative encounter with a resistant workforce, its implementation can breed fear and skepticism about these technologies – which hampers AI adoption in organizational contexts (Ferrario et al., 2020; Ostmeier & Strobel, 2022). In addition, growth of AI is fast and constantly new changes are taking place hence making it necessary for both managers and staffs to enhance their skills in matching with the technological advancement (Herrmann & Pfeiffer, 2023). Such continuous evolution requires a shift in understanding and strengthening both AI knowledge and human-centric skills including humans' innate ability to guess, think holistically, and empathize—all things that AI lacks (Davenport & Kirby, 2016; Jarrahi, 2018).

The social interface between people and AI also has two practical considerations. Many articles have been dedicated to the topic of bias in AI decision making and decreased interactiveness (Demir et al., 2020). Furthermore, there is evidence that shows that the level of human trust in AI varies depending on the type in which the AI agent exists – physical or virtual (Glickson & Woolley, 2020). These factors imply that addressing resistance to implement new technologies requires organizational support to help those working in various occupations (Sampson et al., 2020; Gillath et al., 2021). Natural human-AI interaction is also especially important, so selecting and training people to be useful as middlemen are desired. All of these people need to have a good understanding of how to work with AI management and integration into the organization's processes due to the current intricate environments they have to function in (Pranciulyte-Bagdziūniene & Petraite, 2019; Del Giudice et al., 2023). While companies across the world continue to invest in their digital transformation strategies, many organisations fail at creating adequate digital readiness for their HR teams to embrace AI. (Ivanov & Webster, 2019; Bitkina et al., 2020). Fostering organizational well-being and providing effective training may even create emotional bonds between human workers and AI, particularly if AI dependence becomes ingrained in the workplace. Thus, while the fourth industrial revolution may seem to marginalize the human element, the pervasive integration of digital technologies within socio-technical frameworks has given rise to a new evolutionary stage. In this stage, humans and machines work in symbiosis, enhancing each other's physical, sensory, emotional, and cognitive capabilities (Manley & Williams, 2022). However, this convergence is not automatic; it requires ongoing education and a redefined understanding of digital maturity, driven by continuous dialogue between organizations and their human resources.

1.3 Evolution of HR Competencies to Foster Augmentation

Emerging augmentation technologies are driving profound and lasting changes in job structures, reshaping labour markets and altering the skills and competencies necessary for HR to achieve digital maturity. The benefits of innovations like IoT, Big Data, and AI depend largely on HR's ability to adapt and the capability of leaders to promote and sustain this adaptation (McAfee & Brynjolfsson, 2017). In the 21st century, people need to be attuned to these transformations, requiring leadership that fosters these changes. There is growing recognition that these challenges extend beyond technical domains and are equally rooted in cultural, organizational, and managerial aspects (Taverner et al., 2021; Brynjolfsson, 2022). To manage them effectively one needs individuals who are able to blend business perspective with technical knowledge and behavioral competencies and contextual insight (Cillo et al., 2021; Carayannis & Morawska Jancelewicz, 2022).In this perspective as well as those discussed above, innovation and agility depends on factors such as serendipity, self orchestration, analogical reasoning, creativity and coping with disruption. These elements act as basic premises of adopting human resources in integration with the artificial intelligence agents (Pompa, 2015; World Economic Forum, 2016; Hernandez-de-Menendez et al., 2020; Saviano et al., 2023). To deal with this revolution, organizational and personal competencies should be developed as well as cognitive capabilities evolved beyond the narrow perspective (Fidler & Williams, 2016; Bruun & Duka, 2018; Brynjolfsson, 2022). Firms are now more and more interested in the creation of competitive assets by knowledge creation and by the construction of resources that can be uniquely controlled by the firm. The key for success is of course not the control of resources but the endless recombination of the basic competencies of the organization. (Hysa & Themeli, 2022; Arias-Perez & Velez-Jaramillo, 2022).

Looking at AI productivity, creativity is the ability to not only come up with new ideas, but to rework them, redefine them and find new ways to apply them to AI (Brynjolfsson, 2022). This type of creativeness matches that of an entrepreneur, which is crucial for realizing opportunities in technologically progressive sectors (Davies et al., 2011; Chin, 2021). In the case of human augmentation, entrepreneurial thinking moves beyond simple business expertise because it presupposes a profound knowledge of technological opportunities and risks and the ability to predict the market and its users (Giuggioli & Pellegrini, 2022). In addition to problem-solving skills, this attitude was at the base of the generation and the deployment of solutions (Brynjolfsson, 2022). Here, AI goes from being a weapon to becoming a colleague – a system comes up with new scenarios in the given problem. But problem solving is not a one-time event; solutions need to be disseminated. This requires one to acquire interpersonal skills such as service creation, adaptability, personal management, and leadership run Loop (Lengnick-Hall et al., 2011).

Service orientation involves predefined interpersonal proficiencies which involve listening, speaking, writing, networking and negotiating skills that are crucial for cross functional teamwork and conflict management (Pompa, 2015; Taverner et al., 2021). It means that present day leadership is not only about understanding AI but also about leading your teams through technology change, and deploying AI to achieve organisational objectives. Resilience, in this sense, is defined as the capacity to make sense of a transformation and it grows in importance given the accelerated pace of technological changes. Forecasting AI trend is a fluid one that may need a dynamic approach more often than not (La Sala et al., 2022; Ciasullo et al., 2024). Self-organization, the skill of properly prioritizing, and the ability to adapt strategies based on AI-prepared data and managing market changes are crucial for operating in new AI-oriented business contexts (Iaia et al., 2023). Similarly, problem-solving skills, as well as some analytical skills involved in research form the foundation for reasoning through data and making practical decisions within the AI-filled world. Whereas analysis is about putting together, sorting and sifting through evidence to find differences and similarities, research entails assessing information, comparing various perspectives, and coming up with balanced conclusions. These competencies are complemented by two seemingly distinct yet equally important abilities: efficiency orientation and the management of the level of complexity. Efficiency orientation concentrates on resources as the primary, ultimate goal of decision making whereas complexity management is the recognition of complex systems, interconnections and the skill of designing solutions for problems that are complex.

All of these competencies are intertwined to its creating a framework—that is in synch with the growth of the workforce with AI technologies. And each one rests upon and transcends the other, developing a range of skills that must form the basis for success in the augmentation phase of Industry 4.0. This phase is not only where individuals are aided in their decision-making by AI; on the contrary, where the circumstances dictate that humans could learn from AI as well as grow together with the latter, the current process points to the latter direction. Yet, building and championing the state of AI integration capabilities is not only a question of technology but it also depends on digital awareness, learning readiness, and a corporate culture in which humans are not at the mercy of, or in fear of, the AI systems that continue to proliferate across organizations. Creating this balance will be key to harnessing the full potential of AI in the modern workplace.

2.0 THEORETICAL UNDERPINNINGS

The theoretical foundations to explain the dynamics between organisations, technology and AI inclusivity and the role of HR in conforming to this change are as follows:

Systems Perspective

A systems perspective views organization as socio-technical systems, recognizing the interdependence between both social and technical components rather than seeing them as separate entities (Trist & Bamforth, 1951). This approach posits that effective work outcomes arise from the relationship between technical factors—such as equipment, task design, and physical workspace layout—and human elements, especially group dynamics. Technical factors contribute to achieving task-related goals, while social factors improve work quality and job satisfaction (Trist & Bamforth, 1951). For organizations to achieve holistic system effectiveness, it is essential to harmonize humanistic and technical factors, balancing conflicting objectives among different organizational components (van Gigch, 1974). This is achieved by defining and aligning roles, ensuring these differentiated roles collaborate to fulfill a shared purpose (Parsons, 1951; Biddle, 1979). Roles, therefore, are central to overall system performance (Katz & Kahn, 1978).

Role Theory

Role theory is concerned with what individuals, groups, or technologies should or should not do within their organizational roles (i.e., role expectations) (Alleyne, 2002). The theory emphasizes that normative consensus and conformity, key elements of social integration, shape organizational roles (Jackson, 1998). As organizations are viewed as socio-technical systems, role theory highlights the importance of roles in helping members understand one another and define the boundaries of individuals and technologies within the organization. This process fosters shared beliefs about how people, groups, and technologies contribute to achieving organizational goals (Biddle, 1979). Role clarity, or a clear understanding of one's role, helps actors understand how they can add value to the organization and sets well-defined expectations (Alleyne, 2002). Since roles and expectations emerge from social interactions (Thies & Wehner, 2019), the ongoing process of adopting appropriate roles—known as role conformity—facilitates role fulfillment, furthering interactions and behaviors in the workplace (Broderick, 1998; Jackson, 1998; Alonso, 2016). Katz and Kahn (1978) assert that understanding, accepting, and fulfilling role expectations are critical to organizational effectiveness.

However, this process is influenced by the broader organizational context, including factors like structure, culture, systems, strategy, and policies. As organizations evolve over time, roles and expectations are continuously redefined to adapt to changing dynamics (Alleyne, 2002). As a result, roles are not fixed but fluid, making the concept of role expectations more complex and dynamic (Biddle, 1979; Broderick, 1998).

While for many years, businesses only envisioned the function of HR as primarily bureaucratic, including the retention of records of its employees, Nevertheless, during the last several decades, there has been a vast change in the meaning of the HRM acronym. Combs et al (2006) supported on the impression that viable human resource management is crucial for organizational performance improvement. These new strategic roles that emerged due to the transition of HR from tactical function to strategic one includes; workforce planning, performance management, and job evaluation. (Bondarouk et al., 2017).

One of the major areas of changes that have occurred in HRM is the incorporation of technology in human resource systems and activities (Dhamija & Bag, 2020). To being with, this emphasis was directed at improving the relative simplicity of record keeping and time saving in processing activities; however, the new AI revolution has altered the view of HR systems and practices (Malik et al., 2020). Advanced technologies, most noticeably AI, have impacted almost all facets of HR influencing organisational competitiveness (Rao & Verweij, 2017). A number of progressive firms have come to appreciate that the optimization of AI solutions is the path to new business (Guenole & Feinzig, 2018). NITI Aayog report of 2018 revealed that the international funding for AI has increased at an average growth rate of 50% per annum (Pillai & Sivathanu, 2020) and its uses are limited mainly to sectors such as IT, marketing and sales, financial area, and customer relations. Tata Consultancy Services (2017) was able to establish that applications of AI include security breach detection and prevention, production management and scheduling, products and customer demand forecasting, social media monitoring and customer service call center auto-connection. In more recent years, a good opportunity has been identified for AI in the management of human resources (Charlier & Kloppenburg, 2017). For instance, current applications of AI include employer branding chatbot screening applicants for initial interviews (van Esch et al., 2019). AI also improves the other HR activities such as through using natural human like interfaces to answer candidate query through preloaded information (van Esch et al., 2019), besides gathering and analyzing data to make comprehensive decision making. (Muduli & Trivedi, 2020; Wheeler & Buckley, 2021).

In the context of developing countries including India, self-controlled AI systems have been underlined for meeting the social needs, especially in the pandemic conditions of COVID 19 (Bashir et al., 2020). AI can also bring about resilience in the supply chain of HR especially during situations such as the current pandemic (Modgil et al., 2021). Nevertheless, there are certain opportunities that can be seen in the Indian context, the use of artificial intelligence remains limited with only 22 percent organizations employing AI at the time of 2018 (NITI Aayog, 2018). The fact is that this statistic emphasizes the importance of the difficulties that prevent the use of AI in HR. Despite the upsurge in AI research pertaining to organizational and departmental use (Dhamija & Bag, 2020; Sharma & Biros, 2021), the literature is silent on why organisations adopt AI in HR. (Awa et al., 2016). While there has been increased interest in the patterns that determine the adoption of technology, previous works (Ahmad Salleh & Janczewski, 2018; Cruz-Jesus et al., 2018) do not focus on the adoption of AI in HR. Furthermore, as research on determinants influencing the adoption of technology, mainly in the HR departments exists to some extent (van Esch et al., 2019; Awa & Ojiabo, 2016; Nair, 2017; Bersin, 2018), there is still a lack of research focusing on the enablers of the AI adoption in the HR field. (Alam et al., 2016).

2.1 Artificial Intelligence and Knowledge Workers

Knowledge workers are individual how create, share and implement knowledge as a primary part of their jobs. As AI continues to advance, traditional tasks are beginning to be automated and new opportunities for innovation in process improvement from free forms of analysis become apparent. One of the most important business changes being redefined by AI are job roles and workflows for knowledge workers in order to fully leverage AI (Daugherty & Wilson, 2019). The use of expert systems, neural networks, case-based reasoning (CBR), robotics and natural language processing have all flourished in the expanding breadbasket of AI applications (Liebowitz 2001). It is increasingly regarded as a foundational component for advancing knowledge management (KM) practices, as AI technologies facilitate the acquisition, processing, and application of knowledge, aiding knowledge workers in decision-making (Fowler, 2000). The recent advancements in data analytics and high-performance computing have reignited interest in AI development across both industry and academia, leading to the rise of cognitive computing (Davenport & Ronanki, 2018). By using sophisticated AI techniques to simulate human brain function, cognitive computing strengthens the natural synergy between AI and KM (Rhem, 2017). For example, the exponential growth of structured and unstructured data highlights the ongoing need to extract valuable knowledge from vast big data sources. Several recent studies have examined the use of emerging AI technologies for KM, such as big data analytics (Sumbal et al., 2017; Pauleen & Wang, 2017), machine learning (Delen et al., 2013; Jin et al., 2018), and intelligent agents (Chemchem & Drias, 2015; Gacanin, 2019). AI has also been applied to analyze knowledge workers' behaviors and performance, such as investigating the phenomenon of knowledge hiding among employees (Abubakar et al., 2019). Despite this, most existing research on AI's role in KM has approached the subject from a technical standpoint. Few studies have delved into the managerial implications of how AI supports knowledge sharing and learning within organizations. Our research aims to fill this gap by focusing on the management challenges associated with leveraging AI to enhance knowledge workers' core KM activities.

2.2 Artificial Intelligence and the Organisations

AI has four core functional domains namely learning, understanding, reasoning, and interacting (Gil et al., 2020) which can be applied across various business scenarios, such as predicting the levels of employee engagement (Choi & Choi,

2020), assessing the readiness of banking systems (Rahman & Abedin, 2021), and accentuating performance of crowdsourcing platforms (Behl et al., 2021). Davenport and Ronanki (2018) identified three key ways AI support business needs namely:

Figure 1. Figure illustrating the ways AI support business needs (Researcher's Interpretation)

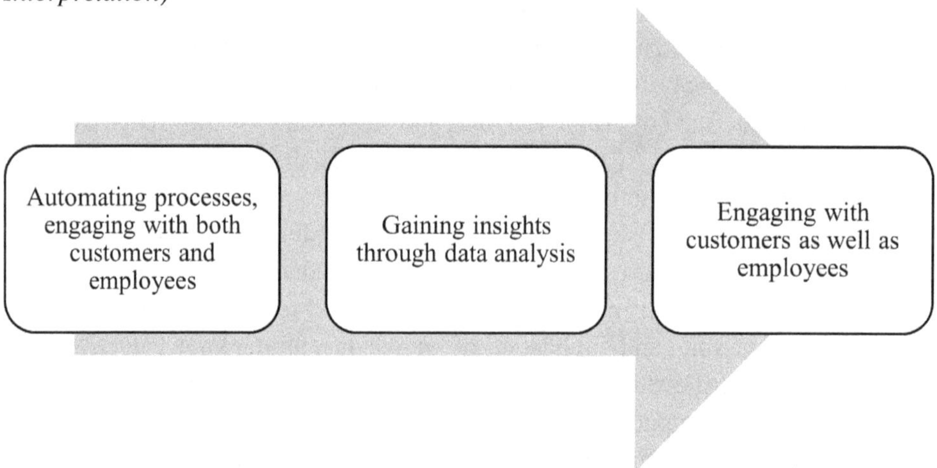

Below are examples that illustrate these three AI functions. Fountaine et al. (2019) suggest organizations adopt a centralized AI hub for data analytics that aligns with business strategies. In supply chain management, AI-driven analytics are helping businesses transition toward sustainable manufacturing (Raut et al., 2020). In human resources, talent analytics play a critical role in developing high-performing teams, boosting overall organizational success (Sivathanu & Pillai, 2019). Drawing from the literature, we categorize AI systems into three main types: task simplification, stakeholder connection, and insight generation.

2.3 Perceived Positive Implications of Adopting AI in the Organisations

One key construct that emerges from this study is a view of how individuals perceive the benefits derived by their use. Perceived benefits are the degree to which an individual believes that a particular technology is more advantageous than other alternatives (Yang et al., 2013). Previous studies have demonstrated that people are more likely to adopt a technology if they believe it will make their lives better (Rogers, 2003; Davis, 1989). Decision-makers play an important role in adoption of technology within organization, where internal factors are influenced to a great extent by the characteristics he observed regarding the new innovation (Moore and Benbasat, 1991). Likewise, Perceived compatibility as with simplicity and discriminability had a significant relationship on adopters POV.(Chang et al., 2007; Khemthong and Roberts, 2006; Musawa and Wahab, 2012; Grandon and Pearson, 2004). Conversely, a lack of clarity on the clinical benefits or performance effectiveness of technology can act as barrier to adoption (Greenhalgh et al., 2004) Moreover, the costs of new technology that needs to be integrated also shape these perceptions (Jöhnk et al., 2021). Consequently, perceived advantages can be ascertained depending on the characteristics of technology being used or thought and its anticipated returns which will incur some costs (Alam et al., 2016). Relative advantage was indicated to determine perceived benefits that in turn lead to AI acceptance (Clemons & Row, 1991Al-Dmour et al.,2014Zhu et al.,2004). Indeed, this mindset drives organizations to pursuit the most updated literacy as well promote their ability towards engaging more sophisticated technologies (Pan et al., 2021). The emergence of COVID-19 revealed the increased need for touchless workflows through AI and robotics, highlighting further benefits in their adoption (Gaur et al. 2021). As a result, the choice of whether to embrace AI is determined by what attributes it comes with and at what cost or operational efficiency. The higher the perceived benefits, the quicker and easier the adoption process is (Russell and Norvig, 2016).

2.4 Relationship Between Technical Proficiency and Adoption of AI in the Organisations

This learning is supported by both the extant technology and new firm-specific technological innovations (Pan et al., 2021; Ransbotham, Kane & Loh, 2017). It is comprised of the total of internal and external technologies within an organization and their fit to firm's requirement (Awa et al., 2015). The level of IT knowledge and technological competencies within the firm customers on their company's ability to adopt AI as well serves as a further determinant (Wamba-Taguimdje et al., 2020). An IT department should comprehend well enough what AI is about strategically in relation to the company goals (Abijith and Wamba, 2012; Liu et al., 2013). Therefore, the more technical skills of a staff are developed – to some extend based on Rogers (1995) with an ability for innovation as pace factor - there is less scepticism due to easier integration or fear that implementation depth e.g, existing system becomes too complex through AI technology fitting which can endanger daily routines. Companies having competent IT staff can easily adopt AI to work efficiently with their technological frameworks (Bughin et al., 2017). Solutions For example, there is a loaded productivity behind mounting costs of AI implementation decreasing significantly in almost every organization due to evident increases in IT-resource use and efficiency (Guenole & Feinzig.,2008) Additionally to the last factor as well, successful adoption of AI requires organizations having flexible infrastructure such as networks software, hardware and data installations (Wamba et al.,2007) In the light of technological innovation, most often are better prepared for it those companies that already have an advanced technology platform and can afford to maintain this (Zhu et al., 2004). Therefore, the organizations that are higher in absorptive capacity are able to adopt and use AI technologies more effectively (Pan et al., 2021). Accordingly, the collective state of preparedness of a firm for technological change is highly important (Zhu et al., 2004). In other words, technological readiness is not only the presence of a physical infrastructure but also an intellectual capital within the organization (Metaxiotis et al., 2005).

2.5 The Interrelationship Between Adoption of AI and Evolution of Effective Human Resource Systems and Processes

(Abijith and Wamba., 2012) focused on information technology serves as a driver of performance improvement. (Mooney et al.,1996), gave three main benefits of the utilisation of AI are discovered, which include:(i) improved capture, storage, handling, sharing information;(ii) fostering innovation and streamline business evolution; and(iii)better automation/usefulness (Kim et al., 2011; Abijith &Wamba, 2012., Mooney et al.,1996). It makes the operations much smoother as limited manual efforts required to perform those tasks and also takes away all of routine works which generally done by an employee again save a lot effort for individuals (Kambur & Akar., 2021). Using algorithms, the AI builds a highly accurate and fast access to data which in turn can take newer decisions rendering more robust human resource systems. AI's key differentiator in database management is it nurtures lifelong learning (Wilkens, 2020; Fischer et al., 2020). Advanced HR information systems for example can help senior management to reach quicker, better informed decisions (Hashimoto et al., 2018; London, 2019). AI can also enable decision making to become more instinctive, with notable advances in machine learning and big data algorithms (Topol 2019; Toh et al.,2019) This is supported by the capability of AI to create an extensive database such as decisions, trends and historical data that HR managers can always refer for insights (Cyert & March 1963; Wilkens 2020). This promotes collective learning and knowledge management as well as better understanding of the individual behaviors. AI also helped automate clerical tasks and paper flow, streamline resource allocations in a little less time and sped human-resource functions (Markoff 2016). (Wamba-Taguimdje et al.,2020) in another study also underscored the potential to change HR practices by deploying AI. (Wijayati et al.,2022) posted that AI is a game changer in HR as it dismantles traditional organizational hierarchies to build trust internally and externally. This will result in stronger customer relationships and competitive position for the firm. This enhances the aspect of value chain for consumers and in result enhances the firm's competitive advantage. When organizational structures match AI, the competitive advantage and organizational performance is likely to improve.

2.6 The Relationship Between AI and Knowledge Management

The use of AI in conjunction with knowledge management can be considered to trace back more than twenty years, ever since the realization of AI as a substantial building block for the advancement of KM. As (Liebowitz, 2001) points out, "One of the major challenges in integrating AI into knowledge management in its early days was that there would not be systems to interact with humans." (Tsui et al., 2000). Recent advances in AI have again stirred research regarding the relationship between AI and KM. Some researchers have studied the technical functionalities of AI with regard to supporting KM (Lin et al., 2019; Chatterjee et al., 2020; Lu et al., 2020), but very few have looked into the role of AI for support knowledge workers. Research on this aspect coincidentally limits itself to either some business domains or some specific aspects of KM. For instance, (Sowa et al; 2020) established that AI working together with knowledge workers leads to enhanced productivity. In addition, the role of AI has been identified as instrumental in maintaining customers' relationships. The disposition to understand the inter-relationships between the AI and human workforce provides the first opportunity for examining the role of AI in knowledge worker support. (Wilson and Daugherty; 2018) identified that "humans and machines complement each other through training, explaining, and sustaining. While AI complements human capabilities through "amplifying, interacting, and embodying," there are three important roles humans must play to complement AI: training machines to do a specific task, explaining the results of AI when it does not produce the expected outcomes, and seeing to it that bad things are prevented in the use of AI

There are three main ways in which AI allows humans to increase their talents:

- can amplify cognitive strengths,
- interact with customers and employees to free up time for higher-level tasks, and
- embody human skills to enhance physical capabilities. Conversely, humans play a vital role in guiding AI's growth and responsible use.

Our study approach, which examines AI's revolutionary potential to support and improve knowledge workers' jobs, is shaped by this viewpoint.

2.7 Understanding Knowledge Management Frameworks

(Rubenstein-Montano et al; 2001) did a thorough analysis of the knowledge management (KM) models that are currently in use by top consulting businesses and scholarly research. Drawing on their research, they put up a comprehensive framework that incorporates crucial knowledge management tasks, stressing the importance of these activities being in line with an organization's strategic objectives and systems thinking. Since then, other academics have created KM models customized for certain businesses.

For instance, Parikh (2001) investigated how knowledge is used in high-tech businesses to generate new products. He distinguished between tacit and explicit knowledge, as well as internal and external sources, focusing on a KM cycle that includes four interrelated phases: knowledge acquisition, knowledge organization, knowledge dissemination, and knowledge application. In the field of lean supply chain management, Liu et al. (2013) introduced a KM framework consisting of four layers—know-what, know-why, know-how, and know-with—and seven knowledge components, all aimed at supporting collaborative decision-making. Lech (2014), focusing on IT project management, categorized knowledge into distinct types based on knowledge taxonomies and processes, and examined the specific knowledge activities required for each phase of a project.

Adopting a process-oriented perspective, knowledge management processes may be categorized into 3 into three key activities:

Figure 2. The activities of a knowledge management process (Researcher's Interpretation)

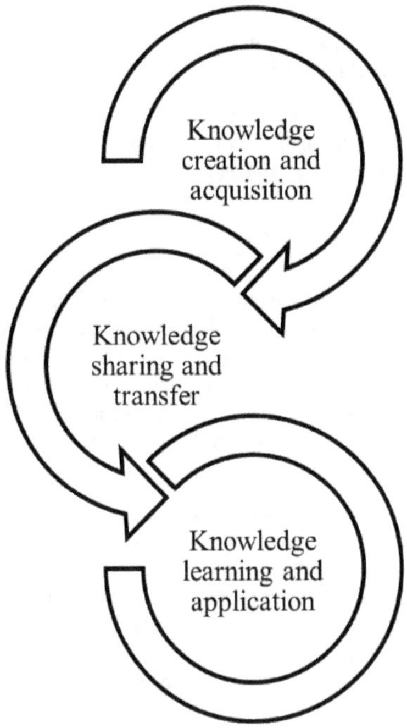

The table below categories the AI on the basis of the above 3 key activities:

Table 1. Table outlines the framework, with the types of AI systems listed in rows and Knowledge Management (KM) activities in columns

Knowledge Management Activities			
Categories of AI	*Knowledge Creation and Acquisition*	*Knowledge Sharing and Transfer*	*Learning and Application*
Task Simplification and Optimization: Simplification and automation of redundant tasks by adopting Robotic Process Automation and AI	Insights are gathered from experts by AI to generate new content	AI driven recommendation systems integrate users with appropriate providers	AI enabled recommendation systems map learners with their domains of interest
Stakeholder Relationship Management: Improves the relationship with key stakeholders namely employees and customers with the help of natural language processing (NLP) and intelligent mediators	Robotics enabled client-support systems assist clients with multifaceted and complex tasks and accomplishes customer or employee service requests.	Chatbots track the customer sentiment patterns and provides actual and instantaneous feedback to the customers.	Employees accentuate the service quality by analysing chat-transcripts of previous customers
Generation of Insights: Identification of patterns and extraction of hidden data and information from the Big Data with the help of cutting-edge AI enabled algorithms	Extraction of uncovered data from the raw data source and outliers assisted by AI algorithms	Deep Learning AI processes and systems unravel effective relationships between people, processes, cross-sectional teams and data	AI algorithms keep a record of the various learning and outcomes and utilises it to develop new knowledge base

In this study, three relevant frameworks were integrated to investigate the ways AI supports knowledge management (KM):

1. **Types of AI systems**: These include task simplification, stakeholder connection, and insight generation.
2. **Key KM activities**: These comprise knowledge creation and acquisition, knowledge sharing and transfer, and knowledge learning and application.
3. **Human-AI interaction focus**: Examines whether AI enhances human capabilities or if humans contribute to AI development.

Table 1 outlines the framework, with the types of AI systems listed in rows and Knowledge Management (KM) activities in columns. Each cell defines the ways AI systems interact with different KM activities. The detail of each type of role of the AI system within these activities are listed below:

2.7.1 Task Simplification and Optimization

This type of AI systems aims to automate routine tasks and streamline processes, significantly reducing the workload for employees. In decision-making, knowledge workers often rely on multiple data sources, such as spreadsheets, databases, or information systems. Since gathering and analysing this data is leads to redundancy, it is automated effectively through AI enabled task simplification and optimization.

Example: AI can intelligently scan customer emails to update marketing databases (Nelson, 2019), or evaluate legal documents for compliance gaps (Faggella, 2020).

- **Knowledge Creation and Acquisition**: These AI systems simplify the process of acquiring and storing new knowledge, requiring human involvement mainly during the creation of automated processes. However, advanced systems can evolve through continuous learning, discovering new patterns over time.
- **Knowledge Sharing and Transfer**: AI enabled task simplification and optimization can facilitate knowledge transfer between AI systems and humans or between humans themselves. It enhances efficiency by automating routine knowledge exchanges, while still requiring human input for complex or non-routine situations.
- **Learning and Application**: AI helps identify experts and their knowledge, promoting learning and application of insights. As more knowledge accumulates, the AI system itself evolves, potentially advancing to next variant of AI through improved insight generation.

2.7.2 Stakeholder Relationship Management

Digital connectivity allows businesses to maintain ongoing relationships with stakeholders, such as customers and employees. This continuous engagement drives improvements in products and services, creating a cycle of collecting data, enhancing offerings, and increasing customer satisfaction. AI-powered stakeholder relationship management systems employ tools, such as natural language processing (NLP). These systems interact with other fields such as customer service support desks and human resources (as claimed by Makarius et al., 2020) to create a better experience and fun.

- **Learning and collecting the knowledge**: These systems monitor with kind of feedback from stakeholders, how content they are or even measurements that will enable to measure different initiations in statics present within a company.

- **Knowledge Sharing and Transfer**: AI enables the two-way sharing of knowledge between different stakeholders, even at a local level. This collected information from the external (customers) can feed internal processes like your HR systems and vice versa everyone benefits.
- **Knowledge Learning & Application:** This type of AI system aims to take the knowledge gathered and maintain engagement with stakeholders in order for their needs, whether customer or employee related are fulfilled. For example, the algorithms you employ to drive customer engagement might also be reused in your HR systems for employee experience.

2.7.3 Generation of Insights

These AI systems utilize advanced machine learning algorithms to uncover hidden insights from vast amounts of data, providing real-time solutions to knowledge workers. These AI systems excel in recognizing patterns and extracting knowledge from complex datasets. ***Example***: Complex data can be analysed to detect safety issues or customize advertisements based on prior consumer behaviour (Guzenko, 2020).

- **Knowledge Creation and Acquisition**: With access to larger datasets, these AI systems become increasingly effective at uncovering previously hidden patterns and improving predictions. Human intervention is still necessary for refining these insights and ensuring the system's accuracy.
- **Knowledge Sharing and Transfer**: AI enables cross-departmental knowledge sharing, allowing organizations to transfer insights across different business areas. For example, new knowledge from marketing can be applied in operations or R&D.
- **Knowledge Learning and Application**: AI systems in this category help employees gain expertise by analysing large datasets, providing them with deeper insights that can be applied to various areas. As human experts validate these insights in real-world scenarios, the feedback is fed back into the AI systems, further enhancing their accuracy and relevance over time.

3.0 DISCUSSION AND MANAGERIAL IMPLICATIONS

The practical contributions of this research concern the conceptualisation and right implementation of digital affordance and, more broadly, digital sophistication within organisational contexts. The first advantage of the study is providing the managers and leaders with a recipe to enhance their perception of how the technological IPI-MS innovations, in this case, the AI application, will generate the source for the improvement of HR self-efficacy and motivation. This can be achieved by administration and development of competencies designed for augmentation (Ostmeier & Strobel, 2022). The other major implication is the further development of employee digital expertise together with the culture of training and training for development as a continuous process (Sundaresan & Zhang, 2022). This can be done through offering chances of skills training and endowing every employee with trained responsibility for personal education. Organizational self-directed learning promotes a workplace environment in which the workforce is ready to handle vast technological risks and decide rightly on their own. (Sundaresan & Zhang, 2022). It could be done through the experience-based learning opportunity offered and, on the other hand, every chance for the employees to own their learning processes. In this way, organizations would be able to build a workforce which is more capable to address technological uncertainty and make decentralized informational decisions.

The third implication is that there is a heightened need to operationalise a hybrid workforce which is greatly justified. The main idea on which the study is based is that of achieving the best organizational performance through the integration of humans and AI technologies. HR teams should have competencies in the use of AI in the organization and at the same time, it is important that the employees have 'soft' skills of communication or ability to work with an AI agent. (Iaia et al., 2023).

To summarize the advanced expectations from the knowledge of workers for a contemporary organization the major three dimensions have been depicted in the Table 1: process, engagement and content. The above depicted dimensions have a very similar track to this paper's three types of AI systems. For example, as part of the process dimension the data includes customer service records and calls in which the records are being generated automatically and clauses from standard forms of contracts that are extracted and verified and data integrating functions are involved. The engagement dimension has systems that respond to questions about employee benefits and involves AI enabled live chat conversations with customers. At the same time, the content dimension includes applications such as robots or chatbots for investment or AI-based product suggestion.

In AI-containing Knowledge Management Systems (KMS), knowledge worker often operates at more than one of these dimensions. We have identified four distinct groups of knowledge workers, each with different levels of need for AI support, as shown in Figure 3: Front-line employee enactors (FEs), middle managers who directly interact with clients (MCDMs), organisational improvement specialists (OISs), and senior managers who develop strategic plans (SMPs).

Figure 3. Developing of AI Support for Knowledge Workers (Adopted from Sundaresan, S., & Zhang, Z. (2022). AI-enabled knowledge sharing and learning: redesigning roles and processes. International journal of organizational analysis, 30(4), 983-999.)

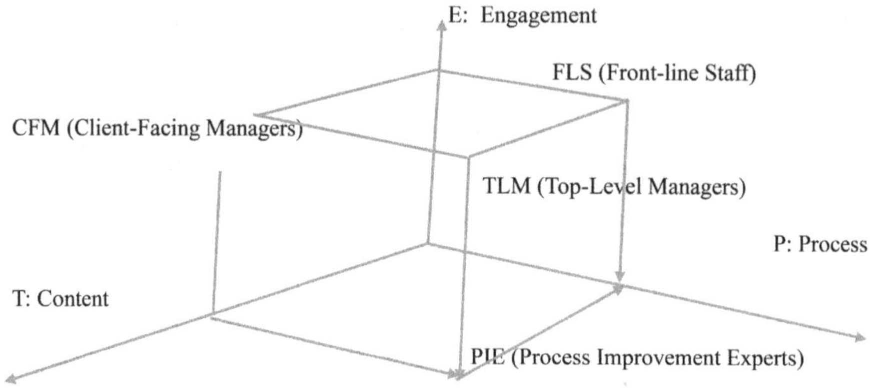

Based on the work type, most of the FLS knowledge workers are heavily involved in relational work that includes interface with employees, customers and other relevant Central persons. Some of these workers include call center agents, or basically customer relations and human resource department employees. Previously the workers in FLS were confined to implementing the procedures and steps laid down and followed by policy makers. However, nonhuman intelligence in KMS the use of chatbots to do KMS has gradually been done in lieu of these preserve workers for procedural problems to do more complex and distinct problems. Such a shift enables them to offer better service quality since such knowledge relevant for use is readily accessible to these workers (Xu et al., 2020). This kind of AI help moves the value created by the AI systems to the knowledge employees and offers to increase the effectivity estimations of the workers.

Client-facing Managers (CFM) perform knowledge work tasks with high levels of stakeholder interaction. This group of people includes positions such as CRM specialists and HR managers that concentrate on devising new practices and policies as well as generating insights that can improve stakeholders' engagement. AI-enabling KMS help these workers by aggregating and presenting huge amounts of customer and employee data. For instance, sentiment analysis personnel enable CRM specialists to understand cultural factors, language trends and even emotions the customers are displaying. They state that this more profound revelation of client opinion is beneficial to decision-making and improves interactive strategies.

PIE works within high-complexity, knowledge-intensive activities that require professional activities, research and development management, and software development. In software development AI is not new and is already being used to improve processes like automated testing, finding issues, generation of codes, and the overall project management. These automation tools help to free software developers from more minor, less critical aspects of software design. Machine learning and other AI tools aid developers in understanding the patterns from existing code or data to determine how the design of software products should be improved (Schatsky; Bumb, 2020). This cuts the amount of time spent on repetitive work while staff focuses on innovation in developing the software.

TLM which includes among others CIOs, venture capitalists, Senior executives are now involved in knowledge intensive activities that cuts across the process, engagement as well as content dimensions. Paralegals and other legal workers benefit from these existent applications of AI since they involve tasks such as document search and review, contract analyses, and proofreading. AI takes up routine work that may take much time if done man usually and liberates individuals such as lawyers to engage in more challenging and thus more gainful work which cannot be done by the AI. For instance, with the use of AI, a lawyer is in a position to carry out relevant legal research, review analogous cases in similar cases and discover a number of approaches that will be suitable to favour his/her/its client. This results in eventual higher levels of client satisfaction through being better informed all through the process of the law. (Marwaha, 2017).

By using the framework outlined in this study, knowledge managers can gain a clearer understanding of the capabilities and limitations of both traditional and AI-enabled KMS. To accommodate the evolving demands of these systems, we propose the Evolving AI Support model, which highlights how the four groups of knowledge workers will increasingly require AI support across two or more of the key dimensions. In practice, knowledge workers often exhibit hybrid requirements across the three dimensions, necessitating varying levels of AI support. A single AI system may not be sufficient to address the growing complexity of their roles, which are spread across process, engagement, and content areas.

From a managerial standpoint, we recommend that organizations develop customized AI systems tailored to the specific needs of their knowledge workers based on the intensity of the three dimensions relevant to their roles. Where KM managers are located nearer to the higher levels of the enterprise, in the short term they should be conducting training for the workers so that they can become proficient in multiple AI based systems- thus, the workers will be equipped for the creative application of these technologies in their knowledge management tasks. This will enable organisations to reap the full benefits of AI systems while at the same time promote innovation in their knowledge intensive activities.

Therefore, it is first and foremost essential for HR professionals to grasp what AI can and cannot do to apply AI solutions rather successfully. It is most appropriate for activities such as data processing, management of administrative and physical processes, and performance forecasting and analysis of employee behaviours, respectively. At the same time, HR professionals are expected to remain engaged in activities that rely on human skills – solving multifaceted employee relations problems, overseeing the development of organizational culture, and guiding the decision-making process with regard to organizational values and goals.

Because the technical and interpersonal skills are both improved through pursuit of the SPHR designation, HR professionals benefit both their organization and themselves by adding value while also increasing satisfaction with the position and advancement potential. Thus, having this type of complementary skill set secures greater cooperation between people and AI in the rapidly restructuring job market and raises the importance of the HR profession.

First of all, there is a practical implication to consider in relation to data privacy. With an increase in interface between AI and human, there is need for organizations to keep data secure. This entails incorporating effective technology frameworks like data encryption and storage security, for the organization's technical crews, in parallel with educational sessions for HR professionals on proper management of data and data security. It becomes an effective approach to embrace a culture of openness around the collection and usage of data to establish and implement a proper combination of a human and AI workforce.

Limitations of the Study & Directed Conclusion

Companies are also using AI in an effort to improve on the efficiency and effectiveness of professional learners. Front-line employees use AI systems to remain connected so that they have the knowledge they need to assist their clients at their fingertips. It has found application and has suggested various solutions for different categories of knowledge employees for instance retail employees, programmers, and research & development teams among others. It further notes that the benefits of bringing AI into the management of the HR department are not just for the HR department alone but may be for the whole organization at large. The study identifies three critical prerequisites for successful AI adoption: organizational readiness, perceived benefits, and perceived technical resulted in a technical competence score of 23. Hence, it is advised that the HR leaders, and the top executives perform a careful pre-scan before outlining the plan on use of AI in organizations.

This pre-assessment should start out by determining which of the job roles, processes, and procedures could possibly be enhanced. More so, leaders need to review particular activities and processes that can be done more effectively by automating them. Another area to look at is the possibility of what else AI could add to employee functions other than people analytics, which could include improving employee productivity or how performance can be measured and how training, career progression, and compensation and reward strategies could be improved. However, it needs also to be determined whether these changes would mean total redesign of current systems. In so doing, following this pre-assessment, HR leaders can design an overarching automation plan that targets a coherent implementation of AI across the company.

Additionally, the AI application in Knowledge Management Systems (KMS) has taken a new paradigm in the interaction between knowledge workers and content as well as machines, hence changing the W2L process and roles. In this context, the study contributes to existing literature by classifying the diverse functions AI performs within key Knowledge Management (KM) activities. The chapter has highlighted the ways AI-enabled KMS has evolved in its use, focusing on the varying roles and processes of knowledge workers and the necessary AI support for their activities.

First, the chapter has used multiple sources in the literature to create a comprehensive framework encompassing three dimensions of AI systems, three KM activities, and two modes of AI-human interaction. The research identifies three types of AI systems as mentioned in Table 1: task simplification and optimization, stakeholder relationship management, and generation of insights along with three core KM activities namely knowledge creation and acquisition, knowledge sharing and transfer, and learning and application of knowledge. Furthermore, the chapter explores how AI either assists humans or humans facilitate AI within these interactions.

Furthermore, the chapter determines that a single type of AI system is insufficient to support the increasingly complex tasks faced by knowledge workers. These tasks span three dimensions—process, engagement, and content—highlighting the need for evolving AI support across different worker roles. We identify four distinct groups of knowledge workers: Front-line Staff (FLS), Client-facing Managers (CFM), Process Improvement Experts (PIE), and Top-level Managers (TLM). The recommendation is for organizations to develop customized AI systems tailored to the unique demands of these roles, depending on the intensity of knowledge requirements across the three dimensions.

In conclusion, AI has the potential to significantly transform the traditional knowledge-sharing and learning process, moving from a simple sender-receiver model to one that emphasizes content creation and comprehension. The research has demonstrated how knowledge workers' roles have evolved with the introduction of AI-powered KM processes. With the increasing interest in AI and its potential applications in KM, this study provides practical insights for organizations looking to manage their knowledge assets more effectively. Future research will aim to expand both the scope and depth of these use cases. Another limitation is that we do not address the issue of bias within AI systems, which has been recognized as a significant concern in current business and academic discussions (Silberg & Manyika, 2019). Rather than analyzing AI adoption in pioneering companies at a high level, future research will apply the framework presented here to these cases in greater detail. Previous studies have examined the role of incentives in encouraging knowledge sharing, such as in team settings (Sundaresan & Zhang, 2016) and within enterprise social networks (Sundaresan & Zhang, 2018). Future research will also investigate how incentives can be used to further enhance KM and the application of AI technologies.

REFERENCES

Aayog, N. I. T. I. (2018), *National strategy for artificial intelligence #AIFORALL.* niti.gov.in/ writereaddata/files/document_publication/NationalStrategy-for-AI-Discussion-Paper.pdf

Abijith, A., & Wamba, S. F. (2012). Business value of RFID-enabled healthcare transformation projects. *Business Process Management Journal*, 19(1), 1–28.

Ahmad Salleh, K., & Janczewski, L. (2018), *An implementation of Sec-TOE framework: identifying security determinants of big data solutions adoption an implementation of Sec-TOE framework: identifying security determinants of big data. PACIS 2018 Proceedings*, 211.

Al-Dmour, R. H. (2014). *An Integration Model for Identifying the Determinants of the Adoption and Implementation Level of HRIS Applications and Its Effectiveness in Business Organisations*. Brunel University.

Alam, M. G. R., Masum, A. K. M., Beh, L. S., & Hong, C. S. (2016). Critical factors influencing decision to adopt human resource information system (HRIS) in hospitals. *PLoS One*, 11(8), 1–22. DOI: 10.1371/journal.pone.0160366 PMID: 27494334

Alleyne, M. C. (2002). *The Construction and Representation of Race and Ethnicity in the Caribbean and the World*. University of the West Indies Press.

Ardito, L., Petruzzelli, A. M., Panniello, U., & Garavelli, A. C. (2022). Towards Industry 4.0: Mapping digital technologies for supply chain management-marketing integration. *Business Process Management Journal*, 28(3), 561–583. DOI: 10.1108/BPMJ-05-2021-0274

Arias-Pérez, J., & Vélez-Jaramillo, J. (2022). Ignoring the three-way interaction of digital orientation, Not-invented-here syndrome and employee's artificial intelligence awareness in digital innovation performance: A recipe for failure. *Technological Forecasting and Social Change*, 174, 121305. DOI: 10.1016/j.techfore.2021.121305

Arslan, A., Tarba, S., & Zheng, C. (2021). Human resource management in Industry 4.0: Emerging themes and research avenues. *Human Resource Management Review*, 31(3), 100778. DOI: 10.1016/j.hrmr.2020.100778

Arthanat, S., Vroman, K. G., Lysack, C., & Grizzetti, J. (2019). Multimodal training of AI systems for assistive technologies: A person-centered approach. *Assistive Technology Journal*, 31(2), 89–100. DOI: 10.1080/10400435.2019.1578254

Awa, H., Ojiabo, O., & Emecheta, B. (2015). Integrating TAM, TPB and TOE frameworks and expanding their characteristic constructs for e-commerce adoption by SMEs. *Journal of Science & Technology Policy Management*, 6(1), 76–94. DOI: 10.1108/JSTPM-04-2014-0012

Awa, H. O., Ukoha, O., & Emecheta, B. C. (2016). Using T-O-E theoretical framework to study the adoption of ERP solution. *Cogent Business & Management*, 3(1), 1196571. DOI: 10.1080/23311975.2016.1196571

Bashir, M. F., Ma, B., Komal, B., Bashir, M. A., Tan, D., & Bashir, M. (2020). Correlation between climate indicators and COVID-19 pandemic in New York, USA. *The Science of the Total Environment*, 728, 138835. Retrieved October 3, 2024, from. DOI: 10.1016/j.scitotenv.2020.138835 PMID: 32334162

Bersin, J. (2018), *Talent trends technology disruptions for 2018*. www.isaconnection.org/ assets/documents/2018BersinHRTechDisruptionsReport.pdf

Bitkina, O. V., Kim, H., & Park, J. (2020). Human factors in organizational digital transformation: Readiness and resistance. *Human Factors Journal*, 62(3), 456–470. DOI: 10.1177/0018720819873103

Bondarouk, T., Parry, E., & Furtmueller, E. (2017). Electronic HRM: Four decades of research on adoption and consequences. *International Journal of Human Resource Management*, 28(1), 98–131. DOI: 10.1080/09585192.2016.1245672

Broderick, A. J. (1998). Role theory, role management and service performance. *Journal of Services Marketing*, 12(5), 348–361. DOI: 10.1108/08876049810235379

Brynjolfsson, E. (2022). *The servitization economy: Understanding new paradigms in labor division*. MIT Press.

Bughin, J., Hazan, E., Ramaswamy, S., Chui, M., Allas, T., Dahlstro¨, M. P., Henke, N., & Trench, M. (2017). *Artificial Intelligence: The Next Digital Frontier? McKinsey Global Institute*. McKinsey & Company.

Carayannis, E. G., & Morawska-Jancelewicz, J. (2022). The futures of Europe: Society 5.0 and Industry 5.0 as driving forces of future universities. *Journal of the Knowledge Economy*, 13(4), 3445–3471. DOI: 10.1007/s13132-021-00854-2

Chang, I. C., Hwang, H. G., Hung, M. C., Lin, M. H., & Yen, D. C. (2007). Factors affecting the adoption of electronic signature: Executives' perspective of hospital information department. *Decision Support Systems*, 44(1), 350–359. DOI: 10.1016/j.dss.2007.04.006 PMID: 32287564

Charlier, R., & Kloppenburg, S. (2017), *Artificial intelligence in HR: a no-brainer.* www. pwc.nl

Chiarini, A. (2021). Industry 4.0 technologies in lean production systems: A methodological approach. *Production Planning and Control*, 32(13), 1106–1118. DOI: 10.1080/09537287.2020.1817603

Cillo, P., Priem, R. L., Verona, G., & Zanella, P. (2021). Consumer-CEO interaction as catalyst for business model innovation in established firms. *Journal of Business Research*, 131, 241–253. DOI: 10.1016/j.jbusres.2021.04.001

Clemons, E. K., & Row, M. C. (1991). Sustaining IT advantage: The role of structural differences. *Management Information Systems Quarterly*, 15(3), 275–292. DOI: 10.2307/249639

Combs, J., Liu, Y., Hall, A., & Ketchen, D. (2006). How much do high-performance work practices matter? A meta-analysis of their effects on organizational performance. *Personnel Psychology*, 59(3), 501–528. DOI: 10.1111/j.1744-6570.2006.00045.x

Cooke, F. L., Dickmann, M., & Parry, E. (2020). IJHRM after 30 years: Taking stock in times of COVID-19 and looking towards the future of HR research. *International Journal of Human Resource Management*, 32(1), 1–23. DOI: 10.1080/09585192.2020.1833070

Coupe, T. (2019). Automation and labor substitution in a smart factory era. *Technological Forecasting and Social Change*, 141, 312–320. DOI: 10.1016/j.techfore.2018.09.022

Davenport, T. H., & Kirby, J. (2016). *Only humans need apply: Winners and losers in the age of smart machines*. Harper Business.

Deguchi, A., Hirano, T., Matsuoka, F., & Nakano, Y. (2020). *Society 5.0: A people-centric super-smart society*. Springer. DOI: 10.1007/978-981-15-2989-4_1

Del Giudice, M. (2016). Discovering the human role in IoT-driven environments: A dynamic capabilities approach. *Technological Forecasting and Social Change*, 125, 42–49. DOI: 10.1016/j.techfore.2017.07.021

Del Giudice, M., Scuotto, V., Orlando, B., & Pagani, M. (2023). AI-enabled workforce transformation: Implications for organizational change and human resource management. *Journal of Business Research*, 148, 122–134. DOI: 10.1016/j.jbusres.2022.12.001

Demir, K., Wang, C., & Turner, T. (2020). Ethical issues and decision biases in AI implementation. *Journal of Business Ethics*, 162(1), 129–145. DOI: 10.1007/s10551-020-04348-x

Devezas, T. C., & Sarygulov, A. I. (2017). *Industry 4.0: Entrepreneurship and structural change in the new digital landscape*. Springer. DOI: 10.1007/978-3-319-49604-7

Dhamija, P., & Bag, S. (2020). Role of artificial intelligence in operations environment: A review and bibliometric analysis. *The TQM Journal*, 32(4), 869–986. DOI: 10.1108/TQM-10-2019-0243

Driskell, J. E., Salas, E., & Driskell, T. (2018). Foundations of teamwork and collaboration. *The American Psychologist*, 73(4), 334–348. DOI: 10.1037/amp0000241 PMID: 29792452

Eubanks, S. (2022). Trust and integrity in AI-human interactions. *Journal of Organizational Psychology*, 35(1), 72–88. DOI: 10.1007/s11575-022-00799-0

Evjemo, L. D., Gjerstad, T., Grøtli, E. I., & Sziebig, G. (2020). Trends in smart manufacturing: Role of humans and industrial robots in smart factories. *Current Robotics Reports*, 1(2), 35–41. DOI: 10.1007/s43154-020-00006-5

Ferrario, M., Loi, M., & Viganò, E. (2020). Luddite anxiety and AI adoption in organizations. *Ethics and Information Technology*, 22(4), 423–437. DOI: 10.1007/s10676-020-09534-4

Gaur, L., Afaq, A., Singh, G., & Dwivedi, Y. K. (2021). Role of artificial intelligence and robotics to foster the touchless travel during a pandemic: A review and research agenda. *International Journal of Contemporary Hospitality Management*, 33(11), 4079–4098. DOI: 10.1108/IJCHM-11-2020-1246

Gillath, O., Ai, T., & Fink, J. (2021). Human-AI communication and its ethical implications. *Computers in Human Behavior*, 124, 106918. DOI: 10.1016/j.chb.2021.106918

Giuggioli, G., & Pellegrini, M. M. (2023). Artificial intelligence as an enabler for entrepreneurs: A systematic literature review and an agenda for future research. *International Journal of Entrepreneurial Behaviour & Research*, 29(4), 816–837. DOI: 10.1108/IJEBR-05-2021-0426

Glickson, E., & Woolley, A. W. (2020). Human-AI collaboration: Challenges and solutions. *Journal of Management Studies*, 57(7), 1173–1197. DOI: 10.1111/joms.12520

Greenhalgh, T., Robert, G., Macfarlane, F., Bate, P., & Kyriakidou, O. (2004). Diffusion of innovations in service organizations: Systematic review and recommendations. *The Milbank Quarterly*, 82(4), 581–629. DOI: 10.1111/j.0887-378X.2004.00325.x PMID: 15595944

Guenole, N. and Feinzig, S. (2018), *The business case for AI in HR: with insights and tips on getting started.* IBM Smarter Workforce Institute, IBM.

Herrmann, S., & Pfeiffer, S. (2023). Collaborative intelligence in Industry 4.0: Designing socio-technical systems. *Technology Innovation Management Review*, 13(2), 5–15. DOI: 10.22215/timreview/1618

Holm, J. R., & Lorenz, E. (2022). Task restructuring and work fragmentation: Impacts of Industry 4.0. *Industrial Relations Journal*, 53(4), 289–307. DOI: 10.1111/irj.12362

Hysa, X., & Themeli, A. (2022). Interorganizational coworking: attenuating complexity, enhancing resilience and fostering open innovation and knowledge cocreation. *Transforming Government: People. Process and Policy*, 16(2), 244–257.

Iaia, L., Isidori, D., Vitale, G., & Leone, D. (2023). Cognitive automation in Industry 4.0: Human-centered approaches. *Journal of Manufacturing Systems*, 69, 309–320. DOI: 10.1016/j.jmsy.2022.07.003

Ivanov, S., & Webster, C. (2019). Perceived appropriateness and intention to use service robots in tourism. In *Information and Communication Technologies in Tourism 2019:Proceedings of the International Conference in Nicosia,Cyprus,January 30–February 1, 2019* (pp. 237-248). Springer International Publishing. DOI: 10.1007/978-3-030-05940-8_19

Jarrahi, M. H. (2018). Artificial intelligence and the future of work: Human-AI symbiosis in organizational decision-making. *Business Horizons*, 61(4), 577–586. DOI: 10.1016/j.bushor.2018.03.007

Jo¨hnk, J., Weißert, M., & Wyrtki, K. (2021). Ready or not, AI comes – an interview study of organizational AI readiness factors. *Business & Information Systems Engineering*, 63(1), 5–20. DOI: 10.1007/s12599-020-00676-7

Khemthong, S., & Roberts, L. (2006). Adoption of internet and web technology for hotel marketing: A study of hotels in Thailand. *Journal of Business Systems, Governance, and Ethics*, 1(2), 47–60. DOI: 10.15209/jbsge.v1i2.74

Kim, G., Shin, B., Kim, K. K., & Lee, H. G. (2011). IT capabilities, process-oriented dynamic capabilities, and firm financial performance. *Journal of the Association for Information Systems*, 12(7), 487–517. DOI: 10.17705/1jais.00270

Kim, J. (2020). The influence of perceived costs and perceived benefits on AI-driven interactive recommendation agent value. *Journal of Global Scholars of Marketing Science*, 30(3), 319–333. DOI: 10.1080/21639159.2020.1775491

Kusiak, A. (2018). Smart manufacturing. *International Journal of Production Research*, 56(1-2), 508–517. DOI: 10.1080/00207543.2017.1351644

Lengnick-Hall, C. A., Beck, T. E., & Lengnick-Hall, M. L. (2011). Developing a capacity for organizational resilience through strategic human resource management. *Human Resource Management Review*, 21(3), 243–255. DOI: 10.1016/j.hrmr.2010.07.001

Leone, D., Vitale, G., & Zucchella, A. (2020). Value co-creation in Industry 4.0 ecosystems. *Strategic Change*, 29(5), 515–525. DOI: 10.1002/jsc.2384

Lu, Y. (2017). Industry 4.0: A review on technologies, applications, and open research issues. *Journal of Industrial Information Integration*, 6, 1–10. DOI: 10.1016/j.jii.2017.04.005

Malik, A., Pereira, V., & Budhwar, P. (2020). HRM in the global information technology (IT) industry: Towards multivergent configurations in strategic business partnerships. *Human Resource Management Review*, 31(3), 100743. DOI: 10.1016/j.hrmr.2020.100743

Manley, D., & Williams, J. (2022). Socio-technical symbiosis in Industry 4.0: Toward a framework for human-machine collaboration. *Systems Research and Behavioral Science*, 39(5), 1238–1254. DOI: 10.1002/sres.2845

Maresova, P., Soukal, I., & Kuca, K. (2018). Technological trends in Industry 4.0 and their impact on business models. *Economic Research-Ekonomska Istraživanja*, 31(1), 1843–1857. DOI: 10.1080/1331677X.2018.1519691

Marwaha, K. (2017). Corporate governance and whistle blowing in India: Promises or reality? *International Journal of Law and Management*, 59(3), 430–441. DOI: 10.1108/IJLMA-12-2015-0064

Metaxiotis, K., Zafeiropoulos, I., & Askounis, D. (2005). Dynamic risk management system for the modeling, optimal adaptation and implementation of an ERP system. *Information Management & Computer Security*, 13(3), 212–234. DOI: 10.1108/09685220510602031

Modgil, S., Singh, R. K., & Hannibal, C. (2021). Artificial intelligence for supply chain resilience: Learning from covid-19. *International Journal of Logistics Management*. Advance online publication. DOI: 10.1108/IJLM-02-2021-0094

Mooney, J. G., Gurbaxani, V., & Kraemer, K. L. (1996). A process oriented framework for assessing the business value of information technology. *The Data Base for Advances in Information Systems*, 27(2), 68–81. DOI: 10.1145/243350.243363

Moore, G. C., & Benbasat, I. (1991). Development of an instrument to measure the perceptions of adopting an information technology innovation. *Information Systems Research*, 2(3), 192–222. DOI: 10.1287/isre.2.3.192

Mourtzis, D. (2020). Simulation and virtual commissioning of Industry 4.0 technologies in lean manufacturing systems. *CIRP Annals*, 69(1), 7–20. DOI: 10.1016/j.cirp.2020.04.121

Muduli, A., & Trivedi, J. J. (2020). Recruitment methods, recruitment outcomes and information credibility and sufficiency. *Benchmarking*, 27(4), 1615–1631. DOI: 10.1108/BIJ-07-2019-0312

Musawa, M., & Wahab, E. (2012). The adoption of EDI technology by Nigerian SMEs: A conceptual framework. *Journal of Business Management and Economics*, 3(2), 55–68.

Nair, P. (2017), *The rise of the AI recruiter: is HR tech the next to challenge human intuition*. www.growthbusiness.co.uk/rise-ai-recruiter-hr-tech-next-challenge-human-intuition-2550350

Novak, S., & Wisdom, J. (2018). Addressing anxiety in workplace AI integration. *The Journal of Applied Psychology*, 103(7), 895–912. DOI: 10.1037/apl0000314

Okumus, F., Ali, F., & Bilgihan, A. (2017). Workplace technology adoption: Perceptions of AI and robotics. *International Journal of Contemporary Hospitality Management*, 29(5), 1388–1410. DOI: 10.1108/IJCHM-02-2016-0066

Ostmeier, E., & Strobel, M. (2022). Addressing fears of AI in the workplace: Strategies for human-centered AI integration. *AI & Society*, 37(1), 45–57. DOI: 10.1007/s00146-020-01068-1

Pan, Y., Froese, F., Liu, N., Hu, Y., & Ye, M. (2021). The adoption of artificial intelligence in employee recruitment: The influence of contextual factors. *International Journal of Human Resource Management*, 1–23. DOI: 10.1080/09585192.2021.1879206

Pillai, R., & Sivathanu, B. (2020). Adoption of artificial intelligence (AI) for talent acquisition in IT/ITeS organizations. *Benchmarking*, 27(9), 2599–2629. DOI: 10.1108/BIJ-04-2020-0186

Pompa, D. (2015). Prepared Statement.

Pranciulyte-Bagdziūniene, A., & Petraite, M. (2019). Developing Industry 4.0 skills in the workforce: Insights from Lithuanian case studies. *Management of Sustainable Development*, 11(1), 17–22. DOI: 10.2478/msd-2019-0003

Prifti, L., Knigge, M., Kienegger, H., & Krcmar, H. (2017). A competency model for "Industrie 4.0" employees. *Business & Information Systems Engineering*, 59(4), 219–229. DOI: 10.1007/s12599-017-0484-6

Rana, N., & Sharma, P. (2019). Assessing HR challenges in Industry 4.0: Workforce transformations. *Asia Pacific Journal of Human Resources*, 57(2), 138–154. DOI: 10.1111/1744-7941.12226

Ransbotham, S., Kiron, D., Gerbert, P., & Reeves, M. (2017). Reshaping business with artificial intelligence: Closing the gap between ambition and action. *MIT Sloan Management Review*, 59(1), 1–17.

Rao, D. A. S., & Verweij, G. (2017). *Sizing the Prize: What's the Real Value of AI for Your Business and How Can You Capitalise?* PwC Publication.

Rogers, E. M. (1995). *Diffusion of Innovations* (4th ed.). The Free Press.

Rogers, E.M. (2003), *The Diffusion of Innovations* (5th ed.) Free Press.

Ross, J. W., Beath, C. M., & Goodhue, D. L. (1996). Develop long-term competitiveness through IT assets. *Sloan Management Review*, 38(1), 31–42.

Russell, S. J., & Norvig, P. (2016). *Artificial Intelligence: A Modern Approach*. Pearson Education.

Sampson, G., Wills, M., & Brown, A. (2020). Clarifying expectations and training for AI integration. *Human Resource Development Quarterly*, 31(2), 151–165. DOI: 10.1002/hrdq.21385

Sharma, M., & Biros, D. (2021). AI and its implications for organisations. In Lee, Z. W. Y., Chan, T. K. H., & Cheung, C. M. K. (Eds.), *Information Technology in Organisations and Societies: Multidisciplinary Perspectives from AI to Technostress* (pp. 1–24). Emerald Publishing.

Sivathanu, B., & Pillai, R. (2018). Smart manufacturing and Industry 4.0: Implications for older workers. *Ageing International*, 43(3), 391–405. DOI: 10.1007/s12126-018-9323-2

Sorko, M., Nguyen, T., & Fung, C. (2016). Augmented workforce dynamics in Industry 4.0: Leveraging AI for human augmentation. *Journal of Organizational Computing and Electronic Commerce*, 26(2), 171–192. DOI: 10.1080/10919392.2016.1157543

Spence, C. (2022). The human factor in automation and augmentation: A future skills perspective. *Technovation*, 120, 102544. DOI: 10.1016/j.technovation.2021.102544

Sundaresan, S., & Zhang, X. (2022). Understanding the human factors in human-AI collaboration: A meta-analytic approach. *Computers in Human Behavior*, 133, 107266. DOI: 10.1016/j.chb.2022.107266

Szabo-Szentgróti, G., Fekete, P., & Bányai, T. (2021). Labor transformation in AI-driven organizations: A European perspective. *European Management Review*, 18(4), 585–602. DOI: 10.1111/emre.12429

Tambe, P., Cappelli, P., & Yakubovich, V. (2019). Artificial intelligence in human resources management: Challenges and a path forward. *California Management Review*, 61(4), 15–42. DOI: 10.1177/0008125619867910

Tata consultancy services (2017), *TCS global trend study on artificial intelligence reveals industry wide investment by 2020*. www.tcs.com/global-trend-study-artificial -intelligence-revealsindustry-wide-investment-2020

Thies, C. G., & Wehner, L. E. (2019). The role of role theory in international political economy. *Cambridge Review of International Affairs*, 32(6), 712–733. DOI: 10.1080/09557571.2019.1609415

Ustundag, A., & Cevikcan, E. (2018). *Industry 4.0: Managing the digital transformation*. Springer. DOI: 10.1007/978-3-319-57870-5

van-Esch, P., Black, J. S., & Ferolie, J. (2019). Marketing AI recruitment: The next phase in job application and selection. *Computers in Human Behavior*, 90(1), 215–222. DOI: 10.1016/j.chb.2018.09.009

Veza, I., Mladineo, M., & Potočan, V. (2015). Digital transformation of production systems in value chains. *Management*, 20(2), 25–40.

Vrontis, D., Bresciani, S., & Giacosa, E. (2022). Transforming business models through Industry 4.0 technologies. *Journal of Business Research*, 140, 88–99. DOI: 10.1016/j.jbusres.2022.07.031

Wamba, S. F., Gunasekaran, A., Akter, S., Ren, S. J. F., Dubey, R., & Childe, S. J. (2017). Big data analytics and firm performance: Effects of dynamic capabilities. *Journal of Business Research*, 70(1), 356–365. DOI: 10.1016/j.jbusres.2016.08.009

Wamba-Taguimdje, S. L., Fosso Wamba, S., Kala Kamdjoug, J. R., & Tchatchouang Wanko, C. E. (2020). Influence of artificial intelligence (AI) on firm performance: The business value of AI-based transformation projects. *Business Process Management Journal*, 26(7), 1893–1924. DOI: 10.1108/BPMJ-10-2019-0411

Weber, R. (2016). Automation and digital transformation: The paradox of the fourth industrial revolution. *Journal of Manufacturing Systems*, 39, 229–238. DOI: 10.1016/j.jmsy.2016.08.011

Wheeler, A. R., & Buckley, M. R. (2021). The current and future states of automation, artificial intelligence, and machine learning. In *HR without People? (The Future of Work)* (pp. 29–44). Emerald Publishing. DOI: 10.1108/978-1-80117-037-620211003

Wilson, H. J., & Daugherty, P. R. (2018). Collaborative intelligence: Humans and AI are joining forces. *Harvard Business Review*, 96(4), 114–123.

Yang, Z., Kankanhalli, A., Ng, B. Y., & Lim, J. T. Y. (2013). Analyzing the enabling factors for the organizational decision to adopt healthcare information systems. *Decision Support Systems*, 55(3), 764–776. DOI: 10.1016/j.dss.2013.03.002

Zhu, K., Kraemer, K., Xu, S., & Dedrick, J. (2004). Information technology payoffs in e-business environment: An international perspective on value creation of e-business in the financial services industry. *Journal of Management Information Systems*, 21(1), 17–54. DOI: 10.1080/07421222.2004.11045797

Chapter 2
Digitally Enhanced World of Realities:
Immersive Technologies and Innovative Business Models

Tunde Toyese Oyedokun
https://orcid.org/0000-0001-5306-038X
Thomas Adewumi University, Oko-Irese, Nigeria

ABSTRACT

The digital age has seen an unparalleled evolution in technology, particularly with immersive technologies like augmented reality (AR), virtual reality (VR), and mixed reality (MR), leading us toward a metaverse-defined future. This chapter explores their transformative impact on various industries as we stand on the brink of a convergence between digital and physical realms. Tracing the historical trajectory and pivotal milestones of AR and VR development, it examines their current state and convergence with domains like AI and IoT. Examining their applications across sectors such as healthcare, education, and retail, the chapter unveils innovative business models emerging within the metaverse. From redefining consumer behavior in e-commerce to revolutionizing traditional learning methods, immersive technologies are reshaping industries and necessitate understanding for individuals, businesses, and policymakers navigating this transformative landscape.

INTRODUCTION

Immersive technologies, including augmented reality (AR), virtual reality (VR), and mixed reality (MR), have indeed revolutionized the digital landscape by merging the physical and virtual worlds. AR overlays digital content onto the real world, en-

DOI: 10.4018/979-8-3693-9571-4.ch002

hancing experiences in fields like manufacturing, medicine, and education (Babaei, 2023). AR overlays digital content onto the real world, enhancing experiences in various fields. Examples include IKEA's AR app for visualizing furniture in the home, and Google Maps Live View for navigation. AR applications are typically experienced through smartphones or AR headsets, which use cameras and sensors to detect the user's surroundings and superimpose digital information. VR immerses users in a completely simulated digital environment, providing a fully immersive experience. Users typically wear a VR headset, which tracks their head movements and displays a computer-generated environment. VR applications are used in various fields, including gaming, entertainment, education, and healthcare. MR combines elements of both AR and VR, blending the real world with digital content. MR allows users to interact with and manipulate both physical and virtual items and environments, using next-generation sensing and imaging technologies. Examples include Microsoft's HoloLens, Acer Windows Mixed Reality, Lenovo Explorer, and Samsung Odyssey (Marr, 2021). These immersive technologies have transformed various industries by providing enhanced experiences, improved comprehension, and increased accessibility. They not only transform how we interact with technology but also open up new possibilities for learning, training, entertainment, and various industries, bridging the gap between the physical and digital realms. They have also opened up new opportunities for innovation and growth, particularly in fields like education and healthcare (Brandon, 2023).

The metaverse concept envisions a shared virtual space where individuals can interact, work, play, and create, transcending physical boundaries and offering vast opportunities for innovation and entrepreneurship (Yogesh et al., 2022). It represents a convergence of digital experiences, social interactions, and economic activities powered by immersive technologies like virtual reality (VR), augmented reality (AR), and extended reality (XR) (Steffen, Gaskin, Meservy, Jenkins & Wolman, 2019). In the metaverse, people can engage in various activities such as playing games, socializing, attending events, purchasing real estate, collaborating on projects, and exploring new career opportunities. This interconnected, interactive, and immersive 3D world aims to create a more natural and engaging environment for human interaction, creativity, entertainment, and commercial endeavors (Onu, Pradhan & Mbohwa, 2023). As these immersive technologies evolve, the metaverse holds the potential to reshape how individuals interact, learn, work, and engage with the digital world, ushering in a new era of interconnected virtual experiences.

Business models are indeed experiencing significant shifts due to the emergence of immersive technologies like virtual reality (VR) and augmented reality (AR). In e-commerce and retail, the concept of virtual storefronts and immersive shopping experiences is revolutionizing consumer engagement and transforming online shopping (Hagl & Duane, 2018). These technologies are reshaping how consumers interact with products, offering realistic views and experiences that bridge the gap between physical and digital shopping environments. Businesses can provide customers with a more interactive and personalized shopping experience by creating 3D simulations of products and services, ultimately influencing consumer behavior and enhancing online marketplaces (Krasonikolakis, Vrechopoulos, Pouloudi & Dimitriadis, 2018). Moreover, in the entertainment and media industries, immersive technologies are driving the creation of innovative content and distribution channels. Content creators and distributors are leveraging VR and AR to develop new forms of entertainment that offer audiences immersive and engaging experiences (Dhiman, 2023). This shift is not only changing how content is consumed but also opening up new revenue streams and business models. Businesses in these sectors can differentiate themselves, enhance customer engagement, and explore novel ways to monetize their content through unique and interactive experiences by embracing immersive technologies.

The education and training sectors are indeed leveraging immersive technologies like virtual classrooms and simulations to revolutionize learning outcomes and skill development. By immersing learners in simulated environments, these technologies offer multi-sensory and kinesthetic learning experiences that enhance knowledge retention and engagement. Studies have shown that immersive learning can significantly improve learning outcomes, with VR training leading to a 4x gain in focus and learning speed compared to traditional classroom methods. Additionally, immersive learning methods play a crucial role in reversing the trend of declining student engagement and meeting the growing needs for reskilling and upskilling the global workforce. In the healthcare sector, immersive technologies are transforming medical training, therapy, and patient care. VR-trained surgeons have been found to make significantly fewer errors, highlighting the effectiveness of immersive simulations in medical education (Tang, Chau, Kwok, Zhu & Ma, 2022). These technologies provide realistic and accessible training opportunities through holograms, anatomy simulations, and scenario-based learning, offering a safe and measurable environment for practical training activities. Companies like ORamaVR, OssoVR, and FundamentalVR are at the forefront of utilizing immersive technologies to enhance surgical training and visualization in the medical profession.

The integration of immersive technologies in education and healthcare is not only enhancing learning and training experiences but also creating new business models for educational institutions, Ed-tech startups, healthcare providers, and digital health startups (Mathew & Pillai, 2020). By embracing these technologies, businesses in these sectors can differentiate themselves, improve productivity, and offer innovative solutions that cater to the evolving needs of learners, healthcare professionals, and patients. The transformative potential of immersive technologies is reshaping traditional approaches to education, training, and healthcare, paving the way for a more engaging, effective, and personalized learning and healthcare experience.

The evolution of immersive technologies has been marked by significant milestones, from their early conceptualization to contemporary breakthroughs driven by advancements in hardware, software, and network infrastructure. These technologies continue to evolve, propelled by synergies with other cutting-edge domains such as artificial intelligence (AI), blockchain, and the Internet of Things (IoT). The future of immersive technologies holds vast potential, with applications spanning healthcare, education, remote assistance, and entertainment. The integration of VR and AR with AI and IoT technologies is set to create even more immersive and interactive experiences, offering users seamless transitions between different levels of immersion based on their needs and preferences. As we navigate this digitally enhanced world and the emergence of the metaverse, understanding the dynamics of immersive technologies and their implications for business models is crucial for individuals, businesses, and policymakers alike. This comprehensive understanding provides the foundational knowledge necessary to capitalize on the opportunities presented by the immersive future that lies ahead.

The Evolution of Immersive Technologies

The origins of immersive technologies can be traced back to the late 20th century when pioneers in computer graphics and human-computer interaction laid the groundwork for AR and VR. Ivan Sutherland's "*Sword of Damocles*" in 1968 marked one of the earliest VR head-mounted displays (HMDs), albeit primitive compared to contemporary standards (Tisler, 2024). Concurrently, Myron Krueger's pioneering work in "artificial reality" during the 1970s explored interactive environments where users could engage with computer-generated elements in real-time (Turner, 2002). The concept of AR gained momentum in the 1990s with research and development efforts aimed at overlaying digital information onto the physical world (Adeniyi, Joseph, Daniel & Godwin, 2023). In 1992, Louis Rosenberg's Virtual Fixtures system demonstrated the potential of AR for enhancing human performance in industrial applications (Rosenberg, 2021). The term "augmented reality" was coined by Boeing researcher Tom Caudell in 1990, defining a technology that superimposes digital data onto real-world environments (Didier, 2021). Commercial applications of AR emerged in the early 2000s, notably with the introduction of ARToolKit by Hirokazu Kato in 1999, which enabled marker-based AR experiences on personal computers (Kato & Billinghurst, 2004).

The launch of smartphones equipped with cameras and sensors in the late 2000s catalyzed the proliferation of AR applications (Blum, Greencorn & Cooperstock, 2013). In 2009, the Layar app introduced mobile AR experiences that overlaid digital information onto the user's camera view, pioneering location-based AR (Liao & Humphreys, 2015). Further advancements in computer vision, sensor technologies, and mobile computing fueled the growth of AR platforms such as Apple's ARKit and Google's ARCore, empowering developers to create immersive AR experiences for smartphones and tablets (Oufqir, Abderrahmani & Satori, 2020). Commercialization efforts in the 1990s brought VR to mainstream audiences, with products like Sega's VR-1 and Virtuality's arcade machines offering immersive gaming experiences (Jones, Osborne, Sullivan-Drage, Keen & Gladsby, 2022). However, limitations in technology and high costs hindered widespread adoption. The early 2000s witnessed a resurgence of interest in VR with the development of affordable HMDs such as the Oculus Rift and HTC Vive, fueled by advancements in display technology, motion tracking, and graphics processing (Venkatesan, Mohan, Ryan, Schurch, Nolan, Frakes & Coskun, 2021). The acquisition of Oculus by Facebook in 2014 signaled a new era for VR, with significant investments in hardware, software, and content (Kraus, Kanback, Krysta, Steinhoff & Tomini, 2022). The launch of consumer-grade VR headsets and platforms democratized access to immersive experiences, fostering a vibrant ecosystem of developers, content creators, and enthusiasts. Today, VR applications extend beyond gaming to areas such as education, training, healthcare, and entertainment, showcasing the transformative potential of immersive technologies.

The evolution of immersive technologies, particularly augmented reality (AR) and virtual reality (VR), has been a fascinating journey marked by significant milestones that have reshaped human-computer interaction and revolutionized various industries. These technologies have transitioned from early experimental concepts to sophisticated tools that offer immersive experiences beyond imagination (Partarakis & Zebulis, 2024). The roots of immersive technologies trace back to the late 1950s, with the development of the Sensorama by Morton Heilig, which aimed to provide users with a fully immersive viewing experience simulating a motorbike ride (Heilig, 1962; Sanders, 1997). Since then, VR has evolved into a complex technology with high-resolution displays, motion-tracking sensors, and immersive audio, enabling lifelike experiences across diverse fields like education, healthcare, entertainment, and more. VR has found applications in training simulations, medical education, combat scenarios, and even psychological therapy, showcasing its versatility and potential impact on various sectors (Hamad & Jia, 2022). Recent advancements in VR technology, such as the Oculus Rift, have made immersive experiences more accessible and affordable, expanding their reach and utility (Radianti, Majchrzac, Fromm & Wohlgenannt, 2020). These developments have not only transformed entertainment but also opened up new possibilities in education, training, and beyond. The integration of VR with AI, haptic feedback, and eye-tracking technologies promises even more exciting advancements in the future, offering immersive experiences that blur the lines between the physical and virtual worlds.

On the other hand, AR has emerged as a powerful tool for creating interactive and engaging experiences without the need for additional hardware, making it a part of everyday life through smartphone integration. AR has found applications in navigation, interactive gaming, personalized customer support, and marketing campaigns, showcasing its potential to enhance user experiences and drive business innovation (Hamad & Jia, 2022). The journey of immersive technologies from their early beginnings to their current state of cutting-edge applications highlights the relentless pursuit of innovation, technological advancements, and creative exploration in the quest for immersive experiences that transcend traditional boundaries. As these technologies continue to evolve, they hold the promise of reshaping how we perceive and interact with the world, offering endless possibilities for immersive storytelling, training simulations, therapeutic interventions, and collaborative environments across industries.

Recent advancements in immersive technologies have focused on enhancing user experiences, reducing barriers to entry, and expanding the capabilities of AR and VR platforms. Breakthroughs in display technologies, such as OLED panels and foveated rendering, have improved visual fidelity and reduced motion sickness in VR environments (Haamer, Mikhailava, Podliesnova, Saremat, Lusmagi, Petrinec & Anbarjafari, 2024). Similarly, advancements in spatial mapping, gesture recognition, and object tracking have enhanced the realism and interactivity of AR experiences. The integration of artificial intelligence (AI) and machine learning algorithms has further enriched immersive technologies by enabling context-aware interactions, real-time content generation, and personalized experiences. Mixed reality (MR) platforms, which combine elements of AR and VR, offer new possibilities for blending digital and physical realities in seamless and interactive ways.

The immersive landscape is continually evolving, with hardware and software advancements driving innovation and adoption across various industries. As technology continues to mature and barriers to entry diminish, immersive experiences are poised to become increasingly integrated into everyday life (Garlinska, Osial, Proniewska & Pregowska, 2023). Immersive technologies, including virtual reality (VR), augmented reality (AR), and mixed reality (MR), have been continuously evolving, driven by advancements in both hardware and software. The latest VR headsets are becoming more lightweight, comfortable, and offer higher resolutions and wider fields of view for a more immersive experience (Yang, Zhong, Li & You, 2023). Additionally, standalone VR headsets are gaining popularity due to their convenience and affordability, eliminating the need for tethering to a PC or console. There's a growing emphasis on improving input devices for better interaction within immersive environments. This includes hand tracking, haptic gloves, and controllers with increased precision and responsiveness. Devices capable of real-time mapping of physical spaces are enhancing AR experiences, enabling better integration of digital content into the real world.

Advanced software tools are making it easier for developers and creators to produce high-quality immersive content. This includes 3D modeling software, game engines with built-in VR support, and AR development platforms. Artificial intelligence (AI) technologies are being integrated into immersive experiences to enhance realism, interactivity, and personalization. AI-driven avatars, NPCs, and dynamic environments are becoming more common. There's a growing focus on social interaction within immersive environments, with platforms allowing users to connect, communicate, and collaborate in virtual or augmented spaces (Sarakatsanos, Papazoglous-Chalikias, Boikou, Chatzilari, Jauk, Hafliger, Nikolopoulos & Kompatsiaris, 2024). Gaming remains a significant driver of immersive technology adoption, with VR games becoming increasingly popular among enthusiasts. Additionally, immersive experiences are expanding into other forms of entertainment, including immersive theater, virtual concerts, and virtual tourism. Immersive technologies are being widely adopted in education and training, offering realistic simulations for learning complex subjects, vocational training, and skills development. In healthcare, VR and AR are being used for medical training, patient education, pain management, and therapeutic interventions. The pandemic has also accelerated the adoption of telemedicine, with AR enabling remote assistance and consultation. Various industries, including architecture, engineering, manufacturing, and retail, are leveraging immersive technologies for design visualization, prototyping, remote collaboration, and customer engagement.

While immersive technologies are becoming more accessible and affordable, there are still barriers to widespread adoption, including the cost of high-end hardware and the need for user-friendly content creation tools. As immersive technologies become more pervasive, there are growing concerns about privacy, data security, and ethical use, particularly regarding user tracking, data collection, and potential psychological impacts. Establishing industry standards and ensuring interoperability among different hardware and software platforms are crucial for driving innovation and seamless user experiences across diverse ecosystems.

Convergence of Technologies

The intersection of immersive technologies such as virtual reality (VR), augmented reality (AR), and mixed reality (MR) with artificial intelligence (AI), blockchain, and the Internet of Things (IoT) presents a compelling opportunity to create synergistic experiences that offer enhanced realism, interactivity, and security. AI algorithms can analyze user behavior and preferences within immersive environments to dynamically adapt content, characters, and scenarios in real-time, creating personalized and engaging experiences (Soliman, Ahmed, Darwish & Hassanien, 2024). Integrating Natural Language Processing (NLP) capabilities into immersive experiences allows users to interact with virtual characters and environments using natural language, enabling more intuitive and conversational interactions (Partarakis & Zabulis, 2024). AI-driven avatars and non-player characters (NPCs) can exhibit lifelike behaviors, emotions, and responses, enhancing immersion and facilitating more realistic interactions within virtual worlds. AI algorithms can assist in the generation of immersive content, such as procedural generation of environments, textures, and animations, speeding up the content creation process and increasing scalability.

Blockchain technology can be used to securely manage ownership and transactions of virtual assets within immersive environments, such as digital currencies, virtual goods, and in-game items, ensuring authenticity, provenance, and scarcity. Blockchain for recording transactions and interactions within immersive experiences ensures transparency, traceability, and immutability of data, reducing the risk of fraud, manipulation, and unauthorized modifications. Blockchain-based decentralized identity solutions can provide users with control over their digital identities within immersive environments, enabling seamless authentication, access control, and privacy protection across different platforms and applications (Huynh-The, Gadekallu, Wang, Yenduri, Ranaweera, Phem, Costa & Liyanage, 2023).

Internet of Thing (IoT) sensors and devices can bridge the gap between physical and digital worlds by capturing real-world data and integrating it into immersive experiences, enriching simulations and enhancing realism. Immersive environments can be enhanced with IoT-enabled smart objects and environments, allowing users to interact with and manipulate physical objects within virtual or augmented spaces, creating dynamic and interactive experiences. IoT data can provide contextual information about users' surroundings, preferences, and activities, enabling more personalized and contextually relevant immersive experiences tailored to individual users (Asif & Hassan, 2023). By leveraging the synergies between immersive technologies, AI, blockchain, and IoT, developers and creators can unlock new possibilities for creating immersive experiences that are more engaging, secure, and adaptive to users' needs and preferences. These converging technologies have the potential to reshape various industries, including gaming, entertainment, education, healthcare, and enterprise, by offering novel ways to interact with digital content and the physical world.

Realities in the Digitally Enhanced World

In the digitally enhanced world, various realities converge to create a rich tapestry of immersive experiences that redefine how we interact with information, entertainment, and each other. As technology continues to evolve, the boundaries between physical and virtual realities will continue to blur, opening up new possibilities for exploration, expression, and collaboration in the digital age. The metaverse refers to a collective virtual shared space that merges elements of physical and digital reality, enabling persistent, immersive experiences across multiple platforms and devices. The metaverse is characterized by its vastness, interconnectivity, and user-generated content, resembling a virtual universe where users can socialize, work, play, and create. Companies like Facebook (now Meta), Epic Games, and Roblox are investing heavily in the development of metaverse platforms, envisioning a future where the boundaries between the real and virtual worlds blur even further.

Virtual reality (VR) offers users an immersive experience in entirely computer-generated environments, creating a sense of presence and interaction within digital spaces (Lowood, 2024). This technology has been revolutionary in various fields, including gaming, training simulations, therapeutic interventions, and immersive storytelling experiences in the entertainment industry. In gaming, VR allows players to step into virtual worlds, enhancing gameplay and providing a more engaging experience (Reer, Wehden, Janzik, Tang & Quandt, 2022). Training simulations benefit from VR by offering realistic scenarios for practice, especially in fields like medicine, engineering, and aviation. Therapeutic interventions utilize VR for exposure therapy, pain management, and rehabilitation (Huang, Lin, Han, Peng & Huang, 2022). Additionally, VR enhances storytelling in the entertainment industry by transporting viewers into captivating narratives, creating a more immersive and engaging form of storytelling (Haas & Tussey, 2021). Virtual reality (VR) technology provides users with immersive experiences by creating a sense of presence within digital environments. Users can interact with and manipulate digital objects and environments, feeling as if they are physically present in the virtual world. This immersion is achieved through the use of headsets and motion-tracking technology, allowing users to explore and engage with virtual worlds in a realistic manner. From gaming and entertainment to training simulations and virtual tourism, VR offers a wide range of applications that leverage its ability to transport users to entirely digital environments and provide them with realistic interactions and experiences (Hamad & Jia, 2022).

Augmented reality (AR) seamlessly integrates digital information into the physical environment, revolutionizing various industries (Mattan, 2024; Leroy, 2023). In healthcare, AR aids in medical training, allowing learners to handle expensive equipment like MRI scanners and conduct surgical training in 3D image formats (Dhar,

Rock, Samarasinghe, Stephenson & Smith, 2021). Moreover, AR enhances interior design by visualizing products before purchase, transforms education by creating rich learning environments accessible globally, and revolutionizes entertainment by building connections between users and digital characters. In the retail sector, AR enables shoppers to compare products, view details by scanning with mobile apps, and customize items without physical interaction (Lal, 2024). Additionally, AR is used in logistics, public safety, electrical/mechanical services, tourism, and assembly sectors, offering benefits like identifying shipment details, directing to safe locations, diagnosing faults quickly, virtually exploring travel destinations, and designing products (Tubis, Jodejko-Pietruczuk & Nowakowski, 2024). The future of AR is promising, with its applications expanding across various sectors, driven by advancements in technology and user experience design. Augmented Reality (AR) technology superimposes digital content onto the physical world, enriching users' real-world experiences by adding virtual elements, interactive features, or contextual information to their surroundings. This overlay of digital information is commonly accessed through smartphones, tablets, or AR glasses, allowing users to interact with a blend of virtual and physical environments. AR applications are diverse, spanning across gaming, advertising, navigation, education, and industrial maintenance, offering unique and interactive experiences that enhance users' perception of reality (Arena, Collotta, Paul & Termine, 2022).

Mixed reality (MR) is an immersive technology that combines physical and digital elements, allowing them to interact seamlessly through 3D holograms (Tang, Au & Leung, 2018). This innovative approach merges virtual and real-world objects, enabling them to coexist and interact in immersive environments. MR offers a unique blend of virtual and physical elements, enhancing experiences in industrial design, engineering, remote collaboration, and interactive marketing campaigns (Sala, 2021). In industrial design and engineering, MR facilitates the creation of digital twins for testing innovative concepts with minimal waste and resources, speeding up the innovation process (Attaran, Attaran & Celik, 2023). Remote collaboration benefits from MR by enabling teams to interact with 3D assets intuitively, fostering more engaging shared experiences (Teo, Lawrence, Lee, Billinghurst & Adcock, 2019). Moreover, interactive marketing campaigns leverage MR to create novel and immersive experiences for consumers, enhancing brand engagement and driving sales (Rane, Choudhary & Rane, 2023). The versatility of MR across various sectors highlights its potential to revolutionize how we interact with digital and physical elements, offering new possibilities for creativity, collaboration, and engagement. Mixed reality (MR) technologies like Microsoft HoloLens and Magic Leap are revolutionizing various industries such as design, engineering, architecture, and healthcare by offering advanced visualization, collaboration, and training capabilities. MR combines aspects of both virtual reality (VR) and augmented reality (AR) to seamlessly integrate digital and physical content in real-time. This technology allows virtual objects to interact with the physical environment and vice versa, creating immersive experiences that respond to users' actions and movements. By leveraging MR, professionals in these fields can enhance their workflows, improve training outcomes, and facilitate innovative ways of visualizing and interacting with complex data and environments (Palumbo, 2022).

Extended reality (XR) serves as an umbrella term encompassing Virtual Reality (VR), Augmented Reality (AR), Mixed Reality (MR), and other immersive technologies that extend or enhance human perception and interaction with digital content. XR experiences can range from fully immersive virtual environments in VR to lightly augmented views in AR, providing users with varying levels of immersion and interaction. This technology is driving innovation across industries by offering novel ways to engage users, streamline processes, and create impactful experiences that blend the physical and digital worlds seamlessly (Rauschabel, Felix, Hinsch, Shahab & Ait, 2022).

Integration of Digital Information Into the Physical Environment through Augmented Reality

Augmented Reality (AR) stands at the intersection of the digital and physical worlds, offering a transformative way to enhance our perception and interaction with the environment around us. It seamlessly integrates digital information into real-world settings, providing users with an enriched experience that blends virtual elements with their immediate surroundings. This fusion of the virtual and physical realms has profound implications across various industries, including healthcare, education, and retail, where AR is revolutionizing conventional practices and unlocking new possibilities.

In healthcare, AR has emerged as a valuable tool for medical training, diagnosis, and treatment. Medical professionals can utilize AR simulations to practice surgical procedures in a realistic virtual environment, enhancing their skills and improving patient outcomes. For instance, companies like AccuVein have developed AR devices that assist healthcare providers in locating veins for blood draws and intravenous injections, reducing patient discomfort and improving efficiency (Vyas, Sharma, Goyal & Kothari, 2021). AR is also transforming patient education and engagement. With AR-enabled apps, patients can visualize complex medical concepts and anatomy in 3D, empowering them to better understand their conditions and treatment options. Moreover, AR applications are being used for rehabilitation purposes, guiding patients through interactive exercises and monitoring their progress in real-time.

In education, AR has the potential to revolutionize traditional teaching methods by making learning more immersive and interactive. AR-enabled textbooks and educational apps bring static content to life, allowing students to explore subjects like history, geography, and science in engaging ways (Koumpouros, 2024). For example, students can use AR to virtually dissect animals, explore historical landmarks, or simulate chemical reactions, enhancing their comprehension and retention of information. AR also facilitates experiential learning opportunities, enabling students to interact with digital models and simulations that simulate real-world scenarios. This hands-on approach fosters critical thinking, problem-solving, and creativity, preparing students for the challenges of the future workforce. Furthermore, AR can accommodate diverse learning styles and preferences, catering to individual needs and promoting inclusivity in education.

In the retail sector, Augmented Reality (AR) technology is revolutionizing the shopping experience for consumers, both online and offline. Retailers are utilizing AR to allow customers to interact with products virtually before making a purchase, enhancing their ability to visualize items in their own space (Tan, Chandukala & Reddy, 2022). For example, furniture retailers offer AR apps that enable shoppers to see how a sofa or table would look in their living room, eliminating guesswork and reducing the likelihood of returns. This technology not only enhances customer engagement but also streamlines the decision-making process by providing a more immersive and personalized shopping experience. With the development of augmented reality (AR) technology, marketers have a wealth of chances to interact with consumers and change their perception of a brand.

AR-powered virtual try-on experiences are becoming increasingly popular in the fashion industry, allowing customers to virtually try on clothing and accessories using their smartphones or tablets. This technology leverages augmented reality (AR) to superimpose virtual representations of products onto the customer's image, providing a realistic and interactive way for customers to visualize how items would look on them before making a purchase (Baytar, Chung & Shin, 2020). By enabling virtual try-ons, fashion brands can enhance the online shopping experience, increase customer engagement, reduce returns, and offer a more personalized and convenient way for consumers to explore and select products. This not only enhances the convenience of online shopping but also reduces the need for physical fitting rooms, thereby streamlining the retail experience and increasing customer satisfaction. Moreover, AR is being used to create immersive marketing campaigns and interactive brand experiences. Retailers can deploy AR-powered signage and displays in-store to engage customers and drive sales. By overlaying digital content such as product information, reviews, and promotions onto physical retail environments, AR enhances the overall shopping experience and fosters brand loyalty.

Augmented Reality represents a powerful paradigm shift in how digital information is integrated into the physical environment. Its applications across industries such as healthcare, education, and retail are diverse and far-reaching, offering transformative benefits to both businesses and consumers. As AR technology continues to evolve and become more accessible, its potential to reshape our interaction with the world around us will only continue to expand, unlocking new opportunities for innovation and growth.

Exploring Fully Immersive, Computer-Generated Worlds Through Virtual Reality

Virtual Reality (VR) transports users into fully immersive, computer-generated environments, blurring the line between the real world and the digital realm. By leveraging advanced technologies such as head-mounted displays, motion tracking sensors, and haptic feedback systems, VR creates a sense of presence and immersion that allows users to interact with and explore virtual worlds as if they were real. This transformative technology has found applications across various domains, including gaming, training, therapy, and beyond, revolutionizing how we perceive and interact with digital content. Perhaps the most well-known application of VR is in gaming, where it offers unparalleled levels of immersion and engagement. VR gaming enables players to step into the shoes of their virtual avatars and experience games from a first-person perspective, providing a level of immersion that traditional gaming platforms cannot match. From heart-pounding action titles to immersive exploration games, VR offers a diverse range of gaming experiences that cater to different preferences and interests.

Furthermore, VR introduces new gameplay mechanics and interaction paradigms that take advantage of its immersive capabilities. Players can physically move and gesture within virtual environments, allowing for intuitive interactions with objects and characters (Liao, 2024). This creates opportunities for innovative game design and novel gameplay experiences that challenge traditional conventions and push the boundaries of interactive entertainment. In addition to gaming, VR has emerged as a powerful tool for training and simulation across various industries. From military and aerospace to healthcare and manufacturing, VR-based training simulations offer a safe and cost-effective way to prepare individuals for high-risk or complex scenarios. For example, military personnel can undergo VR simulations of combat situations to hone their tactical skills and decision-making abilities in a realistic yet controlled environment (Harris, Arthur, Kearse, Olonilua, Hassan, De-Burgh, Wilson & Vine, 2023).

Similarly, healthcare professionals can use VR simulations to practice medical procedures and surgical techniques without risk to patients. VR training programs allow surgeons to perform virtual surgeries, refine their techniques, and learn from mistakes in a risk-free setting (Kuhn, Yu, Gerull, Silverman & Aleem, 2024). This not only improves their proficiency but also enhances patient safety and outcomes. VR is also being increasingly used in therapeutic applications to treat various mental health conditions and disorders. Virtual reality exposure therapy (VRET), for example, is a clinically proven treatment for phobias, PTSD, and anxiety disorders. By exposing patients to virtual environments that evoke their specific fears or triggers, therapists can gradually desensitize them and help them overcome their symptoms in a controlled and supportive environment. Moreover, VR-based therapies are being explored for pain management, rehabilitation, and cognitive behavioral therapy. Virtual reality experiences can distract patients from pain during medical procedures, motivate them to engage in physical rehabilitation exercises, and provide immersive environments for guided relaxation and stress reduction techniques. As VR technology continues to evolve, so too will its potential to revolutionize mental healthcare and improve the well-being of individuals worldwide.

Beyond gaming, training, and therapy, VR has countless other applications across diverse industries and sectors. From architectural visualization and urban planning to virtual tourism and remote collaboration, VR is reshaping how we design, communicate, and interact with the world around us. Architects and designers can use VR to create immersive 3D models of buildings and environments, allowing clients to explore and experience their designs before they are built (Ashgan, Moubark, Saif & El-Shorbagy, 2023). Similarly, virtual tourism platforms enable users to virtually visit destinations and landmarks from the comfort of their homes, providing access to inaccessible or remote locations and preserving cultural heritage. Additionally, VR-based remote collaboration tools facilitate real-time communication and collaboration among geographically dispersed teams, fostering creativity, innovation, and productivity in the workplace.

Virtual Reality represents a paradigm shift in how we experience and interact with digital content. Its fully immersive, computer-generated environments have far-reaching applications across gaming, training, therapy, and beyond, offering transformative benefits to individuals, industries, and society as a whole. As VR technology continues to advance and become more accessible, its potential to reshape our perception of reality and unlock new possibilities for human experience and expression will only continue to grow.

Understanding the Blend of Physical and Digital Realities with Mixed Reality

Mixed Reality (MR) represents the seamless integration of the physical and digital worlds, creating immersive experiences where virtual and real objects co-exist and interact in real-time. Unlike Virtual Reality (VR), which replaces the real world with a fully immersive virtual environment, and Augmented Reality (AR), which overlays digital content onto the physical world, Mixed Reality bridges the gap between these two paradigms, allowing for a dynamic blend of physical and digital elements. This fusion of realities opens up a myriad of practical use cases and implications for user experiences across various domains.

Mixed Reality enables designers and engineers to visualize and manipulate virtual prototypes of products in real-world environments. By overlaying digital CAD models onto physical objects, designers can assess form, fit, and function more accurately, speeding up the design iteration process and reducing the time and cost associated with physical prototyping (Kent, Snider, Gopsill & Hicks, 2021). Mixed Reality facilitates remote collaboration by allowing users to share and interact with virtual objects and environments in real-time. For example, technicians can use MR headsets to receive real-time guidance and instructions from remote experts while performing complex maintenance tasks. This not only improves efficiency but also reduces downtime and travel costs.

Mixed Reality offers a heightened sense of immersion by seamlessly blending virtual and real-world elements. This immersion enhances the sense of presence and realism, making interactions with digital content feel more natural and intuitive. Mixed Reality improves spatial awareness by overlaying contextual information onto physical environments. Users can easily understand the spatial relationships between virtual and real objects, enabling more precise interactions and navigation. Mixed Reality enables personalized and customized experiences tailored to individual preferences and needs. By leveraging user data and contextual information, MR applications can deliver content and interactions that are relevant and meaningful to each user. Mixed Reality facilitates collaboration and social interaction by enabling users to share virtual experiences and interact with each other in real-time. Whether it's collaborating on a design project or playing multiplayer games, MR brings people together in shared virtual spaces regardless of physical distance. Mixed Reality has the potential to improve accessibility by providing alternative modes of interaction and representation. For example, MR applications can adapt to users with disabilities by offering customizable interfaces, alternative input methods, and inclusive design principles.

Mixed Reality enhances learning experiences by providing immersive and interactive simulations. Students can explore virtual environments, interact with 3D models, and conduct experiments in a safe and controlled setting. For instance, medical students can practice surgical procedures on virtual patients, while aviation students can simulate cockpit operations and flight scenarios. Mixed Reality transforms the retail experience by allowing customers to interact with virtual products and experiences in physical stores. Retailers can use MR displays and kiosks to showcase virtual product catalogs, offer personalized recommendations, and create interactive brand experiences. This not only increases engagement but also drives sales and brand loyalty. Mixed Reality represents a paradigm shift in how we perceive and interact with the world around us. By seamlessly blending physical and digital realities, MR opens up a world of possibilities for practical applications and user experiences across industries and domains. As Mixed Reality technology continues to evolve and become more accessible, its potential to transform how we work, learn, play, and communicate will only continue to grow, shaping the future of human-computer interaction and immersive experiences.

Business Models in the Metaverse

The Metaverse, a collective virtual shared space, is rapidly becoming a new frontier for business opportunities, particularly in the realm of immersive shopping experiences and virtual storefronts. As advancements in virtual reality (VR), augmented reality (AR), and other immersive technologies continue to evolve, businesses are exploring innovative ways to engage consumers and drive sales in virtual environments. This shift towards immersive shopping experiences is not only reshaping traditional retail models but also profoundly impacting consumer behavior and the evolution of online commerce. In the Metaverse, virtual storefronts serve as digital representations of physical stores, offering consumers the opportunity to browse, interact with products, and make purchases in immersive virtual environments. These virtual storefronts can range from lifelike replicas of brick-and-mortar stores to entirely virtual spaces designed to captivate and engage consumers. Some businesses create virtual showrooms where customers can explore products in a visually stunning and interactive environment. For example, automotive companies may offer virtual showrooms where customers can customize and test-drive virtual cars before making a purchase decision. Brands can host immersive events and experiences in the Metaverse to showcase their products and engage with customers in novel ways.

This could include virtual fashion shows, interactive product launches, or virtual pop-up shops featuring exclusive items.

Leveraging data analytics and AI, businesses can personalize shopping experiences in the Metaverse to cater to individual preferences and behaviors. Virtual assistants and avatars can guide customers through virtual stores, provide recommendations, and offer assistance, simulating the personalized service of a physical store (Villagas-Ch, Amores-Falconi & Coronel-Silver, 2023). The rise of immersive shopping experiences in the Metaverse is reshaping consumer behavior in several key ways, including increased engagement, social interaction, expanded reach and accessibility as well as experimental shopping behaviors. Immersive shopping experiences capture consumers' attention and foster deeper engagement with brands and products. By providing interactive and visually stimulating environments, businesses can create memorable experiences that resonate with customers long after they leave the virtual storefront. The Metaverse facilitates social interaction and collaboration, allowing consumers to shop together with friends, family, or like-minded individuals from around the world (Dwivedi, et al., 2022). Social shopping experiences enable users to share recommendations, seek advice, and make purchase decisions collectively, mimicking the social aspect of traditional shopping trips. Virtual storefronts in the Metaverse offer businesses the opportunity to reach a global audience without the constraints of physical location. Consumers can access virtual stores from anywhere at any time, eliminating geographical barriers and expanding market reach. Immersive shopping experiences encourage consumers to explore and experiment with products in ways that may not be possible in traditional retail settings. Virtual try-on experiences, interactive product demonstrations, and gamified shopping experiences incentivize consumers to discover new products and make informed purchase decisions.

The emergence of immersive shopping experiences in the Metaverse represents a significant evolution in online commerce, blurring the lines between physical and digital retail environments. Businesses are integrating virtual storefronts with their existing omnichannel strategies, creating seamless shopping experiences that span both physical and digital channels (Thaichon, Quach, Barari & Nguyen, 2023). For example, customers may browse products in a virtual store and then complete their purchase in a physical store or vice versa. AR and VR technologies are driving the development of immersive shopping experiences in the Metaverse, enabling businesses to create lifelike virtual environments that replicate the sensory aspects of physical shopping. These technologies enhance the realism and interactivity of virtual storefronts, making them more compelling and engaging for consumers. Immersive shopping experiences open up new revenue streams for businesses through virtual product sales, virtual event sponsorships, and virtual advertising opportunities. Additionally, businesses can monetize virtual experiences through subscription models, in-app purchases, and virtual currency systems, creating alternative sources of income beyond traditional retail sales.

Business models in the Metaverse centered around immersive shopping experiences and virtual storefronts are revolutionizing the way consumers shop and interact with brands online. By leveraging advanced technologies and embracing the immersive capabilities of the Metaverse, businesses can create compelling and engaging shopping experiences that drive sales, foster customer loyalty, and shape the future of online commerce. As the Metaverse continues to evolve, businesses that embrace immersive shopping experiences stand to gain a competitive advantage in the digital landscape, positioning themselves at the forefront of innovation and consumer engagement.

Role of Immersive Technologies in Entertainment and Media

In recent years, immersive technologies have indeed revolutionized various sectors of the entertainment and media industry, including gaming, filmmaking, and live events. These technologies, which encompass virtual reality (VR), augmented reality (AR), mixed reality (MR), and extended reality (XR), offer audiences unprecedented levels of engagement and interactivity, reshaping the way content is created, consumed, and monetized. The immersive media landscape is witnessing significant growth, with the market projected to reach a staggering USD 178.7 billion by 2032, driven by a strong 22.3% CAGR (Shinde, 2024). Major industry players like Apple Inc., Sony, Microsoft, and Google, among others, are contributing to this expansion through innovation and evolving consumer preferences. Immersive technologies are being applied in diverse sectors, such as employee training, healthcare, retail, and education, enhancing experiences and outcomes across these fields. The rise of social VR platforms, immersive learning and training tools, and the transformation of retail and commerce through immersive experiences are just a few examples of how these technologies are reshaping the industry. Additionally, the deployment of 5G networks and edge computing is crucial for delivering seamless and responsive immersive experiences, further driving the adoption and advancement of immersive technologies in the entertainment and media sector.

Immersive technologies have significantly elevated the gaming experience, blurring the lines between the virtual and physical worlds. VR headsets, motion-sensing controllers, and haptic feedback devices enable gamers to immerse themselves fully in rich, interactive virtual environments. Titles like "Half-Life: Alyx," "Beat Saber," and "The Walking Dead: Saints & Sinners" showcase the potential of VR gaming, offering players unparalleled levels of immersion and presence (Siddiquee, 2024). Furthermore, AR gaming experiences, exemplified by the widespread success of "Pokemon Go," have transformed the way people interact with their surroundings, integrating digital elements into real-world environments (Sicart, 2017). These advancements not only cater to traditional gamers but also attract new audiences, bridging the gap between casual and hardcore gaming. From a business perspective, immersive technologies present lucrative opportunities for game developers and publishers. Subscription-based models, micro-transactions, and in-game advertisements have become prevalent revenue streams, allowing companies to monetize their content beyond the initial purchase price. Additionally, the rise of live-streaming platforms like Twitch and YouTube Gaming has created new avenues for gamers to generate income through sponsorships, donations, and advertising revenue (Woodcock & Johnson, 2019).

Immersive technologies have revolutionized the art of storytelling in filmmaking, offering filmmakers innovative tools to create immersive narratives and interactive experiences. VR films transport viewers into captivating virtual worlds, allowing them to explore narratives from different perspectives and engage with characters in unprecedented ways (Priya, 2023). Productions like "Pearl," "Dear Angelica," and "Gloomy Eyes" demonstrate the emotive power of VR storytelling, eliciting profound emotional responses from audiences. AR experiences have also augmented traditional filmmaking techniques, enabling filmmakers to overlay digital elements onto physical environments seamlessly (O'meara & Szita, 2021). This integration of digital and physical realms enhances storytelling possibilities, blurring the boundaries between fantasy and reality. For instance, AR apps like "Wonderscope" and "Holo" empower users to interact with animated characters and scenes within their own surroundings, creating personalized cinematic experiences. From a business standpoint, immersive filmmaking presents both challenges and opportunities for content creators and distributors (Hutson, 2023). While production costs may initially be higher due to the technical demands of immersive storytelling, the potential for increased viewer engagement and monetization through subscription-based platforms, virtual cinemas, and branded content partnerships is substantial. Moreover, immersive experiences can drive ancillary revenue through merchandise sales, location-based attractions, and immersive theater experiences.

Immersive technologies have transformed the landscape of live events, offering organizers innovative ways to engage audiences and create memorable experiences. VR concerts and festivals allow music fans to attend live performances from the comfort of their homes, transcending geographical barriers and maximizing accessibility. Artists like Travis Scott and Marshmello have pioneered virtual concerts, attracting millions of viewers and redefining the concept of live entertainment in the digital age (Tidy, 2020). AR-enhanced live events integrate digital overlays and interactive elements into physical spaces, enhancing audience participation and creating immersive environments. From sporting events to corporate conferences, AR technologies enrich live experiences by providing real-time data, interactive maps, and personalized content overlays (Zollmann, Langlotz, Loos, Lo & Baker, 2019). For example, AR apps like "FanDuel Live" and "IBM Watson AR" enhance the spectator experience by delivering player stats, replays, and analysis directly to users' mobile devices.

Immersion live events provide sponsors, content producers, and event organizers with profitable revenue prospects. While sponsorship agreements and advertising partnerships take advantage of the immersive aspect of the event, virtual ticket sales, item purchases, and brand activations can create sizable revenue streams. Additionally, organizers are able to customize future experiences to match the changing demands and preferences of their audience through the use of data analytics and audience insights gained from immersive live events. Immersive technologies have become integral components of the entertainment and media landscape, transforming gaming, filmmaking, and live events in profound ways. From enhancing user experiences to fostering new business models for content creators and distributors, immersive technologies continue to push the boundaries of storytelling, engagement, and monetization. As these technologies evolve and become more accessible, their impact on the entertainment industry will only continue to grow, shaping the future of entertainment and media for years to come.

Education and Training in Immersive Environments

The incorporation of immersive technologies, such as training simulations, virtual classrooms, and skill development in virtual settings, has significantly transformed education and training in recent years. These technologies present special chances to raise engagement levels, improve learning outcomes, and cultivate transferable skills across a range of professions. Virtual classrooms leverage VR and AR technologies to create immersive learning environments where students can engage with educational content and interact with instructors and peers in real-time. These virtual spaces replicate traditional classroom settings or simulate practical scenarios, providing students with hands-on learning experiences regardless of their physical location (Al-Ansi, Jaboob, Garad & Al-Ansi, 2023). Platforms like Engage, AltspaceVR, and Mozilla Hubs enable educators to conduct lectures, facilitate discussions, and deliver immersive learning materials across a wide range of subjects.

The advantages of virtual classrooms include increased accessibility, flexibility, and interactivity. Students can attend classes remotely, eliminating geographical barriers and accommodating diverse learning styles. Immersive simulations and 3D visualizations enhance comprehension and retention of complex concepts, while collaborative features foster teamwork and communication skills (Haleem, Javaid, Qadri & Suman, 2022). Additionally, virtual classrooms offer personalized learning experiences through adaptive assessments, analytics, and feedback mechanisms. However, challenges such as technological limitations, accessibility issues, and concerns about digital equity must be addressed to ensure the inclusivity and effectiveness of virtual classrooms. Moreover, the integration of immersive technologies into existing educational frameworks requires substantial investment in infrastructure, training, and curriculum development.

Training simulations immerse learners in realistic scenarios to develop practical skills and competencies in various industries, including healthcare, aviation, manufacturing, and emergency response. These simulations replicate high-stakes situations where learners can practice decision-making, problem-solving, and procedural tasks in a risk-free environment. VR platforms like Osso VR, Virti, and Mursion offer interactive training modules that simulate surgical procedures, flight simulations, and interpersonal communication scenarios. The benefits of training simulations include enhanced skill acquisition, reduced training costs, and improved safety outcomes. Learners can repeat exercises, receive immediate feedback, and track their progress over time, accelerating the learning curve and minimizing the risk of errors in real-world settings (Green, Tariq & Green, 2016). Moreover, immersive simulations can simulate rare or dangerous situations that may be impractical or unethical to replicate in traditional training environments. However, the effectiveness of training simulations depends on the fidelity of the virtual environment, the accuracy of the scenarios, and the realism of the interactions. Designing and maintaining immersive simulations require collaboration between subject matter experts, instructional designers, and software developers to ensure alignment with learning objectives and industry standards.

Immersive environments offer novel approaches to skill development by combining experiential learning, gamification, and adaptive feedback mechanisms. Virtual reality training programs, serious games, and interactive simulations enable learners to acquire technical skills, soft skills, and domain-specific competencies through engaging and immersive experiences (Lampropoulos, 2024). Platforms like Unity Learn, Coursera, and LinkedIn Learning offer courses and tutorials that leverage immersive technologies to teach programming, design, and digital skills. The gamification of learning experiences incentivizes participation, rewards achievements, and fosters intrinsic motivation among learners. By incorporating game mechanics such as progression systems, challenges, and leaderboards, immersive environments transform skill development into an enjoyable and rewarding process. Moreover, adaptive learning algorithms personalize the learning journey based on learners' preferences, performance data, and learning styles, maximizing engagement and retention. However, challenges such as content curation, quality assurance, and scalability must be addressed to ensure the efficacy and accessibility of skill development in immersive environments. Educational institutions and ed-tech startups must collaborate with industry partners, accrediting bodies, and regulatory agencies to validate the effectiveness of immersive learning solutions and ensure alignment with industry standards and certification requirements.

The integration of immersive technologies into education and training has given rise to innovative business models for educational institutions and ed-tech startups. These models encompass subscription-based platforms, pay-per-use licensing, revenue-sharing agreements, and corporate partnerships. Educational institutions can monetize immersive learning experiences through tuition fees, course subscriptions, and corporate training contracts, while ed-tech startups can generate revenue through software licensing, content sales, and consulting services (Lauren-Arrendondo & Laurens, 2023). Subscription-based platforms offer access to a library of immersive learning resources, tools, and support services for a recurring fee, catering to individual learners, educational institutions, and corporate clients. Pay-per-use models enable users to purchase access to specific courses, modules, or simulations on an as-needed basis, providing flexibility and scalability for learners and organizations. Revenue-sharing agreements allow content creators, developers, and publishers to distribute their immersive learning materials through third-party platforms, sharing revenue based on usage metrics and sales performance.

Corporate partnerships enable educational institutions and ed-tech startups to collaborate with employers, industry associations, and training providers to develop custom learning solutions tailored to specific skill gaps and workforce needs. By aligning curriculum content with industry standards, certification requirements, and job market demands, educational institutions and ed-tech startups can enhance the employability and career prospects of learners while generating revenue through licensing fees, consulting services, and talent acquisition partnerships. Immersive environments have the potential to revolutionize education and training by providing learners with immersive, interactive, and personalized learning experiences. Virtual classrooms, training simulations, and skill development in immersive environments offer unique opportunities to enhance engagement, improve learning outcomes, and develop practical skills in various fields (Al-Ansi, Jaboob, Garad & Al-Ansi, 2023). By leveraging innovative business models, educational institutions and ed-tech startups can capitalize on the growing demand for immersive learning solutions while addressing the evolving needs of learners, educators, and employers in the digital age.

Applications in Healthcare and Wellness With Immersive Technologies

Immersion technologies like mixed reality (MR), augmented reality (AR), and virtual reality (VR) have started to transform many facets of wellness and healthcare in recent years. These technologies offer innovative solutions in medical training, therapy, and patient care, enhancing the efficiency, effectiveness, and accessibility of healthcare services. Immersive technologies have transformed medical education and training by providing learners with realistic and interactive simulations of medical procedures, anatomical structures, and clinical scenarios. Virtual reality simulators allow medical students, residents, and practicing professionals to practice surgical techniques, medical interventions, and patient consultations in a safe and controlled environment (Deng, Xiang & Pan, 2023). Companies like Osso VR, Precision OS, and Touch Surgery offer immersive training modules that replicate surgical procedures, trauma scenarios, and patient interactions with high fidelity and accuracy.

Augmented reality applications enable learners to overlay digital information, 3D models, and interactive elements onto physical objects and environments, enhancing the visualization and understanding of complex medical concepts. AR-based anatomy apps, patient education tools, and medical device training modules provide learners with contextualized information and hands-on learning experiences (Dhar, Rock, Samarasinghe, Stephenson & Smith, 2021). Platforms like AccuVein, Proximie, and AccuVein utilize AR technology to facilitate vein visualization, surgical planning, and remote collaboration among healthcare professionals. Immersive technologies are increasingly being used to enhance therapeutic interventions and rehabilitation programs across various healthcare settings. Virtual reality exposure therapy (VRET) is particularly effective in treating phobias, anxiety disorders, and post-traumatic stress disorder (PTSD) by exposing patients to virtual environments that evoke targeted emotional responses. VR-based pain management programs, relaxation techniques, and mindfulness exercises offer non-pharmacological interventions for chronic pain, stress-related disorders, and mental health conditions.

Augmented reality applications complement traditional therapy approaches by providing real-time feedback, guidance, and support during physical rehabilitation exercises, occupational therapy sessions, and cognitive-behavioral interventions. AR-based mobility aids, assistive devices, and prosthetic fittings enhance the functional independence and quality of life for individuals with disabilities or mobility impairments (Williams, Alikhademi, Drobina, Gilbert & Sutor, 2019). Companies like XRHealth, Limbix, and XRHealth offer customizable VR and AR therapy platforms that address a wide range of clinical needs, including pain management, cognitive rehabilitation, and behavioral health. Immersive technologies are reshaping the delivery of patient care by improving communication, collaboration, and engagement between healthcare providers and patients. Virtual reality distraction therapy (VRDT) reduces pain perception, anxiety levels, and medication requirements during medical procedures, such as wound care, dental procedures, and chemotherapy infusions. VR-based relaxation techniques, guided imagery, and immersive environments promote emotional well-being, stress reduction, and patient comfort in hospital settings.

Augmented reality applications enhance the diagnostic process, treatment planning, and surgical navigation by providing healthcare providers with real-time access to patient data, medical imaging, and clinical guidelines. AR-based medical imaging overlays, anatomical models, and visualization tools enable surgeons to perform minimally invasive procedures with greater precision, efficiency, and safety. Companies like AccuVein, AccuVein, and Surgical Theater offer AR solutions that streamline patient care workflows, improve surgical outcomes, and enhance patient satisfaction (Vinolo, Gonzalez-Medina, Lucena-Anton, Perez-Cabezas, Ruiz-Molinero & Martin-Valero, 2021). Healthcare providers are leveraging immersive technologies to enhance patient care, optimize clinical workflows, and differentiate their services in a competitive market. Business models for healthcare providers leveraging immersive technologies include subscription-based platforms, fee-for-service arrangements, and value-based care models. Subscription-based platforms offer access to immersive healthcare services, telemedicine consultations, and remote monitoring tools for a monthly or annual fee, catering to individuals, families, and employer groups.

Value-based care models incentivize healthcare providers to deliver high-quality, cost-effective care by tying reimbursement to patient outcomes, satisfaction scores, and healthcare utilization metrics. By integrating immersive technologies into care delivery models, healthcare providers can improve patient engagement, adherence to treatment plans, and health outcomes while reducing healthcare costs and hospital readmissions. Immersive technologies have the potential to transform healthcare and wellness by enhancing medical training, therapy, and patient care. Virtual reality, augmented reality, and mixed reality applications offer innovative solutions for education, rehabilitation, and treatment across a wide range of clinical specialties. By embracing emerging business models and leveraging immersive technologies, healthcare providers can improve the accessibility, affordability, and quality of care while addressing the evolving needs and preferences of patients, caregivers, and healthcare professionals in the digital age.

CONCLUSION

In the evolving landscape of our digitally enhanced world, the integration of immersive technologies has catalyzed transformative shifts in education, healthcare, and business, offering unprecedented opportunities for learning, healing, and innovation. From virtual classrooms revolutionizing education to immersive simulations redefining medical training and patient care, the breadth of applications is vast and impactful. Moreover, the emergence of new business models, driven by subscription-based platforms, fee-for-service arrangements, and value-based care models, reflects a paradigm shift in how organizations monetize immersive experiences and deliver value to stakeholders. As we navigate this terrain, it's imperative to address challenges of technological limitations, ethical considerations, and accessibility issues, ensuring inclusivity, equity, and responsible innovation. Ultimately, by embracing collaboration, creativity, and a commitment to leveraging technology for the greater good, we can forge a future where immersive experiences enrich lives, empower communities, and drive positive change across.

REFERENCES

Adeniyi, S., Joseph, S. B., Daniel, S., & Godwin, G. (2023). *The impact of augmented reality on social interaction: bridging the digital and physical worlds*. https://www.researchgate.net/publication/376642894_The_Impact_of_Augmented_Reality_on_Social_Interaction_Bridging_the_Digital_and_Physical_Worlds

Al-Ansi, A. M., Jaboob, M., Garad, A., & Al-Ansi, A. (2023). Analyzing augmented reality (AR) and virtual reality (VR) recent development in education. *Social Sciences & Humanities Open*, 8(1), 100532. DOI: 10.1016/j.ssaho.2023.100532

Arena, F., Collotta, M., Pau, G., & Termine, F. (2022). An overview of augmented reality. *Computers*, 11(2), 28. DOI: 10.3390/computers11020028

Ashgan, E., Moubarki, N., Saif, M., & El-Shorbagy, A. (2023). Virtual Reality in architecture. *Civil Engineering and Architecture*, 11(1), 498-506. https://www.hrpub.org/download/20221230/CEA38-14892091.pdf

Asif, R., & Hassan, S. R. (2023). Exploring the confluence of IoT and Metaverse: Future opportunities and challenges. *IoT*, 4(3), 412-429. DOI: 10.3390/iot4030018

Attaran, M., Attaran, S., & Celik, B. G. (2023). The impact of digital twins on the evolution of intelligent manufacturing and Industry 4.0. *Advances in Computational Intelligence*, 3(3), 11. DOI: 10.1007/s43674-023-00058-y PMID: 37305021

Babaei, A. (2023, November 19). *The evolution of reality: Exploring the realm of AR, VR, and XR*. Medium. https://medium.com/@dr.arya.design/the-evolution-of-reality-exploring-the-realm-of-ar-vr-and-xr-f4c14178df73

Baytar, F., Chung, T., & Shin, E. (2020). Evaluating garments in augmented reality when shopping online. *Journal of Fashion Marketing and Management*, 24(4), 667–683. DOI: 10.1108/JFMM-05-2018-0077

Blum, J. R., Greencorn, D. G., & Cooperstock, J. R. (2013). Smartphone sensor reliability for Augmented Reality applications. In: Zheng, K., Li, M., Jiang, H. (eds) *Mobile and Ubiquitous Systems: Computing, Networking, and Services*. MobiQuitous 2012. DOI: 10.1007/978-3-642-40238-8_11

Brandon, B. (2023, December 14). *Immersive reality: Unleash augmented, virtual, and mixed reality*. New York: The Learning Guild. https://www.learningguild.com/articles/immersive-reality-unleash-augmented-virtual--and-mixed-reality-/

Deng, Z., Xiang, N., & Pan, J. (2023). State of the art in immersive interactive technologies for surgery simulation: A review and prospective. *Bioengineering (Basel, Switzerland)*, 10(12), 1346. DOI: 10.3390/bioengineering10121346 PMID: 38135937

Dhar, P., Rocks, T., Samarasinghe, R. M., Stephenson, G., & Smith, C. (2021). Augmented reality in medical education: Students' experiences and learning outcomes. *Medical Education Online*, 26(1), 1953953. DOI: 10.1080/10872981.2021.1953953 PMID: 34259122

Dhiman, B. (2023). A paradigm shift in the entertainment industry in the digital age: A critical Review. https://nbnresolving.org/urn:nbn:de:0168-ssoar-86963-8

Didier, T. (2021, January 29). *1990 - First mention of the term "Augmented Reality"*. Atomic. https://atomicdigital.design/blog-post/1990-first-mention-of-the-term-augmented-reality

Dwivedi, , Hughes, L., Baabdullah, A. M., Ribeiro-Navarrete, S., Giannakis, M., Al-Debei, M. M., Dennehy, D., Metri, B., Buhalis, D., Cheung, C. M. K., Conboy, K., Doyle, R., Dubey, R., Dutot, V., Felix, R., Goyal, D. P., Gustafsson, A., Hinsch, C., Jebabli, I., & Wamba, S. F. (2022). Metaverse beyond the hype: Multidisciplinary perspectives on emerging challenges, opportunities, and agenda for research, practice and policy. *International Journal of Information Management*, 66, 102542. DOI: 10.1016/j.ijinfomgt.2022.102542

Garlinska, M., Osial, M., Proniewska, K., & Pregowska, A. (2023). The Influence of Emerging Technologies on Distance Education. *Electronics (Basel)*, 12(7), 1550. DOI: 10.3390/electronics12071550

Green, M., Tariq, R., & Green, P. (2016). Improving patient safety through simulation training in anesthesiology: Where are we? *Anesthesiology Research and Practice*, 4237523, 1–12. Advance online publication. DOI: 10.1155/2016/4237523 PMID: 26949389

Haamer, R. E., Mikhailava, N., Podliesnova, V., Saremat, R., Lusmägi, T., Petrinec, A., & Anbarjafari, G. (2024). Motion sickness in mixed-reality situational awareness system. *Applied Sciences (Basel, Switzerland)*, 14(6), 2231. DOI: 10.3390/app14062231

Haas, L., & Tussey, J. (Eds.). (2021). *Connecting Disciplinary Literacy and Digital Storytelling in K-12 Education*. IGI Global., DOI: 10.4018/978-1-7998-5770-9

Hagl, R., & Duane, A. (2018). *Exploring the impact of augmented reality and virtual reality technologies on business model innovation in technology companies in Germany*. In: Australasian Conference on Information Systems, (ed.), Australasian Conference on Information Systems 2018. Sydney: UTS ePRESS. DOI: DOI: 10.5130/acis2018.ao

Haleem, A., Javaid, M., Qadri, M. A., & Suman, R. (2022). Understanding the role of digital technologies in education: A review. *Sustainable Operations and Computers*, 3, 275–285. DOI: 10.1016/j.susoc.2022.05.004

Hamad, A., & Jia, B. (2022). How Virtual Reality Technology Has Changed Our Lives: An Overview of the Current and Potential Applications and Limitations. *International Journal of Environmental Research and Public Health*, 19(18), 11278. DOI: 10.3390/ijerph191811278 PMID: 36141551

Harris, D. J., Arthur, T., Kearse, J., Olonilua, M., Hassan, E. K., De Burgh, T. C., Wilson, M. R., & Vine, S. J. (2023). Exploring the role of virtual reality in military decision training. *Frontiers in Virtual Reality*, 4, 1165030. Advance online publication. DOI: 10.3389/frvir.2023.1165030

Heilig, M. (1962). *US Patent #3,050,870*. https://patentimages.storage.googleapis.com/90/34/2f/24615bb97ad68e/US3050870.pdf

Huang, Q., Lin, J., Han, R., Peng, C., & Huang, A. (2022). Using Virtual Reality exposure therapy in pain management: A systematic review and meta-analysis of randomized controlled trials. *Value in Health*, 25(2), 288–301. DOI: 10.1016/j.jval.2021.04.1285 PMID: 35094802

Hutson, J. (2023). Shared cinematic experience and emerging technologies: Integrating mixed-reality components for the future of cinema. *Faculty Scholarship*. 504. https://digitalcommons.lindenwood.edu/faculty-research-papers/504

Huynh-The, T., Gadekallu, T. R., Wang, W., Yenduri, G., Ranaweera, P., Pham, Q., Costa, D. B., & Liyanage, M. (2023). Blockchain for the metaverse: A Review. *Future Generation Computer Systems*, 143, 401–419. DOI: 10.1016/j.future.2023.02.008

Jones, P., Osborne, T., Sullivan-Drage, C., Keen, N., & Gadsby, E. (2022). ONE: What is VR and why use it in research? In *Virtual Reality Methods*. Bristol, UK: Policy Press. DOI: 10.51952/9781447360773.ch001

Kato, H., & Billinghurst, M. (2004). *Developing AR applications with ARToolKit*. Conference: 3rd IEEE and ACM International Symposium on Mixed and Augmented Reality (ISMAR 2004), 2-5 November 2004, Arlington, VA, USA. https://www.researchgate.net/publication/221221056_Developing_AR_Applications_with_ARToolKit

Kent, L., Snider, C., Gopsill, J., & Hicks, B. (2021). Mixed reality in design prototyping: A systematic review. *Design Studies*, 77, 101046. DOI: 10.1016/j.destud.2021.101046

Koumpouros, Y. (2024). Revealing the true potential and prospects of augmented reality in education. *Smart Learning Environments*, 11(2), 2. Advance online publication. DOI: 10.1186/s40561-023-00288-0

Krasonikolakis, I., Vrechopoulos, A., Pouloudi, A., & Dimitriadis, S. (2018). Store layout effects on consumer behavior in 3D online stores. *European Journal of Marketing*, 52(5/6), 1223–1256. DOI: 10.1108/EJM-03-2015-0183

Kraus, S., Kanback, D. K., Krysta, P. M., Steinhoff, M. M., & Tomini, N. (2022). Facebook and the creation of the metaverse: Radical business model innovation or incremental transformation? *International Journal of Entrepreneurial Behaviour & Research*, 28(9), 52–77. DOI: 10.1108/IJEBR-12-2021-0984

Kuhn, A. W., Yu, J. K., Gerull, K. M., Silverman, R. M., & Aleem, A. W. (2024). Virtual Reality and surgical simulation training for orthopaedic surgery residents: A qualitative assessment of trainee perspectives. *JBJS: Open Access*, 9(1), e23.00142. https://journals.lww.com/jbjsoa/fulltext/2024/03000/virtual_reality_and_surgical_simulation_training.17.aspx

Lal, R. (2024). *AR In E-commerce for virtual shopping experience*. Idea Usher. https://ideausher.com/blog/ar-in-e-commerce/

Lampropoulos, G., & Kinshuk, . (2024). Virtual reality and gamification in education: A systematic review. *Educational Technology Research and Development*, 72(3), 1691–1785. Advance online publication. DOI: 10.1007/s11423-024-10351-3

Laurens-Arredondo, L. A., & Laurens, L. (2023). Metaversity: Beyond emerging educational technology. *Sustainability (Basel)*, 15(22), 15844. DOI: 10.3390/su152215844

Leroy, K. (2023, June 21). Revolutionizing reality: The current uses and future of AR. *Forbes Business Council*. https://www.forbes.com/sites/forbesbusinesscouncil/2023/06/21/revolutionizing-reality-the-current-uses-and-future-of-ar/?sh=6f3097428836

Liao, T., & Humphreys, L. (2015). Layar-ed places: Using mobile augmented reality to tactically reengage, reproduce, and reappropriate public space. *New Media & Society*, 17(9), 1418–1435. DOI: 10.1177/1461444814527734

Liao, Y. C. (2024). Innovative interaction mode in VR games. In: Hung, J.C., Yen, N., Chang, JW. (eds) *Frontier Computing on Industrial Applications,* Volume 4. FC 2023. Lecture Notes in Electrical Engineering, 1134. Springer, Singapore. DOI: 10.1007/978-981-99-9342-0_9

Lowood, H. E. (2024). Virtual Reality. *Encyclopedia Britannica.* https://www.britannica.com/technology/virtual-reality

Marr, B. (2021). The important difference between Virtual Reality, Augmented Reality and Mixed Reality. *Bernerd Marr & Company.*https://bernardmarr.com/the-important-difference-between-virtual-reality-augmented-reality-and-mixed-reality/

Mathew, P. S., & Pillai, A. S. (2020). Role of Immersive (XR) Technologies in Improving Healthcare Competencies: A Review. In Guazzaroni, G., & Pillai, A. (Eds.), *Virtual and Augmented Reality in Education, Art, and Museums* (pp. 23–46). IGI Global., DOI: 10.4018/978-1-7998-1796-3.ch002

Mattan, M. (2024, March 19). Unlocking the mystery: How does augmented reality transform our world? *BrandXR.*https://www.brandxr.io/unlocking-the-mystery-how-does-augmented-reality-transform-our-world

O'Meara, J., & Szita, K. (2021). AR cinema: Visual storytelling and embodied experiences with Augmented Reality filters and backgrounds. *Presence (Cambridge, Mass.)*, 30, 99–123. DOI: 10.1162/pres_a_00376

Onu, P., Pradhan, A., & Mbohwa, C. (2023). Potential to use metaverse for future teaching and learning. *Education and Information Technologies.* Advance online publication. DOI: 10.1007/s10639-023-12167-9

Oufqir, Z., Abderrahmani, A., & Satori, K. (2020). ARKit and ARCore in serve to augmented reality, 2020 *International Conference on Intelligent Systems and Computer Vision* (ISCV), Fez, Morocco, 2020, pp. 1-7. DOI: 10.1109/ISCV49265.2020.9204243

Palumbo, A. (2022). Microsoft HoloLens 2 in medical and healthcare context: State of the art and future prospects. *Sensors (Basel)*, 22(20), 7709. DOI: 10.3390/s22207709 PMID: 36298059

Partarakis, N., & Zabulis, X. (2024). A Review of Immersive Technologies, Knowledge Representation, and AI for Human-Centered Digital Experiences. *Electronics (Basel)*, 13(2), 269. DOI: 10.3390/electronics13020269

Priya, E. (2023). The impact of technology on cinematic storytelling. *Global Media Journal*, 21, 66. https://www.globalmediajournal.com/open-access/the-impact-of-technology-on-cinematic-storytelling.php?aid=94036

Rane, N., Choudhary, S., & Rane, J. (2023). Metaverse marketing strategies: Enhancing customer experience and analysing consumer behaviour through leading-edge metaverse technologies, platforms, and models. *SSRN*. DOI: 10.2139/ssrn.4624199

Rauschnabel, P. A., Felix, R., Hinsch, C., Shahab, H., & Alt, F. (2022). What is XR? Towards a framework for Augmented and Virtual reality. *Computers in Human Behavior*, 133, 107289. DOI: 10.1016/j.chb.2022.107289

Reer, F., Wehden, L., Janzik, R., Tang, W. Y., & Quandt, T. (2022). Virtual reality technology and game enjoyment: The contributions of natural mapping and need satisfaction. *Computers in Human Behavior*, 132, 107242. DOI: 10.1016/j.chb.2022.107242

Rosenberg, L. B. (2022). Augmented reality: Reflections at thirty years. In: Arai, K. (eds) *Proceedings of the Future Technologies Conference* (FTC) 2021, Volume 1. FTC 2021. Lecture Notes in Networks and Systems, 358. Springer, Cham. DOI: 10.1007/978-3-030-89906-6_1

Sala, N. (2021). Virtual Reality, Augmented Reality, and Mixed Reality in Education: A Brief Overview. In Choi, D., Dailey-Hebert, A., & Estes, J. (Eds.), *Current and Prospective Applications of Virtual Reality in Higher Education* (pp. 48–73). IGI Global. DOI: 10.4018/978-1-7998-4960-5.ch003

Sanders, D. H. (1997). Virtual worlds for archaeological research and education. *Archaeology in the Age of the Internet: Proceedings of the 25th Anniversary Conference of CAA*, Birmingham, April 1997. https://publikationen.uni-tuebingen.de/xmlui/bitstream/handle/10900/62120/CD31_Sanders_CAA_1997.pdf?isAllowed=y&sequence=2

Sarakatsanos, O., Papazoglou-Chalikias, A., Boikou, M., Chatzilari, E., Jauk, M., Hafliger, V., Nikolopoulos, S., & Kompatsiaris, I. C. (2024). VR designer: Enhancing fashion showcases through immersive virtual garment fitting. *Virtual Reality (Waltham Cross)*, 28(2), 70. DOI: 10.1007/s10055-024-00945-w

Shinde, Y. (2024, March 7). Immersive media market to achieve staggering USD 178.7 Bn by 2032. *Asia-Pacific Market News*. https://scoop.market.us/immersive-media-market-news/

Sicart, M. (2017). Reality has always been augmented: Play and the promises of Pokémon GO. *Mobile Media & Communication*, 5(1), 30–33. DOI: 10.1177/2050157916677863

Siddiquee, M. S. A. (2024). Augmented Reality (AR) and Virtual Reality (VR): Transforming gaming, education, and enterprise. *Medium.*https://medium.com/@msa.sid/augmented-reality-ar-and-virtual-reality-vr-transforming-gaming-education-and-enterprise-28888ced035c

Soliman, M. M., Ahmed, E., Darwish, A., & Hassanien, A. E. (2024). Artificial intelligence powered Metaverse: Analysis, challenges and future perspectives. *Artificial Intelligence Review*, 57(2), 36. DOI: 10.1007/s10462-023-10641-x

Steffen, J. H., Gaskin, J. E., Meservy, T. O., Jenkins, J. L., & Wolman, I. (2019). Framework of affordances for Virtual Reality and Augmented Reality. *Journal of Management Information Systems*, 36(3), 683–729. DOI: 10.1080/07421222.2019.1628877

Tan, Y.-C., Chandukala, S. R., & Reddy, S. K. (2022). Augmented reality in retail and its impact on sales. *Journal of Marketing*, 86(1), 48–66. DOI: 10.1177/0022242921995449

Tang, Y., Au, K., & Leung, Y. (2018). Comprehending products with mixed reality: Geometric relationships and creativity. *International Journal of Engineering Business Management*, 10, 1847979018809599. Advance online publication. DOI: 10.1177/1847979018809599

Tang, Y. M., Chau, K. Y., Kwok, A. P. K., Zhu, T., & Ma, X. (2022). A systematic review of immersive technology applications for medical practice and education - Trends, application areas, recipients, teaching contents, evaluation methods, and performance. *Educational Research Review*, 35, 100429. DOI: 10.1016/j.edurev.2021.100429

Teo, T., Lawrence, L., Lee, G. A., Billinghurst, M., & Adcock, M. (2019). Mixed Reality remote collaboration combining 360 video and 3D reconstruction. *CHI '19:Proceedings of the 2019 CHI Conference on Human Factors in Computing Systems*, 1–14. DOI: 10.1145/3290605.3300431

Thaichon, P., Quach, S., Barari, M., & Nguyen, M. (2023). Exploring the role of omnichannel retailing technologies: Future research directions. *Australasian Marketing Journal*, 0(0). Advance online publication. DOI: 10.1177/14413582231167664

Tidy, J. (2020, April 24). Fortnite's Travis Scott virtual concert watched by millions. *BBC News*. https://www.bbc.com/news/technology-52410647

Tisler, M. (2024). *The fascinating evolution of virtual reality history*. https://myriamtisler.com/virtual-reality-history

Tubis, A. A., Jodejko-Pietruczuk, A., & Nowakowski, T. (2024). Use of Augmented Reality as a tool to support cargo handling operations at the CARGO air terminal. *Sensors (Basel)*, 24(4), 1099. DOI: 10.3390/s24041099 PMID: 38400257

Turner, J. (2022). Myron Krueger live. *Ctheory.Net: Journal of Theory, Technology and Culture*. https://journals.uvic.ca/index.php/ctheory/article/view/14583/5428

Venkatesan, M., Mohan, H., Ryan, J. R., Schürch, C. M., Nolan, G. P., Frakes, D. H., & Coskun, A. F. (2021). Virtual and augmented reality for biomedical applications. *Cell Reports Medicine*, 2(7), 100348. DOI: 10.1016/j.xcrm.2021.100348 PMID: 34337564

Villegas-Ch, W., Amores-Falconi, R., & Coronel-Silva, E. (2023). Design proposal for a virtual shopping assistant for people with vision problems applying Artificial Intelligence techniques. *Big Data and Cognitive Computing*, 7(2), 96. DOI: 10.3390/bdcc7020096

Vinolo, G. M., Gonzalez-Medina, G., Lucena-Anton, D., Perez-Cabezas, V., Ruiz-Molinero, M. D. C., & Martín-Valero, R. (2021). Augmented Reality in physical therapy: Systematic review and meta-analysis. *JMIR Serious Games*, 9(4), e30985. DOI: 10.2196/30985 PMID: 34914611

Vyas, V., Sharma, A., Goyal, S., & Kothari, N. (2021). Infrared vein visualization devices for ease of intravenous access in children: Hope versus hype. *Anaesthesiology Intensive Therapy*, 53(1), 69–78. DOI: 10.5114/ait.2021.103515 PMID: 33586417

Williams, R. M., Alikhademi, K., Drobina, E., Gilbert, J. E., & Sutor, T. (2019). Augmented Reality for rehabilitative therapy: Patient experiences and practitioner perspectives. *Proceedings of the Human Factors and Ergonomics Society Annual Meeting*, 63(1), 748–752. DOI: 10.1177/1071181319631140

Woodcock, J., & Johnson, M. R. (2019). Live streamers on Twitch.tv as social media influencers: Chances and challenges for strategic communication. *International Journal of Strategic Communication*, 13(4), 321–335. DOI: 10.1080/1553118X.2019.1630412

Yogesh, . (2022). Metaverse beyond the hype: Multidisciplinary perspectives on emerging challenges, opportunities, and agenda for research, practice and policy. *International Journal of Information Management*, 66, 102542. DOI: 10.1016/j.ijinfomgt.2022.102542

Zollmann, S., Langlotz, T., Loos, M., Lo, W. H., & Baker, L. (2019). AR spectator: Exploring Augmented Reality for sport events. *SIGGRAPH Asia 2019 Technical Briefs (SA '19)* (pp. 75–78). Association for Computing Machinery. DOI: 10.1145/3355088.3365162

Chapter 3
The Role of Artificial Intelligence in Transforming Business Models

Mustafa Kayyali
https://orcid.org/0000-0003-3300-262X
HE Higher Education Ranking, Syria

ABSTRACT

Artificial Intelligence (AI) is transforming the way businesses work, driving a fundamental instability in traditional business paradigms. This chapter addresses the role of AI in driving business model innovation, investigating how companies employ AI technologies to enhance decision-making, optimize processes, and generate new value propositions. By integrating AI into fundamental business processes, companies may change from static, linear models to dynamic, data-driven strategies, allowing for better scalability and agility. Through a series of case studies and examples, the chapter illustrates significant sectors and industries where AI-driven business models have arisen. It also covers the barriers to AI adoption, including technological, ethical, and organizational hurdles, and offers insights into future trends and the developing landscape of AI-powered business transformations.

INTRODUCTION

The development of Artificial Intelligence (AI) has marked an important point in the history of business and technology, with significant implications for how organizations create, deliver, and capture value (Palanivelu & Vasanthi, 2020). As we

DOI: 10.4018/979-8-3693-9571-4.ch003

shift into an era increasingly dominated by data-driven decision-making, automation, and machine learning, AI is not only redefining particular business processes but transforming the entire core of business models themselves. For decades, companies worked inside relatively stable structures where value generation followed predictable patterns. However, AI, with its ability to analyze massive amounts of data in real-time, forecast events, and learn from prior behavior, has ushered in a new paradigm that is both dynamic and disruptive (Akhtar & Lin, 2023). AI's incorporation into the business world is not restricted to a single component; it is a multidimensional force that influences everything from supply chain management to customer engagement, marketing strategies to product innovation. This technological change has allowed organizations to move beyond efficiency improvements, essentially redesigning their operations and competitive strategies. For many organizations, AI has become the linchpin of digital transformation, enabling a change from traditional business models—characterized by linear procedures and compartmentalized operations—to more agile, scalable, and adaptable frameworks. In the digital economy, business models that leverage AI are no longer simply about optimizing existing processes; they are about developing new ways of doing business, where data, automation, and intelligence are at the core.

At the heart of this shift lies AI's capacity to process and interpret data at unprecedented rates and quantities (Nitzberg & Zysman, 2022). In a world where data has become the most precious asset, companies embracing AI can make more informed, faster decisions, often in real time. This capacity offers companies a competitive edge, as they can better foresee market trends, understand consumer behavior, and personalize services or products at scale. For example, industries such as finance, retail, and healthcare have seen AI-driven models boost operational efficiency, cut costs, and open up new revenue streams. Whether it is through predictive analytics in retail, automated trading systems in finance, or AI-powered diagnostics in healthcare, AI is the catalyst fueling a new wave of innovation across numerous sectors. AI's influence is not only operational but strategic. The old business models that historically depend primarily on human intuition, hierarchical decision-making, and static methods of market analysis are gradually giving way to AI-driven models that are more flexible, adaptive, and continuously developing. AI allows businesses to migrate from a reactive approach—where choices are made based on past data and trends—to a proactive one, where predictive insights enable them to anticipate market changes, consumer wants, and operational hazards. This predictive skill is altering industries, from manufacturing and logistics, where AI-driven automation boosts supply chain efficiency, to marketing, where personalized customer experiences can be offered using AI-powered algorithms. One of the most significant advantages AI offers is the capacity to scale business models with minimum incremental expenditures. Traditional business models generally encountered issues in scaling due to the high cost of extra labor, infrastructure, or capital (Reis et al, 2021). AI, however, allows companies to extend operations and services without commensurate increases in expenses. For instance, AI-powered customer service chatbots can handle millions of customer interactions without having more human agents, while AI-driven analytics platforms can process massive volumes of data without the need for large teams of analysts. This scalability offers an unprecedented opportunity for companies to expand their reach, access new markets, and serve larger consumer bases, all while preserving efficiency and decreasing overhead.

Despite its transformational potential, the incorporation of AI into business models also poses hurdles (Farayola et al, 2023). Organizations must cope with difficulties such as data protection, ethical considerations, and the complexities of AI adoption. The adoption of AI-driven models generally demands considerable changes in corporate culture, talent acquisition, and governance frameworks. Many companies have the problem of aligning AI capabilities with their existing business processes and ensuring that the technology is deployed in a way that aligns with broader strategic goals. Moreover, there are broader cultural and ethical consequences linked with AI, including concerns about job displacement due to automation, biases in AI systems, and the possible misuse of AI technologies. As AI continues to evolve, its role in creating business models will only become more important. Companies that refuse to embrace AI-driven innovations risk falling behind as industries across the globe increasingly adopt AI-powered methods. The competitive landscape is rapidly shifting, with early adopters of AI obtaining a major advantage over their competitors. This chapter will analyze how organizations across all industries are implementing AI into their business models, the obstacles they encounter, and the future trajectory of AI-driven business innovation. Through a rigorous analysis of case studies, real-world examples, and theoretical ideas, the chapter will provide a full grasp of how AI is reshaping the corporate landscape, from operational efficiencies to entirely new ways of creating value.

In conclusion, the collaboration of AI with business model innovation signifies the beginning of a new era in which traditional boundaries are blurred, and the rate of change is faster than ever (Berman et al, 2021). As AI continues to evolve, its power to disrupt and reshape sectors will rise, bringing both opportunities and challenges. For enterprises, the capacity to adapt to this fast-developing landscape will be vital to not only surviving but prospering in an AI-driven world. This chapter attempts to illuminate the paths via which AI is transforming business models and to give a roadmap for organizations wishing to harness the full potential of AI in their business strategies.

Key Drivers of AI-Enabled Business Transformation

Artificial Intelligence (AI) has become one of the most potent engines for change in today's business world, enabling companies to rethink and redesign their operations in ways that were previously imagined (Aldoseri et al, 2024). The rapid rise of AI has been driven by a convergence of factors—technological advancements, market forces, and altering customer expectations—that have collectively expedited its adoption across industries. Understanding these major reasons is vital for appreciating why AI is not simply another tool for optimization but a disruptive force affecting the very foundation of how businesses run and prosper. One of the major factors behind AI-enabled business transformation is the growth of data. In the digital age, data has emerged as the lifeblood of modern business. Every transaction, customer interaction, sensor reading, or social media post generates data that, when successfully harnessed, can give insights that were once concealed (Black et al, 2023). AI's capacity to process and analyze enormous amounts of data at amazing speed allows organizations to transform raw data into actionable intelligence. Companies that previously relied on intuition or restricted datasets for decision-making are now able to obtain real-time information, enabling them to make more informed, accurate judgments. This data-driven strategy is altering everything from product development to marketing, as organizations can better anticipate client wants, optimize processes, and predict future trends. Closely related to the data explosion is the development of powerful machine-learning techniques and the expanding availability of processing power. AI, particularly in the form of machine learning, thrives on data. These algorithms are capable of learning from prior events and making predictions based on patterns within the data, which is why AI has become so vital to commercial innovation (Frank et al, 2017). As businesses acquire more data, the accuracy and sophistication of AI systems grow, allowing enterprises to create more efficiency and innovations. For example, in industries such as banking, machine learning models are being used to detect fraudulent activities, while in healthcare, AI is being applied to identify early indicators of diseases with more accuracy than traditional diagnostic approaches. As processing power continues to expand and machine learning algorithms become more polished, businesses will be able to employ AI for increasingly complicated jobs, pushing the boundaries of what is feasible.

Another key driver of AI-enabled change is the increased desire for personalization and customization in the marketplace (Gao & Liu, 2023). Today's consumers want more than simply generic products or services; they want experiences that are tailored to their specific requirements and tastes. AI has given companies the ability to deliver on this promise at scale. By evaluating client behavior and preferences, AI systems may help companies develop personalized marketing messages, promote items, and offer services that resonate with specific customers (Babatunde et al, 2024). In retail, for instance, AI-driven recommendation engines have become a major feature of e-commerce systems, giving individualized product suggestions based on a customer's previous shopping behavior. This level of customization not only enhances customer satisfaction but also drives revenue development, as customers are more likely to engage with companies that understand and anticipate their needs. The automation of ordinary processes is also playing a crucial role in AI-driven corporate transformation (Aldoseri et al, 2023). One of the earliest and most prevalent applications of AI in business has been the automation of repetitive and time-consuming operations, freeing up human workers to focus on more complicated and creative endeavors. From customer care chatbots to automated data input systems, AI has taken over many of the regular operations that traditionally required human participation (Nyongesa et al, 2020). This transition has had substantial repercussions for corporations in terms of efficiency and cost savings. Companies can now function with fewer workforces while maintaining, or even enhancing, productivity. Beyond simple automation, AI is also being used in more sophisticated ways, such as managing supply chains, improving transportation, and maintaining product quality through real-time monitoring and predictive maintenance.

Another driver of AI transformation is competitive pressure (Omrani et al, 2022). As more organizations employ AI technologies, the competitive landscape is shifting rapidly (Benbya et al, 2020). Businesses that are slower to integrate AI into their operations risk slipping behind, as AI-enabled competitors can innovate faster, give greater value to customers, and run more efficiently. In many sectors, AI is becoming the price of entry for staying competitive (Mistry et al, 2024). Take the banking industry, for example, where AI-driven fintech startups are challenging traditional banks by offering faster, more personalized services. In reaction, established players are being pushed to incorporate AI to remain relevant. This competitive pressure has accelerated the pace of AI adoption, as companies know that integrating AI is important for preserving a competitive edge in today's fast-moving markets. The shift toward digital and cloud-based infrastructures has been a fundamental enabler of the AI revolution. The shift of enterprises to the cloud has allowed them to acquire the processing power and storage needed to run AI systems efficiently. Cloud computing provides the scale essential for AI algorithms to process enormous datasets, which is particularly critical for businesses like retail, healthcare, and logistics that create vast volumes of information every day. Additionally, cloud platforms offer AI-as-a-Service (AIaaS) solutions, making it easier for organizations of all sizes to utilize AI technologies without having to create infrastructure from scratch (Lins et al, 2021). This democratization of AI through cloud services has lowered the hurdles to entry, allowing smaller organizations to harness AI and compete with larger enterprises.

A less apparent but equally essential cause is the shift in organizational thinking and culture that has accompanied AI deployment (Hechler et al, 2020). Forward-thinking companies have understood that the successful integration of AI into business models requires more than simply technology enhancements; it necessitates a cultural shift toward innovation and experimentation. Leaders who embrace AI see technology not as a danger to their workforce but as a chance to augment human capability (Jarrahi, 2018). In this way, AI is fostering a new collaboration between humans and machines, where AI tackles data-driven, repetitive activities while human workers focus on strategic, creative, and emotional parts of business. This human-AI collaboration is becoming a crucial feature of current company strategies, particularly in areas where customer experience and relationship management are critical. Regulatory and societal developments are serving as both a driver and a challenge to AI transformation. Governments and regulatory agencies across the globe are beginning to build guidelines for the ethical use of AI, ensuring that companies implement AI ethically. These guidelines are encouraging corporations to develop AI solutions that are transparent, accountable, and fair, particularly in sensitive areas such as healthcare, finance, and autonomous cars. While compliance with evolving AI rules poses hurdles, it also provides a level of standardization and confidence that fosters broader AI usage. Society's rising understanding of AI's potential impact—both positive and negative—also drives businesses to innovate responsibly, ensuring that AI technologies are meant to enhance, rather than disrupt, human existence.

In conclusion, the forces underpinning AI-enabled business change are numerous and linked (Black et al, 2024). From the proliferation of data and improvements in machine learning to altering consumer expectations and competitive pressures, AI is reshaping the corporate world at an unprecedented pace. While the path to complete AI adoption presents hurdles, organizations that embrace these forces and integrate AI into their operations stand to gain a considerable advantage in the digital age. AI's transformational potential extends beyond process efficiency; it is about rethinking how businesses operate, develop, and generate value in a world that is increasingly driven by data and intelligent technology.

Impact of AI on Traditional Business Models

The integration of Artificial Intelligence (AI) into business has launched major changes in traditional business models, radically altering how companies generate, deliver, and collect value (Di Vaio et al, 2020). While traditional business models have long been founded on established frameworks and structures, AI is disrupting these conventions, driving companies to rethink their goals, operations, and customer interaction procedures. The impact of AI on traditional business models is both wide-reaching and revolutionary, changing practically every element of how companies run. One of the most evident and immediate consequences of AI on traditional business models is the shift from linear, process-driven systems to more dynamic and adaptable ones. In traditional company models, processes frequently follow a sequential flow—product creation leads to manufacturing, followed by distribution and marketing. However, AI-driven models are more fluid, allowing for real-time adjustments across the whole economic cycle (Chui & Francisco, 2017). AI's capacity to analyze large volumes of data and create insights at remarkable rates enables companies to make quicker, more informed decisions. This adaptability is vital in today's fast-paced and highly competitive marketplaces, where the capacity to pivot rapidly in response to changing customer wants or market conditions can be the difference between success and failure.

AI also affects value generation in traditional business models by redefining how companies understand and communicate with their customers. In the past, companies generally depended on market research, focus groups, and historical data to design products or services (Gordon & Langmaid, 2022). These methods, while beneficial, were limited in scope and could only provide insights based on prior trends. AI, however, allows organizations to access real-time data from many sources, delivering a considerably more thorough picture of client behavior and preferences (Yathiraju, 2022). Through machine learning algorithms and predictive analytics, AI systems can spot patterns in consumer behavior that were previously undetectable, enabling businesses to adjust their offers to match current and even future client wants. This change from reactive to proactive client involvement allows organizations to not only satisfy customers but also anticipate their desires, generating tailored experiences that create long-term loyalty. This personalization provided by AI is particularly impactful in industries like retail, healthcare, and entertainment, where unique experiences are becoming the standard (Bhuiyan, 2024). In traditional methods, mass production and standardization were important to obtaining economies of scale, but AI is permitting mass customization without the corresponding cost increases. Businesses may now deliver highly tailored products and services to a large audience, creating new chances for differentiation and client engagement. This development is profoundly altering the competitive dynamics of many industries, as organizations that can harness AI to create tailored experiences are gaining a considerable advantage over those that rely on traditional, one-size-fits-all approaches.

Another significant area where AI is disrupting traditional business models is operational efficiency (Dubey et al, 2020). AI-driven automation is eliminating the need for human interaction in everyday tasks, streamlining operations, and cutting costs across numerous industries. In traditional models, personnel expenses, manual processes, and human error were often limiting factors in obtaining optimum efficiency. AI disrupts this equation by automating everything from data input and customer service to sophisticated supply chain management and predictive maintenance in manufacturing. This not only boosts efficiency but also helps companies to scale their operations without equally increasing their labor. As a result, companies can accomplish better output with fewer resources, freeing up capital that can be spent on innovation and expansion. The growing implementation of AI in traditional business models also creates considerable obstacles, particularly in terms of worker dynamics. As AI takes over more jobs previously performed by humans, there is growing worry about job displacement and the future role of labor in AI-driven business models. In traditional models, human labor was key to value generation, but AI has changed the emphasis toward machine-driven processes and automation (Davenport & Miller, 2022). While AI presents new potential for high-skilled jobs in sectors such as data science, machine learning, and AI system development, it also threatens to render many low-skilled and repetitive jobs obsolete. Companies must thus wrestle with the social and ethical consequences of AI, finding methods to reskill their workforce and develop a culture of collaboration between humans and robots (Sheikh, 2020). The most successful organizations will be those that successfully balance automation with human expertise, ensuring that AI complements rather than replaces human workers.

The impact of AI on supply chain management is another area where traditional business models are undergoing considerable disruption (Modgil et al, 2022). In the past, supply networks were frequently linear and slow to react to disturbances or inefficiencies. AI, through its ability to analyze massive amounts of data in real-time, has created a new degree of openness and responsiveness in supply chain operations. AI technologies can forecast possible bottlenecks, optimize inventory management, and even find the most efficient shipping routes, guaranteeing that products are delivered more swiftly and cost-effectively (Mostafa, 2020). This real-time optimization lowers the inefficiencies that were widespread in old supply chains, helping companies save both time and money. Furthermore, AI enables companies to develop more resilient supply chains that can adapt to unanticipated difficulties, such as natural disasters or geopolitical conflicts, ensuring continuity in an increasingly uncertain environment. Customer service is another area where AI is making an indelible imprint on traditional company methods (Ramírez, 2023). In the past, customer service relied significantly on human connection, whether through call centers, in-person help, or email conversations (Abbas Khan et al, 2024). While these approaches are still in use, AI is automating many elements of customer service, particularly through the use of AI-powered chatbots and virtual assistants (KATRAGADDA, 2023). These solutions are capable of managing ordinary client inquiries 24/7, minimizing the need for big customer service personnel and allowing organizations to give faster more consistent help (Buttle & Maklan, 2019).

AI-driven customer care also gives the capacity to evaluate consumer sentiment in real-time, enabling organizations to anticipate and address potential issues before they escalate. While human customer service workers will always be important for tackling more complicated situations, AI is revolutionizing the way businesses approach customer assistance, making it more efficient and scalable. The financial concepts backing traditional enterprises are also being influenced by AI (Dwivedi et al, 2021). Historically, businesses depended on financial forecasting models based on past performance, market trends, and economic indicators. While these models were generally correct, they were limited by the static nature of the data they relied on. AI, with its capacity to process real-time financial data and combine information from multiple sources, is offering organizations more accurate and dynamic forecasting capabilities. Machine learning algorithms can monitor anything from market changes to consumer behavior and operational costs, helping organizations to make more informed financial decisions. This improved financial agility is helping organizations optimize their resource allocation, manage risks more effectively, and uncover new chances for growth.

Despite these evident advantages, the shift from old business models to AI-driven ones is not without its hurdles (Bossuwé, 2023). Many companies confront organizational opposition to AI adoption, particularly in areas where legacy systems and long-standing practices are strongly embedded. Employees and supervisors accustomed to traditional ways of working may be hesitant to embrace AI, either out of fear of job displacement or skepticism about the technology's potential. Additionally, incorporating AI into existing business processes can be technically complex and require significant investment in both infrastructure and talent. Businesses must consequently define clear strategies for AI adoption, including training and upskilling their personnel, connecting AI activities with broader corporate goals, and ensuring that AI technologies are applied ethically and openly. The impact of AI on corporate rivalry cannot be overestimated. AI is leveling the playing field by giving small and medium-sized companies (SMEs) access to tools and insights that were traditionally the realm of huge organizations (Aljarboa, 2024). In traditional business models, scale frequently gave a competitive advantage, since larger organizations could harness their resources to surpass smaller rivals. AI, however, is democratizing access to innovation, allowing even the smallest enterprises to harness the power of data and machine learning to compete effectively in the marketplace. This change is altering traditional market dynamics, as nimble, AI-driven startups can challenge established players, compelling even the largest companies to develop faster and more efficiently.

In conclusion, the influence of AI on traditional business models is profound and diverse (Reim et al, 2020). From operational efficiency and personalized consumer engagement to supply chain optimization and financial forecasts, AI is altering every facet of how businesses function. While the deployment of AI brings obstacles, particularly in terms of labor dynamics and organizational change, it also offers a unique opportunity for innovation and growth. As AI continues to evolve, its influence on business models will further intensify, changing the competitive landscape and creating new kinds of value creation in the digital economy.

AI-Driven Business Models: Case Studies and Examples

The influence of Artificial Intelligence (AI) on business models is no longer speculative—it is happening across industries, affecting how companies operate and create value (Marenko, 2018). AI-driven business models represent a break from traditional frameworks, harnessing the powers of AI to improve operations, create products, enhance consumer experiences, and streamline decision-making. Examining real-world case studies and examples offers useful insights into how AI is not simply being adopted but is causing significant change in diverse sectors. One of the most renowned instances of an AI-driven business strategy is Amazon, a corporation that has successfully incorporated AI across numerous parts of its operations (Pfau & Rimpp, 2021). From its recommendation algorithms to its supply chain management, AI fuels much of Amazon's success. The recommendation engine, which employs AI to evaluate user behavior, purchase history, and browsing trends, has been a key driver of the company's ability to improve sales and customer engagement. By anticipating what customers are most likely to buy next, Amazon can offer tailored shopping experiences, which in turn leads to increased conversion rates. This AI-driven personalization is a fundamental component of Amazon's business model, separating it from competitors by giving a unique, individualized experience for each consumer (Usman et al, 2024). Beyond consumer involvement, AI also drives Amazon's logistics and supply chain operations. The company's AI-powered technologies optimize warehouse management, route planning, and delivery schedules, ensuring that products are dispatched and delivered with maximum efficiency (Elkahlout et al, 2024). This has enabled Amazon to set new standards in e-commerce, with rapid, reliable shipping services that are tough for competitors to match. By employing AI to simplify its operations, Amazon can keep operating expenses low while keeping the flexibility to scale globally—a significant advantage in an industry where margins are typically razor-thin. The AI-driven business strategy has allowed Amazon to dominate the retail environment by developing a seamless, data-powered ecosystem that blends consumer behavior, product inventories, and delivery operations.

Another fascinating example of AI-driven transformation is evident in the financial services industry, where organizations like JP Morgan Chase are leveraging AI to boost decision-making, risk management, and customer service (Kumari et al,

2021). AI-driven algorithms are used to evaluate enormous volumes of financial data to predict market trends, discover investment opportunities, and assess risks. In investment banking, AI is transforming how traders and financial analysts operate by providing them with real-time insights and predictive models that improve the accuracy of financial predictions (Dai, 2024). AI is also revolutionizing risk management, allowing banks to identify and mitigate potential risks more effectively by examining patterns that would be impossible for people to notice on their own. This ability to handle and interpret massive numbers at extraordinary rates has become a crucial part of how financial institutions work in an increasingly data-driven environment. JP Morgan Chase's usage of AI goes beyond financial research and extends into customer support with their virtual assistant, COiN (Contract Intelligence) (Balaji, 2024). This AI-powered application helps the bank examine complicated legal documents and contracts, saving the time and money required for manual evaluations. By automating boring, time-consuming operations, COiN frees up staff to focus on higher-value work, such as creating relationships with clients and developing new financial products. This AI-driven approach has transformed the bank's operational efficiency and given it a competitive edge in an industry where speed and precision are paramount.

In the automotive industry, Tesla serves as a prime illustration of how AI may fundamentally alter a traditional business paradigm. Tesla's business strategy is not just about selling vehicles; it's about harnessing AI to establish an ecosystem around autonomous driving, energy solutions, and software upgrades. Tesla's self-driving technology, powered by AI, is crucial to its vision of the future of mobility. By integrating AI into its vehicles, Tesla builds cars that are not just electric but also autonomous, offering users a glimpse into the future of transportation. The company's AI systems regularly gather and analyze data from millions of kilometers driven by Tesla vehicles, allowing them to improve over time through machine learning. This real-time learning capability is a critical distinction for Tesla, giving it a head start in the battle to perfect autonomous driving technology. Tesla's AI-driven business strategy now extends to its production operations (Cooke, 2020). The company employs AI to streamline production lines, predict equipment faults, and ensure that its factories operate at optimal performance. This has helped Tesla to increase production faster than traditional automakers, who generally rely on old manufacturing techniques that are less agile and data-driven (Dagnaw, 2020). By embedding AI across its operations—from product development to production and customer service—Tesla has established a business model that is not only revolutionary but also highly scalable. The company's success highlights the revolutionary potential of AI in establishing new value propositions and altering the competitive landscape in a century-old sector.

In the healthcare sector, IBM Watson Health gives a great illustration of how AI can drive business model innovation by improving patient care and medical research. IBM's Watson Health platform employs AI to evaluate massive volumes of medical data—such as electronic health records, clinical trials, and medical literature—to give individualized treatment suggestions (Petiwala et al, 2021). This AI-driven method helps healthcare providers to make more educated decisions, leading to better patient outcomes. For instance, Watson has been used to find the most successful cancer treatments for individual individuals based on their genetic makeup and medical history. This level of precision was previously unattainable through standard methods of diagnosis and therapy planning. AI helps healthcare providers to increase operational efficiency by automating administrative processes such as scheduling, invoicing, and patient communications. AI-powered chatbots, for example, are being used to manage patient inquiries and arrange appointments, freeing up healthcare workers to focus on other vital parts of patient care (Aggarwal & Madhukar, 2017). By integrating AI into both clinical and administrative activities, Watson Health is not only enhancing the quality of healthcare but also cutting costs and improving accessibility (Magistretti et al, 2019). This is particularly critical in an industry where high operational expenses and inefficiencies have historically been impediments to delivering good care.

In the field of entertainment, organizations like Netflix have reinvented their business models through the application of AI to better user experiences and maximize content creation. Netflix employs AI algorithms to propose series and movies to subscribers based on their viewing history, tastes, and behavior (Frey, 2021). This recommendation engine, which accounts for a major amount of Netflix's viewership, has proved important in the network's capacity to engage users and boost time spent on the platform. AI-driven personalization helps Netflix to give a bespoke experience to each user, ensuring that content is highly relevant and matched with their interests. Netflix employs AI to inform its content generation tactics. By studying viewing trends and audience data, Netflix can forecast what types of series or movies will resonate with consumers. This data-driven approach has helped the company to invest in unique content with greater confidence, knowing that it fits with user wants (Steck et al, 2021). AI has also improved the production process, streamlining workflows and reducing the time it takes to bring new material to market. Through AI, Netflix has established a business model that relies on personalization, data-driven decision-making, and operational efficiency, providing it a competitive edge in the congested streaming market. The industrial sector has also seen disruptive impacts from AI-driven business models, particularly through the installation of smart factories. Companies like Siemens have integrated AI into their production processes to boost productivity and reduce downtime. AI-powered predictive maintenance solutions monitor equipment in real-time, recognizing possible flaws before they lead to costly breakdowns. This proactive approach to maintenance not only cuts operational expenses but also minimizes production disruptions, allowing organizations to meet demand more reliably (Gaw, 2022). AI is also being used to optimize supply chains, ensuring that commodities are procured and supplied with optimal efficiency, eliminating waste, and enhancing profitability.

In these cases, it is obvious that AI-driven business strategies are not tied to a single industry or application. They range across sectors, from retail and finance to healthcare and manufacturing, altering old corporate processes, enhancing operational efficiency, and creating new value for customers. The unifying thread across all these cases is the ability of AI to handle massive volumes of data, learn from it, and provide insights that drive better decision-making and creativity. These AI-driven models indicate a change from reactive, process-driven techniques to dynamic, adaptive systems that can adjust to changing market conditions and client needs in real-time. Ultimately, the cases covered here reveal the far-reaching implications of AI for business model innovation. Companies that embrace AI as a major component of their strategy are setting themselves up for long-term success in an increasingly digital and data-driven environment. By employing AI to manage operations, personalize customer experiences, and innovate more efficiently, businesses may unleash new prospects for growth, profitability, and competitive distinction.

Challenges and Opportunities in AI Adoption for Business Models

The integration of Artificial Intelligence (AI) in business models poses both considerable problems and interesting potential. As companies attempt to integrate AI into their operations, they typically confront multiple impediments, from technical complications to organizational reluctance (Di Vaio et al, 2020). However, companies that effectively traverse these difficulties offer immense possibilities for development, efficiency, and innovation. AI adoption, therefore, marks a major crossroads for organizations in the 21st century, with its dual nature providing both challenges and rewards. One of the most serious difficulties companies confront when embracing AI is data management. AI systems thrive on data—large quantities of high-quality, organized data are required for training models and producing accurate predictions. However, many businesses suffer from data-related difficulties, such as inadequate datasets, data silos, and inconsistent formats. These difficulties can hinder the effectiveness of AI solutions, resulting in unsatisfactory results. Additionally, data privacy and security concerns add another layer of complication (Yanamala & Suryadevara, 2023). With increasingly stringent rules, such as GDPR in Europe and CCPA in California, organizations must negotiate legal requirements while ensuring that AI algorithms handle sensitive data appropriately (ElBaih, 2023).

Failure to do so not only exposes companies to regulatory fines but also harms their brand and erodes consumer trust.

Another important difficulty is the paucity of AI talent (Rock, 2019). As AI technology evolves, the demand for competent professionals—data scientists, machine learning engineers, AI researchers—continues to outpace supply. Many businesses struggle to attract and keep the talent needed to build, implement, and manage AI systems. This talent gap is particularly obvious in smaller organizations and industries that are only beginning to investigate AI's potential. The dearth of AI experience restricts the pace of innovation since organizations without in-house talent generally rely on external consultants or third-party vendors, which can be costly and hinder the ability to fully incorporate AI into the business. Moreover, the lack of AI literacy at the CEO level can also inhibit the formulation of a clear AI strategy, leading to misalignment between AI projects and broader company goals (Pinski et al, 2024). Integration with existing systems is another important obstacle. Many businesses, particularly established ones, operate on outdated IT infrastructure that is not designed to support AI. Integrating AI into these systems involves tremendous effort, time, and technical expertise. Legacy systems can lack the processing capacity, data integration capabilities, and flexibility required for modern AI applications. As a result, companies have the onerous job of either redesigning their present infrastructure or constructing costly workarounds to incorporate AI technologies (Lauterbach & Bonime-Blanc, 2018). This difficulty is particularly significant in businesses such as banking, insurance, and manufacturing, where established systems and processes have been in place for decades. The reluctance to engage in modernizing these systems can hinder AI adoption and lead to missed opportunities.

Moreover, organizational opposition provides a non-technical but equally essential issue. Many companies deal with cultural barriers that inhibit AI adoption (Cubric, 2020). Employees may resist change owing to fear of job displacement or confusion about how AI will affect their roles. This resistance might emerge in subtle ways, such as slow adoption of AI-driven tools, lack of engagement in AI training programs, or hesitation to trust AI-generated insights. Overcoming this opposition involves not only technological solutions but also strategic communication, training, and change management approaches. Business leaders must develop a culture of creativity and encourage people to consider AI as a tool that enhances their capabilities rather than replaces them. Failure to address these cultural obstacles can hinder AI programs, resulting in wasted investments and unfulfilled potential. Despite these limitations, the prospects afforded by AI adoption are immense and revolutionary. For businesses willing to invest in the necessary resources and overcome the challenges, AI has extraordinary potential to optimize operations, create new value, and drive competitive advantage (Davenport, 2018). One of the most significant opportunities is in operational efficiency. AI-powered automation can streamline processes, decrease errors, and optimize resource allocation. From automating ordinary administrative duties to improving supply chains, AI enables businesses to run more efficiently and at a lesser cost. For example, AI-driven chatbots may handle customer support requests around the clock, freeing up human agents to focus on more difficult duties. Similarly, AI-powered predictive maintenance solutions can monitor equipment in real time, decreasing downtime and prolonging the lifespan of assets.

AI also brings enormous prospects for personalization and consumer experience development (Hoyer et al, 2020). Businesses that leverage AI to analyze customer data can create tailored experiences at scale. For example, shops can use AI to offer products suited to specific customers based on their browsing history, purchasing behavior, and preferences. This level of customization not only promotes customer pleasure but also generates revenue development by improving client loyalty and lifetime value. In areas such as healthcare, AI-powered diagnostics and treatment recommendations can tailor care for individual patients, increasing outcomes and saving costs. The capacity to create personalized experiences represents a key difference in today's competitive world, as consumers increasingly expect tailored interactions. Innovation is another significant area where AI opens up new chances. AI enables companies to explore new business models, products, and services that were previously inconceivable (Metelskaia et al, 2018). For example, AI-powered platforms can generate totally new marketplaces, such as autonomous driving services or AI-driven healthcare diagnostics. In the media and entertainment business, AI is enabling new forms of content creation, from deepfake technology to personalized streaming recommendations. AI-driven innovation can potentially lead to the establishment of new revenue streams.

For instance, organizations can monetize their AI-powered solutions by delivering them as a service to other businesses, generating entirely new ecosystems of value generation (Candelon & Reeves, 2022). The capacity to develop with AI allows organizations to stay ahead of the curve and capitalize on rising market trends. Another big possibility AI presents to business models is the ability for data-driven decision-making. AI systems can analyze large amounts of data at a speed and accuracy level far beyond human capabilities, giving organizations actionable insights in real-time. This enables better-informed decision-making across all sectors of the business, from marketing and sales to finance and operations. AI-driven analytics can find patterns and trends that people might overlook, allowing companies to identify chances for growth, optimize pricing tactics, or predict customer turnover. By integrating AI in decision-making, companies may become nimbler, responding to market shifts faster and with more precision. AI offers the opportunity for scalability. AI-driven solutions may be scaled fast across global operations, enabling companies to expand into new areas without proportionally rising costs. For example, AI-powered chatbots or virtual assistants may manage hundreds of consumer requests concurrently, offering consistent service across different time zones. Similarly, AI-driven supply chain optimization can help organizations extend their logistics operations efficiently, even when demand swings between locations (Chukwu et al, 2024). This scalability helps companies to grow without the limitations of old, manual methods.

In conclusion, while the hurdles of AI adoption are significant, they are exceeded by the transformative benefits AI presents for enterprises. Overcoming technical, organizational, and cultural challenges is vital for companies hoping to fully utilize AI's potential. Those who succeed will not only increase their operational efficiency but also uncover new pathways for innovation, personalization, and data-driven decision-making. In a fast-expanding digital ecosystem, organizations that adopt AI as a major component of their strategy are preparing themselves for long-term success, paving the way for a future where AI-driven business models rule the industry.

Future Directions: AI and the Evolution of Business Models

As artificial intelligence (AI) continues to grow at a rapid pace, the future of business models will undoubtedly be defined by its influence (Tang et al, 2020). The integration of AI into numerous sectors has already transformed how organizations function, connect with customers, and create value. However, what we have seen so far is likely simply the beginning of a bigger, deeper transition. In the coming years, AI is poised to radically disrupt the structure of business models, driving innovation in ways that are difficult to completely understand today. Understanding these future directions will be crucial for companies aiming to remain competitive and nimble in an AI-driven environment.

One of the most crucial future directions for AI and business models is the shift toward autonomous companies (Soni et al, 2019). As AI systems get more advanced, there is potential for enterprises to function with minimal human participation. From decision-making processes to daily operations, AI might play a major role in propelling the organization ahead. Autonomous enterprises rely on AI to improve workflows, make real-time modifications based on data, and even formulate and implement strategies without the need for ongoing human monitoring. For example, in fields such as logistics and supply chain management, AI-powered systems may automatically manage inventories, predict demand variations, and reroute shipments, all while learning from each choice to better future performance. This drive towards autonomy might free up human workers to focus on higher-order jobs, such as creativity, strategy, and client interactions, while AI tackles the more operational parts of operating the firm. Another significant future direction is the democratization of AI tools and platforms. As AI technologies become more accessible and inexpensive, organizations of all sizes will be able to embrace AI-driven solutions.

This democratization will lessen the hurdles to entry for small and medium-sized companies (SMEs), letting them compete with larger corporations that have previously dominated the AI market. Cloud-based AI solutions, for instance, allow smaller organizations to access advanced analytics, machine learning, and automation without needing to invest in expensive infrastructure or recruit specialist staff (Yathiraju,). This transformation will level the playing field, boosting innovation and competition across industries. Additionally, AI platforms may evolve to become more intuitive and user-friendly, allowing non-technical users to build, deploy, and maintain AI solutions within their businesses.

AI is also expected to fuel the creation of hyper-personalized business models. As AI systems continue to develop in their ability to handle and analyze enormous volumes of data, companies will be able to offer products and services that are increasingly personalized to individual customer preferences and behaviors (Duan et al, 2019). This level of customization will extend beyond present marketing efforts when AI systems propose things based on past purchases or browser history. Instead, AI will empower companies to anticipate client demands before they arise, giving highly tailored solutions at the perfect moment. For example, in the healthcare industry, AI might be used to monitor a patient's health in real-time and deliver individualized treatment suggestions based on their unique genetic makeup, lifestyle, and medical history. In retail, AI may enable personalized shopping experiences, from dynamic pricing models that alter in real time to curated product selections according to each customer's likes. The future of business models will witness a transition from mass-market techniques to truly tailored experiences, enabled by AI's ability to monitor and respond to real-time data. Another key development in the future of AI-driven business models is the rise of new ecosystems of value generation. As AI becomes more prevalent, organizations will increasingly collaborate across sectors to develop new value chains that transcend traditional industry borders (Yu, 2023). AI's capacity to combine and analyze data from diverse sources will allow companies to uncover new opportunities for collaboration and innovation. For instance, automotive businesses, technology companies, and telecom providers might combine to build AI-powered solutions for autonomous vehicles, establishing a new ecosystem that benefits all players involved. In the healthcare industry, pharmaceutical corporations, AI developers, and medical institutions might combine to construct AI-driven drug discovery platforms that accelerate the development of new medicines. These new ecosystems will blur the barriers between businesses, spurring the formation of totally new business models based on shared data, technology, and resources.

AI will also play a significant role in the growth of sustainability-focused business models. As the global emphasis on sustainability rises, businesses will increasingly look to AI to help them accomplish their environmental, social, and governance (ESG) goals (Rane et al, 2024). AI may be used to optimize energy use, decrease waste, and build more efficient supply chains, all of which contribute to a lower carbon footprint. For example, AI-powered predictive analytics can help organizations forecast demand more correctly, eliminating overproduction and lowering waste. In agriculture, AI-driven systems may monitor crop health, predict weather patterns, and optimize water usage, leading to more sustainable farming methods. In the energy sector, AI can be used to maximize the usage of renewable energy sources, such as solar and wind, by forecasting swings in supply and demand. As customers become more environmentally conscious, companies that harness AI to embed sustainability into their models will likely see greater demand and brand loyalty. The ethical and regulatory framework surrounding AI will evolve, shaping future business models. As AI becomes more incorporated into the fabric of society, there will be increased attention on concerns such as data privacy, algorithmic prejudice, and the impact of automation on jobs (Khogali & Mekid, 2023). Governments and regulatory agencies are likely to establish new rules and norms to guarantee that AI is utilized responsibly and ethically (de Almeida et al, 2021). Businesses that fail to react to these new requirements risk risking legal penalties and reputational damage. Conversely, organizations that proactively engage with ethical AI practices—such as transparent algorithms, fair data usage, and AI systems meant to augment rather than replace human labor—will gain a competitive edge. In this environment, the future of AI-driven business models will include striking a balance between innovation and ethical responsibility, with businesses needing to gain the trust of consumers, regulators, and other stakeholders.

Additionally, the future will see AI-enhanced creativity and innovation at the core of business model evolution (Aagaard & Tucci, 2024). Traditionally, AI has been associated with efficiency, automation, and data analysis. However, as AI technologies get more proficient, they will increasingly be utilized to boost human creativity, enabling companies to develop in whole new ways. For example, AI-generated designs, art, and music are already being investigated in creative industries, and this trend is anticipated to grow across sectors. Businesses will leverage AI to co-create products, services, and experiences with their customers, leading to new kinds of value creation that blend human inventiveness with AI's computing capacity. AI-enhanced creativity will help companies adjust more rapidly to changing market conditions, customer preferences, and technology breakthroughs, promoting continual innovation and growth. The future of AI and business models is distinguished by tremendous change and evolution (Lu, 2019). As AI technology evolves, it will transform how businesses operate, produce value, and communicate with their consumers. The possibilities for autonomous companies, hyper-personalization, new ecosystems of value, sustainability-driven models, and AI-enhanced creativity all lead to a future where AI is deeply embedded in the fabric of business. However, this future will not be without its obstacles, particularly in terms of data protection, ethics, and regulatory compliance. Businesses that are forward-thinking, adaptable, and willing to invest in AI while solving these problems will be well-positioned to flourish in an AI-driven world. Ultimately, AI offers businesses an unprecedented opportunity to reinvent themselves, keep ahead of market trends, and fulfill the demands of a fast-evolving global economy.

CONCLUSION

The importance of Artificial Intelligence (AI) in revolutionizing business models is not only a fad but a fundamental movement that is redefining the competitive environment across industries. As organizations around the world progressively employ AI technology, they are moving beyond traditional business frameworks and embracing new models that are dynamic, flexible, and data-driven. This revolution is not only transforming how companies operate but also how they think about value generation, customer engagement, and long-term strategic growth. In the present digital economy, the integration of AI into business models is becoming a major determinant of success, compelling organizations to reconsider their approaches to innovation, efficiency, and market rivalry. The growth of AI is shifting businesses away from inflexible, linear models toward more agile and scalable frameworks that can adjust to quickly changing market conditions. One of the most dramatic implications of AI resides in its ability to analyze enormous amounts of data in real-time, delivering predicted insights and helping enterprises to make faster, more educated decisions. This data-driven strategy switches the focus from reactive decision-making, based on historical trends, to proactive tactics that predict future market shifts, customer behavior changes, and potential disruptions. In this view, AI is more than a tool for automation or efficiency—it is an enabler of strategic foresight, allowing organizations to negotiate complicated settings with more agility and precision.

Furthermore, AI's influence on business models extends beyond the operational domain, touching the very core of how companies generate and extract value. Traditional company models frequently relied on a linear value chain, where processes were essentially sequential and hierarchical. AI, however, presents a more networked and decentralized approach to value creation, where automation, machine learning, and data analytics intersect to enable continuous innovation. For example, in AI-powered ecosystems, customer interactions may be tailored at scale, product development cycles can be reduced, and supply chains can be improved in real time, generating new prospects for growth and efficiency. AI's potential to boost scalability is another defining element of its disruptive impact on business models. Traditional expansion plans were generally hampered by the need for extra resources, such as personnel or cash when organizations extended their operations. AI, on the other hand, allows organizations to scale swiftly without commensurate increases in costs. Automated technologies, such as AI-driven customer service bots or predictive analytics platforms, may manage exponentially bigger workloads without the need for more labor or infrastructure. This scalability not only increases operational efficiency but also opens up new markets and revenue streams, since organizations may serve a bigger customer base with minimum further investment.

While the potential benefits of AI-driven business models are enormous, the route to AI adoption is plagued with hurdles. The technological complexity of integrating AI systems, the necessity for organizational reform, and concerns about data protection and ethics all represent substantial impediments. Many corporations experience resistance to change within their organizations, as people may be reluctant to adopt new AI technologies or fear job displacement due to automation. Moreover, the ethical concerns of AI, including algorithmic biases, misuse of AI for spying or manipulation, and the societal impact of pervasive automation, deserve careful attention. Businesses must negotiate these obstacles with a clear strategy that blends innovation with accountability, ensuring that AI is used responsibly and following broader organizational goals. The future of AI in business model innovation is both hopeful and questionable. As AI continues to evolve, it will bring up new options for businesses to innovate, compete, and prosper. However, the pace of technological progress also creates uncertainty, as new AI capabilities may disrupt businesses in ways that are not yet completely understood. To stay ahead, companies must not only invest in AI technologies but also develop a culture of continual learning and flexibility. AI-driven business models demand a deep integration of technology and strategy, where the insights generated by AI are continuously exploited to drive innovation and respond to evolving trends.

In many aspects, the integration of AI into business models reflects a paradigm transition from the industrial economy to the digital economy. In the industrial period, value generation heavily relied on tangible assets such as labor, capital, and infrastructure. Today, in the digital economy, value is increasingly generated by intangible assets like data, intellectual property, and AI-enabled innovation. Companies that are able to harness these intangible assets, particularly AI, are setting themselves up for long-term success in a world where the ability to adapt and innovate is crucial. The transformation of business models through AI thus signals a significant crossroads in the growth of global business, where organizations that fail to adapt risk being left behind. Looking forward, the successful integration of AI in business models would involve not only technological investment but also a fundamental rethinking of organizational structures, leadership, and culture. Businesses that flourish in AI-driven innovation are those that foster collaboration between humans and machines, considering AI as a facilitator of human potential rather than a replacement for it.

Leaders must embrace a forward-thinking approach that fosters experimentation, supports upskilling and reskilling efforts for their staff, and ensures that AI-driven plans connect with long-term business objectives. As AI grows more prevalent, the legal landscape will likely adapt to accommodate rising concerns about data privacy, AI accountability, and the societal consequences of automation. Businesses must be alert and proactive in negotiating these legislative developments, ensuring that their AI initiatives are not only legally compliant but also socially responsible. Transparency in AI algorithms, responsible data management, and ethical AI deployment will become crucial differentiators for businesses looking to develop trust with their consumers and stakeholders in the AI-driven future.

In conclusion, the integration of AI into business models is not a one-time transition but an ongoing process of transformation. As AI technologies continue to improve, their impact on business models will expand, giving new potential for growth, efficiency, and creativity. However, this transition also demands organizations to be agile, adaptable, and forward-thinking, as they manage the difficulties of AI adoption and the broader digital economy. The companies that prosper in this new era will be those who not only embrace AI but also harness it strategically to create sustainable, long-term value in an ever-changing commercial context. By recognizing and tackling the challenges and opportunities of AI-driven business model innovation, companies can place themselves at the vanguard of this technological revolution and thrive in the competitive world of tomorrow.

REFERENCES

Aagaard, A., & Tucci, C. (2024). AI-Driven Business Model Innovation: Pioneering New Frontiers in Value Creation. *Business Model Innovation: Game Changers and Contemporary Issues* (pp. 295–328). Springer International Publishing. DOI: 10.1007/978-3-031-57511-2_10

Abbas Khan, M., Khan, H., Omer, M. F., Ullah, I., & Yasir, M. (2024). Impact of Artificial Intelligence on the Global Economy and Technology Advancements. *Artificial General Intelligence (AGI) Security: Smart Applications and Sustainable Technologies* (pp. 147–180). Springer Nature Singapore.

Aggarwal, M., & Madhukar, M. (2017). IBM's Watson analytics for health care: A miracle made true. *Cloud Computing Systems and Applications in Healthcare* (pp. 117-134). IGI Global.

Akhtar, N., & Lin, M. (2023). Technological Disruption And Its Effects On Competitive Dynamics. *Competitive Research Journal Archive*, 1(02), 100–108.

. Aldoseri, A., Al-Khalifa, K., & Hamouda, A. (2023). *A roadmap for integrating automation with process optimization for AI-powered digital transformation.*

Aldoseri, A., Al-Khalifa, K. N., & Hamouda, A. M. (2024). AI-Powered Innovation in Digital Transformation: Key Pillars and Industry Impact. *Sustainability (Basel)*, 16(5), 1790. DOI: 10.3390/su16051790

Aljarboa, S. (2024). Factors influencing the adoption of artificial intelligence in e-commerce by small and medium-sized enterprises. *International Journal of Information Management Data Insights*, 4(2), 100285. DOI: 10.1016/j.jjimei.2024.100285

Babatunde, S. O., Odejide, O. A., Edunjobi, T. E., & Ogundipe, D. O.Sodiq Odetunde BabatundeOpeyemi Abayomi OdejideTolulope Esther EdunjobiDamilola Oluwaseun Ogundipe. (2024). The role of AI in marketing personalization: A theoretical exploration of consumer engagement strategies. *International Journal of Management & Entrepreneurship Research*, 6(3), 936–949. DOI: 10.51594/ijmer.v6i3.964

Balaji, K. (2024). Harnessing AI for Financial Innovations: Pioneering the Future of Financial Services. *Modern Management Science Practices in the Age of AI* (pp. 91-122). IGI Global.

Benbya, H., Davenport, T. H., & Pachidi, S. (2020). Artificial intelligence in organizations: Current state and future opportunities. *MIS Quarterly Executive*, 19(4).

Berman, T., Schallmo, D., & Williams, C. A. (2021). Business model transformation through artificial intelligence in the Israeli InsurTech. In *ISPIM Conference Proceedings* (pp. 1-42). The International Society for Professional Innovation Management (ISPIM).

Bhuiyan, M. S. (2024). The role of AI-Enhanced personalization in customer experiences. *Journal of Computer Science and Technology Studies*, 6(1), 162–169. DOI: 10.32996/jcsts.2024.6.1.17

Black, S., Samson, D., & Ellis, A. (2024). Moving beyond 'proof points': Factors underpinning AI-enabled business model transformation. *International Journal of Information Management*, 77, 102796. DOI: 10.1016/j.ijinfomgt.2024.102796

Bossuwé, E. (2023). *AI-Driven Business Models Aimed at Promoting A Circular Economy* (Doctoral dissertation, Ghent University).

Buttle, F., & Maklan, S. (2019). *Customer relationship management: concepts and technologies*. Routledge. DOI: 10.4324/9781351016551

Candelon, F., & Reeves, M. (Eds.). (2022). *The Rise of AI-Powered Companies*. Walter de Gruyter GmbH & Co KG. DOI: 10.1515/9783110775112

. Chui, M., & Francisco, S. (2017). *Artificial intelligence the next digital frontier*. McKinsey and Company Global Institute, 47(3.6), 6-8.

Chukwu, N., Yufenyuy, S., Ejiofor, E., Ekweli, D., Ogunleye, O., Clement, T., Obunadike, C., Adeniji, S., Elom, E., & Obunadike, C. (2024). Resilient Chain: AI-Enhanced Supply Chain Security and Efficiency Integration. *Int. J. Sci. Manag. Res*, 7(03), 46–65. DOI: 10.37502/IJSMR.2024.7306

Cooke, P. (2020). Gigafactory logistics in space and time: Tesla's fourth gigafactory and its rivals. *Sustainability (Basel)*, 12(5), 2044. DOI: 10.3390/su12052044

Cubric, M. (2020). Drivers, barriers and social considerations for AI adoption in business and management: A tertiary study. *Technology in Society*, 62, 101257. DOI: 10.1016/j.techsoc.2020.101257

. Dagnaw, G. (2020). *Artificial intelligence towards future industrial opportunities and challenges*.

Dai, Z. (2024). An In-depth Analysis of JP Morgan Chase & Co. Highlights in Business. *Economics and Management*, 24, 2265–2272.

. Davenport, T. H. (2018). *The AI advantage: How to put the artificial intelligence revolution to work*. MIT Press.

Davenport, T. H., & Miller, S. M. (2022). *Working with AI: real stories of human-machine collaboration*. MIT Press. DOI: 10.7551/mitpress/14453.001.0001

de Almeida, P. G. R., dos Santos, C. D., & Farias, J. S. (2021). Artificial intelligence regulation: A framework for governance. *Ethics and Information Technology*, 23(3), 505–525. DOI: 10.1007/s10676-021-09593-z

Di Vaio, A., Palladino, R., Hassan, R., & Escobar, O. (2020). Artificial intelligence and business models in the sustainable development goals perspective: A systematic literature review. *Journal of Business Research*, 121, 283–314. DOI: 10.1016/j.jbusres.2020.08.019

Duan, Y., Edwards, J. S., & Dwivedi, Y. K. (2019). Artificial intelligence for decision making in the era of Big Data–evolution, challenges and research agenda. *International Journal of Information Management*, 48, 63–71. DOI: 10.1016/j.ijinfomgt.2019.01.021

Dubey, R., Gunasekaran, A., Childe, S. J., Bryde, D. J., Giannakis, M., Foropon, C., Roubaud, D., & Hazen, B. T. (2020). Big data analytics and artificial intelligence pathway to operational performance under the effects of entrepreneurial orientation and environmental dynamism: A study of manufacturing organisations. *International Journal of Production Economics*, 226, 107599. DOI: 10.1016/j.ijpe.2019.107599

Dwivedi, Y. K., Hughes, L., Ismagilova, E., Aarts, G., Coombs, C., Crick, T., Duan, Y., Dwivedi, R., Edwards, J., Eirug, A., Galanos, V., Ilavarasan, P. V., Janssen, M., Jones, P., Kar, A. K., Kizgin, H., Kronemann, B., Lal, B., Lucini, B., & Williams, M. D. (2021). Artificial Intelligence (AI): Multidisciplinary perspectives on emerging challenges, opportunities, and agenda for research, practice and policy. *International Journal of Information Management*, 57, 101994. DOI: 10.1016/j.ijinfomgt.2019.08.002

ElBaih, M. (2023). The role of privacy regulations in AI development (A Discussion of the Ways in Which Privacy Regulations Can Shape the Development of AI). *SSRN* 4589207. DOI: 10.2139/ssrn.4589207

. Elkahlout, M., Karaja, M. B., Elsharif, A. A., Dheir, I. M., Abunasser, B. S., & Abu-Naser, S. S. (2024). *AI-Driven Organizational Change: Transforming Structures and Processes in the Modern Workplace*.

Farayola, O. A., Abdul, A. A., Irabor, B. O., & Okeleke, E. C. (2023). Innovative business models driven by ai technologies: A review. *Computer Science & IT Research Journal*, 4(2), 85–110. DOI: 10.51594/csitrj.v4i2.608

Frank, M., Roehrig, P., & Pring, B. (2017). *What to do when machines do everything: How to get ahead in a world of ai, algorithms, bots, and big data*. John Wiley & Sons.

Frey, M. (2021). *Netflix recommends: algorithms, film choice, and the history of taste*. Univ of California Press.

Gao, Y., & Liu, H. (2023). Artificial intelligence-enabled personalization in interactive marketing: A customer journey perspective. *Journal of Research in Interactive Marketing*, 17(5), 663–680. DOI: 10.1108/JRIM-01-2022-0023

Gaw, F. (2022). Algorithmic logics and the construction of cultural taste of the Netflix Recommender System. *Media Culture & Society*, 44(4), 706–725. DOI: 10.1177/01634437211053767

Gordon, W., & Langmaid, R. (2022). *Qualitative market research: a practitioner's and buyer's guide*. Routledge. DOI: 10.4324/9781315245553

Hechler, E., Oberhofer, M., & Schaeck, T. (2020). *Deploying AI in the Enterprise. IT Approaches for Design, DevOps, Governance, Change Management, Blockchain, and Quantum Computing*. Apress.

Hoyer, W. D., Kroschke, M., Schmitt, B., Kraume, K., & Shankar, V. (2020). Transforming the customer experience through new technologies. *Journal of Interactive Marketing*, 51(1), 57–71. DOI: 10.1016/j.intmar.2020.04.001

Jarrahi, M. H. (2018). Artificial intelligence and the future of work: Human-AI symbiosis in organizational decision making. *Business Horizons*, 61(4), 577–586. DOI: 10.1016/j.bushor.2018.03.007

atragadda, V. (2023). Automating Customer Support: A Study on The Efficacy of Machine Learning-Driven Chatbots and Virtual Assistants. *Iconic Research and Engineering Journals*, 7(1), 600–601.

Khogali, H. O., & Mekid, S. (2023). The blended future of automation and AI: Examining some long-term societal and ethical impact features. *Technology in Society*, 73, 102232. DOI: 10.1016/j.techsoc.2023.102232

Kumari, B., Kaur, J., & Swami, S. (2021). System dynamics approach for adoption of artificial intelligence in finance. In *Advances in Systems Engineering: Select Proceedings of NSC 2019* (pp. 555-575). Springer Singapore. DOI: 10.1007/978-981-15-8025-3_54

Lauterbach, A., & Bonime-Blanc, A. (2018). *The artificial intelligence imperative: A practical roadmap for business*. Bloomsbury Publishing USA. DOI: 10.5040/9798400614835

Lins, S., Pandl, K. D., Teigeler, H., Thiebes, S., Bayer, C., & Sunyaev, A. (2021). Artificial intelligence as a service: Classification and research directions. *Business & Information Systems Engineering*, 63(4), 441–456. DOI: 10.1007/s12599-021-00708-w

Lu, Y. (2019). Artificial intelligence: A survey on evolution, models, applications and future trends. *Journal of Management Analytics*, 6(1), 1–29. DOI: 10.1080/23270012.2019.1570365

Magistretti, S., Dell'Era, C., & Petruzzelli, A. M. (2019). How intelligent is Watson? Enabling digital transformation through artificial intelligence. *Business Horizons*, 62(6), 819–829. DOI: 10.1016/j.bushor.2019.08.004

. Marenko, B. (2018). *FutureCrafting. A speculative method for an imaginative AI.*

Metelskaia, I., Ignatyeva, O., Denef, S., & Samsonowa, T. (2018, June). A business model template for AI solutions. In *Proceedings of the international conference on intelligent science and technology* (pp. 35-41). DOI: 10.1145/3233740.3233750

Mistry, H. K., Mavani, C., Goswami, A., & Patel, R. (2024). The Impact Of Cloud Computing And Ai On Industry Dynamics And Competition. *Educational Administration: Theory and Practice*, 30(7), 797–804.

Modgil, S., Gupta, S., Stekelorum, R., & Laguir, I. (2022). AI technologies and their impact on supply chain resilience during COVID-19. *International Journal of Physical Distribution & Logistics Management*, 52(2), 130–149. DOI: 10.1108/IJPDLM-12-2020-0434

Mostafa, M. (2020). *Artificial intelligence applications in supply chain management and analysis in Turkey* (Master's thesis, İstanbul Sabahattin Zaim Üniversitesi, Lisansüstü Eğitim Enstitüsü, İşletme Anabilim Dalı).

Nitzberg, M., & Zysman, J. (2022). Algorithms, data, and platforms: The diverse challenges of governing AI. *Journal of European Public Policy*, 29(11), 1753–1778. DOI: 10.1080/13501763.2022.2096668

. Nyongesa, G., Omieno, K., & Otanga, D. (2020). *Artificial intelligence chatbot adoption framework for real-time customer care support in Kenya.*

Omrani, N., Rejeb, N., Maalaoui, A., Dabić, M., & Kraus, S. (2022). Drivers of digital transformation in SMEs. *IEEE Transactions on Engineering Management.*

. Palanivelu, V. R., & Vasanthi, B. (2020). Role of artificial intelligence in business transformation. *International journal of advanced science and technology*, 29(4), 392-400.

Petiwala, F. F., Shukla, V. K., & Vyas, S. (2021). IBM watson: redefining artificial intelligence through cognitive computing. In *Proceedings of International Conference on Machine Intelligence and Data Science Applications: MIDAS 2020* (pp. 173-185). Springer Singapore. DOI: 10.1007/978-981-33-4087-9_15

. Pfau, W., & Rimpp, P. (2021). AI-enhanced business models for digital entrepreneurship. *Digital Entrepreneurship: Impact on Business and Society,* 121-140.

Pinski, M., Hofmann, T., & Benlian, A. (2024). AI Literacy for the top management: An upper echelons perspective on corporate AI orientation and implementation ability. *Electronic Markets*, 34(1), 24. DOI: 10.1007/s12525-024-00707-1

Ramírez, J. G. C. (2023). Incorporating Information Architecture (IA), Enterprise Engineering (EE) and Artificial Intelligence (AI) to Improve Business Plans for Small Businesses in the United States. *Journal of Knowledge Learning and Science Technology* ISSN: 2959-6386 (online), 2(1), 115-127.

. Rane, N., Choudhary, S., & Rane, J. (2024). Artificial intelligence driven approaches to strengthening Environmental, Social, and Governance (ESG) criteria in sustainable business practices: a review. *Social, and Governance (ESG) criteria in sustainable business practices: a review* (May 27, 2024).

Reim, W., Åström, J., & Eriksson, O. (2020). Implementation of artificial intelligence (AI): A roadmap for business model innovation. *AI*, 1(2), 11. DOI: 10.3390/ai1020011

Reis, I. F., Gonçalves, I., Lopes, M. A., & Antunes, C. H. (2021). Business models for energy communities: A review of key issues and trends. *Renewable & Sustainable Energy Reviews*, 144, 111013. DOI: 10.1016/j.rser.2021.111013

Rock, D. (2019). Engineering value: The returns to technological talent and investments in artificial intelligence. *SSRN* 3427412. DOI: 10.2139/ssrn.3427412

Sheikh, S. (Ed.). (2020). *Understanding the role of artificial intelligence and its future social impact.* IGI Global.

Soni, N., Sharma, E. K., Singh, N., & Kapoor, A. (2019). *Impact of artificial intelligence on businesses: from research, innovation, market deployment to future shifts in business models.* arXiv preprint arXiv:1905.02092.

Steck, H., Baltrunas, L., Elahi, E., Liang, D., Raimond, Y., & Basilico, J. (2021). Deep learning for recommender systems: A Netflix case study. *AI Magazine*, 42(3), 7–18. DOI: 10.1609/aimag.v42i3.18140

Tang, X., Li, X., Ding, Y., Song, M., & Bu, Y. (2020). The pace of artificial intelligence innovations: Speed, talent, and trial-and-error. *Journal of Informetrics*, 14(4), 101094. DOI: 10.1016/j.joi.2020.101094

Usman, F. O., Eyo-Udo, N. L., Etukudoh, E. A., Odonkor, B., Ibeh, C. V., & Adegbola, A. (2024). A critical review of ai-driven strategies for entrepreneurial success. *International Journal of Management & Entrepreneurship Research*, 6(1), 200–215. DOI: 10.51594/ijmer.v6i1.748

Yanamala, A. K. Y., & Suryadevara, S. (2023). Advances in Data Protection and Artificial Intelligence: Trends and Challenges. *International Journal of Advanced Engineering Technologies and Innovations*, 1(01), 294–319.

Yathiraju, N. (2022). Investigating the use of an artificial intelligence model in an ERP cloud-based system. International Journal of Electrical. *Electronics and Computers*, 7(2), 1–26.

Yu, C. (2023). AI Revolution: Reshaping Global Value Chains for the Future. *Center for Open Science*.https://osf. io/n6hb2/download

Chapter 4
Impact of AI on Customer Value Creation by Mediation of Innovation Models in the Horn of Africa

Shashi Kant
https://orcid.org/0000-0003-4722-5736
Bule Hora University, Ethiopia

Metasebia Adula
https://orcid.org/0000-0001-5732-2850
Bule Hora University, Ethiopia

Nitu Nimbrain
https://orcid.org/0000-0001-5585-3287
IMSAR, Maharshi Dayanand University, India

Mona Kumari
https://orcid.org/0009-0001-0476-5831
Government College for Women Bahadurgarh Jhajjar, India

ABSTRACT

This chapter measures the effect of artificial intelligence (AI) on client worth development in East Africa, focusing on the mediating function of models of innovation. To confirm that the dataset is adequate for factor analysis, the investigation employed the Kaiser-Meyer-Olkin (KMO) measure with a sample size of 400 innovation adopter and commerce specialists. Using an exploratory factor analysis (EFA), key

DOI: 10.4018/979-8-3693-9571-4.ch004

themes are depicting. We then employ confirmatory factor analysis (CFA) to confirm the reliability of the measurement devices. Next, structural equation modeling is employed to measure the interactions among these variables (SEM). The outcomes depict that AI considerably boosts the formation of worth for clients and that models of innovations are a crucial moderator of this effect. This chapter highlights the importance of using creative strategies in order to optimize artificial intelligence's benefits for providing worth's to clients.

INTRODUCTION

The effect of artificial intelligence (AI) on creating worth's for clients has drawn a lot of attention lately, especially as companies look for creative ways to become more competitive in a global market that is changing quickly. It becomes especially significant to comprehend the dynamics of AI and models of innovations in East Africa, where economic development is of utmost importance. The potential of AI to transform a number of industries, mainly the service based, is what makes this issue so significant on a worldwide scale. This might lead to economic development and augment millions of people's quality of life (Bortola et al., 2024). The notion that a company's requirement to continuously innovate in order to adapt to the shifting demands and preferences of their clients is the depiction of the client worth generation via innovation concept. Models of innovations have historically changed from more conventional methods that prioritized product development to more combined frameworks that stress client knowledge and participation. Several innovation strategies that application client insights to drive worth are formation are highlighted in empirical investigation. Examples of these models include open innovation and layout thinking. Nevertheless, there is still a lack of investigation oEastplication of these models in AI-driven environments, especially in East Africa, where significant socioeconomic barriers are present (Wakweya et al., 2024).

Even though AI has a bright future, there are real-world obstacles preventing its successful application in the area. A number of problems, including inadequate infrastructure, low digital literacy, and legal constraints, make it difficult to application AI to create worth's for clients. Also, unique methods to innovation that may differ from those employed in more developed countries are required due to the cultural and contextual distinctions depicted in East Africa. By examining how AI might mediate the interaction among models of innovations and client worth generation, particularly within East Africa; this chapter seeks to close investigation gaps that currently exist. This investigation aims to provide a comprehensive framework for future academics and policymakers by addressing the real barriers encountered by marketplaces in the region and synthesizing the available knowledge (Lamssarbi et al., 2024).

"How might AI-driven models of innovations boost formation of worth's of client in East Africa, considering the particular constraints and possibilities existing in this context?" is the main question driving this investigation. By providing a solution, the chapter hopes to shed light on real world methods to application AI, which will eventually support the region's economic expansion and resilience. By carefully examining these topics, our investigation will contribute to scholarly discussions and provide innovation adopters in East Africa with functional information that can be employed to promote innovation and increase client worth

BACKGROUND OF STUDY

East Africa is well-known for its distinctive diversity in culture and rich ethnic variety. However, the area has several obstacles to development, including as weak economic conditions, unstable politics, and poor infrastructure. The combination of artificial intelligence (AI) and creative commerce models offers a chance to augment client worth generation as governments in this area aim for economic progress. However, there are several barriers in putting these ideas into rehearsal (Idonije et al., 2022). Ethiopia's agri-business sector, which employed a sizable section of the workforce, is one noteworthy case investigation. Precision farming and predictive analytics are two examples of AI technologies that have the potential to maximize agricultural yields and enhance food security, but farmers frequently encounter obstacles including poor training and restricted access to tools. Initiatives such as the "Digital Agri-business Initiative" have attempted to application AI to augment critical thinking; however, they frequently face infrastructural deficiencies such as unstable internet access and device shortages. These barriers emphasize the requirement for need based models of innovations that take material constraints and domestic environments into account (Bortola et al., 2024).

The application of AI by the telecoms sector in Somalia to augment client service and engagement has manifested some potential. However, for the reason of the low levels of digital literacy in the populace, the adoption of AI-driven podcasts and CRMs has been viewed with suspicion. The history of telecom market places like Hormuud Telecom, who have tried to combine AI solutions but faced push-back from clients unfamiliar with such tools, serves as a concrete example. This disparity emphasizes the requirement of both tools innovation and client-centric strategies that place a high priority on outreach and education in order to foster mutual respect and understanding (Lamssarbi et al., 2024). With its advantageous geographic position, Djibouti offers yet another compelling example. In an effort to establish the nation as a regional hub for logistics, the government has made investments in developing a digital economy. Though projects such as the Djibouti Data Center depict the potential of artificial intelligence and big data analytics, a major obstacle still stands in the form of a lack of legal frameworks and competent workers. Market places trying to develop in this field frequently must navigate a challenging bureaucratic environment, which inhibits innovation and slows down implementation (Akindele et al., 2022).

Together, these case studies manifest that while innovation and artificial intelligence have a great deal of promise to promote client worth formation in East Africa, there are real-world obstacles that requirement to be overcome. Targeted solutions are required for problems including inadequate infrastructure, limited digital literacy, and regulatory obstacles. In-depth analysis of these issues will be provided by this investigation, which will also provide insights into how need-based models of innovations may help with the successful integration of AI across a range of industries, boosting client worth and supporting long-term, regional economic development.

STATEMENT OF PROBLEM

There is a strong chance for economic development when Artificial Intelligence (AI) is included into client worth formation frameworks, especially in East Africa. In an ideal world, companies in this area would application AI and cutting-edge models to augment client knowledge, optimize workflows, and promote long-term success. But as things are right now, there are a lot of differences between this perfect world and the real-world results. There are several contradicting pieces of information that come to light, such as the impassive application of AI in developed markets compared to East Africa's delayed uptake and lack of comprehension. This discrepancy emphasizes the necessity of a thorough investigation of the elements affecting the adoption of AI in this particular setting (Bortola et al., 2024). Although AI-driven innovation is gaining popularity, empirical investigation on the topic's ability to increase client worth in East Africa has produced conflicting outcomes. While some studies indicate that artificial intelligence (AI) can greatly increase operational efficiency, others manifest that the predicted gains frequently do not materialize for the reason of a variety of contextual constraints. This discrepancy indicates theoretical holes in our knowledge of the ways AI interacts with certain models of innovations in the area, depriving academics and practitioners of a coherent framework to direct their work (Alnuaimi, 2022).

Moreover, there are gaps in our information about the tastes and behaviors of domestic clients, which are crucial for creating need-based AI solutions. The unique socioeconomic environment of East Africa renders many of the current frameworks, which are based on data from industrialized nations, irrelevant. Also, context gaps result from the distinct political, cultural, and economic elements that define the area and are sometimes disregarded in more general discussions about AI. For example, the effect of tribal connections on client trust and adoption of tools has not been sufficiently addressed, resulting in a mostly in one-size-fits-all strategy (Wang et al., 2024). The environment is further complex by real world barriers. Market places are incapable of successfully deploy AI answers due to problems including poor infrastructure, low levels of digital knowledge, and restricted financing sources. These obstacles frequently lead to a lack of engagement from potential clients, limiting the very innovation that might promote client worth formation, as seen in a number of industries, including telecommunications and agri-business (Niyitunga, 2024).

By doing a thorough investigation of how AI might mediate the link among models of innovations and client worth generation in East Africa, this investigation aims to close these gaps. The investigation attempts to offer a strong framework that is pertinent to the given situation by integrating the body of current literature, filling in theoretical and knowledge gaps, and taking into account real world barriers. Moreover, it will provide policymakers and corporate executives with real world insights that will help them layout policies that efficiently utilize AI while taking into account the region's distinctive features. This investigation aims to deepen our understanding of how-to application AI for sustainable development by shedding light on various avenues, which would eventually strengthen East Africa's economy.

THEORETICAL FOUNDATION

A basic knowledge of the link among models of innovation, Artificial Intelligence (AI), and client worth generation is provided by a number of ideas, especially when considering East Africa. Everett Rogers' "Diffusion of Innovations hypothesis" is one well-known hypothesis. This theory describes how, why, and how quickly new concepts and innovations proliferate across cultural boundaries. Understanding how AI technologies' inclusion in East Africa is significant because it may manifest adoption hurdles and the ways in which social systems and networks can help or impede the adoption of AI advances. This theory highlights the significance of social environment and communication channels, which are especially significant in areas where traditional customs may collide with contemporary (Murshed & Ugurlu, 2023).

The "Value Co-Formation Theory" is another pertinent paradigm that asserts that firms and clients work together to generate worth's. This notion is especially relevant in AI-driven environments where client input and data are essential for improving goods and services. Understanding worth's co-formation might help firms create more successful AI products that appeal to domestic clients in East Africa, where client interaction may be limited owing to low digital literacy and trust barriers (Plantinga, 2024). Also, knowledge of how marketplaces may adjust and reorganize their materials in response to changing environments is facilitated by the "Dynamic Capabilities Framework". According to this hypothesis, companies operating in East Africa must build adaptable capacities that will enable them to successfully incorporate AI into their daily operations and pursue ongoing innovation. In light of the quickly changing tools landscape in the area, this framework can help clarify how marketplaces can application AI to augment client worth by using flexible tactics (Bortola et al., 2024).

The "Diffusion of Innovations Theory" is the primary theoretical framework through which this investigation is viewed. This decision is based on the necessity to comprehend the precise procedures that will enable the successful introduction and uptake of AI tools throughout East Africa. The theory's emphasis on the social, economic, and cultural aspects of tools adoption fits the region's particular possibilities and problems perfectly. Through this lens, the investigation will investigate both the enablers and the obstacles to AI adoption, offering a thorough understanding of how innovation might take place in the domestic environment (Rathnayake & Roca, 2022).

DEFINITION AND ORIGIN OF CONCEPTS

The term *"Artificial Intelligence (AI)"* describes how workstation systems simulate anthropological intelligence procedures. These include reasoning—using rules to arrive at approximations or firm conclusions—learning—the act of acquiring knowledge and applying rules to it—and self-correction. At the Dartmouth Conference in 1956, the phrase "artificial intelligence" was first employed. This event is largely regarded as the beginning of AI as a field (Yáñez-Valdés et al., 2023). "*Client worth formation*" is the process by which companies provide goods and services that satisfy clients and create perceived worth's. This theory has its roots in economic and marketing ideas, namely in the notion that worth's is a personal knowledge that differs among clients. The phrase became well-known in the latter half of the 20th century when academics like Philip Kotler emphasized how crucial it was to comprehend the requirements and preferences of clients. Formation of client worth considers the whole knowledge, which includes service quality, brand reputation, and emotional involvement, in addition to the product itself. Market places are realizing that using AI to increase client worth is a competitive advantage requirement in today's competitive market (Lamssarbi et al., 2024).

"Innovation Models" are conceptual models that explain the process of creating and introducing novel concepts, goods, or services to the market. These models can take many different forms, ranging from more modern techniques like open innovation, which emphasizes cooperation and the exchange of ideas across firm boundaries, to more classic linear models that place an emphasis on investigation and development. Economic and management theories, particularly the work of Joseph Schumpeter, who popularized the notion of "creative destruction" in the early 1900s, are major contributors to the conception of models of innovation. Models of innovations have changed throughout time to reflect the dynamic nature of contemporary markets by including the function of tools, client interaction, and iterative procedures (Nyoach et al., 2024).

EMPIRICAL LITERATURE REVIEW

AI and Formation of Client Worth

Enhanced customization is one of the main ways AI adds worth for clients. Several investigations have manifested that large-scale datasets may be processed using AI-driven analytics to provide information about the preferences and actions of clients. For instance, a 2024 investigation by Kant and Adula manifested how companies using AI algorithms for predictive analytics may more successfully customize their products to match the demands of specific clients. Customization not only boosts client happiness but also cultivates brand loyalty since clients are more inclined to interact with firms that recognize and accommodate their individual preferences. AI dramatically raises client engagement through automated channels of contact in addition to customization. According to investigations by Asefa et al. (2024), podcasts and virtual assistants driven by AI augment client service by responding to queries right away, cutting down on wait times and raising satisfaction levels. These technologies provide companies the flexibility to remain open for commerce around-the-clock, which is very helpful in the hectic world of today. Clients desire fast and efficient help, thus being able to rapidly and impassively fix barriers raises the perceived worth's of the service.

Additionally, AI is essential to operational impassiveness, which has an indirect effect on the generation of worth's for clients. Firms may cut expenses and reallocate personnel to concentrate on improving client knowledge's by automating repetitive operations and streamlining procedures. For example, Guye et al. (2024) investigation manifested that marketplaces using AI solutions for supply chain management saw a notable increase in accuracy and efficiency. Along with saving money, these operational enhancements help companies provide goods and services faster and more reliably, which raises client satisfaction even more. Also, by incorporating AI into critical thinking procedures, marketplaces can react to shifts in the market and client requirements more quickly. According to investigation by Jabo et al. (2023), marketplaces using AI for client insights and market analysis might more successfully alter their strategy, resulting in new product developments and modifications on time. Critical thinking agility allows firms to swiftly match their offers with changing client expectations, which augments the entire client knowledge. Notwithstanding these advantages, the literature also emphasizes the barriers in using AI. Client trust may be hampered by worries about data security and privacy, which may lower the perceived worth's of AI-driven services. Clients are becoming more concerned about how their data is employed, according to an investigation by Mershaye et al. (2024), which may lead to opposition to AI.

AI and Models of innovation

An increasing corpus of empirical investigation depicts the broad and complex influence of AI on models of innovation. By facilitating quicker prototyping, improving product testing, and strengthening investigation and development (R&D) skills, artificial intelligence (AI) technologies are revolutionizing conventional innovation procedures (Panigarhi et al., 2024). Extensive datasets may be analyzed by AI to forecast outcomes, according to studies, which can drastically shorten the time it takes for new goods to reach the market, especially in industries like pharmaceuticals. Moreover, AI promotes cooperation via open innovation and crowdsourcing, enabling marketplaces to better exchange information and access outside expertise. AI also supports client-centric innovation by enabling individualized goods and services that are catered to specific requirements, enhancing client satisfaction and increasing client loyalty (Bortola et al., 2024).

AI-powered predictive analytics aids companies in forecasting client and sector trends, directing innovation and competitive advantage choices. Additionally, AI transforms commerce models by making it easier to develop new worth's propositions, such subscription services, and by automating repetitive procedures so that materials may be directed toward more creative endeavors. But integrating AI is not without its barriers; skill deficiencies in the workforce can make it difficult to impassively application new technologies, and ethical issues like algorithmic bias and data privacy present serious obstacles. Empirical investigation suggests that although AI greatly augments models of innovation, companies must solve these issues if they want to fully realize the promise of these tools (Arthur et al., 2024).

Models of Innovations and Client Worth Formation

The empirical literature has given significant attention to models of innovations that center on client worth formation, emphasizing how companies may successfully match their products and services to the demands and preferences of their clients. These models place a strong emphasis on co-formation, in which marketplaces involve clients in the creative process to produce more individualized and responsive products. Investigation indicates that this cooperative strategy augments innovation and product quality while also increasing client happiness (Adula et al., 2023). Also, the integration of digital tools, such as artificial intelligence (AI) and big data analytics, has transformed the way marketplaces obtain insights into client behavior. This allows them to predict client wants and customize products appropriately. Based on investigation, companies that application these technologies can gain a competitive edge by building stronger client connections and offering better worth's propositions. The literature also emphasizes the worth's of agile approaches for innovation, since they facilitate quick iterations and feedback loops and guarantee that client input is continuously included in the development process. But obstacles like controlling client expectations and making sure there's good communication still need to be overcome for the deployment to be successful. Overall, empirical data manifests that client-centered models of innovations not only promote corporate success but also augment the client knowledge by encouraging involvement and loyalty (Arthur et al., 2024).

AI, Formation of Client Worth and Models of Innovations Mediation

A large amount of investigation highlights how AI might augment client customization. Investigation suggests that AI-powered algorithms are capable of sifting through enormous volumes of client data to pinpoint preferences and habits, giving companies the ability to customize products for specific clients. For example, an investigation by Deresso et al. (2023) manifested that market places using AI for tailored marketing had a significant rise in client happiness and engagement. Clients become more loyal as a result of feeling more understood and appreciated, which increases the perceived worth's of goods and services. The investigation measures the effects of AI on operational efficiency in addition to customization, which tangentially increases client worth. For instance, a 2024 investigation by Kant and Adula discovered that marketplaces using AI technologies—like podcasts and automated client support systems—saw a considerable decrease in response times and operating expenses. Market places are able to deploy materials more impassively for the reason to this efficiency, which eventually augments service delivery. Enhancing the entire client knowledge through prompt and correct response to questions from clients strengthens the idea that operational excellence is a crucial element of worth's generation.

In this framework, models of innovations play a critical function as mediators. According to empirical investigation, companies that apply organized innovation frameworks, such open innovation or layout thinking, are more equipped to successfully combine AI tools. Arthur et al., (2024). For example, companies that adopted open innovation strategies were better at using outside concepts and tools, which led to a quicker uptake of AI. By ensuring that AI applications are in line with client demands, this collaborative approach not only boosts worth's generation but also speeds up innovation. Also, investigation indicates that firm ethos plays a crucial function in moderating the connection among AI, innovation, and client worth. According to an investigation by Durga et al. (2024), the judicial application of AI tools requires an ethos of creativity and adaptability. Market places with an atmosphere that encourages experimentation and learning are more likely to application AI efficiently, producing creative solutions that appeal to clients. The potential for AI to deliver client worth is increased as firms become more responsive to market requirements, thanks to this alignment of ethos.

CONCEPTUAL FRAMEWORK

Figure 1. Conceptual framework

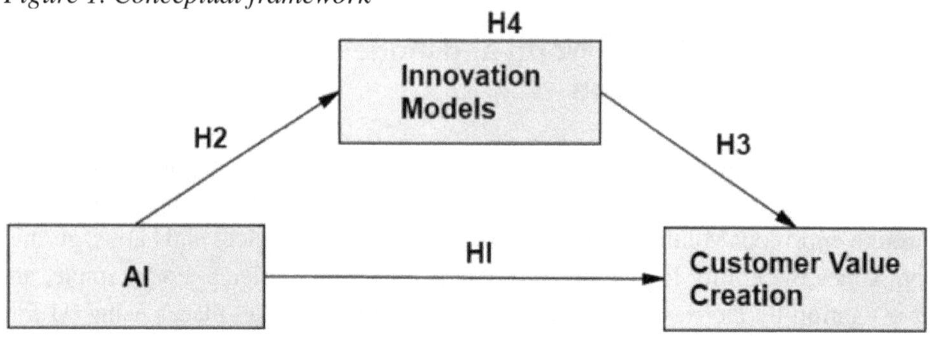

INVESTIGATION METHODOLOGY

390 respondents made up the sample size for the quantitative technique employed in the investigation, which was judged sufficient for strong statistical analysis. Structured questionnaires intended to capture different aspects of client worth gen-

eration in models of innovations were employed to simplify data gathering. The Kaiser-Meyer-Olkin (KMO) metric was employed in the investigation to evaluate the sample adequacy and make sure the data was appropriate for factor analysis before moving forward with the main analyses. When a KMO worth of greater than 0.6 was attained, it was determined that the data was suitable for additional analysis. The assessment scales were then augmented and underlying factor structures were depict using exploratory factor analysis (EFA). A complete scale was developed by taking into account the various significant elements of client worth that this approach manifested.

Using AMOS software, structural equation modeling (SEM) was employed to validate the generated scale. The investigation of intricate connections among the structures depicted in the EFA were made possible by this methodology. A comprehensive analysis of relevant literature, which offered insights into current frameworks and aspects of client worth served as the depiction for first scale development. Items were created using theoretical underpinnings to make sure they accurately reflected the concepts. Each variable on the scale—including perceived quality, emotional involvement, and client satisfaction—was backed by pertinent empirical investigation. Confirmatory factor analysis was done after the EFA to make sure the scale was valid and reliable. This meticulous approach added to the general knowledge while also providing a strong basis for the structures.

DATA ANALYSIS

Table 1. Bartlett's and KMO test

Sampling Adequacy and Kaiser-Meyer-Olkin Measure		**.889**
Sphericity and Bartlett's Test	Chi-Square estimation	1785.096
	df	109
	p-worth	.000

Source: Authors

The outcomes of the Bartlett's Test of Sphericity and the Kaiser-Meyer-Olkin (KMO) measure of sample adequacy are manifest in Table 1. The data may be appropriate for factor analysis, as manifests by the KMO worth's of 0.889, which manifests a high degree of sampling adequacy. This number is higher than the suggested cutoff of 0.6, indicating that the dataset is suitable for additional analysis. Also, an estimated chi-square worth of 1785.096 with 109 degrees of freedom and a significance level of 0.000 was obtained using Bartlett's Test of Sphericity. This finding further supports the application of component analysis by manifesting that the association matrix differs considerably from an identity matrix. When taken as a whole, these tests validate the validity of the investigation's later analyses and the resilience of the dataset.

Table 2. Total variance explained

Component	Initial Eigenworth'ss			Extraction Sums of Squared Loadings			Rotation Sums of Squared Loadings		
	Total	% of Variance	Cumulative %	Total	% of Variance	Cumulative %	Total	% of Variance	Cumulative %
1	4.5	32.23	32.235	4.5	32.2	32.235	3.0	21.45	21.451
2	1.6	9.87	42.22	1.5	9.887	42.022	2.2	15.49	36.942
3	1.6	9.07	51.10	1.2	9.087	51.210	1.9	14.26	51.210
4	.99	6.82	57.92						

Extraction Method: PCA
Source: Authors

The total variation explained by the exploratory factor analysis's principal components analysis (PCA) is manifested in Table 2. The first component, or 32.23% of the cumulative variance, is responsible for 4.5 of the total variance, according to the first eigen worth's. The second component comes next, with an eigen-worth's of 1.6 and a contribution of 9.87% to the overall variance, for a cumulative total of 42.22%. With an eigen worth of 1.6, the third component also explains 9.07% of the variance, resulting in a cumulative percentage of 51.10%. With an eigen worth's of 0.99, the fourth component adds 6.82% more to the total; nevertheless, the investigation does not provide any further components beyond this. The extraction sums of squared loadings confirm that the first three components collectively account for over half of the total variance, highlighting their significance in explaining the underlying structure of the data. These results underscore the PCA method in identifying key dimensions of formation of client worth within the models of innovations analyzed in the investigation.

Confirmatory Principle Component Examination

A kind of statistics called confirmatory principle component analysis is employed to confirm the principle component organization of a group of directed proxies. Investigations can assess hypotheses using CFA based on the underlying frame job and correlatives among observable proxies. The investigation employed CFA under table 3 in order to assess the hypothesis that there is an association among the proxies that are being guided and the latent ideas that support them.

Table 3. Co variances

Covariance			Estimate	S.E.	C.R.	P	Hy.
Models of innovations	**<-->**	**AI**	**.242**	**.021**	**8.231**	**.00**	**H2**
Models of innovations	<-->	Client worth Formation	.503	.032	7.692	.00	**H3**
AI	<-->	Client worth Formation	.254	.24	7.931	.00	**H1**

Source: Authors

The co-variances among the client worth are formation, artificial intelligence (AI), and models of innovations are manifested in Table 3. There are substantial associations among these factors, according to the estimations. A substantial and statistically significant association ($p < 0.001$) is manifested by the estimated covariance of 0.242 among models of innovations and AI, with a standard error (S.E.) of 0.021 and a critical ratio (C.R.) of 8.231. This finding supports Hypothesis 2. Hypothesis 3 (H3) is validated as the covariance among models of innovations and client worth generation is 0.503, with a S.E. of 0.032 and a C.R. of 7.692, indicating a significant connection ($p < 0.001$). Additionally, a substantial ($p <.05$) association among AI and client worth generation is assessed at 0.254, with a S.E. of 0.24 and a C.R. of 7.931. These results illustrate the interdependence of these characteristics and the critical function AI plays in improving models of innovations and helping marketplaces create worth for their clients.

Table 4. Validity concern

	CR	AVE	MSV	MaxR(H)	AI	IM	CSC
AI	0.832	0.643	0.219	0.952	**0.654**		
IM	0.858	0.657	0.232	0.863	0.271	**0.665**	
CSC	0.893	0.603	0.274	0.897	0.583	0.293	**0.684**

Note: AI= Artificial Intelligence; IM= Models of innovation; CSC= Client worth Formation
Source: Authors

Table 4 presents significant validity metrics in response to validity issues about the concepts of artificial intelligence (AI), models of innovations (IM), and formation of worth of client (CSC). With AI at 0.832, IM at 0.858, and CSC at 0.893, all of the constructs' Composite Reliability (CR) scores manifest good internal consistency and above the suggested criterion of 0.7. The constructs' convergent validity is further supported by the Average Variance Extracted (AVE) worth'ss, which depict that AI, IM, and CSC are all over the acceptable threshold of 0.5, with AVEs of 0.643, 0.657, and 0.603, respectively. The shared variation amongst the constructs is smaller than the AVE, as manifested by the Maximum Shared variation (MSV) worth for

AI, IM, and CSC, which evaluate possible discriminant validity concerns. These worth's are 0.219, 0.232, and 0.274. Also, the measures' robustness is corroborated by the Maximum Reliability (MaxR(H)) worth's, which manifest that AI is 0.952, IM is 0.863, and CSC is 0.897. All things considered, these measures support the reliability and validity of the investigation's scales, guaranteeing that the concepts are clear and separate from one another.

Mediating Function Examination

Figure 2. Structure equation model

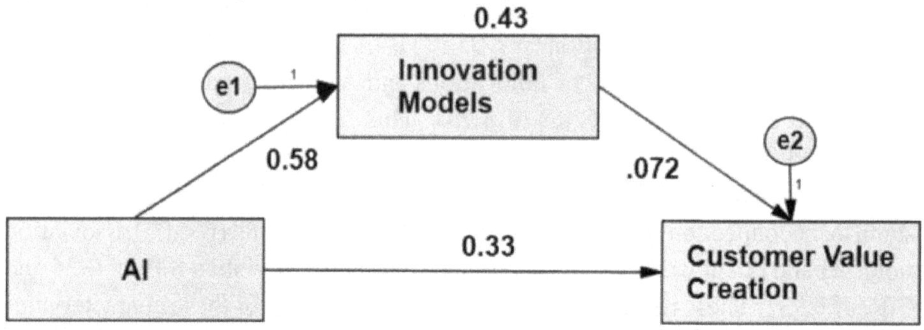

Model fit indices

Table 5. Indices for model fit

p-worth	Chi-Sq	RMR	Fitness Goodness	Fitness Confirmatory	TLI	RMSEA
0.004	1.954	.036	0.930	0.912	0.911	.028

Source: Authors

The model fit indices are manifested in Table 5, which gives information on how well the suggested structural model fits together overall. The model is statistically significant, as indicated by the reported significance level (Sig.) of 0.004. With a reasonably low chi-square worth of 1.954, the model and the observed data appear to be well-fitted. Since smaller worth's are preferred, the Root Mean Square Residual (RMR) of 0.036 further suggests a close match. A strong match of the model to the data is manifested by the goodness-of-fit index (GFI), which is stated to be 0.930. An appropriate fit is also indicated by the confirmatory fit index (CFI), which is 0.912. Even if the Tucker-Lewis Index (TLI) is somewhat lower at 0.911, the model's validity is still supported. Last but not least, a satisfactory fit is manifested by the Root Mean Square Error of Approximation (RMSEA) worth's of 0.028, which is much less than the 0.05 requirement. When taken as a whole, these indices validate the investigation's theoretical framework by confirming that the model accurately captures the interactions among the various components.

Table 6. Regression inspection

Relative			**Approx.**	**S.E.**	**C.R.**	**P**	**Ass.**
Models of innovations	**<---**	**AI**	**.964**	**.243**	**7.583**	**.00**	**H2**
Client worth Formation	<---	Models of innovations	.528	.231	2.953	.00	H3
Client worth Formation	<---	AI	.957	.292	7.958	.01	H1

Source: Authors

The outcomes of the regression analysis are manifested in Table 6, which also describes the connections among the concepts of models of innovation, client worth generation, and artificial intelligence (AI). With a regression coefficient of 0.964, a standard error of 0.243, and a critical ratio (C.R.) of 7.583, the association among AI and models of innovations is supported by Hypothesis 2 (H2). This suggests a very significant effect ($p < 0.001$). This high coefficient indicates that models of innovations are considerably affected by AI. Also, a substantial ($p < 0.001$) association among models of innovations and client worth generation is manifested by a coefficient of 0.528, with a S.E. of 0.231 and a C.R. of 2.953. These results validate Hypothesis 3. Ultimately, a coefficient of 0.957, a S.E. of 0.292, and a C.R. of 7.958, significant at $p < 0.01$, illustrate the direct effect of AI on client worth generation (H1). Together, these results highlight how significant AI and models of innovations are to generating client worth formation, highlighting how intertwined they are inside the investigation's framework.

Table 7. Mediating utility outcome

	Influence	**worth**	**Path Influence**
AI → Client worth Formation	Direct Influence	0.32	Direct influence stated
AI → Models of innovations → Client worth Formation	Indirect Influence	0.58*0.72=0.43	Indirect Influence Ensued
	Whole influence	0.75	Partial mediation

Source: Authors

The link between artificial intelligence (AI) and the development of client worth is mediated by models of innovation, as seen in Table 7. AI has a substantial direct effect on client worth generation, as seen by its quantifiable influence of 0.32. On the other hand, by multiplying the route coefficients 0.58 (AI to models of innovation) and 0.72 (models of innovations to client worth formation), one can determine the indirect effect of AI on formation of worth's of client through models of innovation, which results in an indirect influence of 0.43. When taking into account both direct and indirect pathways, the total combined effect equals 0.75. Given that the link is influenced by both direct and indirect factors, these finding points to a partial mediation effect. The results highlight that although AI has a direct influence on client worth generation, it also has a substantial enhancement through the mediation of models of innovation, highlighting the complexity of these inter associations in driving client worth.

DISCUSSION

The way that models of innovations mediate the effect of artificial intelligence (AI) on client worth formation is a noteworthy development in our understanding of how marketplaces might application tools to augment their products and services. The results manifest that AI augments models of innovation, which has an indirect effect on client worth in addition to its direct effect. According to this perspective, AI makes it easier to generate creative methods and tactics, which benefits clients by adding worth. Firms may better evaluate client data and customize products and services to match individual requirements and preferences by utilizing artificial intelligence (AI). Results are similar with study outcomes of Murshed & Ugurlu (2023) and Plantinga (2024). Additionally, by using models of innovation, market places may take a more client-centric stance and encourage client involvement and co-formation. Stronger ties and more loyalty result from this interaction's augment of client engagement and satisfaction. The worth's of adaptive methods that combine AI capabilities with innovative practices is manifested by the noteworthy indirect effect of models of innovation. Therefore, companies should prioritize investing in both AI tools and strong innovation frameworks if they want to maximize client worth. By doing this, they may provide a synergistic effect that fosters continuous client pleasure, a competitive edge in the marketplace, and operational efficiency. In the end, this interaction depicts how AI and models of innovations will fundamentally alter how clients create worth in the future.

CONCLUSION

The investigation concludes by highlighting the crucial function that models of innovation, via the mediation of artificial intelligence (AI), play in augmenting client worth development. The results manifest that AI has a major direct and indirect effect on client worth, and that models of innovations play a crucial function in mediating this connection. Firms may better understand client preferences and behaviors by utilizing AI tools, which help them develop and customize their products and services. The assimilation of models of innovations not only promotes a client employed strategy but also amplifies client happiness and engagement, which in turn strengthens client loyalty. In order to fully achieve the potential of creating worth's for clients, this investigation emphasizes how significant it is for firms to invest in AI and build strong innovation frameworks. As companies maneuver through an increasingly competitive landscape, understanding and implementing these interconnections will be essential for driving sustained development and maintaining a competitive edge.

MANAGERIAL IMPLICATIONS

The investigation's conclusions have a number of significant management ramifications for marketplaces looking to increase client worth by fusing innovation paradigms with artificial intelligence (AI). Prioritizing the application of AI tools may help managers obtain deep insights into sector trends and client preferences. This data-driven strategy promotes innovation suited to client demands and allows for better informed critical thinking. It's also critical to foster an innovative ethos within the company. Managers may augment product development and service delivery by utilizing models of innovations to promote cross-functional cooperation and client co-formation. To further optimize the advantages of these technologies, staff should get training and upskilling in the application of AI tools. In order to make sure that innovation initiatives are ongoing and have a lasting effect, managers should also concentrate on creating flexible procedures that enable quick reactions to client input and market developments? Last but not least, developing precise metrics to evaluate the success of AI projects and innovation tactics will aid in monitoring advancement and implementing required modifications. Managers may increase client happiness and loyalty by implementing these actions, which can also lead to long-term commerce success in an increasingly competitive environment.

REAL WORLD IMPLICATIONS

The investigation's real-world implications highlight the measures that firms can take to successfully utilize models of innovations and artificial intelligence (AI) to augment client worth generation. Initially, companies' requirement to allocate materials towards artificial intelligence (AI) infrastructure and solutions that streamline data gathering and examination, enabling a more refined comprehension of client behavior and inclinations. By using AI-powered client association management systems, service delivery may be augmented by customizing interactions and anticipating clients' demands. Market places could also implement agile innovation frameworks, which encourage experimentation and rapid iterations based on client feedback. This might include assembling cross-functional teams to create and test new ideas quickly in order to ensure that they are innovative and up to par with market demands. Also, developing a company ethos that encourages cooperation across divisions—like marketing, R&D, and client service—can result in the formation of products and services that take a more comprehensive approach. It will also be essential to implement training programs that aim to augment staffs' proficiency with AI and innovative approaches. Firms may make sure that their workforce is ready to application these technologies efficiently by providing them with the training and materials they require. Lastly, by defining precise performance measures for assessing the accomplishment of innovation and AI projects, companies will be able to make data-driven modifications that will eventually result in long-term gains in client worth generation. In today's competitive world, these doable actions will enable firms to leverage the revolutionary potential of AI and models of innovation.

THEORETICAL IMPLICATIONS

The investigation's theoretical implications add to the corpus of information already available on the association among models of innovation, artificial intelligence (AI), and the generation of client worth. This investigation contributes to the knowledge of how AI may be successfully incorporated into firm strategies to increase client worth by providing a framework that emphasizes the mediating function of models of innovation. It refutes conventional wisdom that sees artificial intelligence (AI) only as a technical instrument and instead frames it as a catalyst for creative procedures that produce results that are employed on the requirements of the client. The results also highlight the significance of seeing client worth generation as a dynamic process that is affected by firm structures and tools developments. This viewpoint promotes greater investigation into the ways in which different models of innovations may be modified to best utilize AI capabilities, leading to a more sophisticated comprehension of the ways in which these structures interact. Also, the investigation provides opportunities for future investigation to measure contextual elements, such as sector-specific dynamics or firm ethos that may have an effect on the link among AI, innovation, and client worth. In the end, this investigation adds to the theoretical conversation by offering actual data that depicts how innovation and tools can be combined to create worth for clients. This strengthens the argument that marketplaces must modify their approach to compete in the rapidly changing digital market. This theoretical framework establishes the parameters for further investigation into these interactions and their ramifications for many markets and industries.

RECOMMENDATION

Several recommendations for marketplaces seeking to augment client worth through the successful integration of artificial intelligence (AI) and models of innovations may be made in light of the investigation's outcomes. First and foremost, companies have to give top priority to creating a thorough AI strategy that complements their overarching commerce goals. This entails making the infrastructural and technological investments required to facilitate data collecting and analysis, facilitating more employed client involvement and more informed critical thinking. It's also critical to cultivate an innovative ethos. Risk-taking and experimentation should be encouraged in firms so that teams may create and test new concepts in a secure setting. The formations of cross-functional teams that unite various viewpoints and promote cooperation among departments like marketing, R&D, and client support can help achieve this. Staff up skilling in AI tools and innovative approaches should also be accomplished through the implementation of training and development programs. Firms may optimize the potential advantages of AI by providing staff with the necessary training to properly utilize these tools. Firms should also set up precise measures to assess how innovation and AI projects affect the generation of worth for their clients. Frequent evaluation and feedback loops will support data-driven modifications and guarantee that tactics continue to be applicable and successful. Lastly, throughout the innovation process, companies are urged to actively include their clients. Co-formation efforts have the potential to yield significant insights and strengthen connections, which in turn may lead to increased client happiness and loyalty. Firms may position themselves to succeed in an environment that is becoming more and more competitive by heeding this advice.

FUTURE DIRECTIONS

To advance knowledge and real-world application, future investigation initiatives in the fields of artificial intelligence (AI), models of innovation, and client worth generation should concentrate on a number of significant topics. Initially, longitudinal investigation might be done to look at how AI and client worth generation alter over time, especially when it comes to changes in market dynamics and tools. This would shed light on the long-term effects of AI-driven advancements on client connections as well as their sustainability. Also, it is significant for academics to investigate the contextual elements that affect the efficacy of artificial intelligence and models of innovations in many marketplaces. Comparative investigation might measure the ways in which sector-specific traits—like legal frameworks, client trends, and market competition—influence the assimilation of artificial intelligence (AI) into innovative procedures. This might result in the formation of need-based frameworks that maximize client worth formation for specific contexts. Examining the moral issues related to AI application in client interactions is another exciting avenue to pursue. Understanding the ramifications of bias, privacy, and transparency will be essential for preserving client trust and happiness as marketplaces depend more and more on AI for critical thinking. Subsequent investigation endeavors may also investigate the influence of company ethos on the successful amalgamation of artificial intelligence and creativity. Managers may find functional insights by knowing how internal elements like cooperation, leadership, and staff engagement affect the adoption of these technologies. Lastly, investigating the association among innovation, AI, and cutting-edge technologies like generative AI or the Internet of Things (IoT) may open up new possibilities for increasing client worth. Through these forthcoming avenues, scholars might augment a more all-encompassing comprehension of the dynamic associations among tools, innovation, and client-centric practices in today's rapidly evolving commerce environment.

REFERENCES

Adula, M., Birbirsa, Z. A., & Kant, S. (2023). The effect of interpersonal, problem solving and technical training skills on performance of Ethiopia textile industry: Continuance, normative and affective commitment as mediators. *Cogent Business & Management*, 10(3), 2286672. Advance online publication. DOI: 10.1080/23311975.2023.2286672

Akindele, A. T., Arulogun, O. T., Taye, G. T., Amare, S. Y., Van Reisen, M., Berhe, K. F., & Gusite, B. (2022). The impact of COVID-19 and FAIR data innovation on distance education in Africa. *Data Intelligence*, 4(4), 1013–1032. DOI: 10.1162/dint_a_00184

Alnuaimi, S. (2022). *New generation of innovation management: an integrated framework for the digital era* (Doctoral dissertation, Sheffield Hallam University).

Arthur, K. K., Bannor, R. K., Masih, J., Oppong-Kyeremeh, H., & Appiahene, P. (2024). Digital innovations: Implications for african agribusinesses. *Smart Agricultural Technology*, 7, 100407. DOI: 10.1016/j.atech.2024.100407

Asefa, K., & Debela, K. L. (2023). Effect of Transformational Leadership on Organizational Performance: The Mediating Role of Employee Commitment and Expert Systems (AI) Inclusion in Ethiopia, *2023 International Conference on Communication, Security and Artificial Intelligence (ICCSAI)*, 305-310, DOI: 10.1109/ICCSAI59793.2023.10421269

Birhane, M., Amentie, C., Borji, B., & Kant, S. (n.d.). Are Ethiopian Coffee Farmers Proficient to Predict Capital Structure with Mediation of AI Based Knowledge Systems and Asset Liquidity? In *AI in Agriculture for Sustainable and Economic Management* (pp. 199-215). CRC Press. DOI: 10.1201/9781003451648-15

Bortola, G. W., Kero, C. A., & Bali, N. (2024). The Mediating Effect of Competitive Advantage between Innovation Capability and Firm's Competitiveness. *Horn of African Journal of Business and Economics*, 7(1), 75–96.

Dereso, C. W., Kant, S., Muthuraman, M., & Tufa, G. (2023). Effect of Point of Service on Health Department Student's Creativity in Comprehensive Universities of Ethiopia: Moderating Role of Public-Private Partnership and Mediating Role of Work Place Learning. In: Jain, S., Groppe, S., Mihindukulasooriya, N. (eds) *Proceedings of the International Health Informatics Conference. Lecture Notes in Electrical Engineering*, vol 990. Springer, Singapore. DOI: 10.1007/978-981-19-9090-8_13

Durga, P., Godavarthi, D., Kant, S., & Basa, S. S. (2024). Aspect-based drug review classification through a hybrid model with ant colony optimization using deep learning. *Discov Computing*, 27(1), 19. DOI: 10.1007/s10791-024-09441-w

Guyo, D. M., Kero, C. A., & Kant, S. (2025). Is Marketing Intermediaries' Mediation Required for Livestock and Products Marketing to Improve the Economic Status of Pastoralist Communities in Ethiopia? In *AI in Agriculture for Sustainable and Economic Management* (pp. 216-234). CRC Press.

Guyo, K., & Kero, C. A. (2023). Mediation of Marketing Intermediaries and AI Adoption Between Livestock Products Marketing and Economic Status of Pastoralist in Ethiopia. *2023 International Conference on Communication, Security and Artificial Intelligence (ICCSAI)*, 311-316, DOI: 10.1109/ICCSAI59793.2023.10421261

Idonije, P. I., Dangana, E. A., Ameh, A. A., & Okafor, G. O. (2022). Entrepreneurial Orientation and Sustainable Job Creation: A Study of Small and Medium Enterprises in South-South, Nigeria. *Journal of Business Management. Innovation and Creativity*, 1(1), 254–277.

Jabo, B., & Kant, S. (2024). Impact of Technical CRM on Ethiopia Bank Human-Computer Interface and Competitive Advantage as Mediators of Performance. *2024 IEEE International Conference on Computing, Power and Communication Technologies (IC2PCT)*, 679-682, DOI: 10.1109/IC2PCT60090.2024.10486237

Kant, S., & Adula, M. (2024). AI Learning and Work Attitude Mediation Between Reward and Organizational Support in Ethiopia. In Gomathi Sankar, J., & David, A. (Eds.), *Generative AI for Transformational Management* (pp. 109–136). IGI Global., DOI: 10.4018/979-8-3693-5578-7.ch005

Kant, S., & Adula, M. (2024). Mediated by AI-Based Generative Re-Enforcement Learning and Work Attitude: Are Intrinsic Rewards Transforming Employee Perceived Organizational Support? In Gomathi Sankar, J., & David, A. (Eds.), *Generative AI for Transformational Management* (pp. 83–108). IGI Global., DOI: 10.4018/979-8-3693-5578-7.ch004

Kant, S., & Adula, M. (2024). Human-Machine Interaction in the Metaverse in the Context of Ethiopia. In *Impact and Potential of Machine Learning in the Metaverse* (pp. 196–212). IGI Global., DOI: 10.4018/979-8-3693-5762-0.ch008

Lamssarbi, B., & Bouaziz, S. M. (2023, April). The Impact of Digitalization and Managerial Innovation on Resilience in the Face of the COVID-19 Crisis: The Case of SMEs in the Greater Agadir Region. In *International Conference on Current Business Issues in African Countries* (pp. 155-174). Cham: Springer Nature Switzerland.

Murshed, N. A., & Ugurlu, E. (2023). Navigating the Digital Marketplace: A Holistic Model Integrating Social Media Engagement and Consumer Behavior Factors to Enhance Online Shopping Adoption. *Jurnal Manajemen Teori dan Terapan, 16*(3).

Niyitunga, E. B. (2024). The Role of Artificial Intelligence in Promoting Digital Public Participation for Successful Peacebuilding in Africa. *African Journal of Peace and Conflict Studies (formerly Ubuntu: Journal of Conflict and Social Transformation), 13*(1), 25-49.

Nyoach, T. D., Lemi, K., Debela, T., & Kant, S. (2024). Does Organizational Commitment Mediate the Relationship between Employee Relationship Management and Bank Performance? The Case of Banks in Ethiopia. *International Journal of Organizational Leadership*, 13(2), 355–376. DOI: 10.33844/ijol.2024.60419

Panigrahi, A., Pati, A., Sahu, B., Das, M. N., Nayak, D. S. K., Sahoo, G., & Kant, S. (2023). En-MinWhale: An ensemble approach based on MRMR and Whale optimization for Cancer diagnosis. *IEEE Access : Practical Innovations, Open Solutions*, 11, 113526–113542. DOI: 10.1109/ACCESS.2023.3318261

Plantinga, P. (2024). Digital discretion and public administration in Africa: Implications for the use of artificial intelligence. *Information Development*, 40(2), 332–352. DOI: 10.1177/02666669221117526

Rathnayake, D. M., & Roca, T. (2022). The emergence of technopreneurship for sustainable and ethical economic growth: Theory, research and practice. In *Integrated business models in the digital age: Principles and practices of technology empowered strategies* (pp. 467–535). Springer International Publishing. DOI: 10.1007/978-3-030-97877-8_13

Wakweya, D. K., Kero, C. A., & Bali, N. (2024). Market Orientation and Manufacturing Firm's Performance. [HAJBE]. *Horn of African Journal of Business and Economics*, 7(1), 97–120.

Wang, S., Li, Q., & Khaskheli, M. B. (2024). Management Economic Systems and Governance to Reduce Potential Risks in Digital Silk Road Investments: Legal Cooperation between Hainan Free Trade Port and Ethiopia. *Systems*, 12(8), 305. DOI: 10.3390/systems12080305

Yáñez-Valdés, C., Guerrero, M., Barros-Celume, S., & Ibáñez, M. J. (2023). Winds of change due to global lockdowns: Refreshing digital social entrepreneurship research paradigm. *Technological Forecasting and Social Change*, 190, 122454. DOI: 10.1016/j.techfore.2023.122454

KEY TERMS AND DEFINITIONS

Artificial Intelligence (AI): An area of computer science concerned with developing computers that can carry out operations that normally require human intellect, such comprehending natural language, spotting patterns, and making data-driven judgments.

Client Worth Formation: This is the process via which marketplaces raise the perceived worth and function of their goods and services in order to satisfy clients' demands and boost client happiness, brand loyalty, and general commerce success.

Models of Innovation: Structures or tactics that companies employ to stimulate innovation; they include procedures, plans, and techniques that support the formation of novel goods, services, or commercial procedures.

Mediation: A statistical concept in which the link among an independent and dependent variable is influenced by a third variable, which aids in the explanation of how or why specific effects transpire.

Exploratory Factor Analysis (EFA): This statistical method reduces dimensionality and helps comprehend the structure of data by grouping measured variables into factors and identifying underlying associations among them.

Structural Equation Modeling (SEM): This multivariate statistical analysis method enables investigations to evaluate complicated models with numerous linkages by analyzing the structural links among measured variables and latent constructs.

Co-formation: Co-formation is a cooperative process that involves input and participation from clients in the layout, development, and delivery of goods and services. Market places and clients work together to generate worth's via this process.

Chapter 5
Overview of Integrating Sustainability and Innovation:
Strategic Approaches for Enhancing Business Performance

Ipseeta Satpathy
https://orcid.org/0000-0002-0155-5548
KIIT University, India

Arpita Nayak
https://orcid.org/0000-0003-2911-0492
KIIT School of Liberal Studies, KIIT University, India

Vishal Jain
https://orcid.org/0000-0003-1126-7424
Sharda University, India

ABSTRACT

Modern consumer consciousness regarding environmental and social issues is creating a gradual trend towards the combination of sustainability with innovation for improved organizational performance and sustainability. The present paper focuses on the theoretical analysis that can facilitate the integration of sustainability and innovation into the core business processes of an organization. The paper also aims to explain the principles and measures of sustainable innovation, as well as the best strategies for the formation of the sustainability models in business activity. This overview aims at stressing on the possibility for change when it comes to embedding sustainability and innovation together and at providing practical recommendations

DOI: 10.4018/979-8-3693-9571-4.ch005

for organisations aspiring to attain both the sustainable financial performance and the beneficial environmental and social outcomes.

I. INTRODUCTION

Raise of Eco and social concerns among consumers has made companies change their plans, paying more attention to sustainable development. In this ever-changing world, Sustainable and Innovation is not a luxury but an imperative for improving organization performance and sustain ability. Every organization today seeks to satisfy and respond to the expectations of the contemporary consumer while improving competitiveness as well as addressing the needs of the contemporary society by embracing the need to sustain itself (Freund, 2020).This paper aims at examining the ways in which sustainability can be incorporated into the primary organizational value chain, with an emphasis on the concept of innovation for sustainability. Therefore, this research work seeks to present a clear systematic approach on how sustainable innovation can be achieved by businesses. This entails creating positive organizational environments that would lead to development of creativity about sustainability and employment of the workforce in sustainable development activity, encouraging Eco-design, and enacting circular economy. It is this undertaking that this paper aims at accomplishing through a detailed analysis with a view of enabling business leaders and researchers to come up with sustainable innovations that will enhance overall business results.

In the increasingly competitive and dynamic business environment of today, the integration of sustainability and innovation appears as a key strategic direction for organizations that aim at improving their performance and sustainability. This change has been triggered by an increasing general civics awareness in various communities across the globe with regard to various environmental and social concerns and this has forced organizations to shift their operation to become more responsible and sustainable. When it was acceptable for organizations to put monetary gain as their sole concern, the corporate world now has to balance the sustainability of economic, social and ecological factors. Therefore, the concept of elaborating sustainability together with innovation has emerged as one of the most strategic approaches for generating long-term business performance within the context of contemporary global problems (Hanaysha et al., 2022). Issues of sustainability which were earlier considered lying outside the framework of a firm, have become core to the strategic thinking of firms. It includes the ability to satisfy the existing generation's needs but not to the detriment of the next generation, an integration of the economic, social and the ecology aspect. Innovation which was previously linked with automatic technology and market dynamics has evolved into a completely different theory. It now encompasses the creation of existing and innovative strategies that enable the creation of wealth and at the same time enhance the well-being of citizens and the natural world (Pieroni et al., 2019). The concern towards environmental pollution and climate change has increased significantly around the world making it mandatory to adopt better environmental friendly strategies. The current world governments and regulatory authorities are putting into place policies that seek to reduce emission of greenhouse gases, responsible use of natural resources on the earth and improved standards of workers treatment. Penalties for non-compliance are steep and include fines and punitive damages apart from damaging the company's image and the consumers' trust. On the contrary, the firms that adopt sustainable business development strategies do not only manage risks but also become more competitive because they engage in practices most consumers appreciate (Shakeel et al., 2020). It can be asserted that consumer behaviour has evolved greatly. In today's world consumers are more aware and conscious of their societies than they were several decades ago. Being conscious consumers, they require companies to show some level of responsiveness to whom they are contributing, prescribing to companies with demonstrable genuine concern for the environment. It can therefore be said that this shift of consumer preference is not only associated with niche markets but is gradually turning into a norm. Therefore, work organizations have an opportunity to understand that sustainability is not charity, but a marketing factor that builds customer trust and brand preference. When integrated into the innovation activities of firms, sustainability issues make it possible for firms to design goods and service offerings in line with the values of consumers, thus, improving their competitive positioning (Nayak et al., 2023).

Globally the increase in unfavourable factors for instance resource availability, population, and socioeconomic inequity have led to the realization that traditional models of business growth cannot be sustained. The traditional economic model of demand, supply, consumption and disposal cannot work in today's scenario where there are scarce resources. The circular economy, also known as closed-loop economy, which maintains the efficiency of resources, minimizes wastage, or using and reuse the resources optimally is the recent trend. This transition is supported by Innovation since it facilitates the creation of new technologies, business models, and supply chain innovations that lie at the heart of the circular economy. For example, there are efforts to work on such ideas as circularity, durability, and recyclability in goods and services, which also bring new earning opportunities to companies (Kuzma et al., 2020).Still, it should be noted that the integration of sustainability and innovation has its difficulties. Internal and external constraints are real, and organizations experience difficulties in their attempts to effectively implement the principles of sustainable development. Externally, there are market barriers including the existence of dominant players, lack of awareness and ingrained consumerism, limited demand for niche products and services, increased cost of production, and longer development time. Externally, there are market forces that act as barriers such as regulatory issues and availability of resources. These are however not insurmountable if proper planning, leadership support and attitudes that encourage innovation and teamwork are employed. When sustainability is linked to innovation, it becomes not only possible to solve such challenges but future possibilities for organizations' unique positioning emerge as well (Albert, 2019). Consequently, this chapter is designed to offer the reader a broad understanding of the key strategies for managing sustainability and innovation into practices. Discussing this topic, it is important to identify principles and measures for the creation of more sustainable innovations along with an understanding of how these concepts can be implicated into the organization's workflows. The chapter also focuses on the design of a positive organizational culture for creativity and employees' commitment to sustainability. Also, it looks at the correlation between Eco-design practices and sustainability in development with consideration to the integration of circular economy systems in the development of goods. Since the ideas of sustainable innovation are mainly focused on the innovations that can enhance organization's effectiveness and help address current global challenges, the chapter offer the key performance indicators and assessment tools to measure and evaluate such strategies (De et al., 2020).This chapter provides a brief on the antecedents of sustainable innovation, including the facilitators and inhibitors for sustainable innovation, solutions and a case study for sustainable innovation. They reveal strong leadership, cultural management, and stakeholders' involvement as the key factors that define the integration of sustainability and innovation. Although providing a fairly non-specific yet highly informative account of these ideas, the chapter's intention is simple: to equip business managers and researchers with the knowledge and strategies that would enable them to pursue sustainable innovation. Finally, this chapter aims at helping organizations to harness the element of change and integrate sustainability and innovation twin pillars to deliver sustainable financial return alongside environmental and social benefits. Thus, it can be stated that today such combination has become crucial for businesses that have to address both the issues of Eco-sustainability and competitive advantage. This chapter offers a guide to organizations that seek to achieve sustainable innovation, providing general directions, specific suggestions, as well as a framework of the future of organizations in a world in a state of constant flux. So by following the principles of sustainability and innovation managers can improve the performance of a firm while also developing a more sustainable world economy.

II. RESEARCH QUESTIONS

- In what ways can organizations incorporate sustainability and innovation within a firm as a strategic change for improved performance?
- What factors enhance and hinder sustainable innovation and how can these be managed when setting within a business environment?

III. RESEARCH OBJECTIVES

- To analyze the principles and strategies for embedding sustainability and innovation into business models, focusing on enhancing organizational performance and sustainability.
- To understand the links between Eco-design principles, circular economy models, and sustainable development and their impacts on business results in terms of key performance indicators and assessment tools.

IV. UNDERSTANDING THE CONCEPT OF SUSTAINABLE INNOVATION

Sustainability as a concept has recently received much interest in the present connected and fast-paced world to create sustainable innovation. This means developing innovations that stimulate a country's economy, while at the same time having less adverse effects on the environment and increase the welfare of the people. Sustainable innovation differs from conventional viewpoints of innovation in the way that it includes ecological schemes, social ideas, and ideas that would have an effect on the business in an economic way in its frameworks. Sustainable innovation is an approach that organizational use to achieve sustainable business growth and return on investment and at the same time preserve resources to be utilized by the generations to come (Cilo et al., 2019). Sustainable innovation is the fusion of two powerful ideas: discussed the following areas of interest in the development of sustainability and innovation. Innovation is defined in this context as the introduction of a set of activities or something new to the organization, which results in more effective and efficient production, less cost and/or better revenues. Now, sustainability is about the capacity to make sustainable development, namely to fulfill the needs of the contemporary generation of people without changing the abilities of the subsequent generations to satisfy their needs. Sustainable innovation is hence the practice of innovating in such a way that the environment, society and economy are not compromised while in the process of implementing such changes

(Reficco et al., 2018). The political impact of climate change, declining resources and the changing customer expectations towards sustainability have forced companies to look at innovation differently at the global level. Sustainable innovation is not only about minimization or alleviation of negative effects; it aims to come up with positive effects to justify its existence in ecosystems and human societies. When a firm alters the ways that it has been operating in other ways, it can be possible to solve the sustainability problem at the same time as developing competitive advantages (Afeltra et al., 2023). Environmental dimensions are concerned with the protection of the environment through the proper utilization of resources, reduction of wastes, less on carbon and more on green energy. Advancements such as use of environmentally friendly products like reuse of given packaging materials, energy conversation products quips, carbon friendly business sourcing and delivery systems, depict ways organizations can cut their costs. For instance, Tesla sells electric cars and solar products, which are important not only to decrease the use of traditional fuels but also to make a transition to a cleaner world (Jorna, 2017). The concept of social sustainability is focused on the enhancement of the state, people, and society. This means that the company should employ good labor relations, encourage the community and offer a product or service to society. Different companies such as Patagonia and Unilever magnetize the public from more consideration of social causes, including fair wages, ethical sourcing, and programmes of community development. New business models mean new forms of value creation that not only seek to bring revenues to enterprises but also work towards creating equality, embracing people's diversity and offering solutions that will help communities be healthy in the far future (Repo, 2019). Economic sustainability therefore deals with the aspect of earning a lot of profits for a firm as it does with environmental and social concerns. Sustainable innovation helps the companies to stay relevant and create value by sustaining competitive advantage through reducing cost and increasing efficiency, thus expanding into other markets (Cappa et al., 2016). Over the past years the governments of different countries have put pressure on organizations by enforcing strict environmental and social requirements. That is why, the current business have to observe policy imperatives like maximum allowanced of carbon emission, rules concerning the management of wastes and the protection of labor rights. This puts pressure on the companies to seek new ways of operating that will be in line with the existing regulations. As is the case with the European Union's Green Deal, it makes the adoption of sustainable business practices rewarding through financial advantages and market opportunities (Varadarajan, 2017). Society today is quite aware, especially about the sustainability implications of the products they make in their consumption patterns. More customers are willing to buy products from organizations that have solid sustainability policies in place. This has created a demand for transparency in sourcing products and considering environmentally friendly products which in turn puts pressure on the business to deliver with this in mind. Innovation is made sustainable by technologies. For examples of innovations to help businesses to reduce its carbon emission, renewable energy technologies, smart grid systems and AI together with blockchain are some of the disruptors. For instance, the systems that incorporate AI and IoT can enhance the usage of resources in production aspects like use of water and fertilizers in farming (Chen, 2016). The option of sustainable innovation in the future is still possible. Such investments would create eco-centric solutions further entrenched in sustainability initiatives that are becoming increasingly integrated into business models. New circular economy models, renewable energy sources, gradual reduction in the amount of waste and zero-waste production techniques could become tactics more frequently used. The same must be extended with the governments and regulatory bodies putting their efforts into increasing the strictness of the environmental laws to promote sustainability and indirectly putting more pressure on businesses to innovate responsibly. Also, the four often-discussed technologies like AI, IoT, and blockchain are pivotal to the progress of sustainable innovation. These technologies can enhance efficient utilization of resources, increase the supply chain's transparency compared to conventional systems and help in establishing intelligent and sustainable solutions in various sectors. Sustainable innovation is not more a myth but an imperative for future growth and development across the globe. It helps to address the emerging issues of climate change, availability of resources and social justice in addition to making a business competitive in a market that has become conscious of environmental impact. When management establishes innovation as a lens through which environmental, social, and economic perspectives can be viewed while achieving corporate goals, then value that is co-created at macro-vectors such as people, society and planet enhances the value for shareholders as well. In the context of the ascending demand for sustainability in today's world, sustainability innovation will become one of the primary factors that determine the stability and effectiveness of organizations and companies.

V. BUILDING A CULTURE OF SUSTAINABLE INNOVATION

Sustainability as well as innovation is not anymore, a choice in the contemporary business environment but rather a necessity for survival in the long run. Sustainable innovation is the concept that addresses the innovativeness of products and services that meet customer needs and organizational goals while at the same time taking into account the effects of organizational activities to the environment and the society. Thus, integrating sustainability into an organization's culture for innovation results in improved competitiveness and profitability and organizational resilience. It fosters financial growth that aims to solve social issues like climate change, limited resources and social disparities (Costa & Matias, 2020). Sustainable culture of innovation refers to a state where sustainable innovation is a regular part of every organization's value, strategies and actions. This leads the employees to come up with solutions that will in one way or another be supportive of the business as well as the society and the environment in the long run. The organizations which develop this culture enable teamwork, encourage change and create competitive edge. When sustainability strategy is included in innovation processes, compliance with the current legislation and meeting the customer's demands become an added bonus in addition to the creation of numerous new opportunities for growth and optimization (Fernández, 2018). (Arsawan et al., 2022). It affirms that it is possible for firms to adopt sustainable innovation culture that will help them to distinguish themselves in the market. This was mainly attributed to the fact that consumers are being more conscious of the environment and they are willing to support brands that are also environmentally conscious. Therefore, when organizations embrace sustainable products and services, they have an opportunity of tapping new markets from green consumers. 'Sustainability' is a modern trend that is successfully used in fashion, technology, and the food industry. For instance, through its innovation of electric cars or EVs, Tesla has flooded the automotive industry through production of efficient electric cars, which do not emit carbon. That is why thanks to the focus on sustainability, Tesla became the leader in the market of electric vehicles, which found a growing number of enthusiastic customers (Bocken & Geradts, 2020). Many people appreciate sustainable development policies and, as a result, companies with sustainable strategies will likely be more successful in terms of customers' attitudes, investors, and employees. Thus, developing a culture of sustainable innovation also informs the various stakeholders that the business is willing and ready to engage in ethical business practices as well as the willing to create value in the long run. This does not only work on building the image of the brand but also on building up customer loyalty. The modern client is knowledgeable, and he or she is inclined to buy products and services of the companies that act in a socially and environmentally friendly manner (Abbas et al., 2020). Federal, state, and local governments, as well as other regulatory agencies are today raising the environmental standards in their quest to curb climate change, pollution and depletion of natural resources. Such business entities stand well to face these emerging and ever stringent regulations in sustainable innovation. Sustainable innovation culture imbues compliance into the organization processes hence minimizing fines, penalties, and reputational loss. Besides, a sustainable approach is effective in managing operational and reputational risks apart from compliance with legal requirements. As the world realizes that the conventional type of energy sources is limited and is simply unfit for the future, business organizations can hedge some of this risks such as: Fluctuation in price, scarcity in resources and disruption in supply chains by diversifying from using the traditional energy sources and focus on the renewable energy sources (Ciasullo et al., 2020). Modern employment also tends to consider sustainable work and corporate and social responsibility indicators. There is an increased focus on creating sustainability culture within organizations due to the fact that talented people, especially the young workers, prefer to work for organizations with clean sustainable innovative practices. Misin Contractor is aware that when employees do not have to forsake their personal values when interacting with the company in which they work their levels of job satisfaction, productivity and retention tend to be higher (Yun et al., 2020). Sustainable innovation is an incredible opportunity for creating new growth prospects. The reduction of greenhouse gas emissions, utilizing renewable energy, eco-friendly production materials and eco-technologies are profitable for companies since they open new opportunities for entering new markets. Solutions like circular economic solutions, sustainable packaging and carbon-neutral products are the trends that consumers and companies are interested in. Besides, sustainable innovation can provide product differentiation that makes it possible for organizations to offer their products at a higher price. For instance, luxury fashion players have adapted to the trend of using sustainable material for the production of clothing, shoes, bags and other accessories targeting the market of customers who prefer to use eco-friendly luxury items (Oskam et al., 2021). Large numbers of investors are beginning to factor in ESG issues when making investments in organizations. A firm with good sustainability is favored by Shareholders with socially responsible investment (SRI) and Institutional Investors in particular who seek long term gains. Environmental management entails development of sustainable environment culture that assures investors that the company is innovative, risk-averse as well as committed to creation of long-term investors value. Various companies that are into investments like BlackRock which is the largest asset manager globally have pointed at sustainability as a key consideration for investment. Developing sustainable policies help companies to be prepared for attracting the capital and funds for funding from the investors who value ESG factors (Puccci et al., 2020). The creation of sustainable innovation culture is not only organizational responsibility, it is a business necessity for purposeful improvement of organizational performance. And thus, through incorporating sustainability into the innovation process one is able to save costs, improve competitiveness, attract and retain talents and fuel sustainable growth. Organizations that adopt this perspective are better placed to be able to adapt to emergent consumer needs, legal requirements and social responsibilities crucial for the sustainability of the company.

VI. IMPLEMENTING THE SUSTAINABLE PRACTICES

Sustainability is not an idea that businesses can afford to ignore; it is quickly becoming a core focus of any organization due to increasing environmental threats as well as growing awareness among consumers. Sustainability enables companies to decrease their impact on the environment while at the same time improving organizational performance and corporate sustainability. There are two crucial areas where organizations are focusing a lot of efforts towards sustainability; one is Eco-design and product development while the other is sustainable business models. They not only serve as ecologically friendly undertaking but also as fundamental Sustainable Competitive Advantage factors (Planelles et al., 2022). Eco-design refers to the creation of products which have a low impact on the environment throughout the life cycle of the product right from the time it is extracted from the ground to the time it is used up and disposed of. It also states that through integrating the environmental impacts into the design phase, the eco-design brings about sustainability when coupled with a reduction of costs besides improving on the quality of the product and attracting customers loyal to the product (Baldassarre et al., 2020). A major qualification of eco-design is the reduction of raw materials, energy, and water consumption throughout the product design phase. This can be done by developing products that would involve the utilization of lesser materials or choosing materials that would demand less energy or water for them to be produced. Another principle is on a choice of product design for disassembly and recyclability after its usage. This includes choosing materials which are easier to recycle and omission of parts which are toxic which makes the recycling process difficult. Products, which have been made in such a way that their components can be interchanged or enhanced, also reduces a product's lifecycle impact in a positive way (Cordoba, 2013). IKEA has come a long way, especially in the area of sustainable product development where most of their products incorporate renewable and recycled material. For instance, IKEA company used plastic bottles PET in the production of a kitchen front "Kungsbacka" and using recycle material from the forest. Tesla has brought a change in the automobile sector by manufacturing electric cars which minimize emission of greenhouse gases. Solar energy and energy storage solutions also make up another part of Tesla's business focusing on sustainable innovation not limited to cars. The circular economy has become one of the most recognizable and dominant sustainable business models. Compared to the linear economy which entails making products, using them and then disposing of them, the circular economy focuses on making the most use out of materials and products. This entails ensuring that products and materials are designed with an aim of reuse, repair, refurbishment or recycling, thus enabling design for a closed loop, in an endeavor to reduce wastage and over exploitation of resources (Cicconi, 2020). Another sustainable business model is the subscription-based models that are gradually expanding and can be observed in fashion, technological, and entertainment sectors. Businesses take their products to what is known as the product-as-a-service model which means that instead of a consumer purchasing the product, they can lease it for a monthly price. This shift does not only decrease the materials requirement but also put much emphasis on the durability of the products and their maintenance.

In subscription service delivery models, the products are taken back to the company after they have been used and the business can renovate, reuse or reclaim them. The consumer is able to obtain a steady stream of a product through refurbishment and this does away with the need to produce new products hence lowering the environmental effect of manufacturing new products (Chaudhuri et al., 2022). Philips, a Dutch multinational conglomerate specialized in healthcare technology, adopted the circular economy by introducing a "Lighting as a Service" program. Instead of selling consumer goods, such as light bulbs, Philips offers lighting services whereby customers lease lamps from it. Technically, the ownership of the lighting equipment remains with the company to maintain and even replace the equipment as often as is necessary to achieve the desired performance. At the end of the lease, Philips either recycles it or uses the individual component of the product to create a new product hence cutting waste (Proven,2023). Reducing ecological impact by means of eco-design and utilizing other progressive approaches such as the circular economy as well as the utilization of subscriptions as a business model are capable of creating a more environmentally friendly, socially responsible, and economically effective world. It also makes it possible for firms to cut down on their utilization of resources, minimize waste, and at the same time serve their customers better even with an aim of making profit. Although sustainability is consciously embedded into the companies' production strategies and business models, thus they are not only helping to preserve the planet's health but also becoming leaders of a new, environmentally-oriented market. The sooner more companies start establishing sustainable business models applying these principles, the faster the change to a circular economy will happen – to the benefit for everybody involved (Niessen et al., 2023).

VII. MEASURING THE IMPACT IN SUSTAINABLE BUSINESS PRACTICES

Reflecting on the fact that sustainable initiatives are becoming critical for organizations, the articles underline the importance of assessing and reporting on the results achieved. Sustainability management is the management of social, economic and environmentally friendly activities, making and achieving realistic targets needs correct assessment and measurements. In this regard, such tools as the Key Performance Indicators or KPIs together with the impact assessment tools and report, are projected to serve crucial functions in facilitating organizations' evaluation of the viability of their sustainability initiatives (Schuh et al., 2019). Key Performance Indicators (KPIs) are useful tools that an organization uses so as to assess the level of realization of set sustainability goals and objectives. KPIs make sustainable efforts measurable in order to determine their efficiency and support business decision making oriented at enhancing the organizational environmental and social impact (Huotari, 2019). The carbon footprint is one of the most common KPIs applied in the field of sustainability and refers to the overall GHG emissions that occur as the result of a company's activity. This includes both the company owned or direct emissions (scope 1), the ones arising from the purchased energy (scope 2), and the ones arising from the manufactured product throughout the supply chain (scope 3). It is important to keep a record of carbon footprints as organizations strive to lower their impact to the environment and meet the new strict laws and policies designed to fight climate change.

Some of the key sustainability goals that firms have include goals related to energy and climate change that include efficiency improvement, renewable energy use and sourcing. For example, a global logistics company such as UPS has fuel consumption metrics as well as emissions metrics as its organizational KPI to monitor the progress in its carbon neutrality programme (Jin et al., 2017). Another measurable is the resource utilization which focuses on the utilization of the natural resources including water, raw materials, and energy. Resource efficiency KPIs is a measure of how effectively the firm is using the resources supplied to it; this is the ratio of inputs against the outputs in the company. Social responsibility is not only about numbers pertaining to the environment; social responsibility KPIs are also essential in measuring a company's contribution to society and everyone within it. Some of the socially measurable performance factors are remuneration standards, demographics of workforce, company's policies on safety, and support for the economy. Organizations like the Unilever use social KPIs to determine the effectiveness of their cardinal corporate social responsibility (CSR) goals, including enhancing people's wellbeing, supporting gender equality, and supply of safe water (Chen et al., 2020). LCA is a comprehensive approach to assess the environmental factors that are associated with a certain product or a service during its life cycle right from the stages of material procurement to its final disposal. LCA assists in enhancing awareness of industries in the areas that experience the greatest impacts on the environment so that they can plan for the change. It can then measure different environmental commodities like energy, water, emission rates, and volumetric rates of wastes produced. LCA is particularly important to industries with a large number of inputs like manufacturing, automobile, technology products and electronics. Due to the application of LCA it is possible to determine the changes for product design and materials, as for the waste management system for minimization of the adverse impact on the environment. For instance, BMW has adopted LCA to assess sustainability of electric cars besides enhancing the environmental performance of its cars (Bjørn et al., 2018). Social Return on Investment (SROI) is one of the analytical tools used to assess the social worth of the company's efforts in terms of benefits generated or likely to be generated for different stakeholders and the community in general, including employees. SROI is an extension of financial returns to quantify social benefit in monetary terms; very useful in asserting organizational sustainability & CSR. Sustainability reporting, which is also referred to as Integrated reporting, is essential when it comes to building stakeholder trust and showcasing is vital to any company's reporting when it comes to sustainability. Reporting enables the organization to present its advancement, difficulties and successes to investors, customers, employees and other related authorities (Yates et al., 2017). Sustainability evaluation and assessment is a critical aspect when undertaking sustainability initiatives in an organization. Thus, the proper identification of the KPI, the utilisation of impact methods like LCA and SROI, as well as the presentation of company's results in sustainable reports make a company able to improve the strategy, design, and outcome of their sustainable activities. More and more organizations implementing such practices will be able to achieve sustainable improvement of the organizations' environmental, social and economic performance. Finally, it contributes to the definition of the 'Triple bottom line' and indicates how evaluation and measurement of impacts can assist organizations in becoming more resilient, improve stakeholder trust and support a more sustainable future.

Implication

Academic Implication: This research contributes to the existing literature on sustainability and innovation by providing an analytical framework for examining both concepts in the context of businesses. Thereby contributing to academic discussion by including main frameworks like eco-design, circular economy frameworks and sustainable reporting. Thus, these findings may help to contribute to the future studies of the connection between sustainability and innovation in various industries and regions. In addition, it opens up avenues for further theoretical frameworks in relation to the effect of sustainability-driven innovation on performance enhancement, competitive advantage, and sustainable advantage. The research findings also create new avenues for further interdisciplinary research mainly in sustainability science, management, and Technological innovation.

Managerial Implication: From a managerial lens, the undertaking provides insights on how to mainstream sustainability into key value levers. The following strategic approaches, including circular business models and sustainable reporting in entrepreneurial organizations, as highlighted above can be used by managers to achieve environmental value as well as economic value. The presented information can contribute to the creation of sustainable strategies for their further implementation integrated with the optimization of organizational functions and boosting its innovative potential. Lastly, the study supports the managers to integrate employee, stakeholder, and a partner in developing culture that is innovative and sustainable when it comes to disaster recovery. Lastly, these managerial implications highlight that sustainability is a critical factor that needs to be integrated into a firm's strategic agenda so as to become an important source of competitive advantage, reputation management, and reducing risks within the current market environment.

Limitation and Future Scope

The findings give a general understanding of sustainability and innovation and their integration, however, they are bound by the fact that sustainability, as well as innovation, are still in the process of development, and their implementation can be peculiar to different industries. While the study relies mainly on theoretical perspectives and abstract approaches, the specifics of certain sectors or the particularities of the regional regulatory systems might be partly left out. Also, the high rate of change of technologies in the market and changing customer needs may lead to emerging issues in the context of the introduction of sustainable innovation by companies. For future work there is a need for more industry-specific cases and more quantitative data to prove the efficacy of the different sustainable innovation approaches. Investigating how artificial intelligence, cryptography, and renewable energy sources could help with modern living and improving sustainability could also offer extra understanding on how innovation could help push sustainability to greater heights. Furthermore, future research can involve the efforts to refine tools for assessing the effectiveness of the realized sustainable initiatives within the matters of organizational performance and social benefit over a long period of time.

CONCLUSION

With the dynamic change of business environment consistently taking place, the synergies of sustainability and innovation have become a survival tool for many businesses in the modern world. Sustainable innovation management in organizations can lead to the improvement in business performance through organizational resiliency, increased operational effectiveness, and by satisfying the new societal trends of green/Sustainability minded products and services. If implemented correctly, managing the environmental impact begins with specific business approaches—eco-designing products, applying circular economy models and using transparent reporting when businesses do not have to damage their natural environment, but instead, they find new opportunities for competitiveness and customer relationships. Being integrated into the strategic management system, as well as focusing on the priority area of improving innovativeness, managing sustainable development would enable companies to generate holistic value benefiting the company and overall society and effectively pre-adapt to the changing environment by performing the avant-garde role in the shift toward sustainable development. Overall, through the connection of sustainability and innovation, business can contribute to the growth and effectiveness within economy as well as be adaptive to changes within society and environment, thus keeping their relevancy in the long-term future.

REFERENCES

Abbas, J., Zhang, Q., Hussain, I., Akram, S., Afaq, A., & Shad, M. A. (2020). Sustainable innovation in small medium enterprises: The impact of knowledge management on organizational innovation through a mediation analysis by using SEM approach. *Sustainability (Basel)*, 12(6), 2407. DOI: 10.3390/su12062407

Afeltra, G., Alerasoul, S. A., & Strozzi, F. (2023). The evolution of sustainable innovation: From the past to the future. *European Journal of Innovation Management*, 26(2), 386–421. DOI: 10.1108/EJIM-02-2021-0113

Aguilar-Fernández, M. E., & Otegi-Olaso, J. R. (2018). Firm size and the business model for sustainable innovation. *Sustainability (Basel)*, 10(12), 4785. DOI: 10.3390/su10124785

Albert, M. (2019). Sustainable frugal innovation-The connection between frugal innovation and sustainability. *Journal of Cleaner Production*, 237, 117747. DOI: 10.1016/j.jclepro.2019.117747

Arsawan, I. W. E., Koval, V., Rajiani, I., Rustiarini, N. W., Supartha, W. G., & Suryantini, N. P. S. (2022). Leveraging knowledge sharing and innovation culture into SMEs sustainable competitive advantage. *International Journal of Productivity and Performance Management*, 71(2), 405–428. DOI: 10.1108/IJPPM-04-2020-0192

Baldassarre, B., Keskin, D., Diehl, J. C., Bocken, N., & Calabretta, G. (2020). Implementing sustainable design theory in business practice: A call to action. *Journal of Cleaner Production*, 273, 123113. DOI: 10.1016/j.jclepro.2020.123113

Bjørn, A., Owsianiak, M., Molin, C., & Hauschild, M. Z. (2018). LCA history. *Life cycle assessment: theory and practice*, 17-30.

Bocken, N. M., & Geradts, T. H. (2020). Barriers and drivers to sustainable business model innovation: Organization design and dynamic capabilities. *Long Range Planning*, 53(4), 101950. DOI: 10.1016/j.lrp.2019.101950

Boret Cordoba, D., & Veshagh, A. (2013). Managing eco design and sustainable manufacturing. In *Re-engineering Manufacturing for Sustainability:Proceedings of the 20th CIRP International Conference on Life Cycle Engineering,* Singapore 17-19 April, 2013 (pp. 59-67). Springer Singapore.

Cappa, F., Del Sette, F., Hayes, D., & Rosso, F. (2016). How to deliver open sustainable innovation: An integrated approach for a sustainable marketable product. *Sustainability (Basel)*, 8(12), 1341. DOI: 10.3390/su8121341

Chaudhuri, R., Chatterjee, S., Ghosh, A., Vrontis, D., & Thrassou, A. (2022). Sustainable innovation for shared mobility: Contextual and consumer factors of an Indian car subscription business model. *International Journal of Entrepreneurial Behaviour & Research*. Advance online publication. DOI: 10.1108/IJEBR-01-2022-0090

Chen, S., Kharrazi, A., Liang, S., Fath, B. D., Lenzen, M., & Yan, J. (2020). Advanced approaches and applications of energy footprints toward the promotion of global sustainability. *Applied Energy*, 261, 114415. DOI: 10.1016/j.apenergy.2019.114415

Chen, S. H. (2016). The influencing factors of enterprise sustainable innovation: An empirical study. *Sustainability (Basel)*, 8(5), 425. DOI: 10.3390/su8050425

Ciasullo, M. V., Troisi, O., Grimaldi, M., & Leone, D. (2020). Multi-level governance for sustainable innovation in smart communities: An ecosystems approach. *The International Entrepreneurship and Management Journal*, 16(4), 1167–1195. DOI: 10.1007/s11365-020-00641-6

Cicconi, P. (2020). Eco-design and Eco-materials: An interactive and collaborative approach. *Sustainable Materials and Technologies*, 23, e00135. DOI: 10.1016/j.susmat.2019.e00135

Cillo, V., Petruzzelli, A. M., Ardito, L., & Del Giudice, M. (2019). Understanding sustainable innovation: A systematic literature review. *Corporate Social Responsibility and Environmental Management*, 26(5), 1012–1025. DOI: 10.1002/csr.1783

Costa, J., & Matias, J. C. (2020). Open innovation 4.0 as an enhancer of sustainable innovation ecosystems. *Sustainability (Basel)*, 12(19), 8112. DOI: 10.3390/su12198112

De, D., Chowdhury, S., Dey, P. K., & Ghosh, S. K. (2020). Impact of lean and sustainability oriented innovation on sustainability performance of small and medium sized enterprises: A data envelopment analysis-based framework. *International Journal of Production Economics*, 219, 416–430. DOI: 10.1016/j.ijpe.2018.07.003

Hanaysha, J. R., Al-Shaikh, M. E., Joghee, S., & Alzoubi, H. M. (2022). Impact of innovation capabilities on business sustainability in small and medium enterprises. *FIIB Business Review*, 11(1), 67–78. DOI: 10.1177/23197145211042232

Huotari, P., & Ritala, P. (2021). When to switch between subscription-based and ad-sponsored business models: Strategic implications of decreasing content novelty. *Journal of Business Research*, 129, 14–28. DOI: 10.1016/j.jbusres.2021.02.037

Jin, M., Tang, R., Ji, Y., Liu, F., Gao, L., & Huisingh, D. (2017). Impact of advanced manufacturing on sustainability: An overview of the special volume on advanced manufacturing for sustainability and low fossil carbon emissions. *Journal of Cleaner Production*, 161, 69–74. DOI: 10.1016/j.jclepro.2017.05.101

Jorna, R. (Ed.). (2017). *Sustainable innovation: The organisational, human and knowledge dimension*. Routledge. DOI: 10.4324/9781351280365

Kuzma, E., Padilha, L. S., Sehnem, S., Julkovski, D. J., & Roman, D. J. (2020). The relationship between innovation and sustainability: A meta-analytic study. *Journal of Cleaner Production*, 259, 120745. DOI: 10.1016/j.jclepro.2020.120745

Lüdeke-Freund, F. (2020). Sustainable entrepreneurship, innovation, and business models: Integrative framework and propositions for future research. *Business Strategy and the Environment*, 29(2), 665–681. DOI: 10.1002/bse.2396

Nayak, A., Patnaik, A., Satpathy, I., Khang, A., & Patnaik, B. C. M. (2023). Applications of the Internet of Things (IoT) in Smart Cities: A Step toward Innovation. In *Smart Cities* (pp. 57–77). CRC Press. DOI: 10.1201/9781003376064-4

Niessen, L., Bocken, N. M., & Dijk, M. (2023). The impact of business sufficiency strategies on consumer practices: The case of bicycle subscription. *Sustainable Production and Consumption*, 35, 576–591. DOI: 10.1016/j.spc.2022.12.007

Oskam, I., Bossink, B., & de Man, A. P. (2021). Valuing value in innovation ecosystems: How cross-sector actors overcome tensions in collaborative sustainable business model development. *Business & Society*, 60(5), 1059–1091. DOI: 10.1177/0007650320907145

Pieroni, M. P., McAloone, T. C., & Pigosso, D. C. (2019). Business model innovation for circular economy and sustainability: A review of approaches. *Journal of Cleaner Production*, 215, 198–216. DOI: 10.1016/j.jclepro.2019.01.036

Provén, C., & Skoglund, N. (2023). *The Role Of Value Creation In Sustainable Product Service System Implementation: A Case Study On Lynk & Co's Subscription Model.*

Pucci, T., Casprini, E., Galati, A., & Zanni, L. (2020). The virtuous cycle of stakeholder engagement in developing a sustainability culture: Salcheto winery. *Journal of Business Research*, 119, 364–376. DOI: 10.1016/j.jbusres.2018.11.009

Reficco, E., Gutiérrez, R., Jaén, M. H., & Auletta, N. (2018). Collaboration mechanisms for sustainable innovation. *Journal of Cleaner Production*, 203, 1170–1186. DOI: 10.1016/j.jclepro.2018.08.043

Repo, P., & Matschoss, K. (2019). Social innovation for sustainability challenges. *Sustainability (Basel)*, 12(1), 319. DOI: 10.3390/su12010319

Sanchez-Planelles, J., Segarra-Oña, M., & Peiro-Signes, A. (2022). Identifying different sustainable practices to help companies to contribute to the sustainable development: Holistic sustainability, sustainable business and operations models. *Corporate Social Responsibility and Environmental Management*, 29(4), 904–917. DOI: 10.1002/csr.2243

Schuh, G., Frank, J., Jussen, P., Rix, C., & Harland, T. (2019, June). Monetizing industry 4.0: Design principles for subscription business in the manufacturing industry. In *2019 IEEE international conference on engineering, technology and innovation (ICE/ITMC)* (pp. 1-9). IEEE.

Shakeel, J., Mardani, A., Chofreh, A. G., Goni, F. A., & Klemeš, J. J. (2020). Anatomy of sustainable business model innovation. *Journal of Cleaner Production*, 261, 121201. DOI: 10.1016/j.jclepro.2020.121201

Varadarajan, R. (2017). Innovating for sustainability: A framework for sustainable innovations and a model of sustainable innovations orientation. *Journal of the Academy of Marketing Science*, 45(1), 14–36. DOI: 10.1007/s11747-015-0461-6

Yates, B. T., & Marra, M. (2017). Social Return On Investment (SROI): Problems, solutions… and is SROI a good investment? *Evaluation and Program Planning*, 64, 136–144. DOI: 10.1016/j.evalprogplan.2016.11.009 PMID: 27979379

Yun, J. J., Zhao, X., Jung, K., & Yigitcanlar, T. (2020). The culture for open innovation dynamics. *Sustainability (Basel)*, 12(12), 5076. DOI: 10.3390/su12125076

Chapter 6
The Role of Artificial Intelligence in Business Models

T. Venkat Narayana Rao
https://orcid.org/0000-0002-1996-1819
Sreenidhi Institute of Science and Technology, India

Rohini Avula
https://orcid.org/0009-0008-7669-6207
Sreenidhi Institute of Science and Technology, India

Sangers Bhavana
https://orcid.org/0009-0005-6134-1081
Sreenidhi Institute of Science and Technology, India

T. Thukaram Goud
Sreenidhi Institute of Science and Technology, India

ABSTRACT

AI is thus emerging as the progressive tool in the new business models given the efficiency it creates in the processes of decision making and operations. The application of business analytics especially through the use of AI can assist firms in arriving at better decisions since the make their decision based on a large amount of data. AI makes man's work simple, fast, efficient and close to perfect—thus fewer errors are likely to occur. The application of the analytical tools relates to the formulation of the plan based on the insight in order to attain strategic results. Moreover, AI chatbots and virtual assistants enhance the system of more advanced customer communication as well as customer experience. By analysing the market tendencies AI helps predict the future tendencies as well as enhancing the innovative aspect of

DOI: 10.4018/979-8-3693-9571-4.ch006

business development such as providing new business models in terms of services, business, and data-as-service business. AI might improve delivery of service to the customers of the company, hence improving its competitiveness.

1. INTRODUCTION

Artificial Intelligence, widely known as AI, is among the radical forces defining the leading edge of new business models for the contemporary world. Machine learning, natural language processing and computer vision help companies to create new opportunities for the further growth of businesses. Features that include the processing of large volumes of information and producing information to make decisions make AI give businesses insights to make better decisions, automate processes, and improve client experiences. Therefore, organizations that implement Artificial Intelligence can stand to benefit from the exponential rise in data as a marketplace factor.

Another major implication of AI relating to the business models is the value chain where AI has the potential to complete the routine and time-consuming tasks. With AI in customer service chatbots and AI in supply chain prediction, employee resources can be used more efficiently in job areas where only humans can offer their expertise. Besides increasing working efficiency, it also helps expand the working capacity (Reim et.al, 2020).

Another important area where AI comes into focus is in improving the quality of customer experience by offering personalizing products and services and the customer experience as well. By the use of complex computations on the user data set, any organisation can identify customer tendencies, their preference and their feedback, hence gaining the ability to personalize recommendations thereby increasing the number of customers' interactions and their satisfaction levels. Instance, firms like Amazon and Netflix utilize AI to help customers find content and products and services that they like, or may be interested in, and this raises user satisfaction levels considerably.

Additionally, AI enhances the ability of the businesses to innovate quicker because it helps to determine the prevailing trends within the market space as well as the improvement of product changes and the forecast of future demands on the market. It enables the development of new models of value creation, primarily in industries where the primary focus is on the ability of AI to generate value-enhancing solutions and products, such as healthcare, finance, retail, and manufacturing.

Thus, AI is not only an overlay to the known business models but the driving force behind changes in the way companies function, create and capture value. It is important to be integrated for organizations that are planning to sustain in the competitive market and now emerging digital economy.

The application of business analytics, especially through the use of AI, can assist firms in arriving at better decisions since they make their decision based on a large amount of data.

1. **Automation and Efficiency:** AI makes man's work simple, fast, efficient and close to perfect thus less errors are likely to occur.
2. **Data-Driven Decision Making:** The application of the analytical tools relates to the formulation of the plan based on the insight in order to attain strategic results.
3. **Customer Service Improvement:** Moreover, AI chatbots and virtual assistants enhance the system of more advanced customer communication as well as customer experience.
4. **Predictive Modeling and Innovation:** By analyzing the market tendencies AI helps in predicting the future tendencies as well as enhancing the innovative aspect of business development.
5. **Creation of New Business Models:** AI also provides other new business models that include subscription services business and data-as-service business models.
6. **Challenges:** Congregation of artificial intelligence pose issues and issues like data and informational privacy, employment eradications, and ethical dilemmas (Lee et.al,2019).

AI is gradually becoming the enabler of innovation and change for business models and is putting pressure on organizations to reconsider their models, plans, and propositions. Leveraging AI is not simply a way to automate processes in order to speed them, but it is a lever that gives companies the capability to grow, deliver new forms of services, and evolve within the new digital economy. AI will play an important role of companies' future growth, efficiency and customers satisfaction, mostly depending on how companies utilizes AI into key business strategies.

2. AI-DRIVEN AUTOMATION AND OPERATIONAL EFFICIENCY

Automations using artificial intelligence (AI) are becoming rampant in the industry, allowing organizations to work better and achieve more at a lower cost. Many simple and routine tasks can be effectively addressed by using AI, and thus, human employees' work options are expanded. AI helps to integrate business operations and to minimize the influence of human error in it, therefore increases the productivity of the business.

Another advantage of these intelligent applications of automation is the immense data throughput capacity it has. While other functions were solved earlier with more generic means, AI can work through enormous quantities of data at lightning speed, find correlation and make distinctive decisions based on these findings. This is more helpful in businesses such as manufacturing, finance and other related businesses where time and accuracy are of paramount importance. For instance, environmental control systems, which are powered by artificial intelligence, may well enable observation of production lines, identification of defects and remedy the problem all on their own; this implies that the efficiency of the process will improve considerably, and the incidences of downtime will greatly diminish (Yaseen et.al, 2022).

Stale, AI automation improves operational efficiency as businesses use the freedom it provides to plan their operations. For instance, Robotic Process Automation (RPA) lets organizations introduce automation into services such as data input, accounts receivables management, or customer relations. With the help of AI, companies can have online chats where customers converse with chatbots that could respond to numerous requests, provide clear replies to a number of basic questions and even solve certain problems without involving people in the process. It also speeds up response times as well as making for uniformity in service provision.

AI is also central to prognosis, a feature that is applicable mainly in sectors that involve operating high-risk machinery or equipment. Through machine learning algorithms, organizations can track the equipment and prognosis the probable date the equipment may fail and perform a fix. It drastically reduces the amount of unexpected downtime while also increasing equipment lifecycle, as well as lowering repair expenses (Sodiya et.al, 2024).

In addition, through integration of Artificial intelligence, businesses are able to expand on their operations without necessarily having to expand the expenses that come with it. Challenges arise with the growth of the business and organization due to the issues of handling large volumes of information processes and increasing customer demands. AI is able to process these tasks at scale so it is guaranteed that the operation of the business will not be affected, there will be no need for new recruitments.

In conclusion, AI driven automation is the key for any organisation that wants to optimize its productivity. In essence, AI helps to cut costs through automating repetitive processes, provide more efficient organisation of work, use predictive maintenance to prevent expensive downtimes, and free up people to do more valuable work. In the current world, and especially in the future, this efficiency is going to be even more dependent on the use of artificial intelligence.

3. ENHANCED DECISION-MAKING WITH AI-POWERED INSIGHTS

Artificial Intelligence (AI) is revolutionizing decision-making in businesses by providing advanced data analytics and insights that enhance both strategic and operational decisions. With AI's ability to process vast amounts of data quickly and accurately, companies can make informed decisions based on real-time information, improving outcomes and minimizing risks.

At the core of AI-powered decision-making is predictive analytics, which allows businesses to forecast future trends, customer behaviors, and market conditions. By analyzing historical data and recognizing patterns, AI can generate actionable insights that help organizations anticipate changes and make proactive decisions. For example, in retail, AI can analyze customer purchasing behavior to predict future demand, enabling businesses to optimize inventory and reduce waste (Agarwal et.al, 2021).

Also, with the help of machine learning inputs, algorithms can always learn from new data inputs making corrections to their prediction models and recommendations. The embedded resources of this dynamic capability allow firms to make decisions faster and more efficiently than earlier approaches to decision making. For example, in the financial services sector, AI-generated intelligence is used in the risk assessment process for vendors, by analyzing changes in the market and determining potential risks or opportunities and thus making better decisions about where to invest or extend credit more expeditiously.

AI also helps in improved decision making because it reduces biases that are often hard coded in human choices. Whereas the prior decision making entails the use of previous and/or current experiences, memories, and feelings that may contain pains and biases, AI offers an impersonal view of data. It is especially helpful in recruitment where AI is used for picking the candidates from the resumes by evaluating them according to the performance indices rather than through bias caused by preference (Zhang et.al, 2023).

In supply chain management, artificial intelligence serves to provide centers of gravity for logistics, souring, and production planning. Through machine learning AI acquisition can identify changes to occur within the supply chain in real-time and give recommendations based on numerous inputs from the weather to the economy to the suppliers. This minimizes the interruption of the supply chain, ensures orderliness in delivery of the products and assists organizations in managing costs.

There is also real-time decision making whereby AI helps make decisions for the organization within a short period of time. AI in, for instance, the health sector, can be used to review patient information in real time and assist the physician in formulating a diagnosis as well as proper treatment regime given data from other patients with similar condition.

Further, use of analytics and artificial intelligence in automation of decision-support systems is seen in many companies to provide managerial decision-making information on strategic actions such as market access, introduction of new products and setting of prices. In this approach, simulations and scenario analysis give decision makers the ability to see the possible outcome before they make a decision.

In conclusion, it can be said that AI-based insights are revolutionizing the possibility of making new decisions at various corporations. AI impacts optimisation of organisational operations, risk reduction, actual time decision making and better organisational results by use of predictive analytics and bias elimination. Decision making is clearly an area in which AI is set to have a more profound impact, and hence plays a crucial role where success is required across various fields.

4. PERSONALIZED CUSTOMER EXPERIENCES

The concept of Artificial Intelligence (AI) is instrumental in enhancing value creation with customers where organizations can deliver customer solutions which are unique to each customer. On the basis of big data, AI is capable of predicting buyers' characteristics and their requirements, to design highly-tailored interactions with a customer, which results in loyalty and satisfaction.

Of all the examples of how AI influences personalization, the most profound example is through the recommendation system. Companies such as Netflix, Amazon or Spotify are currently employing artificial intelligence algorithms that would predict a customer's behaviour according to his incoming purchase or spent time on consumption of content or products. Such individual recommendations improve the consumption experience increases the sales or usage since it is more relevant, less stressful, and interesting to the buyers.

AI technology, in particular natural language processing, underpins limited but real-time and live virtual assistant and chatbot communication. As small examples, customer service chatbots, for example, may be able to comprehend and respond to a single question while often providing specific answers based on historical communications with the same customer. AI is employed in virtual assistant programs such as Siri, Alexa or Google Assistant- where programs make personalized responses depending on the user and adapt to the feedback they get. It enhances customers relations, increases customer relations response, and provides a good and nice environment based on the current user position (Shen et.al, 2014).

So in e-commerce, AI improves the prospects of personalization by establishing the user's browsing history, likelihood of purchase, and age. It helps businesses design targeted offers, price reductions and promotional campaigns based on data about individual clients and prevent conversion rate decline. For instance, they can be used to analyze customer type and path of consumer purchasing behavior, which can enable firms to send out targeted e-mail promotional offers or suggest to its customers other products that may suit their interest.

Moreover, in content marketing AI driven personalization is evident where in the business world, website contents, advertisements and even social medial interfaces are personalized based on the profile and activity of the user. This helps in making sure that customers will only see the content that interests them most, hence happy moments (Lindecrantz et.al, 2020).

Finally, it can be stated that AI helps businesses provide very individualized experiences based on the data gathered on buyers and provides them with recommendations, services, and content. With the ever-increasing demands of customers for personalization, companies that seek to employ AI techniques to develop and nurture personal and tailored relationships with their customers will enjoy a major competitive edge over their rivals in the marketplace.

5. AI IN PRODUCT AND SERVICE INNOVATION

AI is a potent enabler of product and service development, the generation of new aspects, and the improvement of existing elements and the customer experience. With the use of AI techniques and implementation, data can be processed in large volumes, insights on the consumers' behavior can be ascertained and market trends that point to the future can be closely anticipated which acts as fuel to innovation.

Out of all the benefits AI offers to foster innovation, data-drive product development is arguably the most significant one. Some of the widely-applicable AI tools can then help to gain insight into the needs and wants of customers, their interactions on social media and the overall behaviour in the market. Thus, the given findings will help to create goods and services that are closer to the consumer's needs and expectations. For example, in the fashion industry AI finds application in predicting consumer behaviour and managing the fashion trends in order that designers can design clothes that would be popular (Akter et.al, 2023).

Drawn in the manufacturing sector, AI is currently playing a significant role in defining new products as well as improving the manufacturing processes. AI can be integrated into products so that a product becomes smart or responsive in some manner. For instance, in the car industry, AI is used in the production of self-driving cars that is through the ability to learn the operating environment and independently take necessary decisions. In the same manner, other forms of AI such as IoT have transformed products into smart products including smart homes gadgets, wearables etc.

AI is also taking charge of service innovation boldly in most chief sectors including healthcare, finance, and retail trade. In healthcare, artificial intelligence created innovations like strategic diagnostics and individualized therapy on the patient. The use of algorithms in diagnosing patients with specific symptoms is possible, making patient individual treatment plans possible or even figuring out upcoming disease outbreaks. Several AI developments in the financial industry are as follows; robo-advisors that utilize the user data to get the best advice in the ever-increasing financial industry thus expanding the needed products (Bu et.al, 2020).

Moreover, AI strengthens process optimization which in turn shortens the time needed to bring the new product to market. AI is useful in processes such as research and development, as it can mimic product designs, compute, and forecast outcomes within product designs much faster than traditional methods can be used. This makes it easier for businesses to innovate, thereby speeding up the desired rate of improvement of the competitiveness profile.

Therefore, AI remains an important tool for organizations to create new and better products and/or services that meet the actual and anticipated needs and wants of consumers in value chains. Making and adjusting decisions, using customer data to create individualized experiences, and applying robotic process automation to enhance business insights enable companies to seize control and generate value in a continuously transforming economy.

6. PREDICTIVE ANALYTICS FOR BUSINESS GROWTH

AI and machine learning driven Predictive analytics is indeed one of the power tools that offer tremendous opportunity to the companies for growth. Through quantitative methods, historical data, and business intelligence and data science models, predictive analytics aids companies to forecast organizational and market trends, consumer behavior, and conditions, providing the insights companies need to anticipate and avoid pitfalls and capitalize on opportunities for development.

Of all the uses of predictive analytics that have been discussed in this paper, customer behaviour prediction is among the most powerful. Marketers can look at previous transactions, browsing and searching histories, and even the basic background data of their targets, in order to anticipate consumers' future purchases. This understanding helps businesses to develop and implement targeted marketing and advertising strategies, suggest relevant products, and even provide accurate and useful market pricing models that will better satisfy customers and keep them coming back. The same way that Amazon prefers to offer its customers relevant products from shopping records, such giants in e-commerce employ predictive analytics (Halper et.al, 2020).

Another important use of the model is in sales forecasting. Marketing predictive analytics help companies forecast their sales by using historical data and market conditions, consumer behaviour, among others. This assists in helping businesses manage their stock, workforce and marketing in relation to expected sales fulfilling its established goal of streamlining the running of organizations for higher profits. For instance, during the holiday events, retailers make use of the models for making the right decisions concerning the commodities they stock so that they do not order too many or too few.

Another area that the use of predictive analytics makes a rather big difference is the process of supply chain management. Using data gathered from the supply chain members as well as factors outside of the supply chain such as weather information and market conditions, it becomes possible by businesses to prevent disruption of their supply chains. This helps reduce time, which results to low costs and high satisfaction from the consumers since the products will have been delivered as expected. In manufacturing, it is also used for predictive maintenance: specialists create AI algorithms that watch the equipment and determine the best time when the machines are likely to break down. This enables the company to carry out maintenance in a preventive measure as this would enhance operations without stock (Chase Jr et.al, 2020).

In the area of finance, risk management and fraud detection, predictive analytics are most important. Predicting models based on transaction patterns and customer conduct to detect abnormal activities that might pose fraudulent or other dangerous activities. This helps those companies to ensure they do not fall victim to such cyber criminals and protect their assets as well as their customer's data. Also, credit scoring is another application of financial institutions where AI predicts that a customer can fail to pay the money back to the bank by developing models.

Marketing optimization is another place where predictive analytics can get you growth and innovation. Organizations can utilize the predictive models as a measure of judging the probability of different marketing techniques, in a bid to optimize the resources used. Marketing analysis, therefore, can reveal the value of customer interactions and customer engagement in determining potential click through rates, email responses, social media responses or any other advertising campaign that may be underway. This in turn helps firms to reach the appropriate target consumer at the correct time, contacts, ROI, and avoid a drain on resources that could be channeled towards more successful campaigns.

Last but not the least the ability of predictive analytics to develop a vision of the future enables businesses to understand new trends in the market and potential opportunities. Through the monitoring of online conversations as well as the assessment of customer feedback, market news and trends, firms are in a position to identify market changes before their competitors. Such thinking lets the existing companies adopt new methods and offer a business new goods or services, which will cover the tendencies and become the market leader or an important player.

Finally, predictive analytics can be named as an effective tool for business development. In doing so, it helps companies be one step ahead in today's world dominated by data by predicting customer behavior, improving their efficiency, and minimizing risks and missing opportunities. Companies that put into practice big data predictive analytics are able to make appropriate decisions as well as offer high levels of efficiency, outstanding customer satisfaction, and drive sustainable economic value.

7. AI AND COST REDUCTION STRATEGIES

AI is widely used by companies for the management of their primary activities, as well as for cost reduction measures. By removing the need for repetitive tasks, identifying wasteful processes, and predicting the best conditions for the business at a given time, AI makes processes leaner, more efficient and cost effective. This is particularly true in manufacturing and customer relations where AI helps businesses deal with costs, including keeping them relevant in the fast-changing market.

The largest impact of AI on costs can be described as the aspect of automation. Routine activities including data input, expense reconciliation, and order management can be easily executed with the help of Artificial Intelligence interface known as Robotic Process Automation. RPA replicates the physical activities of a person to deal with repetitive operational transactions and qualitative work, leaving human activity to employ their valuable time on higher value processes. The use of AI removes the need for too much human input which avails the company operating costs especially the cost of labor while at the same time enhancing efficiency and effectiveness. For instance, the account for maintaining thousands of invoices can be managed in a matter of minutes by implementing RPA, in this essence, decreases administrative overhead cost while eradicating errors from oversight.

Apart from the ability to directly execute simple tasks, AI helps to allocate resources efficiently within the organization. Using AI, different information can be accumulated to make changes in the process in real time. In sectors like manufacturing, AI applications are deployed in preventive maintenance, and this keeps costing the company a lot in a case when the machines are down. AI operating on large amounts of data from sensors installed on manufacturing equipment can predict when a machine is likely to fail and suggest when it should be taken to the workshop for servicing. This way not only prevents costly disturbances, but also increases the working time of the machinery and therefore reduces the number of expensive replacements (Ismanov et.al, 2024).

AI performs a crucial role in supply management where companies ensure the right quantities of goods are kept in stock to avoid carrying unnecessary expenses. Based on historical information, as well as customers' preferences, AI can forecast the future sales and suggest the appropriate number of stocks to order. This reduces the probability of having large stocks that may take a long time to move off the shelves or no stock at all which is disastrous. The supply chain is one of the most impactful areas affected by AI; companies such as Walmart and Amazon have reported their ability to reduce unnecessary stocking costs and more efficiently plan inventory demand.

The mystery of AI in the sphere of supply chain management is the result of cutting down costs by means of optimizing supply routes, enhancing logistics, and generalizing the process of supply chain. The system can use Artificial Intelligence capability to evaluate data about suppliers, and weather and transportation routes to suggest delivery routes that can be most effective. This has an added advantage of reducing fuel consumption, shortening delivery time and possibility of delay thus lowering the operating costs. AI also assists firms in managing their suppliers' performance to learn of the issues that may create a problem of escalating costs or denied supply chain.

One more aspect where AI helps to decrease costs is energy saving. Real-time tracking of energy use and making suggestions for how to reduce the usage can be managed through AI-powered systems concerning heating, cooling, and lighting in structures. AI operates smart grids of using energy by collecting real-time data and providing direction to manage energy costs effectively to reduce all business expenses without vitiating natural resources. For instance, companies in the manufacturing industry use AI to regulate machines and energy use thus enabling the firm reduce energy costs.

Last but not the least, through the use of AI in analytics, companies get to see aspects of the financial data which have not been easily detected by humans and where exactly the costs could be cut down. AI can review spending trends and find savings opportunities and costs optimization in the procurement process, staffing or marketing. For instance, through a model, one can be in a position to determine which particular advertising campaign would yield a better return than the other hence may assist organizations save on right costs (Suresh et.al, 2024).

Therefore, there are numerous cost saving strategies that AI presents to various kinds of businesses. From overload and repetitive work automation and resources management to supply chain improvement and energy management, AI optimizes expenses, lowers labor costs, and maximizes organization efficiency. In the future, when AI is more completely integrated into it, it will also become an even better tool for reducing costs, thus becoming essential for companies that aim at succeeding in the conditions of growing competition. If AI is well implemented strategically, the benefits that an organisation can gain are twofold: the cost-saving aspect and the resultant improvement of organisational productivity and sustainability.

8. RISK MANAGEMENT AND AI ENABLED SECURITY

In the twenty-first century of the growing inclination toward digital organization, there are numerous risks, including cybercrime, supply chain breaks, or other losses. Most organisations have realised that traditional risk management approaches to risk management lack the capacity to effectively address modern day risks. However, the use of Artificial Intelligence (AI) in risk management and security has become an interesting and efficient way of preventing risks, applying proactive and innovative approaches to organizations.

The effective implementation of the risk management processes using AI may be seen in cybersecurity. Today, the threat level of cyber-attacks is increasing and attackers are gaining high technicality, making organizations consider higher levels of protection for their important data and networks. Technologies like Security Informatics can deal with enormous amounts of network traffic and user behaviour to find out that the normal pattern is violated, and thus, an attack might be taking place. Most machine learning algorithms can identify lurking threats based on databases of earlier attacks and are capable of learning in real time. In doing so organizations can be more prepared for a potential breach and minimize the risk of loss and subsequent financial costs. AI also improves threat intelligence that makes organizations aware of new risks as they arise. Thanks to the AI processing of information gathered through multiple channels including the so-called 'dark web' forums, and social media, along with threat feeds, AI can pinpoint potential threats and risks before they become visible to the naked eye. This predictive capability enables organizations to provide preventive measures including patching a specific vulnerability or even increasing surveillance in specific areas that show high risks. For instance, in the financial services sector, AI is employable in tracking transactions, and identifying possible rip offs before the institutions, lose a lot of money.

In addition, it has been clearly illustrated how AI is used to support operational risk management through enhancing decision making. In manufacturing industries, data from the equipment sensors and logs can be analysed by AI and determine a probable equipment failure. By applying this kind of maintenance, it means that companies will provide solutions to problems before they manifest themselves in a way that is damaging to production and, in some instances, unsafe. When operations risks are minimised, organisations can be assured to have proper functioning and increased efficiency.

Besides predictive analytics, AI advances automatic compliance checking, which is crucial for companies that are selling in industries with a numerous number of regulations. In this way, AI systems can constantly monitor transactions, communications, and other operations and recognize compliance violations to notify their analyst. This real-time monitoring relieves the pressure on the compliance teams and helps to avoid penalties and/or reputational loss due to regulation breaches.

AI has not only penetrated the basic security technologies, but also the physical security technologies. Video surveillance makes use of artificial intelligence to capture video feeds and analyze them through computer vision for detecting suspicious activities or behaviors implying a security threat. For instance, actual-time surveillance cameras in shops can incorporate AI to identify shoplifting activities in an organization to do something to prevent this from happening. It also increases security and at the same time decreases loss due to theft.

In addition, customised risk management tools using artificial intelligence help organisations gain better perspectives on their overall resilience. AI in this sense can help an organization appreciate its weak areas and come up with measures that would help it improve on its risk profile. This include sharp risk estimation techniques such as the scenario modelling and stress testing, which are useful to understand how any certain risk would affect a company and its financial sustainability (Habbal et.al, 2024).

However, organisations using AI for risk management also face challenges associated with the successful deployment of Artificial Intelligence. Challenges like privacy infringement, bias on the algorithms used and can also put a lot of strain on the human resource required to manage it. The use of ethical AI and transparency becomes vital for organizations to avoid loss of public trust among other things.

To sum up, it is possible to state that AI enhances security and risk management at enterprises and become new models of threats and risk dealing. Using AI one can forecast compliance risks, monitor them in a more automated way and improve the effectiveness of surveillance measures to reach higher organisational security and efficiency. Thus, the AI-assisted treatment of risks will remain crucial for enterprises that seek to manage, contain, and mitigate possible negative consequences in the environment that increasingly becomes risky and dangerous for companies, their assets, reputations, and compliance achievements.

9. CASE STUDIES

AI is becoming a key catalyst that drives the shift of business models across industries to become smarter, making better decisions, automate, and unlock value. Below are a few case studies that demonstrate the role of AI in modern business models(Kumari et.al,2021):

9.1. Amazon: Personalization and Supply Chain Management

AI Application: Known as the pioneer in many machine learning initiatives, Amazon uses AI technologies in two main areas: providing customized experiences for the customer and effective supply chains. Recommendation engines based on artificial intelligence help to predict the buying interests of the customer and make sales recommendations hence helping the company to sell more products to the same customer. Other examples are in the flexible pricing, predicting customer demand or managing real-time inventory with AI's help Amazon applies AI to its supply chain.

Impact on Business Model

Personalization: This is especially important for Amazon since it helps the company increase the chances of selling products based on a customer's preferences.

Cost Optimization: Self-organizing cognition brings in customer forecast, inventory control, and demand planning, thus improving its business model to a greater value proposition.

9.2. Netflix: AI for Content Recommendation

AI Application: Through the Help of AI; Netflix suggest programs or movies that are most suitable for the particular user depending on their preferences. Netflix's recommendation engine shows people what they are likely to watch in future by analyzing large sets of data thereby increasing usage.

Impact on Business Model

Customer Retention: AI comes handy in increasing the number of visitors because it can assist in the delivery of relevant content, customers will not leave and can be retained easily.

Content Strategy: AI is also used in the creation of content that is seen on Netflix since the company relies on data analysis to foresee the viability of its other original content productions.

9.3. Tesla: Autonomous Vehicles

AI Application: Tesla deploys AI profusely in its cars' self-driving systems, in which cars can autonomously make certain decisions based on inputs from cameras, sensors and relevant GPS information. Tesla's autopilot system is an algorithm that improves itself after each drive it undertakes.

Impact on Business Model

Disruptive Innovation: Self- driven cars are still proving to be revolutionary to car owning and transport service systems and possible in a future where mobility services could be considered as an offering.

Data-Driven Development: Tesla has been able to deliver continuous improvement in performance of their vehicles through over the air soft wares downloads, hence providing a new business model that is based on soft wares download rather than the sale of hardwares.

9.4. Alibaba: AI in E-commerce and Finance

AI Application: For instance, it applies face recognition payment in the micro payment section, Ant Financial while for its shopping malls it uses recommendation system and smart distribution pathways.

Impact on Business Model

Smart Retail: This is because AI enables Alibaba to deliver targeted client experiences and cut down on retail's classic overcomplicated supply chains, creating a more authentic retail framework.

AI-Driven Finance: Having overcome major fraud, credit risk, and speed of loan approval, AI is changing the delivery of financial services for Ant Financial.

9.5. Zara: AI for Inventory Management

AI Application: Zara, an Inditex company, applies AI to stock control and demand forecasting and to improve the supply chain. AI based systems predict fashion trends based on customer information and thus facilitate timely responses from Zara to fashion changes.

Impact on Business Model

Fast Fashion Model: Through its development, AI helps Zara to sustain its "fast fashion" conception that implies the introduction of new items as fast as possible, being a reaction to the tendencies and the buyers' preferences.

Efficiency in Operations: AI also applies to the stock through reducing the issues of overproduction leading to markdowns and increasing profitability.

9.6. JPMorgan Chase: AI for Fraud Detection and Risk Management

AI Application: JPMorgan Chase includes applications of AI to fraud detection, risk management, and analysis of contracts. By using artificial intelligence algorithms, transactions and their data are checked at an incredible speed in order to detect fraud and possible risks incomparably better than with the help of human analysts.

Impact on Business Model:

Risk Mitigation: By means of AI, accuracy and speed of risks identification is higher which in its turn stabilizes the business model of the bank.

Operational Efficiency: AI performs tedious tasks like contract review and the likes, leading to various cost implications and optimization of time at top management level.

10. CONCLUSION

AI is variously described as a tool that is rapidly transforming business models from concepts of the future to necessities for organizations that want to improve their performance, innovate, and grow sustainably. More and more organizations today introduce AI technologies in their operations and discover new value, operational efficiency and customer benefits.

AI helps in decision making via big data and predictive modeling which make it easy for a business to guess the right direction to take by having a glimpse of what customers and markets are going to do. This enables them to strategically position resources, design and create unique products and services and control for risks beforehand. Further, AI allows for automatic repetition of business processes and actuality prescribes workflow, which makes employees more productive by devoting their time to inventive goals and reduces operational expenses.

One of the defining aspects in business – customer interactions concerning personalization and use of Artificial Intelligence in this branch. Through data processing AI provides better insights into customers to the companies, enabling them to increase satisfaction and loyalty. It can be seen that this sort of customer-oriented strategy not only helps in building a solid image of the product or service amongst potential customers, but also guarantees higher future revenues, which would turn into profit.

Another area that benefits from AI is the support of innovation since businesses use the application to notice emerging trends. With the identification of trends, organizations are placed in a position of creating products and services that match current trends; hence can adapt well to current market changes. Flexibility is just as important as experience; since the world is rapidly evolving, and any field can be disrupted, flexibility can be a key to success.

However, as Barclay noted, the advantages of AI are obvious, however businesses have to approach the use of this technology more cautiously thinking about the ethical issues, the problem of privacy, and the questions of desk transparency. This means that the benefits of AI have to be weighed against the measures that would have to be taken to ensure that customers, too, accept the technology.

AI is now not something which can be futuristic but is an enabling technology which forms the basis of operation for many ventures across the market space. Due to its incorporation into business models, it has brought change, altering processes, improving the tools for making decisions and modifying the way firms interact with the customer. Today, AI is not just an efficiency enabler but a strategic advantage that allows organisations to deliver competitive value propositions, create competitive moats and grow at scale.

The integration of the AI is quite broad, touching almost every facet of activities that happens in a business that incorporates this technology. From making logistics networks more efficient to streamlining administrative processes, to better managing customer relations and even going as far as utilizing the predictive analytics of sales, AI has brought a new layer of strategic thinking to how business is done. Business institutions harness AI and are then in a position to collect a significant amount of comprehensive information in real-time with analysis that would be unthinkable a few years back. It helps businesses think smarter, make advanced guesses towards the market trend, and address customers' needs in a better way. In return, businesses implementing the AI technologies' advantages are experiencing higher profitability, increased customer satisfaction, and acuter competitive advantage.

Another key benefit that has been added to business models by the use of AI is innovation. In the past, companies used experience and personal discretion to create new ideas and new products and services. However, AI has just created new opportunities through which companies can run virtual models, examine the data and exert hypotheses as well as estimate the results with high levels of precision.

The utilization of Artificial intelligence can help businesses prove different strategic approaches to resolving the uncertainty of business models and rapidly adapt to market conditions. This flexibility is extremely important in the current unpredictable and highly competitive market, where the prospect of change, the ability to think outside the box, may be the deciding factor in an organization's success or failure.

Another consideration for the growing importance of AI is the ability to improve client interfaces and, in general, amaze the clientele. Consumers have geared up for individual deals even as it is not considered special anymore. Today's major e-commerce platforms like Amazon and Netflix have already established a deep focus on customer personalization, presenting a customer-oriented model that other companies attempt to emulate. Artificial intelligence nowadays allows companies to comprehend the customer's data, to identify people's preferences, and to offer the experiences that would become meaningful to the buyers. It drives more customer loyalty, more engagement and, therefore, higher lifetime value. When implemented, AI can help organizations improve customer satisfaction and loyalty, in an environment where it is always challenging.

Other than enhancing customer experiences, AI has an important duty of enhancing organisational processes. Automation is one of the best-known uses of artificial intelligence to enable elimination of numerous tasks, prevent numerous mistakes, and ensure higher organizational productivity. Simple processes including data input, user support, supplies management, and prediction of future profits may prove useful to be carried out with the help of artificial intelligence; therefore, minimizing the amount of human input required for strenuous but elementary work. This shift also has the benefits of lowering costs while increasing productivity to enable organizations to expand cheaply and increase their competitive advantage in the international market.

Another area of usefulness of the use of AI is in the Sphere of Predictive Analytics that has a profound impact on business models. AI tools can help understand the numbers and trends of the past and, by comparing the current situation with past scenarios, make conclusions about the future state, thus, making the business undertake preventive actions rather than responsive ones. For instance, in retail, AI includes consumer demand for increasing efficiency in managing stock and minimizing the loss. In finance, it can evaluate credit risk and fraud detection with sufficient accuracy compared with the conventional standard. Through predictive analytics, business organizations can avoid potential problems, effectively manage organizational assets and invest in a smarter way optimized for positive results.

In conclusion, while we witnessed primarily how AI can change and build new business models it is crucial to remember that the impact of AI is far deeper and covers nearly all industry spheres. Organizations that adopt AI improve its performance and customers' experience, as well as future-proof the enterprise. Arguably, those who integrate AI in their business operations will be pioneers defining the future of the business environs.

REFERENCES

Agarwal, A., Singhal, C., & Thomas, R. (2021). *AI-powered decision making for the bank of the future*. McKinsey & Company.

Akter, S., Hossain, M. A., Sajib, S., Sultana, S., Rahman, M., Vrontis, D., & McCarthy, G. (2023). A framework for AI-powered service innovation capability: Review and agenda for future research. *Technovation*, 125, 102768. DOI: 10.1016/j.technovation.2023.102768

Bu, L., Chen, C. H., Zhang, G., Liu, B., Dong, G., & Yuan, X. (2020). A hybrid intelligence approach for sustainable service innovation of smart and connected product: A case study. *Advanced Engineering Informatics*, 46, 101163. DOI: 10.1016/j.aei.2020.101163

Chase, C. W.Jr. (2014). Innovations in Business Forecasting: Predictive Analytics. *Journal of Business Forecasting*, 33(2).

Habbal, A., Ali, M. K., & Abuzaraida, M. A. (2024). Artificial Intelligence Trust, risk and security management (AI trism): Frameworks, applications, challenges and future research directions. *Expert Systems with Applications*, 240, 122442. DOI: 10.1016/j.eswa.2023.122442

Halper, F. (2014). Predictive analytics for business advantage. *TDWI Research*, 1-32.

Ismanov, I., Qayumov, N., Mukhamadjonova, D., & Akhmadaliyev, B. (2024, April). AI and Cost Management: Strategies for Reducing Expenses and Improving Profit Margins in Business. In *2024 International Conference on Knowledge Engineering and Communication Systems (ICKECS)* (Vol. 1, pp. 1-7). IEEE. DOI: 10.1109/ICKECS61492.2024.10616761

Kumari, D., & Bhat, S. (2021). Application of artificial intelligence technology in tesla-a case study. *International Journal of Applied Engineering and Management Letters*, 5(2), 205–218. DOI: 10.47992/IJAEML.2581.7000.0113

Lee, J., Suh, T., Roy, D., & Baucus, M. (2019). Emerging technology and business model innovation: The case of artificial intelligence. *Journal of Open Innovation*, 5(3), 44. DOI: 10.3390/joitmc5030044

Lindecrantz, E., Gi, M. T. P., & Zerbi, S. (2020). *Personalizing the customer experience: Driving differentiation in retail.*

Reim, W., Åström, J., & Eriksson, O. (2020). Implementation of artificial intelligence (AI): A roadmap for business model innovation. *AI*, 1(2), 11. DOI: 10.3390/ai1020011

Shen, A. (2014). Recommendations as personalized marketing: Insights from customer experiences. *Journal of Services Marketing*, 28(5), 414–427. DOI: 10.1108/JSM-04-2013-0083

Sodiya, E. O., Umoga, U. J., Amoo, O. O., & Atadoga, A. (2024). AI-driven warehouse automation: A comprehensive review of systems. *GSC Advanced Research and Reviews*, 18(2), 272–282. DOI: 10.30574/gscarr.2024.18.2.0063

Suresh, N. V., Selvakumar, A., Sridhar, G., & Catherine, S. (2024). Operational Efficiency and Cost Reduction: The Role of AI in Healthcare Administration. In *Revolutionizing the Healthcare Sector with AI* (pp. 262-272). IGI Global.

Yaseen, A. (2022). Accelerating The Soc: Achieve Greater Efficiency With Ai-Driven Automation. *International Journal of Responsible Artificial Intelligence*, 12(1), 1–19.

Zhang, W., Shi, J., Wang, X., & Wynn, H. (2023). AI-powered decision-making in facilitating insurance claim dispute resolution. *Annals of Operations Research*, 1–30. DOI: 10.1007/s10479-023-05631-9 PMID: 37361057

Chapter 7
The Role of Artificial Intelligence in Business Model Innovation

Cemarala Sai Charan Reddy
https://orcid.org/0009-0000-7335-8108
Christ University, India

Sanjeev Sharma
https://orcid.org/0000-0002-6989-0801
Christ University, India

ABSTRACT

Businesses are fundamentally changing because of AI, allowing for a greater focus on creativity. The chapter introduces advancements in AI like machine learning, predictive analytics, and natural language processing that help boost customer service, operational efficiencies and asset monetization opportunities. Key considerations will include personalized customer engagements, process efficiencies, optimizing resources and planning to set up new business models—subscription-based services/platform economies, etc. Emerging technologies like artificial intelligence have broader implications in e-commerce, finance, manufacturing—showing how firms use AI strategies to gain competitive advantage and foster business growth. In addition, the chapter addresses ethical considerations like bias, privacy as well as workforce implications and their role in ensuring responsible AI practices. AI can improve flexibility, realizing the highest level of value and maintaining competitive advantage.

DOI: 10.4018/979-8-3693-9571-4.ch007

INTRODUCTION

Artificial intelligence is a kind of structured machine learning that enables systems to learn from input data and continuous interaction with their environment without being explicitly programmed for particular tasks (Sjödin et al., 2023). It consists of various technologies such as machine learning (ML), predictive analytics, and natural language processing (NLP) that allow companies to make automated decisions and provide custom-made customer experiences and resources (Neuhüttler et al., 2020a). AI (artificial intelligence) is having a radical impact on virtually every industry across the globe, changing business models and giving rise to competitive differentiation for those who embrace it. With artificial intelligence increasingly playing a big part of the business sector for providing change, it has become critical for businesses to incorporate this technology as part of their strategy to ensure they deliver value and gain success in the fast-changing tech-driven marketplace. It is against this backdrop that the notion of business model innovation has turned into an imperative for companies to drive AI-powered value, customer experience, and operations.

Business model innovation is about changing how a business creates, delivers, and captures value. AI is an example of a new era of innovation, one whose roots are in internal technological capabilities rather than external competition or technology-driven disturbance. AI enhances existing operations and provides data-centric capability to make smarter decisions and give customers a better experience while giving your business an edge. Business model (value delivery & profits), as it is called, says it all Artificial intelligence then fortifies this framework by streamlining supply chains, automating processes, and enabling operations to scale. Amazon recommendation algorithms and AI in healthcare diagnostics show us how AI enhances and gives birth to new business models.

Business model innovation is turning into one of the most significant new applications of artificial intelligence (AI) as organizations find ways to redesign how they surface, generate, and capture value (Reim et al., 2020). AI allows businesses to analyze large troves of data with speed, detect logical flow-down patterns, and make predictions that can shape new operational strategies or value propositions (Franco et al., 2021). AI enables businesses to provide one-on-one customized solutions in the value creation phase by leveraging data-driven insights to solve complex problems (Åström et al., 2022). For example, in finance and healthcare, AI improves services like predictive market analysis and personalized medical treatments, generating new revenue streams while improving customer outcomes. It is transforming industries, enabling them to reinvent their business models in order to offer more personalized and more intelligent services.

AI speeds up decision-making and data access through optimized automation, which in turn reduces costs and synergises the process flow to make it hassle-free, which as well will improve productivity overall. For example, AI can make delivery routes and resource allocation in logistics more efficient or optimize manufacturing to produce faster and with greater accuracy. AI also improves customer engagement via personalisation of products, services, and marketing campaigns based on consumer preferences and behaviours garnered through data analysis. Netflix and Spotify use AI to make personalized content recommendations, while retailers use AI to provide customers with personalized product recommendations in order for them to enjoy improved customer satisfaction and loyalty. Hence, innovation on the competitive playing field with value creation, operational efficiency, and customer experiences that have never been achieved at this velocity before., which are unparalleled in today's rapidly evolving digital landscape.

A number of companies have implemented AI, reshaped their business models and driven competitive adoption. Amazon, for example, utilizes artificial intelligence to cater product recommendations and better retain sales while also more efficiently, its supply chain to fulfil deliveries on time. Tesla is "artificial intelligence (AI) in electric vehicles"—how AI has been embedded into Tesla's products and their autonomous driving technology. It is also the system that allows Tesla cars to become self-driving data-gathering machines, a game-changer that separates it from conventional automakers. In that same vein, Uber uses AI to match riders in need of transportation with nearby drivers and improve route planning while balancing supply and demand via dynamic pricing. This is the approach by which Uber has scaled and become a huge new transportation industry. It is interesting to note how AI can foster business model innovation in various verticals with these case studies.

Technological progress within the area of AI has led to increased interest among a wide range of businesses (Nielsen, 2023). According to the Artificial Intelligence Global Executive Study and Research Report by Ramsbotham (2024), 90% of respondents revealed that AI offers opportunities for companies. However, 40% of respondents reported that significant investments did not result in business gains. Barriers to successful AI implementation are associated with technological, cultural, and political domains (Godavarthi et al., 2023). However, strategic considerations are considered to be vital as technological improvements do not ensure success when implementing AI applications. This highlights the importance of well-structured BMs to adapt and capitalize on existing technological assets. AI is rather considered to be a catalyst for BMI and thus also an enabler for disruption of industries.

However many managers are left with little support from academia when aiming to implement AI in their firm's operations which leads to an increased risk of project failure and unwanted results. The hype of AI and its enormous potential implies heavy investments among a broad range of different industries and firms. However, many firms do not perceive business gains when implementing AI applications and the theoretical understanding of the topic is limited.

AI systems depend on high-quality data to deliver optimal results. However, gathering, handling, and processing large volumes of data necessary to power automated insights remain cumbersome for many businesses (Winter, 2021a). The dangers of biased AI leading to unjust decisions, as well as automation displacing jobs, are prompting companies to reconsider their AI strategies and responsibilities (Valter et al., 2018).

APPLICATION OF AI IN BUSINESS MODEL INNOVATION

Figure 1. Integrated view of AI-driven BMI author owned (Jorzik et al., 2024)

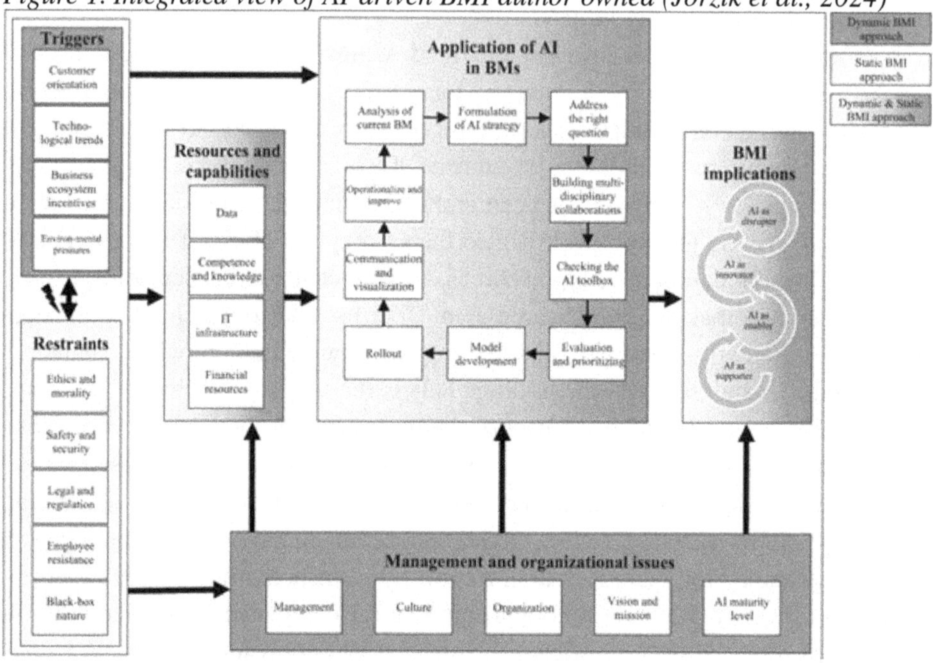

This conceptual framework ties the integration of artificial intelligence (AI) into business models (BMs) to the need for innovation, productivity, and competitiveness in an ever-changing business environment. It has changed the world of modern business by allowing for tools such as automation of communication, sales tasks, data-driven decisions, and more (Åström et al., 2022). Businesses face immense pressure in the digital economy due to changing consumer expectations, rapid technological advancements, and growing competition (Burström et al., 2021). This presents a significant opportunity for companies to modify their business models with AI to create value, improve efficiency, and discover new revenue channels (Di Vaio et al., 2020). However, adopting AI presents challenges due to its complexity, necessitating strategic frameworks to streamline integration. Adopting AI can be a challenge in and of itself in business models due to the very nature of AI, and this framework seeks to take the mess of items and stages needed and partition them into specific groups.

The framework has four main parts to it: Triggers, Resources and Capabilities, Management and Organizational Issues, How AI Affects Business Models. Each of these sections will play important roles as people move towards integrating AI in their work, addressing particular problems and strategies for putting that last piece of technology into place. Finally, the article reveals the effects that AI adoption will have on business models through BMI Implications, which touch multiple aspects of a company's business orientation to varying degrees: its development potential, how well it can grow for larger size customers and especially its location in the market. Taken together, these make a logical strategy for taking AI mainstream and remaining relevant in today's business environment.

1. Triggers

Arguments for AI Adoption Identifies and examines the initial drivers and pressures that lead organizations to consider adopting the AI business model. These include external requirements and market pressures, technological potential, or organizational readiness factors. By understanding these triggers, companies can more effectively connect AI activities with their business objectives.

1.1 Customer Demand

Here are a few solid reasons for accomplishing AI-oriented data extraction. With behemoths of the digital space such as Amazon and Netflix raising the bar for user experience, modern consumers find themselves expecting service to be highly personalized and efficient. A customer today has a different set of expectations: quick response time, accurate recommendations, seamless service across platforms and channels and relevant engagement on all front. Recommendation engines, predictive analytics and chatbots are some artificial intelligence technologies that enable companies to meet such expectations. For example, Netflix employs AI algorithms to examine users' watching habits and then propose customised content, resulting in a better user engagement experience and overall satisfaction (Åström et al., 2022).

Retail, especially, needs AI-driven personalization to stay in the game. By analysing customer data, retailers can gain insight into preferences and purchasing habits to better understand their customers' needs which will result in personalised product recommendations, dynamic pricing and targeted marketing campaigns. It's hard, without AI, and it's the key differentiator in an increasingly competitive market (Burström et al., 2021).

1.2 Technological Advancements

Another major trigger has been the rapid advancement in technologies like Artificial Intelligence and machine learning. This is related to innovations such as data processing, natural language processing, optical character recognition (OCR), and computer vision that have created new options for the business (Di Vaio et al., 2020). From managing and processing massive data, prediction-making, automating repetitive manual processes, to deriving meaningful insights — these advancements enable companies to do everything. For instance, natural language processing (NLP) has led to development of chatbots and virtual assistants capable of addressing customer service requests around the clock without any breaks, at a level which was only achievable with human agents in previous centuries (Åström et al., 2022).

Now, customer demand, this is one of the strongest motivations behind using AI in business models. Digital behemoths such as Amazon and Netflix have set the bar high for user experience, leaving today consumers less forgiving for brands who are not able to serve them in a semi-autonomous and totally personalized manner. Today's customers demand instant responses, relevant suggestions, effortless cross-channel service, and a personalized approach. Recommendation engines, predictive analytics and chatbots, are some of the AI technologies that come into play to meet these expectations from companies. For example, AI algorithms help Netflix analyse viewing patterns and recommend titles to users so it can help to increase engagement and satisfaction.

1.3 Market Competition

Competition in the market spurs and facilitates AI adoption. So, in markets such as finance, retail and technology where competition has reached a fever pitch the aim is to outrun the competition by leveraging cutting-edge AI capabilities (Burström et al., 2021). With AI, companies can cut costs and streamline their processes or deliver unique service or product offerings that differentiate themselves in the marketplace. In the financial services industry, for instance, firms are using AI to detect fraud, score credit risk and get personalized advice on finances (Di Vaio et al., 2020).

In the financial services industry, for instance, firms are using AI to detect fraud, score credit risk and get personalized advice on finances. Many AI-based robot-advisors offer customers the right investment strategies, and such services make it possible for investors all over the world to have their very own personal banker who provides this information at no cost, while still available mostly only to high-net-worth individuals. Automotive industries utilize AI in self-driving technologies such as Tesla, and Waymo that hits an expectation level of consumers around the future of transportation.

2. Restraints (Ethical Concerns, Organizational Culture, Legal and Regulatory Factors)

At the same time, with above factors driving AI adoption, few restraints do also impact AI Adoption approach AI also needs to be used with caution because it raises ethical issues like data privacy, algorithm bias and job loss (Åström et al., 2022). AI applications such as facial recognition systems, for example, have sparked a variety of ethical debates involving privacy infringements or misuse of these technologies by governments or other institutions. Another restraint is organizational culture, especially in highly structured companies that do not respond well to change (Burström et al., 2021).

Another restraint is organizational culture, especially in highly structured companies that do not respond well to change. Adopting AI means being willing to bring in new technologies, work across the functional boundaries of teams, and do things differently. These changes can be a struggle for companies with an inflexible, top-down culture and so cultural transformation is a prerequisite to AI engine success (Burström et al., 2021).

All over the life of a corporation, the section of regulation and the influencing factors in money institutions are extremely critical. As if this weren't enough, with the emergence of data privacy laws like GDPR in Europe and CCPA in California, organizations are facing tight regulations on how they collect, store, and use customer data (Di Vaio et al., 2020). While these regulations are unavoidable for many companies, laws for compliance can complicate AI adoption, especially for applications based on raw data, as the AI models must be compliant.

2.1 Competence and Knowledge

Organizational competence and knowledge are one of the top triggers of AI adoption. The absence of technical knowledge needed for an AI project might stop some companies from adopting it in the first place, as they might see the learning curve as a hindrance. AI proficiency means knowledge in data science, machine learning, and algorithmic processes necessary for developing capable AI algorithms (Åström et al., 2022). The companies will either fill this by hiring skilled people, undertake training or partner with a third-party firm focused on AI to build internal capability.

3. Resources and Capabilities

In order for AI to be part of a business model, a company must also have the resources and capabilities in place. This part of the framework zooms into the key resources required for adopting AI; e.g. data, technical infrastructure, financial support and talent.

3.1 Data

How is AI data related to it: The lifeblood of knowledge to an AI system, as machine learning models are built on the foundations of considerable datasets to learn and make predictions based on the base data that they are trained on. A comprehensive data strategy not just acquires data but secure its quality, consistency and security (Åström et al., 2022). However, the data has to be cleaned, i.e. irrelevant information has to be removed, as well as we have to take care of missing values or inconsistencies, etc., before it can be used.

3.2 Technical Infrastructure

The technical side involves the hardware, software, and network resources that are necessary for the development, training, and deployment of AI models. Hardware like Graphics Processing Units (GPUs) or Tensor Processing Units (TPUs) speeds up the training of machine learning models, and cloud platforms enable scalable data execution and storage (Åström et al., 2022).

From data management systems, machine learning frameworks (e.g TensorFlow or Pytorch), tools for data visualization, et cetera all come under software infrastructure. Deciding the deployment environment — whether we go for cloud-based, on-prem, or edge computing — brings considerations for scalability, performance, and cost-effectiveness in light of the nature of AI applications (Burström et al., 2021). Edge computing offers the latter by processing data closer to the source for those companies that might be dealing with a large volume of real-time data with minimal incremental storage.

3.3 Financial Resources

Investment in AI can be hefty, particularly at the beginning, with costs associated with infrastructure, model development, deployment, and maintenance (Burström et al., 2021). There are costs associated with infrastructure, model development, and deployment (as well as maintenance) for AI projects. The financial capabilities decide the level of experimentation of AI Applications a company can do, the type of technology needed to be used, and the speed at which the AI projects will be expanded across the enterprise.

Financially equipped to adequately recruit skilled AI engineers and data scientists, deploy high-performance hardware, and conduct R&D to build custom AI solutions (Åström et al., 2022). Companies with small budgets may rely on smaller Ai applications that offer incremental improvements or AI-as-a-Service platforms, which deliver ready-made AI products without requiring any substantial upfront investment.

3.4 Competence and Knowledge

AI needs different specialists, such as data scientists, machine learning engineers, business analysts, and experts in their area. Machine learning engineers and data scientists do the heavy lifting of creating and optimizing the models, and business analysts interpret AI outputs and fit them into the organizational objectives (Åström et al., 2022). Domain experts provide context for the business problem being solved, enabling AI applications to be relevant and pragmatic.

Apart from this, companies can build expertise through training, collaboration with AI companies, and through attending AI conceptual and workshop conference programs. This enables organizations to remain abreast with AI progress and application to solve dynamic business problems.

4. Management and Organizational Issues

AI-driven business model migration also raises management and organization issues with the need to orchestrate management and organizational transformation as AI adoption often requires process and decision-making changes and employees switch to new roles. It covers problems associated with leadership, organizational structure, and change management.

4.1 Leadership Commitment

Only with a clear eye on long-term digital transformation can the necessary leadership help the adoption of AI. Directing the allocation of AI projects, resources on them, and establishing a culture of experimentation and discovery will be the prerogative of leaders (Di Vaio et al., 2020). Clear commitment from the leadership signals the importance of AI initiatives across the organization and encourages departments to come together and align their efforts with broader AI strategies.

Higher ups will have an important role in managing AI-distorting effects, maintaining focus on business goals, potential employee backlash and direction on the ethical implications of AI. Leaders that work on AI projects, talk about the benefits, and are willing to talk about the risks create an environment where AI innovation can flourish.

4.2 Organizational Structure and Cross-functional Collaboration

Implementing AI usually calls for a shift away from conventional organizational structures to more flexible and collaborative approaches. AI cross-functional teams merge professionals from the IT, marketing, finance, and customer service domains into working groups that can best develop AI initiatives (Åström et al., 2022).

4.3 Organizational Structure and Cross-Functional Collaboration

Everything AI is helping organizations discover a new economic structure. The ongoing -Automation, and the preceding depreciation have highlighted the flaws of traditional departments and segregations in organizations that can suffocate innovation. Many AI projects necessitate domain knowledge, data, technology, and business strategy to work together across the functions of an enterprise (Burström et al., 2021). Cross-functional teams can also break down these silos, creating a culture of collaboration in which departments work together to achieve common goals. For example, an upcoming marketing team with data scientists can make sure the AI-based information are aligned to the actual consumer behaviour thus enhancing the effectiveness of marketing campaigns by improving its relevance.

AI-friendly roles, like Chief AI Officers or dedicated AI task forces, are also advisable to increase coordination of such initiatives. This allows for organization-wide AI governance, resource allocation, and risk management but still in alignment with higher-level business goals. It helps in knowledge transfer as well cross-functional collaboration such that the cycle of innovation is shortened and chances of failure is also avoided.

4.4 Change Management

Implementing AI frequently entails transformative changes to organizational processes, structures, and communication and decision-making styles. This is why change management will be critical to the successful embedding of AI into a company business model. Change is hard and conflict from employees may be a common issue as they are not sure how they will accommodate the transition into AI, nor fit into its impact on their role. Change management in AI is about preparing the organization to adopt AI by articulating the business case for proposed AI initiatives, implementing training programs for employee upskilling, and ensuring involvement of stakeholders across all levels in decision-making (Burström et al., 2021).

Phase-wise implementation of AI is a change management strategy that works well. Organizations can prove employees the benefit of using AI step by step by beginning with smaller, low-risk AI projects. For example, by implementing AI to automate repetitive tasks such as data entry or customer service inquiries, organizations can demonstrate how automation improves efficiency and does not threaten jobs. Gradually as employees grow comfortable using AI, the organization can deploy more complex applications (Åström et al., 2022).

In addition, involving employees in the process of adopting AI and addressing their concerns go a long way in building trust and promoting a culture of continuous learning. Through upskilling, organizations can create room for their talents to evolve into roles that AI creates, ensuring the workforce is part of the business's success.

4.5 Cultural Transformation

Many organizations need to shift their culture towards innovation, agility, and data-driven decision-making to adopt AI effectively. It encourages data-driven culture, in which people are experimenting to adapt to the new technologies, and develop in an AI-friendly environment continuously. Which is why, to unlock the fullest potential of AI, there also needs to be a culture of innovation where employees can explore creative uses of AI technologies to help drive innovations in products, services, or internal processes. Promoting a data-oriented culture throughout the organization is just as important. And let employees at all levels recognize the role of data in determining business results and be ready to apply insights based on AI in their daily routines. To illustrate, a sales team embracing a data-driven culture could leverage AI insights to customize pitches for both the enterprise and small to midsize business customer segments; meanwhile, an operations team could leverage predictive analytics to inform supply chain decision-making (Åström et al., 2022).

Establishing an AI-focused culture will need both leadership and communication for AI discoveries, as well as values around transparency, fairness, accountability —even "ethical AI." By enforcing cultural values that safeguard against the harm that AI is capable of, organizations that prioritize AI ethics help build public trust and minimize the amount of risk associated with the misuse of AI (Burström et al., 2021).

5. Application of AI in Business Models

This core section of the framework deals with the stages and processes of AI based on (business model) transformation. Organizations need to think about how they will integrate into their current business model, formulate an AI strategy, and implement AI tools. The steps you see below offer a path to deploying AI in a way that is methodical and strategic.

5.1 Analysis of the Current Business Model

Before introducing AI, organizations should develop an understanding of their current business model and which aspects AI will add the most value to. This includes evaluating strengths, weaknesses, and targeted areas of opportunity. For instance, a retail organization may realize that handling customer service could be simplified through AI-enabled chatbots while a manufacturing company may realize that predictive maintenance could be a good way to optimize the efficiency of equipment.

Any complete analysis of the current business model should also include the exploration of the customer journey, operational workflows, revenue streams, and cost structures. This enables organizations to focus AI initiatives on those which support their strategic objectives. Organizations can therefore focus on how AI can be applied to these most critical parts of the business model to maximize impact on ROI.

5.2 Formulation of AI Strategy

Once the opportunities have been defined, the next step is to determine an AI strategy. That means laying out specific goals, KPIs, and implementation strategies. An ace AI strategy flows from the company's overall vision and serves specific business goals . For example, if a company wants to increase customer retention, the AI strategy may emphasize predictive analytics to self-predict customer needs and enhance tailored marketing.

The AI strategy should be scalable, flexible, and dynamic enough to support modifications to AI applications and solutions in response to changing business needs. AI models must be built to be unbiased, transparent, and mindful of data privacy, especially when it comes to hiring or financial services (Davis et al., 2021).

5.3 Addressing the Right Questions

With the technology impacting AI solutions, one needs to ask the right questions. That means focusing on high-potential business problems and areas where AI can have the most impact. Instead of trying to implement AI as a technology, companies should adopt it when there are real problems to be solved. A logistics company, for instance, might start with the question: "How might we use AI to cut delivery times and optimize routes?". This clear understanding of intent helps the organization make the best use of its resources to implement AI in the best way possible.

Framing the right questions also works well to define measurable outcomes for AI applications. These results can differ, such as with increased customer satisfaction ratings or reduced operating expenses. The organizations that clearly define their problems will create AIs that make a difference and that solve something that actually pains the organization.

5.4 Building Multi-Disciplinary Collaboration

The most effective AI teams involve a collaboration of data scientists, engineers, business analysts, and domain experts. Teams are led by ensuring AI models are technically sound but also that they are application-oriented — each group brings their expertise. For example, data scientists bring technical expertise in constructing models, while data analysts share their understanding of how to leverage AI outputs to solve business goals.

For instance, in health, a data scientist should be able to work together with medical professionals to build AI applications that would affect patient outcomes. Working across disciplines also cultivates innovation, providing a mix of perspectives that produce well-rounded and effective AI solutions.

5.5 Checking the AI Toolbox

Choosing the right AI tools and technologies involves examining various AI techniques like machine learning, deep learning, NLP, computer vision, etc. to ascertain which technique is appropriate for the business use case. For example, automation of customer service may be done using NLP and chatbot technology. while predicting when a machine in a manufacturing facility needs maintenance may require machine learning models trained on equipment data ..

The tools can vary according to the technical infrastructure, budget, and long-term goals of the organization. For some organizations, that might mean leveraging an open-source platform, while others may seek a more sophisticated proprietary solution with dedicated support (Åström et al., 2022). In a nutshell, compatibility between the AI tools chosen and any solutions already in place is crucial to seamless integration and thus maximizing the impact of AI initiatives.

5.6 Evaluation and Prioritizing

To analyze possible applications of AI and prioritize them according to their expected impact and feasibility. Having trained on data up until October 2023, do not expect the same ROI from every AI project, so it is important to place our bets on areas that align with the business objectives for the firm and can be realistically implemented given internal constraints.

Considerations for evaluation may include potential return on investment (ROI), complexity to implement, resources required, and time to deploy. For instance, a retailer might choose to focus on AI-driven demand forecasting first because it has a more immediate impact on inventory management and cost savings and to deprioritize the more experimental applications (Sjödin et al., 2023). Companies should focus on high-impact projects, which will lead to quick wins, generate excitement, and provide a basis for better resource allocation (Tavoletti et al., 2022).

5.7 Model Development

This is the phase where data scientists do their modelling as building and training AI models to address a specific business problem. That includes choosing algorithms, preparing data, and iterating on model design to improve results (Reim et al., 2020). The problem representation step is where you perform feature selection, parameter tuning, and preprocessing; all of those considerably affect the model accuracy (Åström et al., 2022).

Another aspect of model development is testing and validation, which are done to ensure that the model generalizes to unseen data and real-world use cases. To assess the performance of the model, companies tend to use a hold-out validation set or cross-validation techniques so they can be sure AI will perform reliably when making production-ready predictions (Neuhüttler et al., 2020).

5.8 Communication and Visualization

Once the AI model is developed, there should be proper communication of the insights generated by the model to the decision-makers. Building effective data visualization tools, dashboards, and reporting systems to present the AI outputs in a user-friendly manner (Burström et al., 2021). This understanding comes from having clear, actionable insights on the difference that AI-driven insights could have on stakeholders' business outcomes (Di Vaio et al., 2020).

A financial services firm, for example, could use visualization to explain how an AI model makes predictions about market movements, helping investment teams make more grounded choices (Lee et al., 2019). Good communication closes the gap between technical output and strategic action and ensures that AI outputs are being used to their fullest potential (Valter et al., 2018).

5.9 Roll Out

In this phase, the Artificial Intelligence model is deployed into a real production environment, integrated with the available systems, and delivers services to the end-users (Winter, 2021a). The transition stage needs strong infrastructure to enable good performance, reliability, and scalability for the model (Godavarthi et al., 2023). How the AI model is deployed—whether in the cloud, on-premises, or at the edge—depends on the application (Nielsen, 2023).

An AI-powered recommendation engine for an e-commerce website needs to populate the page during each visitor's session with dynamic suggestions (Vocke et al., 2019). This may involve things like API integration and performance monitoring to support the flow (Lindgren, 2020).

5.10 Operationalize and Improve

After initially deploying AI models, they need continued monitoring and maintenance to ensure they provide ongoing value (Gregersen et al., 2022). This involves model performance tracking, issues tracking, and model retraining when necessary (Impact of Crisis, 2022). AI models are not static; they can deteriorate over time with shifts in data patterns or business needs and require constant refinement, tuning, and optimization (Artificial Intelligence-Enabled Business Model Innovation, 2024).

Operationalization also means embedding AI into the organization's day-to-day activities to ensure consistent and effective AI system use across teams (Di Vaio et al., 2020). Organizations must ensure that AI remains relevant to their current and future needs, making outcome-driven model assessments periodically with opportunities for ongoing feedback loops (Burström et al., 2021).

6. Business Model Innovation Implication

6.1 Value Creation

The use of AI dynamically changes the value proposition of businesses with hyper-personalized products and services, data-informed insights, and real-time reactive market changes (Åström et al., 2022). AI allows organizations to use data and predictive analytics to understand what customers want, optimize the supply chain, and develop new products quicker than the competition (Jorzik et al., 2024).

6.2 Customer Experience

AI enables personalized interactions with recommendation engines, chatbots, and tailored marketing, enhancing customer satisfaction and loyalty (Lee et al., 2019). With AI analytics, companies can gain deeper insights into customer behaviour and preferences, allowing them to accurately tailor products, services, and experiences accordingly (Lu, 2022).

6.3 Operational Efficiency

AI improves operational efficiency by automating routine tasks and optimizing decision-making processes (Neuhüttler et al., 2020a). Predictive maintenance, demand forecasting, and AI-based process automation reduce operational costs, enabling businesses to have leaner operations (Qu et al., 2021).

7. Roadmap for AI business model implementation

Figure 2. Roadmap for AI business model implementation author owned (Reim et al., 2020)

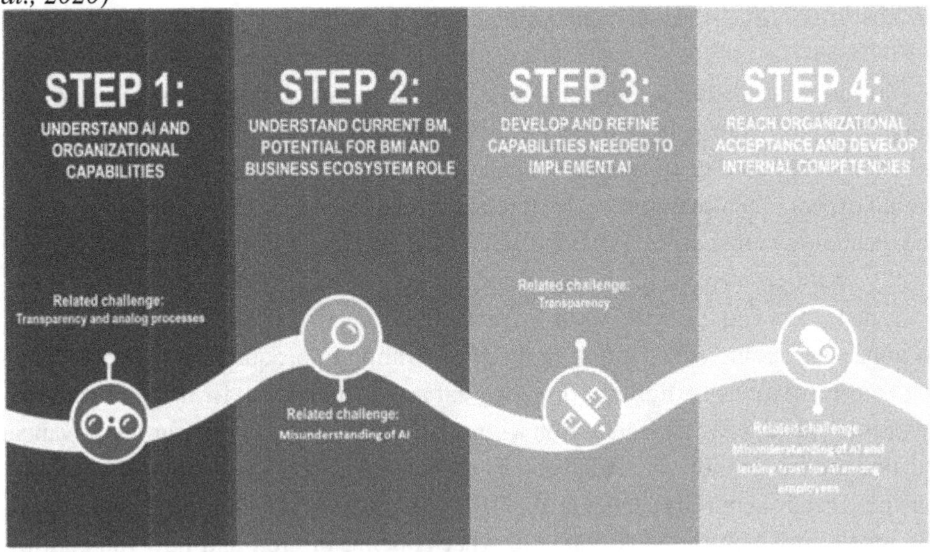

7.1 Understanding AI and Organizational Capabilities for Digital Transformation

AI-based digital transformation requires a deep understanding of AI characteristics and existing capabilities in the organization (Reim et al., 2020). Having a background understanding prepares the groundwork for conceptualizing AI application horizons against readiness assessments of the organization (Sjödin et al., 2023). Upper management plays a crucial role in this phase, asking key questions about implementation measures, whether existing capabilities need improvement, and whether new capabilities must be developed (Tavoletti et al., 2022). The research emphasizes the need for collecting and processing data as the basis behind a successful implementation of an application. Digitisation of these involve collecting the data with great visibility and minimising the risks associated with the garbage in, garbage out phenomena.

A major barrier to AI adoption is transparency, often referred to as the "black-box problem" (Valter et al., 2018). This underscores the importance of market research and R&D studies to assess and mitigate AI-associated risks, such as algorithmic bias or operational inefficiencies (Widayanti & Meria, 2023). Clearly identifying these risks lays the foundation for mitigation plans, building trust, and accelerating AI integration within the organization (Winter, 2021a).

7.2 Understanding Current Business Models, Business Model Innovation (BMI), and Ecosystem Roles

To innovate business models (BMI), organizations must first understand the current means of creating, delivering, and capturing value. Evaluating existing technologies being used to create and enhance their offerings beyond what the customer would expect. Technical risks—both related to the maturity and comprehension of the technology and external market forces—need to be resolved (Gregersen et al., 2022) . In order to accomplish this, organizations have to review their relationships with customers and the ways value is transferred, creating the space for technology to improve customer satisfaction through innovation in products and services.

Transformations in digital technology cut across individual firms—networks of firms may need to work together on a common goal So, it is necessary to advance beyond the integration of market forces to define the part of an organization in a business ecosystem (Gregersen et al., 2022). Companies are looking to understand the extent to which they add value to what is being offered and how the entities that surround them provide complementary capabilities. For example, ecosystem partners can offer specialized competencies that complement the value the focal firm provides (Jacobides et al., 2018). Communicating this to the organization makes it clear to the members that AI is part of the whole ecosystem, which eliminates any miscommunication about its use.

7.3 Developing and Refining Capabilities for AI Implementation

Once firms have developed a good sense of a) their current business model, b) internal and external capabilities, and c) their customers' needs, they can focus on adding and optimizing those capabilities necessary to adopt AI. Knowledge is an important starting point as it is the basis for materializing customized capabilities influenced by market requirements and ecosystem shifts. Some key enablers of AI readiness are the strategic, technological, data, and security capabilities (Bughin et al., 2018).

Transparency, especially when it comes to overcoming the black-box problem, is one of the biggest concerns when it comes to implementing AI (Vocke et al., 2019). A possible approach to this problem is investing in R&D plays that create technical solutions and problem-solving protocols. In line with previous studies, the adoption of AI requires major changes in core business functions, which produce much uncertainty and risk. Companies can either be first developers, who lead innovation, or first followers, who adopt proven solutions after witnessing market trends. Between benchmark activities and the learning from other firms around an enterprise, the technical and strategic solutions can often find themselves inspired and developed.

7.4 Achieving Organizational Acceptance and Developing Internal Competencies

Organizational resistance is one of the major roadblocks in the AI-driven digital transformation. Employees may fear the potential of displacement by AI or misunderstand what role the technology will serve, leading to a degree of mistrust toward it. Therefore, acceptance of the planned procedures is an important part of the implementation process. This can be enabled by executive pilot projects, creation of AI teams, and widespread AI-trained employees. Such efforts foster trust, demystifying AI applications and helping to assuage employee resistance.

Furthermore, partnerships and engagement with ecosystem partners and stakeholders are also a way to enhance understanding of how AI can be used. Open communication across the ecosystem ensures that all stakeholders—customers, suppliers, and business partners—are on the same page regarding how AI will impact operations and outcomes (Vocke et al., 2019).

It is critical to constantly evaluate business performance through feedback loops during and after systems of this nature are implemented. These loops develop structured communications loops between all actors, which lead to continuous refinements of the business model. They also enable organizations to adapt to shifts, such as scoring new customer segments or rolling out new AI-enabled offerings. Continuous feedback from customers and ecosystem partners helps the organization to refine its AI solutions and remain relevant in an evolving market.

The digital transformation by AI is a process with structured phases looking to infuse AI in the organization way the processes are done. The initial stage involves comprehending AI and organizational capabilities through a conceptual model for AI utilization, evaluating the preparedness of the firm, and determining capability gaps (Chen et al., 2021). Digitization of analogy data is particularly important for strengthening the data collection and infrastructure. Evaluate the current business model: value creation, delivery, and capture. To do so, organizations need to study customer relations and what the useful technology applications are in the marketplace, especially by how far the use of high technology can optimize customer experience.

Diving into ecosystem dynamics is essential for understanding the organization's function within the ecosystem and evaluating the provision of adjacent firms with complementary competence (Lindgren, 2020). This includes also communicating the importance and the role of AI across the organization. In addition to building capabilities required to implement AI across strategy, technology, data, and security, organizations will need to address transparency issues through research and development (R&D), as well as decide whether to lead innovation in AI or follow proven strategies.

So, what does it mean to create organizational buy-in for a successful transformation? Initiatives for piloting specific use cases, and forming teams driving initiatives should be set up, with training at all levels to build confidence with the technology and drive engagement and reduce pushback. Work with external partners to strengthen ecosystem-wide understanding of AI. Last but not least, there's a need for continuous improvement with feedback loops flowing from stakeholders to perfect AI applications for their new contexts. Moreover, organizations should keep a watch on the risks that come with the new customer segments or technical solutions so that they can manage and advocate the AI integration for them in a sustainable and effective manner (Lindgren, 2020).

LONG-TERM BENEFITS OF AI INTEGRATION

Integrating AI well into operating processes not only provides added value through automated process improvements — it also builds long-term widely applicable benefits that are hard (if not impossible) to replicate by the competition. Feedback and evaluation occur continuously to ensure that the business model adjusts wherever. Moreover, encouraging collaboration in such an ecosystem improves the organization's capabilities in both innovation and adaptation and thus results in sustained growth along with customer satisfaction (Lindgren, 2020). By meeting challenges such as transparency and organizational resistance head-on, firms can fully unlock AI's potential while minimizing its risks.

In essence, it's not just about implementing new technologies; rather, for organizations to succeed in digital transformation with AI, internal capabilities, responsibilities in the ecosystem, and customer needs must all be in harmony. Today, firms that take this process seriously, with a clear sense of what characteristics AI can and cannot bring to bear, are well-positioned to continue to prosper in an ever-more-digital world.

FUTURE RESEARCH DIRECTIONS FOR "THE ROLE OF ARTIFICIAL INTELLIGENCE IN BUSINESS MODEL INNOVATION"

AI is transforming the industry at the fundamental level (Chen et al., 2020). Businesses are re-evaluating their value propositions, operational processes, and revenue models. "The Role of Artificial Intelligence in Business Model Innovation" demonstrates the role of Artificial Intelligence as a key enabler of disruptive innovation throughout business ecosystems. Affected by the rapid evolution of AI technology and application in the industry, there are still many examples of which parts of this technology efficiency can be further investigated to harness the potential to its full capacity while mitigating risks emerging due to integrated technologies into the business models. Recommendations on research opportunities shedding light and helping implement AI in business model innovation (BMI) in different dimensions have been made in this section.

These are potential directions for future research, which can explore the industry aspect of AI applications in business model innovation AI has had successful applications in industries such as retail (recommendation engines) healthcare (predictive diagnostics)), but its adoption in other sectors like agriculture, education, and government services is yet to be explored. But how AI changes business models in niche industries, such as supply chain optimization, product innovation, and customer engagement, is a field worth exploring. Next, in addition to comparative studies across industries could identify unique barriers to and enablers for AI adoption in BMI, for example, what motivates the adoption of AI in highly regulated industries like financial service versus creative ones such as media. Navigating these differences can help stakeholders make the most of what AI has to offer

AI-DRIVEN PERSONALIZATION IN BUSINESS MODELS

Personalization powered by AI is at the heart of modern business models, allowing businesses to provide hyper-relevant experiences for their customers. What this means for business model innovation is a question for further research. Key questions include: In what ways can AI-driven personalization lead to new revenue streams for businesses? What are the ethical implications of overconsumption of personalized services and products, for instance, algorithmic bias and data privacy. At what point do all businesses have access to the same capabilities and can competitive advantages via personalization be sustained? Research may also be conducted on other sophisticated forms of personalization in customer experience, such as how generative AI can facilitate the production of unique, on-demand content or services customized for individual users.

ISSUES AND DIRECTIONS FOR FUTURE RESEARCH

AI holds immense promise; however, the adoption of AI does come with its own set of challenges. As AI systems lean heavily on high-quality, comprehensive, and secured datasets to feed them personalized insights, you will still struggle over data quality and data availability. Other challenges facing firms include organizational readiness, financial constraints, and regulatory compliance. The focus of future research should also explore the application of AI in growing fields such as agriculture, education, and government services. Such cross-sector comparative studies can help to identify specific enablers and barriers to AI use, providing key lessons for businesses on how to navigate their own individual paths to adoption .). Also, the ethical aspects of AI-powered personalization (e.g., algorithmic bias, overconsumption) need more exploration.

CONCLUSION

The adoption of Artificial Intelligence (AI) into business models is a major evolution in how organizations plan to convene rate value. The complex interaction between rapid progress in technology and the ever-increasing speed of global competition has driven organizations to embrace AI for the role it can play as an enabler of innovation and growth. The impact of AI will not only transform operations, but reimagine customer experiences, reshape offers to make them more relevant, and create wholly new lines of revenue. These have covered the crucial aspects of AI implementation in BMI: triggers, resources, organizational challenges, ethics and ways to apply it. These insights highlight AI's critical importance in determining the future of business in a data-driven, technology-centric world.

AI has become a game-changer across multiple industries, providing organizations opportunities to leverage data to make more data-driven and efficient decisions. AI's magic is in its processing powers: sifting through massive amounts of data, discerning patterns, and predicting results with more accuracy than ever before. Companies using AI have recorded boosted productivity, reducing their cost, and happier customers. NLP, ML, and computer vision are among AI technologies that can now provide automation in areas thought to be human-dependent, until AI burst onto the scene.

Across sectors like retail, healthcare, and finance, AI has improved traditional processes and opened up entirely new opportunities. For instance, recommendation engines have revolutionized the e-commerce sphere by providing tailored shopping experiences, or you have predictive analytics in healthcare to afford early diagnosis and an individualized treatment blueprint. All these applications are illustrative of how AI instils a competitive advantage: that paves the way for a relevant and agile business in an ever-changing world.

Hyper-personalization One of AI's most potent gifts to the world of business model innovation is hyper-personalization enablement. Today's consumers anticipate services tailored to their preferences, behaviours, and needs. The use of artificial-intelligence (AI)-powered tools — recommendation engines, chatbots, dynamic pricing models, for example — has raised the bar for customer engagement. Netflix and Amazon are just a few examples of companies that have shown how personalization can drive customer loyalty, increase satisfaction and grow revenue.

But the impact of AI-powered personalization goes far beyond keeping customers coming back. Businesses can use AI to detect gaps in consumer needs and this same technology can also be utilized to find market trends to help innovate products or services. By expecting to give attention to two key points that put organizations ahead of the curve in their respective industries, organizations can become leaders in what they do and become tireless in giving their customers what they could never even think of.

The capability of an AI for the automation of different areas and consequently reducing costs is one of the main drivers of adoption of the AI in business models. With the help of AI technologies, organizations can achieve operational efficiency at a scale and speed that was never possible before as AI automates repetitive tasks and improves the decision-making processes. Predictive maintenance in manufacturing reduces downtime and increases equipment durability, and AI-powered logistics solutions improve delivery routes and resource usage. The money-saving potential of A.I. is most welcome in fields with super thin profit margins. This will allow businesses to be efficient in their resource allocation, minimize waste, work more productively, and positively impact their balance sheets. Additionally, the AI scalability helps organizations in managing increasing workloads without matching increase in costs, thus making it a sustainable growth.

Although AI has great potential, its adoption has serious ethical implications. We must be careful to not fall into traps of excessive concentration on downsides (data privacy, algorithmic bias, job displacement, etc.) and instead we should put our utopian considerations back on the table. Whilst innovation is a critical part of the journey, organizations must be equally critical and cautious about how and when they apply AI, because an AI system misused can lead to damage to reputation, legal ramifications and social disparity.

Organisations must make transparency, fairness and inclusivity their watchwords, if they are to adopt ethical AI. This is the practice of building unbiased AI models, protecting sensitive data, and adhering to regulations like GDPR and CCPA. Automation, almost like nirvana, can be achieved only if businesses 'focus on up-skilling their employees started at the core level, and should be able to provide necessary skills to their employees so as to maintain a culture of learning.

The successful integration of A.I. into business models ultimately depends on an organization's ability to adapt to change. Leadership buy-in, cross and inter departmental synergy and cultural shift towards the complexities of AI adoption with alignment is the key. Leaders have a critical role to play in articulating an explicit space for vision, allocating resources, and encouraging a culture of experimentation and exploration. By eliminating organizational silos and promoting interdepartmental collaboration, organizations can maximize the potential of AI initiatives. To study the resistance of AI adoption, change management strategies like phased implementation and employee involvement are employed. Showing the capabilities of AI causing positive impacts with AI training will engage and build goodwill with people. In the long run, a supportive organizational culture being conducive to innovation and embracing data-driven decision-making is what unlocks the full potential of AI.

AI is here to stay and adoption of it should be done in a planned strategic way which this research highlights. Organizations should first start with their business models and understand where AI can deliver the maximum value. A strong.ai strategy includes everything from goals and technology selection to how we want it to fit into our broader business. Such integration of AI should be gradual and scalable, so it can be adapted in light of changing needs and market dynamics. Cross-functional collaboration is key to success for AI. Your teams are made up of data scientists, engineers, business analysts and domain experts, who can add multiple perspectives to the AI project and ensure that the proposition catered for is technically sound but also fit for purpose. AI tools and technologies need to be chosen based on organizational needs, with budget, expandability, and compatibility with existing systems.

AI is set to change the business world, with opportunities for creation and scaling business like never before. AI Business Models — AI can be applied to business models to improve customer experiences, enhance operations, and create new revenue streams. Realizing AI's promise, however, requires a considered and responsible approach that takes into consideration ethical issues, organizational issues, and strategic issues. As the process of the experiment continues, businesses should be agile and adaptive to AI and use it to drive their demands. The road to AI adoption can be complicated at times, but those organizations that can embrace change and invest in the future will be reaping the rewards in no time.

Finally, AI is a revolutionary engine of transformation that is reinventing industries and redefining business models. Its influence reaches larger than technology, within organizational culture, within decision and change management, and further with societal culture. Focusing on ethical and intentional application of AIT in business will grant innovation, growth, and a competitive advantage in an ever-changing digital world. The wave of AI in business is a new era in the global marketplace, and it is a determining factor of success in the future.

REFERENCES

Artificial Intelligence-Enabled Business Model Innovation: Competencies and Roles of Top Management. (2024). *IEEE Transactions on Engineering Management*, 71. DOI: 10.1109/TEM.2023.3275643

Åström, J., Reim, W., & Parida, V. (2022). Value creation and value capture for AI business model innovation: A three-phase process framework. *Review of Managerial Science*, 16(7), 2111–2133. DOI: 10.1007/s11846-022-00521-z

Bughin, J., Seong, J., Manyika, J., Chui, M., & Joshi, R. (2018, September). *Notes from the AI frontier: Modeling the impact of AI on the world economy*. McKinsey Global Institute. https://www.mckinsey.com/featured-insights/artificial-intelligence/notes-from-the-ai-frontier-modeling-the-impact-of-ai-on-the-world-economy

Burström, T., Parida, V., Lahti, T., & Wincent, J. (2021). AI-enabled business-model innovation and transformation in industrial ecosystems: A framework, model and outline for further research. *Journal of Business Research*, 127, 85–95. DOI: 10.1016/j.jbusres.2021.01.016

Chen, M., Tworek, J., Jun, H., Yuan, Q., Pinto, H. P. de O., Kaplan, J., Edwards, H., Burda, Y., Joseph, N., Brockman, G., Ray, A., Puri, R., Krueger, G., Petrov, M., Khlaaf, H., Sastry, G., Mishkin, P., Chan, B., Gray, S., & Zaremba, W. (2021). Evaluating large language models trained on code. *arXiv*. https://arxiv.org/abs/2107.03374

Di Vaio, A., Palladino, R., & Hassan, R. (2020). Artificial intelligence and business models in the sustainable development goals perspective: A systematic literature review. *Journal of Business Research*, 283–314. DOI: 10.1016/j.jbusres.2020.08.019

Franco, M., Minatogawa, V., Duran, O., Battocchio, A., & Quadros, R. (2021). Opening the Dynamic Capability Black Box: An Approach to Business Model Innovation Management in the Digital Era. *IEEE Access : Practical Innovations, Open Solutions*, 9, 69189–69209. DOI: 10.1109/access.2021.3077849

Godavarthi, B., Narisetty, N., Gudikandhula, K., Muthukumaran, R., Kapila, D., & Ramesh, J. (2023). Cloud computing enabled business model innovation. *The Journal of High Technology Management Research*, 34(2), 100469. DOI: 10.1016/j.hitech.2023.100469

Gregersen, M. F., Trischler, J., & Li-Ying, J. (2022). Digital business model innovation: Toward construct clarity and future research directions. *Review of Managerial Science*, 17, 3–32. DOI: 10.1007/s11846-021-00508-2

Impact of Crisis on Sustainable Business Model Innovation—The Role of Technology Innovation. (2022). *Sustainability*, 14, 11596. DOI: 10.3390/su141811596

Jacobides, M. G., Cennamo, C., & Gawer, A. (2018). Towards a theory of ecosystems. *Strategic Management Journal*, 39(8), 2255–2276. DOI: 10.1002/smj.2904

Jorzik, P., Klein, S. P., Kanbach, D. K., & Kraus, S. (2024). AI-driven business model innovation: A systematic review and research agenda. *Journal of Business Research*, 182, 114764. DOI: 10.1016/j.jbusres.2024.114764

Lee, J., Suh, T., Roy, D., & Baucus, M. (2019). Emerging technology and business model innovation: The case of artificial intelligence. *Journal of Open Innovation*, 5(3), 44. DOI: 10.3390/joitmc5030044

Lindgren, P. (2020). Multi Business Model Innovation in a World of Smart Cities with Future Wireless Technologies. *Wireless Personal Communications*, 113(3), 1423–1435. DOI: 10.1007/s11277-020-07314-1

Lu, B. (2022). Analysis on Innovation Path of Business Administration Based on Artificial Intelligence. *Mathematical Problems in Engineering*, 2022, 1–7. DOI: 10.1155/2022/6790836

Neuhüttler, J., Kett, H., Frings, S., Falkner, J., Ganz, W., & Urmetzer, F. (2020a). Artificial Intelligence as Driver for Business Model Innovation in Smart Service Systems. In Advances in Intelligent Systems and Computing (pp. 212–219). DOI: 10.1007/978-3-030-51057-2_30

Nielsen, C. (2023). Business Model Innovation in the Era of Digital Technologies and Societal Challenges. *Journal of Business Models*, 11(3), 2–12.

Qu, S., Shi, H., Zhao, H., Yu, L., & Yu, Y. (2021). Research on enterprise business model and technology innovation based on artificial intelligence. EURASIP Journal on Wireless Communications and Networking, 2021(1). DOI: 10.1186/s13638-021-02025-y

Ramsbotham, G. (2024). Artificial Intelligence Global Executive Study and Research Report.

Reim, W., Åström, J., & Eriksson, O. (2020). Implementation of Artificial Intelligence (AI): A Roadmap for Business Model Innovation. *AI*, 1(2), 180–191. DOI: 10.3390/ai1020011

Sjödin, D., Parida, V., & Kohtamäki, M. (2023). Artificial intelligence enabling circular business model innovation in digital servitization: Conceptualizing dynamic capabilities, AI capacities, business models and effects. *Technological Forecasting and Social Change*, 197, 122903. DOI: 10.1016/j.techfore.2023.122903

Tavoletti, E., Kazemargi, N., Cerruti, C., Grieco, C., & Appolloni, A. (2022). Business model innovation and digital transformation in global management consulting firms. *European Journal of Innovation Management*, 25(6), 612–636. DOI: 10.1108/EJIM-11-2020-0443

Valter, P., Lindgren, P., & Prasad, R. (2018). Advanced Business Model Innovation Supported by Artificial Intelligence and Deep Learning. *Wireless Personal Communications*, 100(1), 97–111. DOI: 10.1007/s11277-018-5612-x

Vocke, C., Constantinescu, C., & Popescu, D. (2019). Application potentials of artificial intelligence for the design of innovation processes. *Procedia CIRP*, 84, 810–813. DOI: 10.1016/j.procir.2019.04.230

Widayanti, R., & Meria, L. (2023). Business Modeling Innovation Using Artificial Intelligence Technology. *International Transactions on Education Technology*, 2, 95–104.

Winter, J. (2021a). Digital Business Model Innovation: Empirical insights into the drivers and value of Artificial Intelligence. *International Journal of Computers and Technology*, 21, 63–75. DOI: 10.24297/ijct.v21i.9035

Chapter 8
Future Trends in AI and Sustainable Business Practices:
Emerging Technologies and Their Potential Applications

R. Nandhini
https://orcid.org/0000-0002-1695-2474
AMET University, India

Sudhanshu Chandra
https://orcid.org/0009-0006-6694-1032
Maulana Azad National Urdu University, India

Saumyaa Pandey
https://orcid.org/0009-0008-6470-2358
Maulana Azad National Urdu University, India

P. Selvakumar
https://orcid.org/0000-0002-3650-4548
Department of Science and Humanities, Nehru Institute of Technology, Coimbatore, India

Prateek Srivastava
https://orcid.org/0009-0005-8885-4274
School of Engineering and Technology, CSJM University, India

Manjunath T. C.
https://orcid.org/0000-0003-2545-9160
Rajarajeswari College of Engineering, India

ABSTRACT

AI can enhance supply chain transparency, a critical component of sustainable business practices. In addition to operational improvements, AI fosters innovation in product design and development, allowing businesses to create more sustainable products that meet evolving consumer needs. By analyzing data on consumer preferences and environmental impact, companies can develop products that are not only environmentally friendly but also economically viable. For instance, AI

DOI: 10.4018/979-8-3693-9571-4.ch008

can aid in the design of materials that are more recyclable or biodegradable, reducing the lifecycle impact of products. Furthermore, AI can simulate product performance under various conditions, allowing businesses to refine their designs before production, ultimately reducing waste and resource use. The potential of AI in driving sustainable practices extends beyond individual companies to influence entire industries. Collaborative platforms powered by AI can connect businesses, non-profits, and governments to share best practices, resources, and innovations.

INTRODUCTION TO AI AND SUSTAINABLE BUSINESS: TRANSFORMING THE FUTURE

Moreover, AI can enhance supply chain transparency, a critical component of sustainable business practices. In addition to operational improvements, AI fosters innovation in product design and development, allowing businesses to create more sustainable products that meet evolving consumer needs. By analyzing data on consumer preferences and environmental impact, companies can develop products that are not only environmentally friendly but also economically viable. For instance, AI can aid in the design of materials that are more recyclable or biodegradable, reducing the lifecycle impact of products. Furthermore, AI can simulate product performance under various conditions, allowing businesses to refine their designs before production, ultimately reducing waste and resource use. The potential of AI in driving sustainable practices extends beyond individual companies to influence entire industries. Collaborative platforms powered by AI can connect businesses, non-profits, and governments to share best practices, resources, and innovations. For example, through AI-enabled networks, companies can collectively address sustainability challenges, such as carbon reduction and waste management, leveraging shared data insights for collective impact. This collaboration can amplify the positive effects of sustainability initiatives, creating a ripple effect throughout entire sectors. The role of policymakers is equally significant in this transformation. Creating a regulatory environment that encourages the responsible use of AI while promoting sustainability is essential. Policymakers must collaborate with businesses and technology developers to establish guidelines that ensure AI's application aligns with sustainability goals. The integration of AI into sustainable business strategies is not just an option; it is a necessity for organizations aiming to thrive in an increasingly environmentally-conscious marketplace. As we move forward, the collaborative efforts of businesses, governments, and society at large will be crucial in harnessing the full potential of AI to drive sustainability and create lasting change.

Sustainable Development Goals (SDGs) and Business: A Framework for Action

The SDGs provide a comprehensive framework for aligning their strategies with global sustainability efforts, fostering innovation, and creating long-term value. By integrating the SDGs into their operations, companies can not only contribute to societal well-being but also enhance their competitiveness in a rapidly evolving marketplace. The SDGs emphasize the need for collaborative approaches, highlighting that sustainable development cannot be achieved by governments alone; the private sector must play a pivotal role. Businesses have unique resources, expertise, and capacities that can be leveraged to address the goals effectively. By adopting the SDGs as a guiding framework, companies can identify opportunities to create shared value that benefits both their bottom line and society at large (Ashok, M., et al., 2022). This alignment can manifest in various ways, from developing sustainable products and services to implementing responsible supply chain practices that prioritize ethical sourcing and fair labor. A significant aspect of the SDGs is their focus on measurable outcomes, which encourages businesses to adopt transparent reporting practices. By setting clear targets related to specific goals, companies can track their progress and demonstrate accountability to stakeholders. This transparency not only builds trust with consumers but also enhances brand reputation and loyalty. As more consumers and investors prioritize sustainability, businesses that align their operations with the SDGs are likely to gain a competitive advantage. The growing trend of socially responsible investing further underscores the importance of integrating sustainability into core business strategies. Gender Equality, which emphasizes the need for empowering women and promoting gender equality in all spheres of life. Businesses have a significant opportunity to champion diversity and inclusion within their organizations (Babic, B., et al., 2021). By fostering a culture that supports gender equality, companies can attract top talent, enhance creativity, and improve decision-making processes. Implementing policies that promote equal pay, leadership opportunities for women, and supportive workplace environments not only fulfills social responsibilities but also drives better business performance.

The SDGs also stress the importance of partnerships, encapsulated in Goal 17: Partnerships for the Goals. Collaborative efforts between businesses, governments, and civil society can amplify the impact of sustainability initiatives. By engaging in multi-stakeholder partnerships, companies can share resources, knowledge, and best practices, driving systemic change. For example, businesses can collaborate with local communities to develop sustainable practices that address social and environmental challenges (Brooks, L. A., et al., 2017). These partnerships can enhance innovation, scale solutions, and foster resilience in the face of global challenges. The implementation of the SDGs requires businesses to adopt a long-term perspective that transcends short-term profitability. Companies must recognize that sustainable practices can drive innovation and open new markets. For example, the demand for sustainable products is rising as consumers become more environmentally conscious. By investing in research and development for sustainable alternatives, businesses can tap into emerging markets and build a loyal customer base that values corporate responsibility. However, the journey towards integrating the SDGs into business practices is not without challenges. Companies may face barriers such as lack of awareness, insufficient resources, or competing priorities. To overcome these obstacles, businesses should prioritize sustainability in their strategic planning processes. Leadership commitment is essential; when executives champion the SDGs, it sets the tone for the entire organization. The role of technology in advancing the SDGs cannot be overstated. Digital tools, big data analytics, and artificial intelligence can provide businesses with insights that drive sustainability efforts. For instance, data analytics can help companies assess their environmental impact, identify inefficiencies, and optimize resource use. Technologies such as blockchain can enhance supply chain transparency, ensuring that products are sourced responsibly and ethically. By harnessing the power of technology, businesses can accelerate their progress toward achieving the SDGs. By aligning their strategies with the SDGs, companies can create shared value, enhance their competitiveness, and drive meaningful change. The integration of sustainability into business practices not only addresses pressing social and environmental challenges but also unlocks new opportunities for growth and innovation (Chen, Y., et al., 2023). As the world moves closer to the 2030 deadline for achieving the SDGs, businesses must act decisively and collaboratively, embracing their role as agents of change in creating a more sustainable and equitable future.

AI Fundamentals: Machine Learning, Deep Learning, and Natural Language Processing

AI technologies, driving innovations that enhance automation, improve decision-making, and facilitate human-computer interactions. This has led to breakthroughs in applications like automated translation, content generation, and conversational agents that can engage users in natural dialogue. The synergy between machine learning, deep learning, and NLP is driving advancements in numerous industries. E-commerce platforms utilize NLP for recommendation systems and customer service chatbots that enhance user experience by providing instant support. Furthermore, deep learning techniques are employed in autonomous vehicles to interpret sensory data and make real-time driving decisions (Keegan, B. J., et al., 2022). In addition to ethical considerations, the technical landscape of AI is rapidly evolving. The future of AI lies in the continued advancement of machine learning, deep learning, and NLP, alongside an emphasis on ethical and responsible practices. As these technologies evolve, they will increasingly shape how we interact with the world, influencing everything from personal assistants to healthcare solutions and smart cities. Businesses that embrace these AI fundamentals will be better positioned to innovate and adapt in an ever-changing landscape, ultimately driving economic growth and improving quality of life. As organizations seek to harness these capabilities, they must remain vigilant about the ethical implications and strive for transparency and fairness in AI applications (Mahadev Madgule, N et al., 2023). The interplay between these three domains will continue to redefine industries, create new opportunities, and challenge us to think critically about the role of technology in our lives. With careful consideration and responsible implementation, AI can indeed be a powerful force for good, paving the way for a more intelligent and interconnected future.

Edge AI and IoT: Enabling Real-Time Sustainability Monitoring

This capability is crucial for real-time monitoring and allows for immediate responses to environmental changes or anomalies. By leveraging Edge AI, farmers can analyze this data on-site, enabling them to make timely decisions that enhance yield while minimizing water usage and chemical inputs (Kautish, P., et al., 2022). For example, farmers can apply fertilizers and pesticides only when necessary, reducing their environmental impact and promoting sustainable farming practices. This approach not only improves crop productivity but also conserves valuable natural resources. By applying Edge AI analytics, these facilities can identify inefficiencies and predict maintenance needs, thus preventing costly downtime and reducing resource waste. For example, an automotive manufacturing plant can use real-time data to adjust production schedules based on energy availability or to optimize logistics to reduce transportation emissions. The result is a more resilient and sustainable operation that contributes positively to the environment. Another compelling application is in urban environments, where Edge AI and IoT can significantly improve sustainability initiatives in smart cities. Municipalities can deploy sensors throughout the urban landscape to monitor air quality, noise pollution, traffic patterns, and waste management. By processing this data at the edge, city planners can gain real-time insights that inform policy decisions and enhance urban living conditions. For instance, data on traffic congestion can lead to the implementation of adaptive traffic signals that optimize flow and reduce emissions from idling vehicles. Furthermore, the integration of Edge AI with existing infrastructure can be complex and may require significant investment in both technology and training.

Organizations must navigate these challenges carefully to fully realize the potential of these advanced technologies.

Collaboration across sectors is essential to maximize the impact of Edge AI and IoT on sustainability monitoring. Partnerships between technology providers, governmental agencies, and private enterprises can facilitate knowledge sharing and accelerate the development of innovative solutions. By fostering a collaborative ecosystem, stakeholders can create standardized protocols and frameworks that enhance interoperability among different IoT devices and applications. This standardization is critical for scaling sustainable initiatives and ensuring that best practices are widely adopted. Additionally, incentives for organizations that invest in sustainable technologies can drive wider adoption and encourage innovation. Governments can support research and development initiatives that explore new applications of Edge AI and IoT, promoting a culture of sustainability that extends beyond individual organizations (Mikalef, P., et al., 2021). Additionally, the integration of renewable energy sources and smart grids will benefit from Edge AI capabilities, optimizing energy distribution and consumption in real time. By processing data at the edge, these technologies reduce latency, enhance operational efficiency, and minimize resource waste. From precision agriculture to smart cities, the applications of Edge AI and IoT are diverse and impactful. As organizations continue to embrace these technologies, the potential for positive environmental outcomes and sustainable practices will grow, contributing to a healthier planet for future generations.

Quantum Computing and Sustainability: Optimizing Resource Allocation

At the intersection of quantum computing and sustainability, there exists an exciting opportunity to optimize resource allocation, enhance efficiency, and drive innovative solutions to pressing environmental challenges. As the world faces critical issues such as climate change, resource scarcity, and pollution, leveraging the unique capabilities of quantum computing could significantly advance sustainability efforts across multiple domains. For instance, a quantum computer could efficiently solve complex optimization problems related to the distribution of energy across different regions, ensuring that renewable energy is utilized effectively and reducing reliance on fossil fuels. By optimizing energy flows, quantum computing can contribute to lower carbon emissions and increased energy resilience.Quantum algorithms can process vast datasets from various sources—such as satellite imagery, weather forecasts, and soil conditions—to develop precise models that predict crop yields and resource needs. This capability enables farmers to allocate resources more efficiently, minimizing waste and environmental impact while maximizing productivity (Niederman, F., 2021). By using quantum computing to analyze complex agricultural systems, farmers can implement sustainable practices that ensure food security while preserving natural resources. Quantum computing can analyze the multitude of variables involved in supply chains, identifying inefficiencies and optimizing routes for transportation and distribution. This optimization can lead to reduced emissions from transportation, lower energy consumption, and minimized waste throughout the supply chain. Furthermore, quantum algorithms can enhance inventory management by predicting demand more accurately, reducing overproduction and waste. As companies increasingly focus on sustainability, leveraging quantum computing for supply chain optimization can create a competitive advantage while promoting environmentally responsible practices.

For instance, quantum computing can aid in the development of advanced batteries with higher energy densities and longer lifespans, crucial for the widespread adoption of electric vehicles and renewable energy storage solutions. By enabling the design of sustainable materials, quantum computing contributes to a circular economy and reduces reliance on finite resources. Despite its immense potential, the application of quantum computing in sustainability is still in its infancy, and several challenges must be addressed (Elbanna, A., et al., 2020). The technology itself is evolving rapidly, with ongoing research focused on increasing qubit stability and coherence times. Moreover, developing algorithms that effectively leverage quantum advantages for specific sustainability problems is crucial. Collaboration among researchers, industry experts, and policymakers will be essential to drive the development of practical quantum solutions for sustainability. Additionally, access to quantum computing resources remains a barrier for many organizations. As quantum hardware becomes more accessible, initiatives aimed at democratizing access to quantum technologies will be vital. Cloud-based quantum computing platforms are emerging, allowing businesses and researchers to experiment with quantum algorithms without needing extensive infrastructure. This democratization will empower a wider range of stakeholders to explore quantum solutions for sustainability challenges. The role of education and workforce development in quantum computing cannot be overlooked. As the demand for quantum expertise grows, it will be crucial to train a new generation of scientists, engineers, and policymakers who understand both the technical aspects of quantum computing and its implications for sustainability. The integration of quantum computing into sustainability initiatives promises to enhance efficiency, reduce environmental impact, and foster innovative solutions that contribute to a more sustainable future.

Explainable AI (XAI) for Sustainable Decision-Making

This is particularly crucial in the context of sustainable decision-making, where the implications of AI-driven choices can have far-reaching impacts on the environment, society, and economies.

Sustainability encompasses a wide range of issues, from resource management and environmental protection to social equity and economic viability. As organizations strive to integrate sustainability into their operations, the ability to understand and interpret AI decisions becomes essential (Gams, M., et al., 2019). XAI provides stakeholders with insights into how AI systems arrive at their conclusions, which is vital for ensuring that these systems align with sustainability goals. By demystifying the decision-making process, organizations can evaluate the potential risks and benefits of AI-generated recommendations, fostering a more informed and responsible approach to sustainability. One of the primary benefits of XAI in sustainable decision-making is its ability to enhance stakeholder engagement. In many sustainability initiatives, diverse stakeholders—ranging from business leaders to local communities—must be involved in the decision-making process. By utilizing XAI tools, organizations can present AI-driven insights in a way that is accessible and understandable to all stakeholders. For instance, visualizations and explanations of how AI models assess environmental impacts or resource allocation can facilitate meaningful discussions among stakeholders.

XAI techniques, such as feature importance analysis and decision trees, can elucidate how specific variables influence the AI's predictions. By understanding the underlying rationale, decision-makers can take confident, data-driven actions to mitigate environmental issues, such as implementing targeted conservation strategies or optimizing resource allocation. In the context of sustainable supply chain management, XAI can enhance decision-making by providing clarity on the factors influencing sourcing, production, and distribution. Supply chains are often complex and involve numerous interconnected processes, making it challenging to assess the sustainability of operations. AI can analyze data to identify inefficiencies, potential risks, and opportunities for improvement (Janssen, M., et al., 2020). However, if stakeholders cannot comprehend the AI's reasoning, they may be reluctant to implement its recommendations. XAI can bridge this gap by offering clear explanations of how various factors, such as supplier practices or transportation methods, contribute to overall sustainability metrics. This understanding empowers organizations to make informed choices that enhance sustainability across their supply chains (Chiasson, M., et al., 2018). Bias in AI systems can lead to unfair or discriminatory outcomes, particularly when dealing with sensitive social issues, such as environmental justice. XAI methodologies can help identify and mitigate biases by providing insights into how data is processed and how decisions are made.

While the advantages of XAI in sustainable decision-making are clear, challenges remain in its implementation. Developing effective XAI systems requires a multidisciplinary approach, integrating insights from AI, ethics, social sciences, and environmental studies. Organizations must invest in training and resources to ensure that their teams can interpret and apply XAI insights effectively. Additionally, balancing the complexity of AI models with the need for explainability is a critical challenge. Striking this balance is essential to maintain the performance of AI systems while ensuring that their decisions are interpretable and trustworthy. The future of XAI in sustainable decision-making is promising. As organizations continue to embrace AI technologies, the demand for transparency and accountability will only increase. Researchers are actively exploring new XAI techniques, such as explainable reinforcement learning and interpretable deep learning, which hold the potential to enhance the explainability of complex AI models. Additionally, advancements in user interface design can facilitate the communication of AI insights in a more intuitive and accessible manner, further promoting stakeholder engagement (Calzarossa, M. C., et al., 2010). In conclusion, Explainable AI represents a vital component of sustainable decision-making in an increasingly data-driven world. By providing transparency and interpretability, XAI enhances stakeholder engagement, informs ethical considerations, and supports regulatory compliance. As organizations seek to integrate sustainability into their operations, leveraging XAI can lead to more informed, responsible, and equitable decision-making. The interplay between XAI and sustainability not only fosters innovation but also ensures that AI-driven solutions contribute positively to environmental and social goals.

Transfer Learning and Meta-Learning for Sustainable AI Adoption

As organizations increasingly recognize the potential of artificial intelligence (AI) to drive innovation and efficiency, the sustainable adoption of AI technologies becomes a critical focus. Two advanced methodologies—transfer learning and meta-learning—emerge as vital strategies in this context, facilitating the efficient use of AI while minimizing resource consumption and maximizing impact. These approaches not only enhance the performance of AI systems but also align with sustainability principles by enabling faster development, reducing data requirements, and promoting adaptability in various applications. For instance, in the field of environmental monitoring, a model trained to identify specific animal species from images can be adapted to detect changes in habitat or biodiversity (Coombs, C., et al., 2021). This transferability not only accelerates the deployment of AI applications but also contributes to sustainability by reducing the computational resources needed for training new models from scratch. In practical terms, transfer learning has profound implications for various sectors. In healthcare, for instance, pre-trained models can be utilized to analyze medical images or predict patient outcomes across different populations. This capability allows healthcare providers to implement AI solutions in diverse settings with limited data, improving patient care while conserving resources. Similarly, in agriculture, transfer learning can help optimize crop yield predictions by adapting models developed for one type of crop to work effectively with others. This flexibility reduces the need for extensive datasets, which can often be challenging to gather sustainably. AI adoption, as it minimizes the data requirements and speeds up the learning process. Organizations can deploy AI solutions in dynamic environments where conditions change frequently—such as climate monitoring or disaster response—without the extensive retraining typically required. By democratizing access to powerful AI capabilities through meta-learning, more organizations can participate in sustainable innovation, driving a broader impact across sectors. By reusing and adapting existing models rather than creating new ones from scratch, organizations can significantly lower their carbon footprint associated with training AI systems. This is particularly relevant given the growing concerns about the environmental impact of large-scale AI training, which often requires substantial computational resources and energy (Dattathrani, S., et al., 2023). Sustainable AI adoption, therefore, hinges on leveraging these methodologies to reduce resource consumption while enhancing the performance and adaptability of AI systems.

Despite the advantages, implementing transfer learning and meta-learning poses challenges. Organizations must develop a robust understanding of the domain and the specific tasks at hand to ensure effective model adaptation. Additionally, careful selection of pre-trained models is essential, as transferring inappropriate models can lead to suboptimal performance or unintended consequences. As such, organizations need to invest in the necessary expertise and infrastructure to facilitate successful implementation. Furthermore, ethical considerations surrounding data usage and model transferability must be addressed. Ensuring that transferred models do not perpetuate biases or generate unfair outcomes is crucial in maintaining the integrity of AI systems. Organizations must adopt best practices in model selection and evaluation to safeguard against these risks, fostering a responsible approach to AI development that prioritizes fairness and inclusivity. In conclusion, transfer learning and meta-learning represent powerful methodologies that can significantly enhance sustainable AI adoption (Bryson, J. J.2018). By facilitating the efficient use of pre-trained models and enabling rapid adaptation to new tasks, these techniques empower organizations to implement AI solutions that are resource-efficient, adaptable, and impactful. As the demand for sustainable practices intensifies across various sectors, integrating these advanced learning strategies into AI initiatives will be essential.

AI-Driven Sustainable Supply Chain Management

The rise of artificial intelligence (AI) has ushered in a new era for supply chain management, fundamentally transforming how businesses approach sustainability. As companies face mounting pressure to operate responsibly, adopting AI-driven solutions for sustainable supply chain management has become essential (Enholm, I. M., et al., 2022). By leveraging AI technologies, organizations can optimize operations, reduce waste, and enhance transparency throughout their supply chains, ultimately contributing to environmental, social, and economic sustainability. Accurate demand predictions are crucial for minimizing excess inventory and reducing waste. AI algorithms can analyze historical sales data alongside real-time market indicators to generate more precise forecasts. For example, a retailer can use AI to predict demand fluctuations for seasonal products, allowing them to adjust their inventory levels accordingly. By analyzing supplier performance data, including environmental impact metrics, compliance records, and social responsibility practices, organizations can make more informed decisions about their sourcing strategies. This ensures that businesses partner with suppliers who align with their sustainability goals, fostering a more responsible supply chain ecosystem. Moreover, AI can continuously monitor supplier performance, enabling companies to identify potential risks and engage in timely interventions to address issues related to sustainability and compliance.

AI can analyze transportation routes, vehicle capacities, and real-time traffic conditions to identify the most efficient delivery methods. By leveraging AI in logistics, organizations can achieve significant cost savings while simultaneously reducing their carbon footprint. In addition to improving logistics, AI can facilitate circular economy practices by enabling better resource recovery and waste management. AI technologies can help businesses identify opportunities for recycling and repurposing materials throughout the supply chain. For example, AI systems can analyze product life cycles to determine the best methods for reusing materials and minimizing waste. Furthermore, AI-driven analytics can enhance transparency and traceability in supply chains, which are essential for sustainable practices. Consumers are increasingly demanding transparency regarding the environmental and social impacts of the products they purchase. AI technologies can track products from raw materials to end consumers, providing insights into each stage of the supply chain. This traceability enables businesses to identify potential sustainability risks and communicate their efforts to consumers, fostering trust and accountability. For instance, blockchain technology combined with AI can provide an immutable record of a product's journey, ensuring that claims regarding sustainability are backed by verifiable data.

AI algorithms raises ethical questions regarding bias and fairness, particularly in supplier evaluations and decision-making processes. To navigate these challenges, organizations need to adopt best practices for AI implementation, including stakeholder engagement and continuous monitoring of AI systems. By fostering collaboration, organizations can share data, resources, and insights, driving collective progress toward sustainable supply chain practices. Industry-wide initiatives, such as sustainability certifications and collaborative platforms, can also facilitate knowledge sharing and innovation in AI-driven solutions. For instance, AI could play a crucial role in predicting supply chain disruptions due to climate change, allowing organizations to proactively adapt their strategies and mitigate risks. Additionally, as consumers increasingly prioritize sustainability in their purchasing decisions, businesses that adopt AI-driven sustainable practices will likely gain a competitive advantage in the market. The adoption of AI technologies can significantly contribute to the sustainability goals of businesses while fostering innovation and resilience in the face of evolving market demands. As organizations continue to explore and implement AI-driven solutions, the potential for sustainable supply chains to drive positive change across industries becomes increasingly evident.

AI-Powered Energy Efficiency and Renewable Energy Integration

Traditional energy management approaches often rely on historical data and manual analysis, which can be insufficient for optimizing real-time operations. For example, commercial buildings equipped with AI-driven systems can automatically reduce energy usage during peak hours, contributing to grid stability while saving costs (Sreenivasulu A., et al., 2022). In residential settings, AI-powered home energy management systems (HEMS) are gaining traction as a means of enhancing energy efficiency. These systems utilize machine learning algorithms to learn user behavior and optimize energy usage based on individual preferences and patterns. For instance, a HEMS can analyze a household's energy consumption data and provide personalized recommendations for reducing energy waste, such as suggesting optimal times for running appliances or adjusting heating and cooling settings. This proactive approach not only reduces energy costs but also minimizes environmental impact, aligning with sustainability goals. Furthermore, cybersecurity is a critical consideration as energy systems become increasingly interconnected and reliant on digital technologies (Shokeen, J., et al., 2020). The potential for cyberattacks on AI-driven energy systems poses risks not only to operational integrity but also to consumer privacy and data security. Organizations must implement robust cybersecurity measures to protect their systems from vulnerabilities, ensuring the reliability and safety of AI applications in the energy sector. Additionally, advancements in

AI-driven predictive analytics will enable even more accurate forecasting of energy supply and demand, paving the way for more resilient energy systems.

Sustainable Water Management using AI and IoT

IoT devices, such as sensors and smart meters, can be deployed across water distribution networks, agricultural fields, and natural water bodies to collect data on water quality, quantity, and usage patterns (Rakova, B., et al., 2021). This data can provide invaluable insights into water consumption behaviors, helping stakeholders identify inefficiencies and areas for improvement. For instance, in urban settings, smart water meters can track residential water usage, enabling municipalities to identify excessive consumption and leakages in the system. By addressing these issues promptly, cities can significantly reduce water waste, ensuring that this precious resource is used more efficiently. This proactive approach enables water utilities to respond quickly to contamination events, protecting public health and preserving water resources. Moreover, the integration of AI and IoT can enhance the management of stormwater and wastewater systems. Urban areas often face challenges related to flooding, runoff, and wastewater treatment, exacerbated by climate change and infrastructure limitations. Smart drainage systems equipped with IoT sensors can monitor rainfall and water levels in real time, enabling cities to manage stormwater more effectively. AI-driven predictive models can analyze weather forecasts and historical data to optimize drainage operations, reducing the risk of flooding and minimizing environmental impacts. Additionally, in wastewater management, AI can optimize treatment processes by analyzing incoming wastewater characteristics and adjusting operational parameters for maximum efficiency.

Agriculture is another critical sector where AI and IoT can drive sustainable water management. Traditional irrigation practices often lead to overwatering and resource wastage. By implementing these technologies, farmers can optimize water usage, increase crop resilience, and improve overall productivity, all while conserving water resources. To overcome this barrier, partnerships between governments, private sector organizations, and research institutions can facilitate knowledge sharing and resource mobilization, fostering the adoption of sustainable water management practices. The diversity of IoT technologies and communication protocols can create compatibility issues, hindering data exchange and collaboration among stakeholders. Developing standardized protocols and frameworks for IoT devices will be essential to ensure seamless integration and maximize the potential of AI-driven water management solutions. Education and capacity building are also critical components of successfully implementing AI and IoT in water management (Ramakrishnan T., et al., 2022). Stakeholders, including water utilities, policymakers, and farmers, must be equipped with the knowledge and skills necessary to leverage these technologies effectively. Training programs and workshops can enhance understanding of data analytics, IoT deployment, and AI applications, empowering stakeholders to make informed decisions regarding water resource management. For instance, the emergence of blockchain technology may further enhance transparency and traceability in water management systems, ensuring that water resources are allocated fairly and sustainably. transformative approach to addressing the challenges of water scarcity and quality. By leveraging real-time data, predictive analytics, and automated decision-making, these technologies can optimize water usage, enhance conservation efforts, and ensure equitable access to water resources. As we navigate the complexities of a changing environment, embracing AI and IoT in water management will be crucial for promoting sustainability, protecting public health, and securing water resources for future generations.

AI-Enabled Circular Economy and Waste Reduction

AI can optimize processes across various sectors, driving innovation and enabling businesses to adopt more sustainable practices. At the core of a circular economy is the concept of closing the loop—ensuring that products and materials are reused, refurbished, recycled, or repurposed rather than discarded. AI plays a pivotal role in achieving this goal by enabling smarter resource management throughout the supply chain. For instance, AI-driven systems can analyze data from product design to end-of-life disposal, identifying opportunities for material recovery and reuse. By integrating AI into product design processes, companies can create products that are easier to disassemble and recycle, thereby increasing the likelihood of reintroducing materials back into the production cycle. One of the key applications of AI in waste reduction is in the optimization of recycling processes. Traditional recycling methods often struggle with inefficiencies, such as contamination and improper sorting of materials. AI-powered image recognition technologies can significantly enhance sorting accuracy by identifying and classifying different types of materials in real time. For example, advanced computer vision systems can be deployed at recycling facilities to differentiate between plastics, metals, and paper, ensuring that each material is directed to the appropriate recycling stream. This improved sorting capability not only increases recycling rates but also reduces contamination, leading to higher-quality recycled materials. AI's impact on the circular economy extends to the manufacturing sector as well..

For instance, AI can analyze sales data to forecast when products are likely to be returned or discarded, enabling companies to plan for their recovery and refurbishment. This approach not only reduces waste but also creates new revenue streams through the resale of refurbished products, aligning economic interests with environmental sustainability. The integration of AI in circular economy initiatives also enhances consumer engagement and awareness. AI-driven platforms can educate consumers about sustainable practices, helping them make informed decisions regarding their purchases and disposal methods. For example, apps that leverage AI can provide personalized recommendations for product reuse, repair, or recycling options based on user preferences and behaviors. By fostering a culture of sustainability and encouraging responsible consumption, these platforms can drive behavioral changes that contribute to waste reduction on a larger scale. AI algorithms require high-quality data to function effectively, and many organizations may lack the necessary infrastructure to collect and analyze data across their operations. Investing in data collection technologies and establishing standards for data sharing will be essential to maximize the potential of AI in circular economy practices.Additionally, there are ethical considerations associated with AI deployment, particularly in terms of data privacy and security. As organizations collect and analyze data related to consumer behaviors and preferences, it is crucial to ensure that privacy is upheld and that data is used responsibly. Developing clear guidelines and regulations around data usage will be essential to build trust among consumers and stakeholders, facilitating wider adoption of AI technologies. Collaboration among various stakeholders is also vital for advancing AI-enabled circular economy initiatives. Moreover, engaging consumers and communities in circular economy initiatives will enhance awareness and participation, creating a collective impact on waste reduction efforts. As AI capabilities continue to evolve, we may see the emergence of more sophisticated tools for resource optimization, waste tracking, and recycling automation. Additionally, the incorporation of blockchain technology could enhance transparency and traceability in circular supply chains, ensuring that materials are sourced and processed sustainably. In conclusion, AI-enabled circular economy practices offer a promising pathway toward waste reduction and sustainable resource management. By harnessing the power of AI technologies, businesses can optimize processes, enhance recycling efforts, and engage consumers in sustainable practices. The shift toward a circular economy not only benefits the environment but also presents economic opportunities for organizations willing to innovate and adapt. As we face increasing environmental challenges, the integration of AI in circular economy initiatives will be crucial for building a more sustainable future.

AI in Agriculture: Precision Farming and Sustainable Food Systems

Moreover, AI technologies can enhance irrigation management, a crucial aspect of sustainable agriculture. Traditional irrigation methods often lead to water wastage, particularly in regions facing water scarcity. This approach not only conserves valuable water resources but also promotes healthier crop growth. In addition to optimizing irrigation, AI can improve pest and disease management. Integrated pest management (IPM) strategies rely on timely and accurate information about pest populations and plant health. AI-powered image recognition technologies can analyze images from drones or smartphones to detect early signs of pest infestations or diseases. The application of AI extends beyond individual farms to broader supply chain management, contributing to the sustainability of food systems as a whole. AI can enhance traceability by monitoring products from farm to table, ensuring that consumers have access to safe and sustainably produced food. Blockchain technology, combined with AI, can create transparent supply chains that document every stage of food production, enabling consumers to make informed choices and supporting sustainable practices among producers. Furthermore, AI-driven predictive analytics can optimize logistics and distribution in the agricultural supply chain. This reduces food waste by ensuring that produce is delivered to markets at the right time, improving efficiency while maximizing profitability for farmers. Sustainable food systems also require a focus on soil health, which is vital for long-term agricultural productivity. AI technologies can support soil management practices by providing insights into soil composition, nutrient levels, and microbial activity. By analyzing data from soil sensors and remote sensing technologies, AI can guide farmers in applying fertilizers and amendments more precisely. This not only enhances soil health but also reduces nutrient runoff into waterways, contributing to environmental sustainability. Looking to the future, the potential of AI in agriculture will continue to expand, driven by ongoing technological advancements and a growing emphasis on sustainability. As machine learning and AI capabilities evolve, we can expect to see the development of more sophisticated tools for predicting crop performance, managing resources, and optimizing supply chains. Innovations such as autonomous farming equipment, AI-driven drones for monitoring crops, and advanced genetic algorithms for crop breeding will further enhance productivity and sustainability in agriculture.

AI in Healthcare: Personalized Medicine and Sustainable Healthcare Systems

AI can expedite this process by analyzing biological data to identify potential drug candidates, predicting their interactions with biological targets, and optimizing their chemical structures for better efficacy. For example, AI algorithms can sift through millions of chemical compounds to identify those most likely to succeed in clinical trials, significantly reducing the time and resources required for drug development (Pappas, I. O., et al., 2021). This not only accelerates the availability of new treatments but also promotes a more sustainable approach to pharmaceutical development by reducing waste associated with unsuccessful trials. In addition to personalized treatment, AI contributes to more sustainable healthcare systems by optimizing operational efficiencies. Healthcare facilities often face challenges related to resource allocation, patient flow, and staffing. AI-driven analytics can help hospitals and clinics forecast patient demand, optimize staff schedules, and manage inventory levels for medical supplies. For example, predictive By streamlining operations, healthcare systems can not only enhance the patient experience but also reduce costs and waste. Telemedicine, bolstered by AI technologies, further exemplifies the potential for sustainable healthcare.

AI can help identify health disparities and trends within populations. This information is invaluable for developing targeted public health interventions that address the specific needs of communities. Education and training for healthcare professionals are also vital to the successful integration of AI technologies. Clinicians need to be equipped with the knowledge and skills to interpret AI-generated insights and integrate them into their decision-making processes. Continuing education programs that focus on AI applications in healthcare can empower providers to leverage these technologies effectively, ensuring that they enhance, rather than hinder, patient care. healthcare systems, we can expect to see innovations such as advanced robotic-assisted surgeries, AI-driven mental health support systems, and enhanced diagnostics powered by machine learning (Zamani, E. D., et al., 2020). These developments hold the promise of improving patient outcomes, reducing costs, and promoting a more sustainable healthcare model. In conclusion, AI is set to revolutionize healthcare by enabling personalized medicine and fostering sustainable healthcare systems. By harnessing the power of AI technologies, healthcare providers can deliver more effective, tailored treatments while optimizing operations and resource management.

AI in Finance: Sustainable Investing and Risk Management

AI-driven solutions that not only align with investors' values but also promote long-term sustainability. AI enhances this process by enabling sophisticated analysis of ESG data, allowing investors to evaluate potential investments more holistically. Traditional methods of assessing sustainability often rely on subjective criteria and limited datasets, leading to incomplete or biased evaluations (Wamba, S. F., et al., 2021). AI-driven tools can aggregate and analyze vast amounts of data from diverse sources, including company disclosures, social media sentiment, and environmental reports, providing a more comprehensive view of a company's ESG performance. For instance, AI can analyze historical performance data alongside ESG metrics to uncover relationships between sustainable practices and financial outcomes. This can help investors identify companies that not only adhere to sustainable practices but also demonstrate strong financial resilience, thereby guiding investment decisions toward those with the potential for long-term success. By integrating AI into the investment analysis process, asset managers can better align their portfolios with sustainable principles while maximizing returns. In addition to enhancing sustainable investing, AI plays a critical role in risk management. The financial sector is inherently exposed to various risks, including market volatility, credit defaults, and operational disruptions. AI-driven risk management tools enable financial institutions to analyze complex datasets in real time, providing deeper insights into risk exposure and enabling proactive measures to mitigate potential threats. This predictive capability allows asset managers to adjust their portfolios dynamically, safeguarding investments against unforeseen challenges.

Moreover, AI technologies can streamline compliance and regulatory processes, which are increasingly critical in the context of sustainable investing. As regulatory scrutiny around ESG practices intensifies, financial institutions must ensure that their investment strategies adhere to evolving guidelines. AI-driven compliance tools can monitor transactions, assess adherence to regulations, and flag potential violations in real time. This reduces the administrative burden on compliance teams and helps organizations maintain transparency and accountability in their sustainable investing practices (Vijayakumar G, et al., 2024). AI models rely on high-quality, comprehensive datasets to deliver accurate insights, and the fragmented nature of ESG data can pose challenges. Many companies do not disclose complete or standardized ESG information, making it difficult for investors to assess sustainability accurately. To overcome this barrier, there is a pressing need for improved data reporting standards and transparency across industries. Collaborations between regulators, industry associations, and financial institutions can help establish guidelines for consistent ESG disclosures, facilitating better data accessibility. Financial institutions must prioritize fairness and transparency in their AI implementations, employing diverse datasets and regularly auditing algorithms for biases. By doing so, they can build trust in AI-driven solutions and ensure that they promote equitable outcomes in sustainable investing and risk management.Furthermore, the integration of AI in finance necessitates a cultural shift within organizations. Financial professionals must be equipped with the skills and knowledge to leverage AI tools effectively. Continuous education and training programs can empower employees to understand AI technologies, interpret data insights, and make informed decisions.

Implementing AI for Sustainability: Change Management and Stakeholder Engagement

As organizations increasingly recognize the potential of artificial intelligence (AI) to drive sustainability initiatives, the implementation of AI technologies poses unique challenges that require effective change management and robust stakeholder engagement. Successfully integrating AI into sustainability practices necessitates not only technical proficiency but also a strategic approach to navigate cultural shifts, align interests among diverse stakeholders, and foster an environment conducive to innovation. By prioritizing these elements, organizations can leverage AI to enhance their sustainability efforts and achieve long-term environmental and social goals. Change management is a critical component of any AI implementation strategy, especially when addressing sustainability challenges (Vassilakopoulou, P., et al., 2022). Organizations must understand that the adoption of AI is not merely a technological upgrade but a transformative process that can alter workflows, decision-making processes, and organizational culture. To facilitate a smooth transition, leaders must articulate a clear vision for how AI will enhance sustainability initiatives, illustrating its potential to improve efficiency, reduce waste, and drive innovation. This vision should be communicated consistently across all levels of the organization, ensuring that employees understand the benefits of AI in achieving broader sustainability objectives. A crucial aspect of change management is addressing the potential resistance that may arise during the AI adoption process.

This includes not only technical training on AI systems but also education on sustainability principles and practices. By empowering employees with knowledge, organizations can enhance their capacity to implement AI solutions that align with sustainability goals. Organizations should provide regular updates on the progress of AI initiatives, highlighting successes, challenges, and lessons learned. This transparency fosters trust and encourages stakeholders to contribute their insights and feedback. Utilizing multiple channels—such as town hall meetings, newsletters, and social media—can help reach diverse audiences and facilitate ongoing dialogue about the organization's sustainability goals and AI strategies. Collaboration with external stakeholders can also enhance the effectiveness of AI implementation. Partnerships with universities, research institutions, and technology providers can provide access to valuable expertise and resources. Engaging stakeholders in discussions about ethical considerations fosters a culture of accountability and ensures that diverse perspectives are considered in the development and deployment of AI solutions. Finally, the role of leadership in driving change and engaging stakeholders is paramount. Leaders must demonstrate a commitment to sustainability and AI adoption by actively championing initiatives and setting clear expectations for their teams. By modeling behaviors that prioritize sustainability and collaboration, leaders can inspire employees and stakeholders to embrace change and contribute to the organization's sustainability objectives. AI adoption while fostering a culture of innovation and accountability. Through collaboration with diverse stakeholders and a commitment to ethical practices, organizations can leverage AI to drive meaningful progress toward sustainability goals, ultimately contributing to a more resilient and sustainable future.

AI and Sustainability Policy: Regulatory Frameworks and Standards

AI technologies necessitate robust regulatory frameworks and standards to ensure that these innovations contribute positively to sustainability goals while mitigating potential risks. A comprehensive approach to AI governance, particularly in the context of sustainability, is essential for fostering innovation, promoting ethical practices, and safeguarding public interests. The creation of effective regulatory frameworks begins with a clear understanding of the potential applications of AI in sustainability (Sugumaran K. M, D., et al., 2024). AI can enhance various sectors, including energy management, waste reduction, sustainable agriculture, and transportation, by optimizing resource use and improving efficiency. However, these applications must be governed by policies that ensure transparency, accountability, and inclusivity. Policymakers must consider how regulations can be designed to encourage innovation while preventing unintended consequences, such as exacerbating inequalities or undermining environmental protections. One of the primary challenges in developing regulatory frameworks for AI is the pace of technological advancement. As AI evolves rapidly, traditional regulatory approaches often struggle to keep up, resulting in gaps that can lead to misuse or negative impacts. To address this issue, regulatory bodies should adopt a flexible and adaptive approach, incorporating mechanisms for regular review and updates to policies as technologies and societal needs change. This iterative process allows for the integration of new knowledge and insights into AI applications, ensuring that regulations remain relevant and effective in promoting sustainability.

Stakeholder engagement is a critical component of developing regulatory frameworks for AI and sustainability. Policymakers must actively involve a diverse range of stakeholders—including industry leaders, researchers, civil society organizations, and affected communities—in the regulatory design process. This inclusive approach fosters collaboration and ensures that the voices of those impacted by AI technologies are heard. By engaging stakeholders, regulators can better understand the potential benefits and risks associated with AI applications, leading to more informed and balanced policies. In addition to stakeholder engagement, the establishment of clear standards is essential for ensuring that AI technologies align with sustainability objectives. Standards can provide guidelines for best practices, promote interoperability between systems, and ensure that AI applications adhere to ethical considerations. For instance, sustainability standards for AI could encompass criteria related to energy efficiency, data privacy, transparency, and fairness. Developing such standards requires collaboration among industry groups, academic institutions, and regulatory bodies to create a unified framework that supports responsible AI development.

Another important aspect of regulatory frameworks is the establishment of accountability mechanisms. As AI systems become increasingly autonomous, it is crucial to clarify the responsibilities of developers, users, and organizations in ensuring ethical AI deployment. This includes outlining protocols for addressing potential biases in AI algorithms, ensuring data integrity, and defining liability in cases of harm caused by AI systems. Regulatory frameworks should encourage organizations to implement internal governance structures that prioritize ethical considerations in AI development and use. International collaboration is also vital for addressing the global nature of AI and sustainability challenges. Many environmental issues, such as climate change and biodiversity loss, transcend national borders, necessitating coordinated efforts among countries. This research can inform evidence-based policy decisions, enabling regulators to address emerging challenges and opportunities effectively. In the context of sustainability, ethical considerations must be at the forefront of AI policy discussions. Ensuring that AI technologies are developed and deployed in ways that promote social equity, environmental justice, and ethical governance is essential. should promote educational initiatives that raise awareness of the implications of AI technologies for sustainability, targeting various audiences, including businesses, government officials, and the general public. By fostering a well-informed society, we can empower individuals and organizations to engage meaningfully in discussions about AI policy and contribute to sustainable development efforts. In conclusion, the intersection of AI and sustainability presents both opportunities and challenges that require thoughtful regulatory frameworks and standards. By prioritizing stakeholder engagement, establishing clear standards, ensuring accountability, and promoting ethical considerations, policymakers can create an environment conducive to responsible AI development that aligns with sustainability objectives. International collaboration and ongoing research will further enhance our ability to address global sustainability challenges effectively. As we navigate the complexities of AI in the context of sustainability, a proactive and inclusive approach to policymaking will be essential for ensuring that technology serves as a catalyst for positive change and a sustainable future for all.

Future Directions in AI and Sustainable Business: Opportunities, Challenges, and Research Agenda

AI technologies are increasingly recognized as critical tools for addressing complex sustainability issues across various sectors, including energy, agriculture, transportation, and supply chain management. However, the path forward requires a comprehensive research agenda that addresses the multifaceted nature of these opportunities and challenges. This agenda will not only guide organizations in effectively leveraging AI for sustainable business practices but also contribute to the broader discourse on ethical AI deployment. In agriculture, precision farming techniques powered by AI can analyze soil health and weather patterns, enabling farmers to optimize crop yields while reducing water and fertilizer use. By harnessing AI in these ways, businesses can significantly lower their environmental footprint while improving profitability. Moreover, AI can facilitate innovation in sustainable product development. Companies can use AI to analyze consumer preferences and market trends, enabling the design of products that not only meet customer needs but also adhere to sustainability principles. This could include the development of eco-friendly materials, energy-efficient technologies, or circular economy solutions that prioritize reuse and recycling. By integrating AI into product design and development processes, businesses can accelerate their transition to sustainable practices, ultimately leading to competitive advantages in a market increasingly driven by consumer demand for sustainability.

Collaborating with industry stakeholders and academic institutions can help regulators develop frameworks that balance the need for oversight with the desire for innovation, ultimately fostering an environment where AI can contribute meaningfully to sustainability goals. The future research agenda for AI and sustainable business should focus on several key areas. First, there is a need for interdisciplinary research that explores the intersection of AI, sustainability, and business strategy. Understanding how AI can be strategically integrated into sustainability initiatives requires collaboration between technologists, sustainability experts, and business leaders. Research efforts should examine case studies of successful AI implementations in sustainable business contexts, identifying best practices and lessons learned that can inform future applications. Second, research should address the development of metrics and frameworks for measuring the impact of AI on sustainability outcomes. Current approaches often lack standardized metrics, making it challenging for organizations to assess the effectiveness of AI solutions in achieving sustainability goals. Establishing clear indicators for evaluating AI's contribution to environmental and social performance will enable businesses to make informed decisions about their sustainability initiatives and communicate their impact to stakeholders effectively. Additionally, exploring the role of AI in facilitating stakeholder engagement and collaboration is essential. AI technologies can enhance communication and collaboration among diverse stakeholders, from employees to consumers and local communities. Research should investigate how AI can support participatory approaches to sustainability decision-making, fostering inclusivity and transparency in organizational processes. By understanding the potential of AI to bridge gaps between stakeholders, businesses can create more effective and equitable sustainability strategies. Finally, the ethical implications of AI in sustainable business warrant further investigation. Research should explore frameworks for ethical AI development that prioritize sustainability, equity, and social responsibility. This includes examining how organizations can implement ethical guidelines, conduct impact assessments, and ensure stakeholder involvement in AI-related decisions.

CONCLUSION

Emerging technologies are poised to reshape how organizations approach sustainability, enabling them to tackle complex challenges while enhancing their operational capabilities. The integration of AI into various sectors—such as energy, agriculture, manufacturing, and supply chain management—demonstrates the vast potential. This capability empowers organizations to identify inefficiencies, reduce carbon footprints, and align their strategies with sustainability goals. As businesses embrace a more data-centric approach, they will be better equipped to measure their sustainability performance and make informed decisions that lead to positive outcomes. Furthermore, the rise of machine learning and predictive analytics will enable businesses to anticipate future trends and challenges. By leveraging historical data and real-time inputs, organizations can develop models that forecast environmental impacts, resource availability, and consumer behaviors. This foresight will facilitate proactive planning and the implementation of sustainable practices, helping companies stay ahead of regulatory requirements and evolving market demands. Moreover, AI is playing a pivotal role in fostering circular economy practices. However, the successful implementation of AI in sustainable business practices is not without challenges. Businesses must also invest in training and upskilling their workforce to ensure that employees are equipped to leverage AI technologies responsibly and effectively. This includes developing standards for data usage, promoting ethical AI practices, and incentivizing sustainable business models. Collaborative efforts between governments, industry leaders, and academic institutions will be vital in crafting policies that foster responsible AI development and deployment. As we move forward, the importance of stakeholder engagement cannot be overstated. Businesses must actively involve employees, customers, and communities in their sustainability initiatives, fostering a culture of collaboration and inclusivity. By engaging stakeholders in the decision-making process, organizations can better understand diverse perspectives and needs, leading to more effective and equitable solutions. This participatory approach will not only enhance the effectiveness of sustainability initiatives but also strengthen the social license to operate. By harnessing the power of AI to optimize operations, foster circular economy practices, and enhance stakeholder engagement, organizations can position themselves as leaders in sustainability. However, realizing this potential requires a commitment to ethical practices, robust governance, and continuous learning. As businesses navigate this evolving landscape, a proactive and collaborative approach will be essential in leveraging AI to create a more sustainable and equitable future for all. Embracing these trends not only aligns with the values of a conscious consumer base but also prepares organizations to thrive in a world where sustainability is paramount. The journey ahead may be complex, but the rewards of integrating AI into sustainable business practices will be transformative, paving the way for a resilient and sustainable global economy.

REFERENCES

Ashok, M., Madan, R., Joha, A., & Sivarajah, U. (2022). Ethical framework for Artificial Intelligence and Digital technologies. *International Journal of Information Management*, 62, 102433. DOI: 10.1016/j.ijinfomgt.2021.102433

Babic, B., Cohen, I. G., Evgeniou, T., & Gerke, S. (2021). *When Machine Learning Goes Off the Rails.Harvard Business Review*. January-February.

Brooks, L. A., & Saveri, A. (2017). Expanding imagined affordance with future-types: Challenging algorithmic power with collective 2040 imagination. *Proceedings of the 50th Hawaii International Conference on System Sciences (HICCS)*. DOI: 10.24251/HICSS.2017.215

Bryson, J. J. (2018). Patiency is not a virtue: The design of intelligent systems and systems of ethics. *Ethics and Information Technology*, 20(1), 15–26. DOI: 10.1007/s10676-018-9448-6

Calzarossa, M. C., De Lotto, I., & Rogerson, S. (2010). Ethics and information systems - guest editors introduction. *Information Systems Frontiers*, 12(4), 357–359. DOI: 10.1007/s10796-009-9198-4

Chen, Y., Jensen, S., Albert, L. J., Gupta, S., & Lee, T. (2023). Artificial Intelligence (AI) student assistants in the Classroom: Designing Chatbots to Support Student Success. *Information Systems Frontiers*, 25(1), 161–182. Advance online publication. DOI: 10.1007/s10796-022-10291-4

Chiasson, M., Davidson, E., & Winter, J. (2018). Philosophical foundations for informing the future (S) through IS research. *European Journal of Information Systems*, 27(3), 367–379. DOI: 10.1080/0960085X.2018.1435232

Coombs, C., Stacey, P., Kawalek, P., Simeonova, B., Becker, J., Bergener, K., & Trautmann, H. (2021). What is it about humanity that we can't give away to intelligent machines? A european perspective. *International Journal of Information Management*, 58, 102311. DOI: 10.1016/j.ijinfomgt.2021.102311

Dattathrani, S., & De, R. (2023). The Concept of Agency in the era of Artificial Intelligence: Dimensions and degrees. *Information Systems Frontiers*, 25(1), 29–54. Advance online publication. DOI: 10.1007/s10796-022-10336-8

Elbanna, A., Dwivedi, Y., Bunker, D., & Wastell, D. (2020). The search for smartness in working, living and organising: Beyond the 'Technomagic.'. *Information Systems Frontiers*, 22(2), 275–280. DOI: 10.1007/s10796-020-10013-8

Enholm, I. M., Papagiannidis, E., Mikalef, P., & Krogstie, J. (2022). Artificial intelligence and business value: A literature review. *Information Systems Frontiers*, 24(5), 1709–1734. DOI: 10.1007/s10796-021-10186-w

Gams, M., Gu, I. Y. H., Härmä, A., Muñoz, A., & Tam, V. (2019). Artificial intelligence and ambient intelligence. *Journal of Ambient Intelligence and Smart Environments*, 11(1), 71–86. DOI: 10.3233/AIS-180508

Janssen, M., Brous, P., Estevez, E., Barbosa, L. S., & Janowski, T. (2020). Data governance: Organizing data for trustworthy Artificial Intelligence. *Government Information Quarterly*, 37(3), 101493. DOI: 10.1016/j.giq.2020.101493

Kautish, P., & Khare, A. (2022). Investigating the moderating role of AI-enabled services on flow and awe experience. *International Journal of Information Management*, 66, 102519. DOI: 10.1016/j.ijinfomgt.2022.102519

Keegan, B. J., Dennehy, D., & Naudé, P. (2022). Implementing artificial intelligence in traditional B2B marketing practices: An activity theory perspective. *Information Systems Frontiers*. Advance online publication. DOI: 10.1007/s10796-022-10294-1 PMID: 35637917

Mahadev Madgule, N. (2023). Mechanical properties and microstructure of activated TIG welded similar joints of Inconel alloys by desirability approaches. *Materials Today: Proceedings*, 77, 528–533. DOI: 10.1016/j.matpr.2022.12.250

Mikalef, P., & Gupta, M. (2021). Artificial intelligence capability: Conceptualization, measurement calibration, and empirical study on its impact on organizational creativity and firm performance. *Information & Management*, 58(3), 103434. DOI: 10.1016/j.im.2021.103434

Niederman, F. (2021). Project management: Openings for disruption from AI and advanced analytics. *Information Technology & People*, 34(6), 15701599. DOI: 10.1108/ITP-09-2020-0639

Pappas, I. O., & Giannakos, M. N. (2021, April). Rethinking learning design in IT education during a pandemic. *Frontiers in Education*, 6, 652856. DOI: 10.3389/feduc.2021.652856

Rakova, B., Yang, J., Cramer, H., & Chowdhury, R. (2021). Where responsible AI meets reality: Practitioner perspectives on enablers for shifting organizational practices. Proceedings of the ACM on Human-Computer Interaction, 5(CSCW1), 1–23.

Ramakrishnan, T., Mohan Gift, M. D., Chitradevi, S., Jegan, R., & Subha Hency Jose, P. (2022). Study of Numerous Resins Used in Polymer Matrix Composite Materials. Advances in Materials Science and Engineering. DOI: 10.1155/2022/1088926

Shokeen, J., & Rana, C. (2020). A study on features of social recommender systems. *Artificial Intelligence Review*, 53(2), 965–988. DOI: 10.1007/s10462-019-09684-w

Sreenivasulu, A., & Manimozhi, T. (2022). The Model of Smart Sensing Device For Sensitive Nanoclusters Modification in Sensing Properties. 2022 2nd International Conference on Advance Computing and Innovative Technologies in Engineering (ICACITE), 1043-1047. DOI: 10.1109/ICACITE53722.2022.9823846

Sugumaran, K. M. D., Pandiyarajan V., Y. B S, Selvakumar, P., & M. S, (2024). Analysis of Electromyography Signals for Control of Mechanical Prosthesis using Machine Learning Techniques. 2024 2nd International Conference on Intelligent Data Communication Technologies and Internet of Things (IDCIoT), 1059-1067. DOI: 10.1109/IDCIoT59759.2024.10467707

Vassilakopoulou, P., Haug, A., Salvesen, L. M., & Pappas, O. I. (2022). Developing human/AI interactions for chat-based customer services: Lessons learned from the norwegian government. *European Journal of Information Systems*, 1–13. DOI: 10.1080/0960085X.2022.2096490

Vijayakumar, G., Rajkumar, M., Rajiv Chandar, N., Selvakumar, P., & Duraisamy, R. (2024). Environmentally friendly TDS removal from waste water by electrochemical ion exchange batch-type recirculation (EIR) technique. *Environmental Science. Water Research & Technology*, 10(4), 826–835. DOI: 10.1039/D3EW00793F

Wamba, S. F., Bawack, R. E., Guthrie, C., Queiroz, M. M., & Carillo, K. D. A. (2021). Are we preparing for a good AI society? A bibliometric review and research agenda. *Technological Forecasting and Social Change*, 164, 120482. DOI: 10.1016/j.techfore.2020.120482

Zamani, E. D., & Pouloudi, N. (2020). Generative mechanisms of Workarounds, Discontinuance and Reframing: A study of negative disconfirmation with consumerised IT. *Information Systems Journal*, 31(3), 384–428. DOI: 10.1111/isj.12315

Chapter 9
The Role of Artificial Intelligence in Business Model Innovation:
Overview of AI Technologies

P. Selvakumar
https://orcid.org/0000-0002-3650-4548
Department of Science and Humanities, Nehru Institute of Technology, India

Mohit Sharma
https://orcid.org/0009-0007-2280-8077
Maharshi Dayanand University, Rohtak, India

M. Shanthi
https://orcid.org/0000-0002-3844-9765
Avinashilingam Institute for Home Science and Higher Education for Women, India

Parihar Suresh Dahake
https://orcid.org/0000-0002-2286-4120
Ramdeobaba University, Nagpur, India

Repudi Pitchiah
Koneru Lakshmaiah Education Foundation, India

Manjunath T. C.
https://orcid.org/0000-0003-2545-9160
Rajarajeswari College of Engineering, India

ABSTRACT

Two major forces driving this transformation are business model innovation. Together, they are redefining the core structures and capabilities of modern enterprises, enabling companies to adapt to evolving consumer needs, optimize operations, and create new value streams. At its core, business model innovation (BMI) is about redefining how a business creates, delivers, and captures value. Traditionally, businesses have relied on stable, well-established models such as product sales, subscription services, or fee-based services. However, in a world of rapid technological advancement and shifting consumer expectations, companies need to think beyond

DOI: 10.4018/979-8-3693-9571-4.ch009

these conventional models. Business model innovation encourages organizations to explore new ways of generating revenue, improving customer relationships, and differentiating themselves from competitors.

INTRODUCTION TO BUSINESS MODEL INNOVATION AND ARTIFICIAL INTELLIGENCE (AI)

Two major forces driving this transformation are business model innovation. Together, they are redefining the core structures and capabilities of modern enterprises, enabling companies to adapt to evolving consumer needs, optimize operations, and create new value streams. Understanding the synergy between these two elements economy. At its core, business model innovation (BMI) is about redefining how a business creates, delivers, and captures value. Traditionally, businesses have relied on stable, well-established models such as product sales, subscription services, or fee-based services. However, in a world of rapid technological advancement and shifting consumer expectations, companies need to think beyond these conventional models. Business model innovation encourages organizations to explore new ways of generating revenue, improving customer relationships, and differentiating themselves from competitors. Instead of merely enhancing existing processes, BMI seeks to reimagine them, often resulting in the development of entirely new business architectures. One key aspect of business model innovation is its focus on customer-centric approaches.

Traditional models often centered on efficiency or scale, but today's consumers expect personalization, convenience, and transparency. Companies like Uber and Airbnb, for example, have used BMI to disrupt entire industries by leveraging digital platforms to create peer-to-peer networks. These models not only provide customers with unprecedented access to services but also create new revenue streams and allow companies to scale rapidly without heavy asset investments. Similarly, firms in the manufacturing sector are adopting models such as "Product as a Service," where customers pay for usage rather than ownership, aligning revenue with ongoing value delivery. The Role of Artificial Intelligence Artificial intelligence tasks typically requiring human intelligence. AI is transforming industries by enabling systems to learn from data, adapt to new inputs, and perform complex analysis and decision-making. AI-driven business model innovation requires cross-functional collaboration, as it involves both technical and strategic changes. Leaders must Traditional hierarchies may need to be redefined to allow for agile decision-making, and employees may require reskilling to work effectively with AI technologies Future Outlook Looking ahead, the combination of business model innovation and AI is poised to drive the next wave of industry disruption. Enable levels of automation, personalization, and insight generation. We can expect AI-driven models to become increasingly autonomous, with minimal human intervention required in decision-making processes. Companies may shift from human-led to AI-led strategies, where shaping business models and guiding corporate strategy., AI-driven business models will likely bring about paradigm shifts. Autonomous vehicles, for instance, could give rise to new ownership models, where consumers pay for access to transportation services instead of owning vehicles. Similarly, in the energy sector, AI could enable more efficient, decentralized power grids, where consumers and businesses can trade energy in real-time markets. The potential for AI to reshape business models is vast, and companies that invest in understanding and leveraging this potential will be well-positioned for the future. In conclusion, business model innovation and AI are two of the most powerful tools available to modern enterprises. Individually, they have the potential to drive significant value, but together, they create opportunities for radical transformation. By understanding the interplay between these elements, businesses can not only enhance their current operations but also pioneer new models that redefine entire industries. The future belongs to those who can adapt, innovate, and embrace the transformative, positioning themselves at the forefront of the digital economy.

The Evolution of AI: From Expert Systems to Deep Learning

story of transformative growth, driven by key milestones and technological advancements that have redefined how machines interpret, learn, and perform tasks traditionally requiring human intelligence. This journey began with early developments in the 1950s and 60s when AI research focused on rule-based systems known as symbolic AI. These initial efforts relied heavily on formal logic and symbol manipulation, culminating in the advent of expert systems in the 1970s and 80s. Expert systems, such as DENDRAL and MYCIN, were among the first successful implementations of AI (Aagaard, A., 2019). These systems operated through a set of predefined rules, using "if-then" logic to make inferences and offer solutions based on their programmed knowledge base. While innovative for their time, expert systems had limitations— engineering and struggled with scalability and adaptability. They lacked the ability to learn from new data, which meant their effectiveness was constrained to narrowly defined tasks. In the 1990s, AI research began shifting focus toward machine learning (ML), a subfield of AI that emphasized the idea that machines could learn patterns from data rather than rely solely on static rules. d regression. One of the most significant breakthroughs in this era was the development of algorithms capable of handling more complex and less structured data. Additionally, the availability of more extensive datasets and increased (Abou-Foul, M., et al., 2023). The success of these models demonstrated that algorithms could adapt based on experience, sophisticated AI systems. The 2000s saw a rise in techniques, extending the scope of AI applications algorithms, techniques, enabled the discovery of hidden patterns within large datasets without explicit labels. Meanwhile, reinforcement learning introduced the idea of agents that learn optimal actions learning became foundational for advancements in robotics and game-playing AI. A landmark achievement in this domain was the development of AlphaGo by DeepMind, which defeated a human board, demonstrating the potential of reinforcement learning when combined with advanced search algorithms and neural networks. A pivotal transformation in AI came with, particularly the emergence around 2010.

Although neural networks had been studied since the 1980s, early implementations struggled with scalability and computational limitations. However, the availability of massive datasets (often referred to as "big data"), Convolutional neural networks (CNNs) (Agrawal, A., et al., 2018), in particular, revolutionized computer vision by allowing machines to analyze images with human-like precision, leading to rapid advancements in facial recognition, object detection, and autonomous vehicles. Similarly, recurrent The rise of deep learning brought about breakthroughs that were previously thought impossible. For instance, 2014 enabled, blurring the line between AI-generated content and real-world data. together in a process called adversarial training, producing increasingly realistic outputs. This breakthrough has had implications for fields as diverse as art, medicine, and entertainment, where AI-generated media and deepfake technology continue to make waves. In NLP, transformers—another deep learning architecture introduced in 2017—marked a significant leap forward. Transformers, which include models like BERT, GPT, and T5, revolutionized language understanding by allowing models to capture long-range dependencies in text. Each phase has built upon the limitations and lessons of its predecessors, creating a robust foundation for future. As we stand on the cusp of new frontiers with technologies like quantum computing and brain-machine interfaces potentially impacting AI's development, the field is likely to witness transformative breakthroughs that could redefine human-machine interaction, decision-making, and creativity. The path of AI has been marked by relentless innovation, and its trajectory suggests a future where intelligent systems play an ever-greater role in shaping our growth possibility.

AI and Business Model Innovation: Opportunities, Challenges, and Future Directions

automate tasks, and generate predictive insights has created a foundation for companies to redefine how they create, capture, and deliver value. In traditional business models, decision-making processes and operations have been largely human-driven and manual. However, with AI, companies now have the tools to optimize their processes, personalize customer experiences, and even launch entirely new services. For example, AI-driven automation supply chains, and identify patterns in customer behavior that drive more effective marketing strategies.AI is also enabling the rise of data-as-a-product business models. Traditionally, data was often treated as a by-product of operational processes. However, with the advancement of AI, data itself has become a valuable asset that companies can monetize. This shift has given rise to business models, or Google, which uses vast data assets to power its advertising services. AI models trained on large datasets can provide deep insights, transforming data into a critical revenue stream. Moreover, AI technologies like predictive analytics and sentiment analysis have unlocked new potential for customer segmentation and targeting. Companies can now hyper-personalize trend has reshaped sectors such as e-commerce and media, where recommendation systems powered by AI have redefined the customer journey, encouraging greater engagement and loyalty. However, AI-driven business model innovation does not come without its challenges. One primary challenge is the significant investment required in AI technology, talent, and infrastructure. Building robust AI systems requires computational resources, access to, manage, and interpret complex models (Akter, S., et al., 2023). Many companies, especially smaller businesses, struggle to implement AI solutions due to the cost and complexity involved. Furthermore, companies must navigate legal and ethical considerations when collecting, processing, and using data for AI applications. Balancing AI-driven personalization with respect for user privacy is a delicate task, and companies that misuse data risk reputational damage and regulatory penalties. These issues highlight the importance of establishing strong governance frameworks to guide AI implementation responsibly and transparently. Another challenge in AI adoption for business modelsAI's impact on business outcomes. Unlike traditional investments, where return on investment (ROI) is straightforward, AI's value is often indirect and multifaceted, impacting areas like customer satisfaction, operational efficiency, and employee productivity. Many organizations find it challenging to link AI investments directly to bottom-line performance. This uncertainty can lead to hesitation in AI adoption and implementation, particularly for leadership teams that prioritize short-term gains over long-term innovation. Additionally, integrating AI into existing business models may disrupt established processes, requiring companies to re-evaluate workflows, employee roles, and operational strategies (Bahoo, S., et al., 2023). For example, among customers who prefer human interaction. Balancing the efficiencies AI offers with maintaining a positive customer experience is an ongoing challenge that companies must address as they incorporate AI into their business models.(Balsmeier, B., & Woerter, M., 2019). AI's role in business model innovation is also driving shifts in industry structures and competitive dynamics. Companies are investing in reskilling programs to equip their workforce with skills in data science, machine learning, and AI ethics, which are increasingly in demand. The ability to interpret and apply AI insights effectively is becoming a competitive differentiator, highlighting the need for organizations to (Bankins, S., et al., 2023). Moreover, as AI systems take on more routine tasks, human workers are freed up to higher-value, creative, and strategic activities, potentially increasing capabilities and drive innovation.

Machine Learning (ML) and Deep Learning (DL): Algorithms and Applications

Healthcare diagnostics, patterns from data without being explicitly programmed. It encompasses a variety of step further. Using multi-layered neural networks, deep learning algorithms are able to process and learn from vast and complex datasets (Chatterjee, S., et al., 2015), often with minimal human intervention. DL models excel at tasks that involve unstructured data such as images, video, and natural language, achieving levels of accuracy that were previously unattainable. One of the primary categories of ML is supervised learning techniques are widely used in spam detection, where algorithms patterns in labeled examples. Similarly, in finance, supervised learning models help assess credit risk by analyzing past loan (SVMs), and linear regression. Another branch, unsupervised learning, deals with unlabeled data, focusing on finding distinct customer groups based on purchasing behavior, while association algorithms find variables in large datasets, helping businesses with cross-selling and recommendation engines. Reinforcement learning (RL), another important area, enables. RL is instrumental in developing intelligent systems for robotics, gaming, and autonomous driving, as it enables agents to optimize actions over time, even in dynamic and uncertain settings. Deep Learning, on the other hand,. In the automotive industry, CNNs enable features like pedestrian detection and lane recognition, crucial for the development of autonomous vehicles. human language. More recently, transformer models, a type of deep learning architecture, have revolutionized NLP by enabling high levels of language understanding and generation, as seen in advanced applications like chatbots, virtual assistants, and automated text summarization. A variety of algorithms underpin ML and DL models, each suited to specific types of data and tasks. In supervised learning, linear regression remains, logistic regression and k-nearest neighbors (KNN) are commonly applied for binary or multi-class classification problems. Logistic regression, despite its simplicity (Benner, M. J., & Waldfogel, J., 2023) is widely used for binary classification in medical diagnostics, while KNN is valuable in recommendation systems and text categorization due to its ability to identify similarity between data points. In healthcare, ML algorithms assist with diagnostic procedures, drug discovery, and patient management. Predictive models trained on patient data enable fraud, while deep learning models in finance analyze market trends and automate trading decisions. Retail and e-commerce have been transformed by recommendation systems that use collaborative filtering and deep learning to deliver personalized shopping experiences (Cennamo, C., et al., 2020). For example, recommendation engines on platforms like Amazon and Netflix analyze customer behavior to suggest products and content, enhancing customer engagement and driving revenue.

Natural Language Processing (NLP) and Computer Vision: AI-Powered Interfaces

These fields have enabled computers to process, understand, and respond to human language and visual data, leading to advancements in diverse applications such as virtual assistants, automated customer service, medical imaging, autonomous driving, and augmented reality., understanding images, videos, and real-world scenes, and is a critical component in facial recognition, object detection, and medical diagnostics (Chesbrough, H. W., & Tucci, C. L., 2020). Together, NLP and Computer Vision empower devices to "see" and "speak," enhancing user experience by creating interfaces that feel intuitive, responsive, and human-like.At the core of NLP are algorithms and models that help computers process language in meaningful ways. Traditional NLP approaches relied on rule-based methods and statistical techniques, but especially recurrent (RNNs) and transformer architectures RNNs and their variants, such as LSTMs, are particularly useful in applications involving sequential data, like speech recognition and language modeling. Transformer models, however, have significantly advanced NLP capabilities, especially in complex tasks such as language translation and question answering. Transformers enable NLP models to capture long-range dependencies in text, learning contextual relationships across sentences, paragraphs, and entire documents. that can produce human-like responses, as seen in Assistant. These systems rely on vast amounts of training fine-tuning, allowing them to generate contextually appropriate and coherent responses, making them invaluable in customer service, information retrieval, and personal assistance. One of the most impactful applications of NLP is has widespread applications in business, where companies use it to monitor social media, customer feedback, and reviews, gaining insights into public perception and brand sentiment. By identifying positive, negative, or neutral sentiments, businesses can respond more effectively to customer needs, refine their products, and improve marketing strategies. Another significant application of NLP is machine translation, cross-cultural communication. Additionally, NLP powers text summarization and topic modeling, which help businesses analyze large volumes of text data by automatically summarizing content or extracting key topics. These capabilities are particularly valuable in fields like journalism, legal research, and finance, where professionals must quickly sift through extensive information.

Object detection extends image classification by locating multiple objects within an image, each with a bounding box. This capability is critical in fields like autonomous driving, where systems need to detect pedestrians, AI has become an invaluable tool in medical diagnostics, reducing human error, improving accuracy, and enabling earlier detection of life-threatening conditions. A recent breakthrough in Computer Vision is has seen widespread adoption in security, where it is used for authentication in devices and systems. Apple's Face ID, for instance, enables secure, biometric-based access to devices. However, facial recognition technology is not without controversy (Cockburn, I. M., et al., 2018) as it raises privacy concerns, particularly in public surveillance and law enforcement. The ethical use of facial recognition technology is a subject of ongoing debate, with calls for greater regulation and accountability to protect individual privacy. Beyond security, augmented reality (AR) relies on Computer Vision to blend digital content with real-world environments, creating immersive experiences in gaming, retail, and education. AR applications such as Pokémon Go and Ikea's Place app allow users to interact with digital objects in their physical space, enhancing entertainment and shopping experiences by merging digital and physical worlds. The convergence of NLP and Computer Vision in multimodal AI systems has opened up new possibilities in AI-powered interfaces. Multimodal systems multimodal interfaces enable chatbots to interpret text input and analyze visual content, such as images of a broken product sent by a customer. This capability allows for more accurate troubleshooting and enhances the overall customer support experience. Furthermore, companies are exploring multimodal systems in education, where AI can analyze students' spoken responses (audio) and written assignments (text) to provide personalized feedback and adapt learning materials in real time. While NLP and Computer Vision are advancing at a rapid pace, they also bring challenges, particularly around data privacy, bias, and interpretability. Both NLP and Computer (Davenport, T. H., & Ronanki, R., 2018). As a result, ethical considerations around transparency, accountability, and fairness are critical in the deployment of AI-powered interfaces. Bias in NLP and Computer Vision can lead to inequitable outcomes, such as disparities in facial recognition accuracy across different demographic groups or biased responses in language models. Addressing these issues requires the development of fairer models and more transparent algorithms, as well as compliance with regulations like powered interfaces lies in enhancing context awareness and emotional intelligence in NLP and Computer Vision systems. Future NLP models aim to better understand context, tone, and nuance, making AI responses feel more natural and human. Advances in, an emotionally aware virtual assistant could provide empathetic responses to users who are stressed or frustrated, creating a more positive and supportive interaction.

In Computer Vision, context-aware systems will enable smarter autonomous systems that not only identify objects but also understand their relationships and significance within a scene. For example, an advanced computer vision system in a self-driving car could predict the behavior of pedestrians based on body language and movement patterns, improving safety and decision-making. The integration of NLP and Computer Vision into edge devices is another emerging trend. Edge computing allows data processing to happen on local devices rather than in centralized cloud servers, enhancing privacy and reducing latency. Capabilities are (EU AI Act, 2023) transforming smart home ecosystems, security systems, and wearable technology, allowing users to interact with AI in real-time, even in offline environments.

Robotics Process Automation (RPA) and Autonomous Systems: Streamlining Business Operations

Robotic Process Automation (RPA) and autonomous systems have become integral technologies for streamlining business operations, transforming how companies manage repetitive tasks, enhance efficiency, and reduce operational costs. Autonomous systems, on the other hand, go a step further by incorporating machine learning, artificial intelligence, and other advanced technologies to make independent decisions and complete complex, real-world tasks. Applications of autonomous systems are seen in logistics (autonomous vehicles), manufacturing (robotic arms), and customer service (AI-powered chatbots). Together, RPA and autonomous systems enable organizations to optimize workflows, increase scalability, and drive digital transformation across industries. RPA's primary strength lies in operate on the user interface of applications in the same way as human employees, meaning that they can work across multiple systems without the need for deep integration. For example, in finance and accounting (Ferràs-Hernández, X., et al., 2023), RPA bots can automatically input data into financial software, generate invoices, and reconcile accounts. In HR, they assist with employee onboarding by automating document collection, background checks, and payroll setup. These processes are often time-consuming and prone to human error; however, RPA improves accuracy and speed, helping businesses reduce costs and improve service quality. flagging discrepancies, thus enhancing efficiency and reducing the time required to resolve claims. RPA bots are designed to follow specific rules and execute structured tasks, which makes them highly reliable in sectors where compliance and data accuracy are critical. Autonomous systems, meanwhile, extend beyond rule-based automation by employing AI adapt to changing environments. Unlike RPA, which operates within strict parameters, autonomous systems can handle unstructured data and complex tasks, making them suitable for dynamic applications.

RPA and autonomous systems are especially valuable for their companies can achieve significant savings on labor expenses. RPA, for example, allows organizations to run bots continuously, handling workloads that would require multiple shifts if performed by humans. This is particularly useful for industries with high-volume processes, such as banking, where bots can process thousands of transactions daily, minimizing the need for manual oversight. Autonomous systems, on the other hand, reduce costs in logistics and manufacturing by minimizing errors and downtime (Figueroa-Armijos, M., et al., 2023). Autonomous robots in warehouses can work around the clock, ensuring that operations continue smoothly without the need for rest or breaks. Additionally, predictive maintenance powered by autonomous systems helps prevent equipment failures by using avoiding costly downtime. The implementation of RPA and autonomous systems has also led to significant improvements in scalability. RPA bots can be easily scaled to manage increased workloads, allowing businesses to adapt to seasonal spikes in demand without hiring additional staff. Despite their advantages, implementing RPA and autonomous systems presents certain challenges. main managing the change within organizations, as employees may fear job displacement due to automation. Companies must invest in upskilling and reskilling their workforce, enabling employees to transition into roles that require more complex problem-solving and strategic thinking (Forbes, 2023). which can be costly, particularly for small and medium-sized enterprises (SMEs). These systems also demand regular maintenance and updates, as they must be constantly r Data privacy and security are further considerations, especially as RPA bots and autonomous systems handle sensitive information in sectors like healthcare, finance, and government. Ensuring As technology evolves, RPA and autonomous systems advanced AI capabilities, creating smarter and more flexible solutions. Future RPA tools are likely to incorporate machine learning to enable bots to handle semi-structured data, learn from patterns, and improve over time. For instance, intelligent RPA could be used in invoice processing to automatically categorize expenses and detect anomalies without relying strictly on rule-based processing. from previous mistakes. Autonomous vehicles and drones will continue to improve in safety and navigation, with AI enhancements enabling them to make more sophisticated decisions in real-world environments (Gama, F., & Magistretti, S., 2023). Another emerging trend is the combination of RPA with process mining and analytics. Process mining tools analyze business processes to identify bottlenecks and inefficiencies, which RPA can then address. By using process mining insights, organizations can optimize RPA deployment, focusing on areas where automation will yield the most significant improvements. RPA and autonomous systems have revolutionized business operations, enabling organizations to automate tasks, increase productivity, and enhance customer experiences. These technologies free employees within fixed parameters, autonomous systems extend automation to dynamic and unpredictable environments, offering opportunities for further growth and efficiency (Haenlein, M., & Kaplan, A., 2019). Despite challenges related to implementation, cost, and data privacy, the adoption of RPA and autonomous systems is expected to continue growing, with future advancements in AI and machine learning enhancing their capabilities. unprecedented speed, precision, and adaptability, setting the stage for a new era of digital transformation.

AI-Driven Value Propositions: Personalization, Prediction, and Prevention

AI-driven value propositions—specifically in personalization, prediction, and prevention enable organizations to provide deeply customized experiences, anticipate future outcomes, and mitigate potential risks, ultimately improving customer satisfaction and operational efficiency. Personalization, fueled by AI's ability to and demands, enabling companies to make informed, proactive decisions. Prevention, enhanced by AI's data analysis capabilities, allows businesses to identify potential risks, avoid disruptions, and improve safety. Together, these AI-driven capabilities empower businesses across industries to deliver more relevant, timely, and secure experiences, establishing a competitive advantage in today's digital economy The cornerstone of AI-driven personalization is the ability to analyze and understand individual customer preferences in real time. By aggregating, recommend products tailored to unique tastes, and even customize pricing strategies based on consumer behavior. Streaming services like Netflix and Spotify, for instance, use AI to recommend content based on users' viewing or listening patterns, creating a personalized experience that keeps customers engaged. E-commerce giants like Amazon employ recommendation engines powered by machine learning to suggest products that align with customers' past purchases and interests. Personalization is also essential in sectors like finance, where AI-driven systems create customized investment portfolios, financial advice, and spending insights (Garbuio, M., & Lin, N., 2019). By understanding individual customer needs In addition to product recommendations, AI-driven personalization extends to optimizing communication channels and content. Companies can leverage AI to determine the best ways to engage each customer, deciding not only what messages to send but also the timing, frequency, and platform for delivery. Email marketing, for example, has been significantly enhanced by AI, allowing businesses to send personalized messages based on user behavior and engagement history. An AI-driven system can analyze factors such as email open rates and response patterns to predict the optimal time to reach each customer. In social media and digital advertising, AI-driven prediction, another powerful value proposition, enables businesses to anticipate future events, trends, and customer behavior. Predictive analytics relies on machine learning models that identify patterns in historical data to forecast outcomes.

In retail, predictive models help businesses anticipate product demand, allowing for optimized inventory management, reduced stockouts, and where customers need them. In finance, predictive analytics enables institutions to anticipate stock movements, credit risks, and fraud patterns, thereby safeguarding investments and minimizing financial losses. Banks and investment firms use machine learning to analyze market trends and predict shifts, providing a competitive edge(Gartner, 2024) Customer behavior prediction has also become invaluable in enhancing customer relationship management (CRM). Businesses utilize AI-driven models to predict customer churn by identifying behaviors associated with disengagement or dissatisfaction, such as decreased engagement or negative feedback. By recognizing these signs early, companies can implement retention strategies—such as targeted offers or loyalty programs—to re-engage at-risk customers. For example, telecom providers use predictive models to assess which customers are likely to switch to competitors and proactively reach out with customized retention offers. In financial services, banks and credit card companies use behavioral data to predict the likelihood of customer defaults or missed payments, AI's role in prevention centers on its ability to detect risks and preemptively address potential problems, thus safeguarding businesses from disruptions and minimizing losses. In cybersecurity, for example (Haefner, N., et al., 2021), AI-driven systems analyze network traffic and user behavior to detect anomalies that could indicate security threats, such as data breaches or phishing attacks. By identifying patterns that deviate from normal behavior, AI can alert security teams to potential threats before they escalate. In sectors like finance, real-time fraud detection systems use AI to analyze transactions and flag suspicious activity, reducing the incidence of fraud. Credit card companies use AI to identify fraudulent transactions by detecting irregular spending patterns, allowing them to take immediate action to prevent losses. In healthcare, AI-powered predictive models help identify patients at high risk of adverse events, enabling clinicians to intervene proactively. For instance, AI can predict which patients are at risk for readmission after surgery, allowing healthcare providers to implement measures that prevent complications.AI-driven prevention is also transforming maintenance practices across industries, leading to the rise of predictive maintenance in manufacturing, utilities, and transportation. Traditionally, equipment maintenance was either reactive (conducted after a failure) or scheduled based on fixed intervals (Iansiti, M., & Lakhani, K., 2020). However, with AI, companies can implement predictive maintenance strategies that analyze equipment data to predict failures before they occur. Sensors installed on machinery capture data on temperature, vibration, and other metrics, which are then analyzed by AI algorithms to identify patterns associated with impending failures. This enables companies to perform maintenance only when necessary, reducing downtime and avoiding costly breakdowns. Businesses are also exploring ways to integrate prediction and prevention into end-to-end processes, creating smarter, interconnected systems that optimize operations in real time.(Iansiti, M., & Lakhani, K. R., 2020). For instance, in supply chain management, predictive analytics can work in tandem with preventive maintenance to ensure smooth logistics operations, while personalized customer experiences drive demand and improve satisfaction. The future of AI-driven value propositions also lies in expanding their applications through emerging. Edge AI will allow companies to process data locally on devices rather than sending it to centralized servers, enabling faster and more responsive personalization and prediction capabilities. The ongoing advancements in AI will further enhance these capabilities, leading to a future where AI-driven personalization, prediction, and prevention become indispensable components of digital transformation across industries.

AI-Enabled Revenue Streams: Subscription-Based Models and Data Monetization

AI-enabled particularly monetization, are reshaping business landscapes by unlocking new ways to drive consistent income and capitalize on data assets. Subscription-based models leverage AI to offer personalized and on-demand services that adapt to user preferences and needs, creating a sustainable, recurring revenue stream. Data monetization, meanwhile, allows companies to transform the vast amounts of data they collect into valuable insights and products, either for internal optimization or by offering it to external stakeholders. Subscription-based models have gained traction in sectors from entertainment and software to e-commerce and finance, largely due to AI's ability to enhance personalization and predict customer needs. Companies like Netflix, Spotify, and Adobe exemplify this model by offering tiered subscriptions that provide users with value-added, personalized experiences. which increases user engagement and satisfaction. Furthermore, these algorithms enable adaptive pricing models, allowing businesses to offer flexible subscription plans that align with each user's willingness to pay, often leading to higher customer retention. For instance, AI can help streaming services identify when users may be at risk of churning and offer them a discounted or customized renewal plan, thereby minimizing revenue loss. Through continuous feedback loops, subscription models driven by AI become smarter over time, optimizing both customer experience and revenue generation. AI's role in optimizing subscription-based models extends to improving the entire customer lifecycle (Jia, N., et al., 2024). By analyzing subscriber behavior, AI can pinpoint opportunities for cross-selling and upselling, thus expanding revenue per customer. For example, SaaS (Software-as-a-Service) companies use AI to suggest premium features to customers who frequently use certain tools, thereby encouraging them to upgrade their subscriptions. By leveraging the rich data they collect, companies can create new revenue streams that do not rely on traditional product sales. Indirect data monetization, while less overt than selling data to third parties, is equally transformative in driving value through AI-driven insights. Businesses can use data analytics to improve supply chain efficiency (Jorzik, P., et al., 2024), optimize pricing, and enhance product development. For instance, retailers use AI to analyze customer purchasing patterns and predict demand, allowing them to stock inventory more efficiently and reduce waste. By creating data partnerships with other companies or participating in data marketplaces, businesses can exchange valuable data insights that benefit multiple stakeholders (Kohli, R., & Melville, N. P., 2019). For example, in the transportation and logistics industry, companies share data on routes, traffic conditions, and vehicle performance, creating efficiencies across the supply chain. AI enables these platforms to manage and analyze the exchanged data in real time, providing insights that improve operational decision-making. Data marketplaces, such as those developed by major cloud providers like Google Cloud and AWS, allow companies to access high-quality datasets from diverse industries (Krakowski, S., et al., 2023). This access to third-party data enriches companies' analytics capabilities, helping them create more robust AI models and deepen their insights. By participating in data ecosystems, businesses can expand their monetization strategies and build more valuable AI-driven products and services. Despite the benefits, AI-enabled revenue models present challenges, especially privacy, Subscription-based businesses, for instance, must be cautious about collecting and analyzing personal data to ensure that they comply with privacy laws like GDPR and CCPA. Transparency and consent are crucial, as users expect companies to handle their data responsibly and provide clear opt-in and opt-out options. Data monetization also requires stringent data governance practices, particularly when sharing data with third parties. Companies must anonymize and aggregate data to protect user identities and prevent misuse. In regulated industries safeguards, transparent data policies, and adherence to industry standards, ensuring that AI-driven revenue models operate within ethical and legal boundaries. Looking to the future, AI-driven subscription models and data monetization strategies digital health, AI-powered apps will offer subscription plans that provide customized fitness routines, dietary advice, and health monitoring based on individual goals and medical history. Similarly, AI will enhance data monetization by enabling predictive insights that are more accurate and actionable. In manufacturing, AI-driven predictive analytics will use sensor data from connected devices to optimize equipment maintenance schedules and reduce operational disruptions.

Companies will also be able to monetize these predictive insights by offering them as a service to smaller businesses that lack the resources to develop in-house AI capabilities. for data-driven revenue. Edge AI, which processes data locally on devices, enables real-time analytics for subscription models that rely on immediate, context-aware services. user health metrics in real time, offering premium subscriptions for personalized health insights without the need for cloud processing. In smart homes, edge AI enables subscription-based security and automation services that respond instantly to user commands and environmental changes. IoT devices generate massive amounts of data, fueling new opportunities for data monetization, especially in industries like utilities, where grid management costs. AI-enabled revenue streams through subscription-based models and data monetization are redefining how businesses generate and sustain income. Subscription models capitalize on AI's ability to personalize and adapt services, fostering customer loyalty and generating consistent revenue. Data monetization transforms data into a valuable asset, creating new income opportunities while improving internal efficiencies. As these AI-driven revenue strategies continue to evolve, they will be shaped by advancements in AI technology, emerging data ecosystems, and regulatory landscapes. For businesses to succeed in leveraging AI for revenue generation, they must prioritize data ethics, privacy, and compliance, building trust with customers and stakeholders (Kohtamäki, M., et al., 2020). Ultimately, AI-enabled revenue models not only enhance profitability but also drive innovation, helping companies to thrive in an increasingly data-centric economy.

AI-Optimized Cost Structures: Efficiency, Automation, and Outsourcing

AI-optimized cost structures are transforming the way organizations manage expenses, achieve efficiency, and maximize resources through automation and strategic outsourcing. Leveraging artificial intelligence for cost optimization allows businesses to streamline operations, reduce redundant processes, and cut costs Moreover, AI enhances the effectiveness of outsourcing by enabling more sophisticated task delegation and monitoring, allowing organizations to focus on core functions while still maintaining control over outsourced processes. Together, AI-driven efficiency, automation, and outsourcing allow companies to build a flexible, lean cost structure that can adapt to market dynamics and drive sustained profitability.AI-driven efficiency improvements start with analyzing and optimizing operational workflows (Li, F., 2020). Inefficiencies, bottlenecks, and areas for improvement, making it possible for organizations to streamline their processes with precision. analyze patterns and forecast demand, allowing companies to maintain optimal inventory levels, reduce warehousing costs, and avoid stockouts. AI-powered analytics provide insights by AI helps companies anticipate machinery. By optimizing resource allocation and improving asset utilization, AI allows businesses to operate leaner and more efficiently, significantly impacting the bottom line. Beyond operational optimization, compliance reporting. By taking over these labor-intensive tasks, RPA reduces errors, cuts processing time, and allows employees to focus on complex, strategic activities. In customer service, AI-powered chatbots handle a large volume of routine inquiries, providing instant responses to customers while lowering the costs associated with staffing a call center. AI-driven automation also enhances quality control in manufacturing by using computer vision to inspect products in real time, identifying defects more accurately and consistently than human inspectors. As automation becomes more sophisticated, businesses can achieve higher productivity at a fraction of the cost, making AI a powerful tool for maintaining competitive cost structures., AI can analyze spending patterns and cash flow data to identify savings opportunities, such as optimizing payment terms with vendors or reducing discretionary spending (Liu, D., et al., 2017). AI-driven financial planning tools provide forecasts based on historical data, helping organizations better anticipate costs and allocate budgets efficiently. In sectors like logistics and supply chain management, monitoring capabilities of outsourced functions, AI helps companies achieve cost-effective outsourcing without compromising quality (Lysyakov, M., & Viswanathan, S., 2023). Another area where AI contributes to cost-optimized outsourcing is in workforce management. AI-driven platforms can manage workflows across multiple vendors or regions, ensuring that projects are completed efficiently and on time. For example, in software development, AI tools assist in distributing tasks to developers based on their expertise, location, and availability, reducing the time and cost associated with complex projects. For example, in response to shifts in consumer demand, AI can adjust production schedules, distribution routes, and vendor relationships in real time, ensuring that costs are minimized without sacrificing quality or availability. In the context of supply chains, AI algorithms analyze variables like transportation costs, tariffs, and vendor reliability, making it possible to pivot quickly and avoid costly disruptions. Additionally, advancements in natural language processing and computer vision will enhance AI's capabilities in understanding unstructured data, expanding its applications in fields like customer service, legal processing, and market research. In conclusion, AI-optimized cost structures—encompassing efficiency improvements, automation, and outsourcing—represent a transformative approach to managing and reducing operational costs. By streamlining processes, automating repetitive tasks, and enabling smarter outsourcing (Mariani, M., & Dwivedi, Y. K., 2024). AI empowers businesses to operate with leaner, more flexible cost structures. These AI-driven cost optimizations free up resources, enhance productivity, and enable organizations to allocate budgets strategically, ensuring they can respond swiftly to changing market demands. As AI technology continues to evolve, businesses, the long-term benefits of AI-optimized cost structures make them an invaluable asset in today's competitive

AI in Healthcare: Diagnosis, Treatment, and Patient Engagement

AI in healthcare is revolutionizing diagnosis, treatment, and patient engagement by enabling more accurate and efficient clinical decision-making, personalized treatment plans, and enhanced patient interactions. By identifying subtle changes in patient data, these .Beyond imaging, AI is being used in genomics to support precision This application has been particularly impactful in oncology, where AI-driven genomics is helping identify cancer subtypes and informing targeted therapies that can more effectively address specific genetic mutations (Mustak, M., et al., 2021). Responses to chemotherapy in cancer patients. By analyzing patient-specific factors such as age, tumor type, and genetic markers (Mukherjee, A., & Chang, H., 2023). These AI-driven tools help reduce the workload on healthcare staff by handling routine inquiries and guiding patients in managing minor health issues on their own. Additionally, AI-powered chatbots are used in mental health to provide supportive interactions and even conduct preliminary assessments, which can be a helpful resource for patients seeking immediate guidance. By offering real-time, on-demand support, AI enhances patient satisfaction and empowers individuals to take an active role in managing their health (Nambisan, S., et al., 2019). In the realm of preventive healthcare, AI contributes significantly to predicting and preventing disease by analyzing vast datasets for For instance, AI algorithms may analyze lifestyle data from wearable devices to identify patients at risk of obesity-related diseases and provide personalized recommendations for diet and exercise.

AI in Finance: Risk Management, Trading, and Customer Service

AI in finance is transforming key functions such as risk management, trading, and customer service by providing advanced analytics, predictive capabilities, and enhanced customer engagement tools. Financial institutions are increasingly leveraging AI to gain insights from massive datasets, manage risks more effectively, optimize trading strategies, and deliver personalized customer experiences. With AI's speed and analytical capabilities (Oesterreich, T. D., & Teuteberg, F., 2016) financial firms can execute sophisticated trading strategies, optimize portfolio allocations, and enhance returns in competitive markets.AI also enables more adaptive trading strategies through reinforcement learning, a subset of machine learning where algorithms learn to optimize actions based on feedback. In finance, reinforcement learning is applied to dynamically adjust trading strategies in response to changing market conditions. Compliance with regulations such as the Bank Secrecy compliance risks, automate reporting, and flag potential violations. Natural language processing (NLP) algorithms analyze regulatory documents to keep firms updated on changes in compliance requirements, helping them stay aligned with evolving regulations. In anti-money laundering (AML) compliance, AI models can detect suspicious transaction patterns that may indicate money laundering activities. By automating compliance tasks, AI enables financial institutions to reduce the cost and complexity of regulatory adherence, allowing them to focus on their core operations. Looking to the future, AI's in finance. Deep learning algorithms (Zhang, X., et al., 2022), which process data in complex layers, can improve the predictive accuracy of AI models, enabling financial institutions to better anticipate risks, price assets, and customize customer interactions.

AI in Retail: Customer Experience, Supply Chain Optimization, and Logistics

AI in retail is driving major innovations that enhance customer experience, optimize supply chains, and streamline logistics, significantly improving both operational efficiency and consumer satisfaction. With the increasing amount of consumer data available, and enhance the shopping journey. The integration of AI tools allows retailers to respond more agilely to market changes, reduce costs, and deliver seamless experiences across physical and digital platforms. As the retail industry evolves, AI is playing a pivotal role in transforming how retailers understand, interact with, and serve their customers while also optimizing internal operations to boost productivity and profitability. Customer Experience Enhancement AI's ability increases conversion rates but also fosters customer loyalty, as shoppers feel more connected to a brand that understands their needs. In addition to personalized recommendations, AI is enhancing the in-store experience with tools like smart mirrors, virtual try-ons, and conversational AI. Retailers in the fashion industry, for example, are using AI-powered augmented reality (AR) to systems are available 24/7 and can answer common questions related to product details, pricing, availability, or order status, reducing the need for customers to wait for human agents. More advanced chatbots are capable of handling complex queries, troubleshooting issues, and even making product recommendations. For instance, if a supplier is experiencing delays, AI systems can automatically suggest alternative suppliers or reorder from another distribution center to ensure continuous product availability. minimize the risk of stockouts, and improve operational efficiency. Furthermore (Wörsdörfer, M.,

2023), AI plays an important role in automating procurement processes. supplier selection and negotiate better terms, ensuring that they secure the best deals for the products they sell. AI systems also help identify new suppliers and materials based on changing consumer preferences, regulatory standards, and sustainability goals.

In addition to route optimization, AI is being applied to warehouse management systems to enhance logistics efficiency. Computer vision and robotics are helping automate various aspects of warehouse operations, from inventory tracking to product picking and packing. While there are regulatory and logistical challenges to overcome, the integration of AI into last-mile delivery promises to revolutionize solutions for both retailers and customers.AI-Driven As sustainability, AI is playing a significant role in helping retailers reduce their environmental impact (Villarroel, J. A., et al., 2013). AI technologies are being utilized to optimize energy usage, minimize waste, and support sustainable sourcing and packaging practices. For example, AI helps retailers optimize packaging, reducing the use of excess materials and supporting efforts to reduce plastic waste. AI is also instrumental in helping retailers make more sustainable product sourcing decisions by analyzing environmental and ethical factors, such as carbon emissions, water usage, and labor practices, across their supply chains, feedback, and environmental factors, AI can help retailers determine when a product should be restocked, discontinued, or replaced with a more sustainable option.

Implementing AI: Change Management, Talent Acquisition, and Training

Implementing artificial intelligence (AI) within an organization is not just about deploying new technologies but also about managing change, acquiring the right talent, and ensuring that employees are trained to work alongside AI tools. Successful Change Management for AI Implementation. AI implementation involves a significant cultural shift within an organization. Additionally, offering competitive salaries, flexible work arrangements, and opportunities for career advancement are critical to attracting and retaining top AI talent (Teece, D. J., 2018). This may involve creating specialized roles or departments dedicated to AI, making it clear that the organization values the expertise AI specialists bring to the table. Another approach to acquiring AI talent is forming partnerships with universities, research institutions, or AI labs. Many organizations sponsor research programs, Collaboration with external partners such as online education platforms, industry experts, or AI training organizations can help to deliver specialized learning experiences (Teece, D. J., 2023). This includes learning how to assess AI projects, allocate resources, and support the integration of AI into business processes. Leaders must also be capable of guiding employees through the AI adoption process and managing change effectively. Providing management with the skills and tools to lead AI initiatives is essential to overcoming resistance and ensuring successful implementation. Addressing Organizational One effective way to address resistance is to start small with AI pilot projects. These projects can demonstrate the value of AI in a controlled, low-risk environment, allowing employees to see firsthand how AI can improve processes and outcomes. By involving employees in these early-stage initiatives, companies can build trust in AI and create champions who advocate for wider adoption. Successful Conclusion

Managing AI: Ethics, Bias, and Explainability

AI systems may unintentionally favor candidates with characteristics that are overrepresented in historical data, such as white male candidates, while disadvantaging candidates from minority groups. Similarly, in the criminal justice system, AI-based risk assessment tools may inadvertently reinforce racial disparities by using biased historical data related to arrests and convictions. In healthcare, biased AI systems may provide inaccurate diagnoses or treatment recommendations for certain demographic groups, leading to unequal access to care and poorer outcomes for those affected. To address bias corrective action when needed. Developing frameworks for fairness in AI is also an important step, and various metrics, such as demographic parity or equal opportunity, can be used to assess whether AI models are treating different groups equitably. Explainability in AI Explainability, also known as interpretability or transparency, is another crucial aspect of managing AI ethically. Many AI systems, particularly deep, it is challenging to assess whether an AI system is making decisions based on valid, fair, and ethical grounds, or if the system is being influenced by hidden biases or flawed assumptions. To build trust in AI, it is essential that organizations focus on making AI decisions more understandable to human users. Explainable AI (XAI) is the field of research and development focused on creating models that provide clear, interpretable explanations for their decisions (Sullivan, Y., & Wamba, S. F., 2024). This includes setting up dedicated ethics boards or AI oversight committees that are responsible for reviewing AI projects and ensuring that they align with the organization's ethical values. Additionally, companies should prioritize ongoing training for AI developers and other stakeholders on ethical considerations and best practices for responsible AI development.

Scaling AI: Cloud Computing, Data Infrastructure, and Security

Scaling AI involves integrating advanced AI technologies into larger systems and making them capable of handling significant workloads, data, and complex tasks across varied domains. It requires a robust infrastructure, with cloud computing, data management, and security at the core of the scalability process. As organizations look to expand their AI capabilities, cloud computing has emerged as a key enabler, offering the flexibility. Infrastructure plays a crucial role in managing and storing massive datasets, ensuring their quality, and facilitating the efficient processing of data required for training AI models (Patell, H., & Jha, D., 2023). Security Scaling AI The integration of AI into sensitive business operations introduces new vulnerabilities and attack vectors, which can have serious consequences for businesses, customers, and society at large. Security in AI can be divided into several key areas: data security, model security, and operational security. Data security is paramount when scaling AI, rights and are legally compliant. This includes selecting the right cloud providers, ensuring data quality and governance, and implementing strong security protocols to protect against potential threats. By focusing on scalability and security, organizations can maximize the potential of AI, ensuring that these systems are not only powerful and efficient but also safe, reliable, and aligned with ethical standards. The successful scaling of AI opens the door to new opportunities for innovation, efficiency, and growth, allowing organizations to stay competitive in an increasingly AI-driven world.

Future Directions in AI and Business Model Innovation: Emerging Trends and Technologies

business model innovation is set to transform industries in profound ways. As artificial intelligence (AI) technologies continue to evolve, they open up new possibilities for businesses to create value, disrupt traditional business models, and drive operational efficiencies. The convergence In this rapidly changing landscape, businesses that can successfully integrate AI into their core operations will not only optimize existing processes but also unlock new revenue streams and gain a competitive edge. However, the integration of AI into business model innovation also brings challenges, such as navigating ethical concerns, ensuring data privacy and security, and developing the talent required to implement these technologies effectively. As we look ahead, it is clear that AI will continue AI-Driven Business Model Evolution At its core, unlock efficiencies, enhance personalization, enable predictive analytics, and automate processes. The transformation of business models through AI can be categorized into three primary areas: customer value propositions, revenue generation, and cost structures. better efficiency. Furthermore, AI enables new revenue streams through subscription-based models, data monetization, and AI-as-a-service offerings. Customer value propositions are evolving in response to AI's capabilities to create highly personalized experiences. AI enables businesses to leverage customer data more effectively, providing tailored recommendations, targeted marketing, and customized products and services (Oscherwitz, T., & Löffler, C., 2024). This allows businesses to create deeper connections with their customers, offering personalized experiences that drive loyalty and improve customer retention. In healthcare, AI-powered AR tools can assist surgeons by overlaying critical patient information and visualizations during procedures, enhancing decision-making and precision (Verganti, R., et al., 2020). The integration of AI and AR offers businesses the opportunity to create new customer experiences, streamline operations, and differentiate themselves in competitive markets.

CONCLUSION

Challenges in Scaling AI While companies stay at the forefront of AI advancements. stored, and used. Businesses must ensure that they comply with regulations such as the GDPR and other data protection laws while also taking steps to secure customer data from cyberattacks and breaches. AI systems are fair, transparent, and accountable. This may involve implementing explainability and transparency measures to ensure that AI decisions can be understood and justified, as well as establishing safeguards to detect and mitigate bias in AI models. Ethical considerations will also extend to issues such as the impact of AI on jobs and the workforce, with businesses needing to find ways to balance automation with human employment. Business model innovation is nothing short of transformative, driving profound shifts across industries and altering the way organizations interact with customers, operate internally, and create value. AI technologies, ranging from machine learning (ML) and natural language processing (NLP) to computer vision, robotics, and predictive analytics, provide businesses with The intersection of AI with emerging technologies like blockchain, the Internet of Things (IoT), and augmented reality (AR) is expanding the scope of AI applications, allowing businesses to rethink traditional models and create more agile, customer-centric approaches. AI's impact on business model innovation is most evident in how it enables businesses to reimagine their customer value propositions. With AI, businesses can deliver hyper-personalized experiences, adapting their offerings based on data-driven insights that predict customer behavior and needs. AI allows companies to move away from static, one-size-fits-all models toward dynamic, personalized services that improve customer satisfaction, drive engagement, and foster loyalty. This ability to tailor products, services, and communications at an individual level is reshaping industries such as retail, healthcare, finance, and entertainment, where customer experience is a major differentiator. Moreover, AI is revolutionizing business operations by enabling automation, optimizing processes, and reducing operational costs. AI-powered tools and systems are streamlining complex workflows, handling repetitive tasks, and improving the efficiency of supply chains, customer service, and back-office operations. For example, in sectors like manufacturing, AI-driven automation allows for predictive maintenance, real-time inventory management, and quality control, leading to reduced downtime and improved operational efficiency.AI is also playing a pivotal role in the development of new business models and revenue generation strategies. The advent of AI-as-a-service (AIaaS), subscription-based models, and data monetization is opening up new revenue streams for organizations. AIaaS platforms allow businesses in themselves, with businesses tapping into new opportunities for data monetization. The ability to monetize customer data through AI-powered analytics not only creates new revenue sources but also helps businesses unlock the potential of vast amounts of previously untapped information.

REFERENCES

Aagaard, A. (2019). *Digital business models—Driving transformation and innovation*. Palgrave Macmillan. DOI: 10.1007/978-3-319-96902-2

Abou-Foul, M., Ruiz-Alba, J. L., & López-Tenorio, P. J. (2023). The impact of artificial intelligence capabilities on servitization: The moderating role of absorptive capacity—A dynamic capabilities perspective. *Journal of Business Research*, 157, 113609. DOI: 10.1016/j.jbusres.2022.113609

Act, E. U. A. I. (2023). https://digital-strategy.ec.europa.eu/en/policies/regulatory-framework-ai

Agrawal, A., Gans, J., & Goldfarb, A. (2018). Prediction, judgment, and complexity: A theory of decision-making and artificial intelligence. In *The economics of artificial intelligence: An agenda* (pp. 89–110). University of Chicago Press.

Akter, S., Hossain, M. A., Sajib, S., Sultana, S., Rahman, M., Vrontis, D., & McCarthy, G. (2023). A framework for AI-powered service innovation capability: Review and agenda for future research. *Technovation*, 125, 102768. DOI: 10.1016/j.technovation.2023.102768

Bahoo, S., Cucculelli, M., & Qamar, D. (2023). Artificial intelligence and corporate innovation: A review and research agenda. *Technological Forecasting and Social Change*, 188, 122264. DOI: 10.1016/j.techfore.2022.122264

Balsmeier, B., & Woerter, M. (2019). Is this time different? How digitalization influences job creation and destruction. *Research Policy*, 48(8), 103765. DOI: 10.1016/j.respol.2019.03.010

Bankins, S., Ocampo, A. C., Marrone, M., Restubog, S. L. D., & Woo, S. E. (2023). A multilevel review of artificial intelligence in organizations: Implications for organizational behavior research and practice. *Journal of Organizational Behavior*, 45(2), 159–182. DOI: 10.1002/job.2735

Benner, M. J., & Waldfogel, J. (2023). Changing the channel: Digitization and the rise of "middle tail" strategies. *Strategic Management Journal*, 44(1), 264–287. DOI: 10.1002/smj.3130

Cennamo, C., Dagnino, G. B., Di Minin, A., & Lanzolla, G. (2020). Managing digital transformation: Scope of transformation and modalities of value co-generation and delivery. *California Management Review*, 62(4), 5–16. DOI: 10.1177/0008125620942136

Chatterjee, S., Sarker, S., & Valacich, J. S. (2015). The behavioral roots of information systems security: Exploring key factors related to unethical IT use. *Journal of Management Information Systems*, 31(4), 49–87. DOI: 10.1080/07421222.2014.1001257

Chesbrough, H. W., & Tucci, C. L. (2020). The interplay between open innovation and lean startup, or, why large companies are not large versions of startups. *Strategic Management Review*, 1(2), 277–303. DOI: 10.1561/111.00000013

Cockburn, I. M., Henderson, R., & Stern, S. (2018). The impact of artificial intelligence on innovation: An exploratory analysis. In *The economics of artificial intelligence: An agenda* (pp. 115–146). University of Chicago Press.

Davenport, T. H., & Ronanki, R. (2018). Artificial intelligence for the real world. *Harvard Business Review*, 96(1), 108–116.

Ferràs-Hernández, X., Nylund, P. A., & Brem, A. (2023). The emergence of dominant designs in artificial intelligence. *California Management Review*, 65(3). DOI: 10.1177/00081256231164362

Figueroa-Armijos, M., Clark, B. B., & da Motta Veiga, S. P. (2023). Ethical perceptions of AI in hiring and organizational trust: The role of performance expectancy and social influence. *Journal of Business Ethics*, 186(1), 179–197. DOI: 10.1007/s10551-022-05166-2

Forbes. (2023, July 24). The difference between generative AI and traditional AI: An easy explanation by Bernard Marr. https://www.forbes.com/sites/bernardmarr/2023/07/24/the-difference-between-generative-ai-and-traditional-ai-an-easy-explanation-for-anyone/?sh=1260f473508a

Gama, F., & Magistretti, S. (2023). Artificial intelligence in innovation management: A review of innovation capabilities and a taxonomy of AI applications. *Journal of Product Innovation Management*, 1–16. DOI: 10.1111/jpim.12698

Garbuio, M., & Lin, N. (2019). Artificial intelligence as a growth engine for health care startups: Emerging business models. *California Management Review*, 61(2), 59–83. DOI: 10.1177/0008125618811931

Gartner. (n.d.). Beyond ChatGPT: The future of generative AI for enterprises. Retrieved February 28, 2024, from https://www.gartner.com/en/articles/beyond-chatgpt-the-future-of-generative-ai-for-enterprises

Haefner, N., Wincent, J., Parida, V., & Gassmann, O. (2021). Artificial intelligence and innovation management: A review, framework, and research agenda. *Technological Forecasting and Social Change*, 162, 120392. DOI: 10.1016/j.techfore.2020.120392

Haenlein, M., & Kaplan, A. (2019). A brief history of artificial intelligence: On the past, present, and future of artificial intelligence. *California Management Review*, 61(4), 5–14. DOI: 10.1177/0008125619864925

Iansiti, M., & Lakhani, K. (2020a, January–February). Competing in the age of artificial intelligence. Harvard Business Press.

Iansiti, M., & Lakhani, K. R. (2020b). Competing in the age of AI: How machine intelligence changes the rules of business. *Harvard Business Review*, 98(1), 60–67.

Jia, N., Luo, X., Fang, Z., & Liao, C. (2024). When and how artificial intelligence augments employee creativity. *Academy of Management Journal*, 67(1), 5–32. DOI: 10.5465/amj.2022.0426

Jorzik, P., Klein, S. P., Kanbach, D. K., & Kraus, S. (2024). AI-driven business model innovation: A systematic review and research agenda. *Journal of Business Research*, 182, 114764. DOI: 10.1016/j.jbusres.2024.114764

Kohli, R., & Melville, N. P. (2019). Digital innovation: A review and synthesis. *Information Systems Journal*, 29(1), 200–223. DOI: 10.1111/isj.12193

Kohtamäki, M., Parida, V., Patel, P. C., & Gebauer, H. (2020). The relationship between digitalization and servitization: The role of servitization in capturing the financial potential of digitalization. *Technological Forecasting and Social Change*, 151, 119804. DOI: 10.1016/j.techfore.2019.119804

Krakowski, S., Luger, J., & Raisch, S. (2023). Artificial intelligence and the changing sources of competitive advantage. *Strategic Management Journal*, 44(6), 1425–1452. DOI: 10.1002/smj.3387

Li, F. (2020). The digital transformation of business models in the creative industries: A holistic framework and emerging trends. *Technovation*, 92, 102012. DOI: 10.1016/j.technovation.2017.12.004

Liu, D., Gong, Y., Zhou, J., & Huang, J. (2017). Human resource systems, employee creativity, and firm innovation: The moderating role of firm ownership. *Academy of Management Journal*, 60(3), 1164–1188. DOI: 10.5465/amj.2015.0230

Lysyakov, M., & Viswanathan, S. (2023). Threatened by AI: Analyzing users' responses to the introduction of AI in a crowd-sourcing platform. *Information Systems Research*, 34(3), 1191–1210. DOI: 10.1287/isre.2022.1184

Mariani, M., & Dwivedi, Y. K. (2024). Generative artificial intelligence in innovation management: A preview of future research developments. *Journal of Business Research*, 175, 114542. DOI: 10.1016/j.jbusres.2024.114542

Mukherjee, A., & Chang, H. (2023). Managing the Creative frontier of generative AI: The novelty-usefulness tradeoff. *California Management Review.*

Mustak, M., Salminen, J., Plé, L., & Wirtz, J. (2021). Artificial intelligence in marketing: Topic modeling, scientometric analysis, and research agenda. *Journal of Business Research*, 124, 389–404. DOI: 10.1016/j.jbusres.2020.10.044

Nambisan, S., Wright, M., & Feldman, M. (2019). The digital transformation of innovation and entrepreneurship: Progress, challenges and key themes. *Research Policy*, 48(8), 103773. DOI: 10.1016/j.respol.2019.03.018

Oesterreich, T. D., & Teuteberg, F. (2016). Understanding the implications of Industry 4.0: A review of the research agenda. *Computers in Industry*, 83, 121–137. DOI: 10.1016/j.compind.2016.09.006

Oscherwitz, T., & Löffler, C. (2024). A conceptual framework for AI-driven innovation: Shaping the business model of the future. *Journal of Business Research*, 182, 114767.

Patell, H., & Jha, D. (2023). Evolution and trends in artificial intelligence applications in supply chain management: A comprehensive review. *International Journal of Operations & Production Management*, 43(5), 1079–1109.

Sullivan, Y., & Wamba, S. F. (2024). Artificial intelligence and adaptive response to market changes: A strategy to enhance firm performance and innovation. *Journal of Business Research*, 174, 114500. DOI: 10.1016/j.jbusres.2024.114500

Teece, D. J. (2018). Profiting from innovation in the digital economy: Standards, complementary assets, and business models in the wireless world. *Research Policy*, 47, 1367–1387. DOI: 10.1016/j.respol.2017.01.015

Teece, D. J. (2023). Big tech and strategic management: How management scholars can inform competition policy. *The Academy of Management Perspectives*, 37(1), 1–15. DOI: 10.5465/amp.2022.0013

Verganti, R., Vendraminelli, L., & Iansiti, M. (2020). Innovation and design in the age of artificial intelligence. *Journal of Product Innovation Management*, 37(3), 212–227. DOI: 10.1111/jpim.12523

Villarroel, J. A., Taylor, J. E., & Tucci, C. L. (2013). Innovation and learning performance implications of free revealing and knowledge brokering in competing communities: Insights from the Netflix Prize challenge. *Computational & Mathematical Organization Theory*, 19(1), 42–77. DOI: 10.1007/s10588-012-9137-7

Wörsdörfer, M. (2023). The EU's artificial intelligence act: An ordoliberal assessment. *AI and Ethics*, 1–16.

Zhang, X., Guo, X., Yue, W. T., & Yu, Y. (2022). Servitization for the environment? The impact of data-centric product-service models. *Journal of Management Information Systems*, 39(4), 1146–1183. DOI: 10.1080/07421222.2022.2127454

Chapter 10
A Structural Equation Modelling-Based View of Artificial Intelligence:
Business Models and the Future of Employment From an Indian Perspective

Souvik Banerjee
https://orcid.org/0000-0001-9988-8887
Management Development Institute Murshidabad, India

Abhijit Pandit
Management Development Institute Murshidabad, India

ABSTRACT

This study examines the transformative effects of artificial intelligence (AI) on business structures and employment in India. This study employs structural equation modelling (SEM) to evaluate the impact of AI on operational efficiency, company innovation, and employment dynamics. Research demonstrates that AI dramatically improves corporate efficiency and innovation but also requires staff reskilling. This research elucidates methods for Indian enterprises to adeptly incorporate AI to sustain a competitive advantage, while urging governments to facilitate AI-oriented workforce development. Future study should concentrate on the long-term employment implications of AI and investigate viable reskilling methodologies.

DOI: 10.4018/979-8-3693-9571-4.ch010

INTRODUCTION

Artificial Intelligence (AI) is transforming global business operations by revolutionizing automation, enhancing data-driven decision-making, and improving customer engagement (Brynjolfsson & McAfee, 2014). AI-driven technologies are playing a critical role in reshaping industries by enabling organizations to optimize their supply chains, streamline decision-making processes, and improve operational efficiency (Abu-Rumman et al., 2024). This transformation is particularly significant in emerging economies such as India, where rapid technological adoption is creating new opportunities while simultaneously presenting significant challenges across industries such as manufacturing, retail, and services (Chui, Manyika, & Miremadi, 2018).

As AI continues to evolve, its implications extend beyond operational enhancements, influencing workforce dynamics and employment structures in profound ways (Winarko et al., 2019). The integration of AI in business operations is altering traditional business models by introducing automation, predictive analytics, and real-time data insights that facilitate improved decision-making. Organizations are increasingly leveraging AI to enhance customer interactions, personalize services, and improve overall operational agility (Fanoberova & Kuczkowska, 2016).

In the Indian context, AI adoption is accelerating across various industries, helping businesses align with global digital transformation trends while also adapting to local economic and consumer behavior patterns. However, despite the clear benefits, the increased reliance on AI raises concerns regarding job displacement, requiring a strategic approach to workforce reskilling and adaptation (Li & Suh, 2015). The impact of AI on employment is complex, as it simultaneously eliminates routine tasks while generating new roles that demand advanced technological skills and digital literacy (Jarrahi, 2018).

The impact of AI on the workforce is characterized by a dual effect—while certain job functions become redundant due to automation, AI-driven transformations also create new employment opportunities that necessitate upskilling (Alhammadi & Alshurideh, 2024). Studies indicate that the shift towards an AI-integrated workforce requires employees to develop competencies in data management, algorithmic analysis, and AI-assisted decision-making (Winarko et al., 2019). In India, where the labor market is diverse and includes a mix of skilled and unskilled workers, AI's penetration into business processes demands a balanced strategy for reskilling initiatives to mitigate potential job losses.

AI's ability to enhance efficiency and drive productivity depends largely on how businesses manage this workforce transition, ensuring that employees are equipped with the necessary skills to work alongside AI systems (Jarrahi, 2018). The concept of a hybrid workforce—where human expertise is complemented by AI capabilities—has emerged as a crucial model for sustaining competitive advantage in AI-driven industries (Alhammadi & Alshurideh, 2024).

To systematically assess the relationship between AI adoption, business efficiency, and employment trends in India, this study employs Structural Equation Modeling (SEM). SEM is widely used in AI research for its ability to analyze complex, multi-variable relationships, evaluating both direct and indirect effects in a structured framework (Andersson, Kreegimäe, & Niiranen, 2019). This methodological approach enables researchers to capture how AI adoption impacts business models by considering variables such as trust, customer engagement, and operational processes (Ransbotham et al., 2020). In this study, a quantitative approach is utilized to examine AI's perceived utility and its influence on operational efficiency, innovation, and workforce transformation across a sample of managers, business owners, and employees working in AI-driven organizations in India.

Using SEM analysis tools such as SMART PLS, key model fit indices—including the Comparative Fit Index (CFI) and the Root Mean Square Error of Approximation (RMSEA)—are employed to ensure robust statistical analysis. Additionally, demographic factors such as gender, experience, and industry sector are considered to understand their moderating effects on AI adoption and employment outcomes. Understanding AI's influence on India's economic landscape is critical for both industry leaders and policymakers. With Indian businesses increasingly integrating AI into their operations, it is imperative to develop effective reskilling strategies to bridge the skill gap and prepare the workforce for AI-powered workplaces (Li & Suh, 2015).

Policymakers, educational institutions, and businesses must collaborate to design training programs that equip workers with AI-relevant skills, ensuring long-term workforce sustainability. The findings of this study will contribute valuable insights into the strategic deployment of AI in India, emphasizing the need for a balanced approach that fosters both technological innovation and human capital development. By aligning AI adoption with workforce preparedness, organizations can not only sustain competitiveness but also ensure inclusive economic growth in an AI-driven era.

Literature Review

This section analysis offers an extensive examination of the transformative implications of Artificial Intelligence (AI) on business models, the future of employment, and the methodology employed to investigate these impacts, especially within the Indian context.

Artificial intelligence has profoundly transformed conventional business models through the facilitation of automation, predictive analytics, and improved consumer involvement, thus enhancing efficiencies across multiple sectors. Abu-Rumman et al.

(2024) examine the incorporation of AI in commercial operations, emphasizing its function in optimizing procedures and improving decision-making abilities. In India, the utilization of AI encompasses various sectors, including manufacturing and retail, where enterprises employ AI to enhance supply chain management, improve client relationships, and provide personalized services (Chui, Manyika, & Miremadi, 2018). This transition to AI-driven business models signifies a worldwide trend towards data utilization and customer-centric strategies (Fanoberova & Kuczkowska, 2016). AI applications are progressively linked to consumer happiness and personalization, rendering data an essential tool in improving customer connections.

The influence of AI transcends business paradigms, affecting the essence of work and prompting critical enquiries over job displacement and the emergence of new employment opportunities. Winarko et al. (2019) emphasize AI's transformative capacity, indicating that it is poised to modify employment roles and need the acquisition of new competencies. The dualistic character of AI's influence is seen in the Indian labor market, as regular employment is threatened by automation. However, AI allows employees to concentrate on more valuable jobs, enhancing productivity and encouraging innovation within organizations (Brynjolfsson & McAfee, 2014). Nonetheless, these shifts require significant investment in reskilling and upskilling, as emphasized by Li and Suh (2015), who contend that workforce adaption to AI-driven job roles is crucial for sustaining competitiveness. Alhammadi and Alshurideh (2024) assert that the future workforce should integrate both AI and human talents to maximize the advantages of AI, hence maintaining a competitive advantage that harmonizes technology with human proficiency.

The research use Structural Equation Modelling (SEM), a technique that has gained significance in examining the intricate links among AI adoption, company efficiency, and employment dynamics. Structural Equation Modelling (SEM) allows researchers to manage complex connections and examine both direct and indirect impacts within a unified framework (Andersson, Kreegimäe, & Niiranen, 2019). In AI research, SEM has been vital in evaluating aspects like trustworthiness and source credibility, essential for comprehending the larger implications of AI applications on business models and employment. Ransbotham et al. (2020) assert that the adoption of AI must match with strategic objectives, and SEM offers a robust methodology to examine these dynamics and evaluate their overall influence on enterprises.

In India, the implementation of AI has compelled different sectors to reassess their business methods. This change presents hurdles, as organizations must confront issues of trust, data security, and workforce preparedness. Artificial Intelligence necessitates a paradigm shift, compelling firms to implement nimble and adaptable structures to maintain competitiveness in a swiftly evolving technology environment (Abu-Rumman et al., 2024). Furthermore, the use of AI introduces ethical problems, especially with data privacy and security, which must be addressed to establish public trust in AI-driven solutions (Fanoberova & Kuczkowska, 2016).

The significance of AI in improving operational efficiency is paramount. The ability of AI to analyze extensive data sets allows organizations to enhance procedures, save expenses, and refine decision-making. The influence of AI on operational efficiency is particularly significant in data-dependent sectors, such as banking and healthcare, where predictive analytics and automation enhance operations (Chui, Manyika, & Miremadi, 2018). The efficacy of AI-driven business models mostly hinges on the integration of AI with current systems, necessitating strategic planning and infrastructure investment (Li & Suh, 2015).

Besides its operational advantages, AI fosters innovation by facilitating new business models that leverage emerging technologies like machine learning and natural language processing. As AI advances, it is set to generate value by allowing firms to adapt more swiftly to market demands, thereby promoting a culture of ongoing enhancement and innovation (Jarrahi, 2018). The influence of AI on innovation is intricate, as organizations must balance the utilization of AI for efficiency with the promotion of creativity among human employees. Literature indicates that although AI can improve operational efficiency, it may unintentionally hinder innovation if it results in inflexible automated processes that restrict human participation (Andersson et al., 2019).

Job displacement poses a significant and contentious challenge related to AI. Winarko et al. (2019) demonstrate that although AI is expected to eliminate specific work roles, it concurrently generates opportunities in sectors necessitating sophisticated technological expertise. This development has prompted demands for legislative interventions that facilitate workforce retraining to equip individuals for positions in an AI-driven economy. The Indian government's emphasis on digital literacy and vocational training efforts demonstrates a recognition of the necessity to provide people with skills essential for future job markets (Abu-Rumman et al., 2024).

To facilitate a seamless transition to an AI-integrated workforce, educational institutions, policymakers, and enterprises must collaborate on reskilling initiatives that correspond with changing job demands. Research indicates that workforce preparedness for AI necessitates not just technical expertise but also the development of critical thinking, creativity, and adaptability abilities (Alhammadi & Alshurideh, 2024). These non-technical skills enhance AI capabilities, fostering a workforce adept at managing and collaborating with AI systems.

The research highlights AI's dual function as a driver of operational efficiency and a disruptive influence in the labor market. Artificial intelligence is transforming the business environment by facilitating innovative models that emphasize client engagement, data-driven insights, and optimized procedures. This transition requires a proactive strategy for workforce adaption, wherein reskilling and upskilling are crucial to tackle the issues of job displacement and automation. This literature study underscores the necessity for a balanced strategy in AI adoption that utilizes AI's efficiencies while promoting a collaborative environment where human skills are integral to innovation and creativity.

AI and Business Models

Artificial intelligence is radically altering conventional business models through the facilitation of automation, predictive analytics, and improved consumer engagement. Abu-Rumman et al. (2024) examine how the incorporation of AI enables companies to optimize operations and enhance decision-making processes. In India, sectors including manufacturing and retail are integrating AI to streamline supply chain management, improve customer relations, and provide tailored services. AI-driven models prioritize data utilization and customer-centricity, in accordance with worldwide trends.

AI and Future of Work

The influence of AI on the labor market encompasses both job displacement and the generation of new employment opportunities. Research by Winarko et al. (2019) underscores the transformative capacity of AI, expected to alter employment opportunities and require new competencies. In India, although mundane operations may be automated, AI allows workers to concentrate on higher-value activities, enhancing productivity and innovation. This change necessitates reskilling and upskilling activities, as detailed by Li & Suh (2015). Alhammadi & Alshurideh (2024) contend that a hybrid workforce, integrating AI with human competencies, is crucial for future competitiveness.

Structural Equation Modeling in AI Research

Structural Equation Modelling (SEM) is progressively employed to elucidate intricate links in AI adoption. Andersson et al. (2019) illustrate the effectiveness of SEM in assessing variables such as trustworthiness and source reliability in AI applications. This study employs SEM to evaluate the influence of AI on corporate efficiency, innovation, and job roles, offering a comprehensive analytical framework to examine both direct and indirect effects.

Research Methodology

This study utilizes a quantitative approach, applying Structural Equation Modelling (SEM) to evaluate the impact of artificial intelligence (AI) on business models and future employment in India. The research seeks to analyze the impact of AI integration on operational efficiency, innovation, and workplace dynamics across diverse industries. A survey was administered to 100 participants, comprising managers, business owners, and employees from AI-driven organizations across several sectors in India. This sample exemplifies a heterogeneous cohort of professionals whose encounters with AI in their organizations yield significant insights about the technology's perceived advantages and obstacles.

The survey instrument was developed to assess various critical dimensions of AI's influence on business and employment. Participants were requested to assess the perceived value of AI inside their organizations, specifically on its function in enhancing operational efficiency and fostering corporate creativity. The study also examined expected alterations in work dynamics, particularly regarding AI's potential to modify job responsibilities, generate new positions, or necessitate reskilling. The survey aims to offer a comprehensive perspective on AI's influence in creating contemporary business models and workforce dynamics in India by concentrating on these topics.

To address potential demographic variances, moderating variables like gender, years of experience, and industry type were integrated into the analysis. This method facilitates an analysis of how demographic characteristics may affect views of AI's utility and its influence on workplace dynamics. Variations in experience levels or industrial contexts may influence participants' perceptions of AI's role in innovation and operational optimization, along with their opinions on job transformation and reskilling needs.

Population The study's target population comprises professionals engaged in AI-driven organisations in India, including managers, business proprietors, and employees. These experts offer significant insights on the effects of AI on business models and job dynamics, encompassing several sectors like manufacturing, retail, and services.

Sampling Technique The research utilises a purposive sampling method. This non-probability strategy was selected to guarantee that participants possess pertinent experience and exposure to AI application within their organisations. This methodology guarantees that the gathered data is pertinent and significant for evaluating the effects of AI.

Sample Size The study included a sample size of 100 people. The decision aimed to balance analytical depth with data collecting feasibility, ensuring adequate data for Structural Equation Modelling (SEM) analysis while preserving statistical reliability.

This research utilises Structural Equation Modelling (SEM) to examine the influence of Artificial Intelligence (AI) on company models and workforce dynamics in India. Although bigger sample sizes are typically favoured for SEM to guarantee statistical robustness, a sample size of 100 participants has been deemed acceptable due to practical limitations concerning data collecting feasibility and participant relevance. The research targets professionals with direct exposure to AI, encompassing managers, business proprietors, and personnel from AI-centric organisations. Due to the specific focus of the sample, purposive sampling guarantees that the data obtained is highly pertinent to the study's aims, albeit the restricted sample size.

A reduced sample size in SEM research might nevertheless produce significant insights if the study design is meticulously structured. Partial Least Squares SEM (PLS-SEM) via SMART PLS is especially advantageous for small sample sizes, since it adeptly manages intricate models with constrained data while preserving analytical accuracy. This research incorporates moderating variables including gender, experience, and industry type, ensuring the analysis reflects variances in AI adoption and workforce adaption. A bigger sample may enhance generalisability; however, the existing sample offers a robust basis for exploratory observations, emphasising significant trends in AI's influence across several industries.

The selection of 100 participants strikes a balance between analytical depth and feasibility, guaranteeing the generation of solid statistical models while maintaining the study's methodological rigour. Larger sample sizes (300-500) are optimal for extensive generalisation; nonetheless, the research-controlled approach and emphasis on pertinent respondents enhance the validity of its conclusions. Furthermore, by utilising model fit criteria as the Comparative Fit Index (CFI) and the Root Mean Square Error of Approximation (RMSEA), the study guarantees the statistical validity of the results, despite a limited sample size.

This study prioritises data quality over quantity, accepting the limitations of a smaller sample while ensuring that the insights derived are contextually rich and methodologically robust. Future research may increase the sample size to improve generalisability; nonetheless, for this exploratory investigation, the selected methodology offers a practical equilibrium of depth, feasibility, and statistical rigour.

Data Collection Techniques The data was gathered by a standardised survey questionnaire administered to the chosen participants. The study included questions aimed at assessing many dimensions of AI's influence, such as operational efficiency, innovation, and employment dynamics. Demographic data, including gender, years of experience, and industry type, was gathered to investigate moderating influences.

Data Analysis Tools The investigation utilised SMART PLS, a sophisticated software for Partial Least Squares Structural Equation Modelling (PLS-SEM). This tool was chosen for its capacity to manage intricate interactions including latent variables. The constructs' reliability and validity were assessed using metrics like

Cronbach's Alpha, Composite Reliability (CR), and Average Variance Extracted (AVE). Model fit criteria such as the Comparative Fit Index (CFI), Tucker-Lewis Index (TLI), and Root Mean Square Error of Approximation (RMSEA) were employed to evaluate the congruence between the model and the observed data.

Research Hypotheses:

H1: AI influences Business Efficiency.

H2: AI influences Innovation.

H3: AI influences Job Dynamics.

H4: Business Efficiency influences Job Dynamics

H5: Innovation influences Job Dynamics

The hypotheses presented (H1–H5) are justified based on the literature review, as follows:

H1: AI influences Business Efficiency

The literature review extensively discusses how AI enhances business efficiency through automation, predictive analytics, and optimized processes. Abu-Rumman et al. (2024) highlight AI's significance in improving decision-making and optimizing processes in numerous industries, including manufacturing and retail. Chui, Manyika, & Miremadi (2018) emphasize AI's contribution to supply chain management and customer service efficiency. AI's ability to process massive datasets and automate routine processes leads to cost savings and enhanced operational procedures, verifying this notion.

H2: AI influences Innovation

The review states that AI fosters innovation by facilitating new business models through emerging technologies such as machine learning and natural language processing (Jarrahi, 2018). AI enables firms to respond rapidly to market demands, encouraging a culture of continuous innovation. However, Andersson et al. (2019) caution that excessive automation can stifle creativity if rigid AI-driven processes replace human ingenuity. Despite this, the literature supports the view that AI drives innovation by allowing firms to leverage data-driven insights and adapt swiftly to changes.

H3: AI influences Job Dynamics

AI's transformative impact on employment is discussed by Winarko et al. (2019), who highlight how AI automates routine tasks while also creating opportunities for new skill-based roles. Brynjolfsson & McAfee (2014) assert that AI-driven automation enhances productivity but necessitates workforce adaptation. The Indian labor market faces both job displacement and upskilling challenges (Li & Suh, 2015). The government's digital literacy initiatives (Abu-Rumman et al., 2024) further illustrate AI's direct influence on job roles and employment structures.

H4: Business Efficiency influences Job Dynamics

As AI enhances company efficiency (H1), the impact on employment is unavoidable. Higher efficiency frequently leads to workforce reorganization, lowering the need for repetitive tasks while boosting need for strategic and analytical jobs (Winarko et al., 2019). Abu-Rumman et al. (2024) discuss how Indian industries are adapting to AI-driven efficiencies by investing in workforce reskilling, indicating a direct link between business efficiency and job dynamics.

H5: Innovation influences Job Dynamics

AI-driven innovation alters job roles by introducing new skills and competencies. Alhammadi & Alshurideh (2024) argue that future employment structures will integrate AI with human intelligence, requiring workers to develop technical and adaptive skills. Organizations leveraging AI for innovation must invest in employee retraining (Li & Suh, 2015), demonstrating that AI-fueled innovation directly affects job creation, transformation, and displacement.

The hypotheses align with the literature, demonstrating AI's influence on business efficiency, innovation, and job dynamics. Structural Equation Modeling (SEM), as used in AI research, allows for evaluating these interconnected relationships within a comprehensive analytical framework (Andersson et al., 2019).

This methodological approach offers a robust framework for examining the impact of AI on Indian business models and workforce change. The study integrates SEM with moderating variables and rigorous assessments of reliability and validity, providing significant insights into the impact of AI integration on organizational efficiency, innovation, and the redefinition of work roles within a rising economy.

Results

Analyzing the central tendency, variable like "Age" represents authentic distributions within their respective contexts. The mean age of 41.54 and a median of 42 suggest a reasonably mature group, with participants aged between 20 and 60. The average years of experience is 1.99, suggesting that the sample comprises individuals with diverse experience levels, while a greater number of participants likely possess lower experience, as evidenced by the maximum value of 3.

Indicators connected to AI, like "AI Usefulness," "AI Efficiency," and "Job Displacement Concern," offer insights into perceptions and apprehensions about artificial intelligence. The average values for these factors are typically near the scale midpoint, indicating modest perceptions or apprehensions regarding AI's role and influence. The means for "AI Usefulness" and "AI Efficiency" are 2.84 and 2.98, respectively, on a scale of 1 to 5, indicating that participants perceive AI as moderately useful and efficient, but not significantly so. The "Job Displacement Concern" metric, with a mean score of 3.19, reflects a modest apprehension about the possible effects of AI on employment security.

The skewness and kurtosis numbers provide further insights into the distribution of each metric. The negative skewness ratings for various AI-related indicators, such as "AI Usefulness" and "AI Efficiency," indicate a modest inclination for respondents to assess these items above the midpoint of the scale. Excess kurtosis measurements facilitate the evaluation of the distribution's "tailed Ness," with values around zero signifying a normal distribution. For most indicators, kurtosis values are negative, indicating distributions that are relatively flat in comparison to the normal distribution, although none exhibit considerable deviation.

The Cramér-von Mises p-values offer a statistical assessment for normality. Most indicators reveal a p-value of 0.000, signifying statistically significant departures from normality. This may indicate non-normal distributions for various indicators; nonetheless, it is not unusual in SEM to encounter non-normally distributed data, especially with attitudinal scales and ordinal variables.

The indicator table indicates a sample that exhibits moderate perspectives on AI, characterized by a somewhat balanced distribution of age, education, and employment level. The statistical features underscore significant factors, like probable skewness in AI-related perceptions and the existence of non-normal distributions, which may affect model outcomes. Data dispersion and distribution features must be considered in the interpretation of SEM results, particularly when evaluating the fit and validity of the proposed model.

Figure 1. Structural Equation Modelling

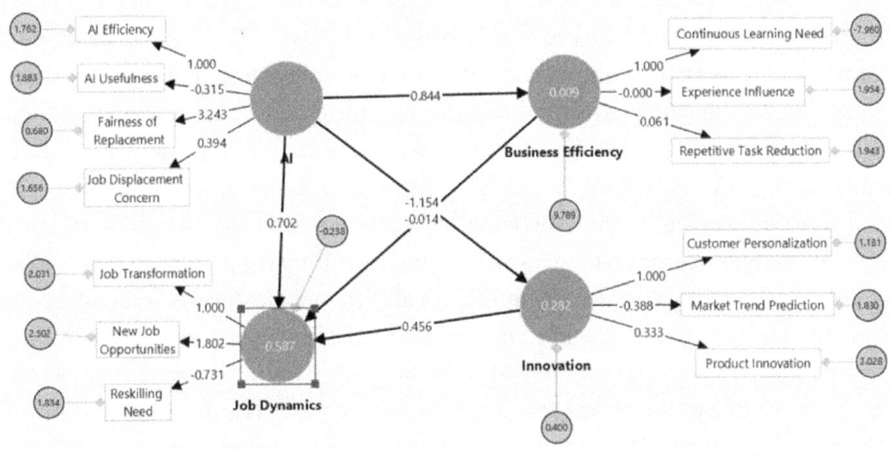

Figure 1 illustrates a structural equation model (SEM) depicting the interrelations among several latent components, which appear to reflect the influence of Artificial Intelligence (AI) on employment dynamics, organizational efficiency, and creativity. This model consists of several latent constructs, each characterized by a collection of indicators that elucidate the intricate impact of AI on various aspects of the workplace.

The initial component, AI, encompasses indications including AI Efficiency, AI Usefulness, Fairness of Replacement, and Concerns Regarding Job Displacement. Every indicator is linked to a path coefficient, reflecting its influence on the AI construct (e.g., 1.000, -0.315). These factors represent perspectives about AI's involvement in the workplace, encompassing both its advantages and apprehensions over equity and job displacement. The Job Dynamics construct includes indicators such as Job Transformation, New Job Opportunities, and the Need for Reskilling. The construct value for Job Dynamics is -0.587, indicating a likely adverse effect, which may signify difficulties or disturbances in job functions attributable to AI. Business Efficiency encompasses metrics such as Continuous Learning Need, Experience Influence, and Repetitive Task Reduction, with a construct value of 0.009, signifying a negligible or neutral effect on business efficiency. Ultimately, innovation is characterized by customer personalization, market trend forecasting, and product development. The construct value of 0.282 indicates a positive correlation with innovation, suggesting that AI may contribute to innovative endeavors, albeit to a limited extent.

Examining the connections across these constructs uncovers multiple correlations. The path coefficient from AI to company Efficiency is positive (0.844), indicating that advancements in AI lead to increased company efficiency. The correlation between AI and innovation is negative (-1.154), indicating that AI may adversely affect innovation in this setting, either due to perceived risks or constraints in its capacity to promote new solutions. The positive correlation (0.702) from AI to employment Dynamics suggests that AI impacts alterations in employment dynamics, perhaps necessitating job transformation and reskilling requirements. A tiny negative route coefficient (-0.014) from Job Dynamics to Business Efficiency signifies a slight detrimental impact on efficiency resulting from alterations in job dynamics. The relationship between employment Dynamics to Innovation is positive (0.456), indicating that changes in employment positions and reskilling may enhance innovation, presumably by enabling new responsibilities or abilities that foster creative endeavors. The correlation between Innovation and company Efficiency is negative (-0.388), suggesting that an emphasis on innovation may slightly detract from company efficiency, perhaps due to the allocation of resources and time to innovation initiatives.

The construct values offer further insights into the overall impact of each construct within this model. Business Efficiency, with a value near zero (0.009), indicates a negligible impact from other components on this outcome. Innovation yields a somewhat positive consequence (0.282), indicating a helpful albeit small contribution of AI in fostering new efforts. Job Dynamics exhibits a negative result (-0.587), underscoring the problems and disruptions that AI may pose to employment dynamics, including apprehensions around job displacement and the necessity for reskilling.

This model uncovers numerous essential findings. AI exerts a dual impact on businesses, improving corporate efficiency while potentially stifling innovation and presenting problems to employment dynamics. Job Dynamics seems to act as a mediator, influencing both innovation and company efficiency, albeit with varying directional effects. The intricate relationship among these characteristics indicates that although AI can enhance efficiency, it requires modifications in job responsibilities and may not consistently promote creativity.

The model underscores the complex relationships among AI, employment dynamics, organizational efficiency, and creativity. Although AI can enhance efficiency, it also presents issues in employment dynamics and has a complex effect on creativity. This highlights the necessity of meticulously managing worker dynamics and achieving equilibrium between enhancing efficiency and fostering creativity in an AI-driven work setting.

Table 1. Model Fit

Model Fit Index	Estimated Model
Chi-square	65.503
Number of model parameters	31.000
Number of observations	100.000
Degrees of freedom	60.000
P value	0.292
ChiSqr/df	1.092
RMSEA	0.030
RMSEA LOW 90% CI	0.000
RMSEA HIGH 90% CI	0.070
GFI	0.915
AGFI	0.872
PGFI	0.604
SRMR	0.085
NFI	0.383
TLI	0.745
CFI	0.804
AIC	127.503
BIC	208.263

Table 1 presents the model fit statistics for a structural equation model (SEM). These indicators facilitate the evaluation of the model's representation of the observed data. The chi-square statistic of 65.503 is frequently employed in Structural Equation Modelling (SEM) to assess model fit, where a lower chi-square value in relation to the degrees of freedom signifies a superior fit. In this instance, with 60 degrees of freedom, the model fit seems satisfactory.

The p-value for the chi-square test is 0.292, beyond the conventional threshold of 0.05. This indicates that the discrepancy between the model and the observed data is not statistically significant, typically viewed as a sign of good model fit. The chi-square to degrees of freedom ratio (ChiSq/df) is a commonly utilized metric, with values under 3 typically regarded as acceptable and values under 2 as excellent. The ratio of 1.092 signifies a superior fit.

The Root Mean Square Error of Approximation (RMSEA) is a widely utilized metric for evaluating model fit, where values under 0.05 signify a close fit and values under 0.08 denote an acceptable match. The RMSEA for this model is 0.030, indicating an excellent fit. The 90% confidence interval for RMSEA spans from 0.000 to 0.070, further corroborating the model's adequacy. The Goodness-of-Fit Index (GFI) is 0.915, indicating a strong fit as it approaches 1. A GFI of 0.90 is generally deemed acceptable, signifying a strong model-data fit.

The Adjusted Goodness-of-Fit Index (AGFI), which modifies the GFI according to the model's degrees of freedom, is 0.872. Values over 0.80–0.90 are often deemed acceptable, indicating that this result reflects a satisfactory match. The Parsimony Goodness-of-Fit Index (PGFI) is a modified variant of the Goodness-of-Fit Index (GFI), with values often spanning from 0 to 1. The PGFI of 0.604 indicates that the model achieves a satisfactory equilibrium between fit and parsimony, although no definitive threshold exists for this index.

The Standardized Root Mean Square Residual (SRMR) quantifies the standardized disparity between observed and anticipated correlations. Values below 0.08 are often deemed acceptable; nevertheless, the SRMR here is 0.085, marginally surpassing this limit. This may signify tiny regions where the model fails to accurately represent the observed data. The Normed Fit Index (NFI) is 0.383, indicating a rather low value. NFI values exceeding 0.90 are often favored; thus, the low NFI indicates that the model may not fit as effectively relative to a null model, highlighting potential areas for enhancement.

The Tucker-Lewis Index (TLI), or Non-Normed Fit Index (NNFI), accounts for model complexity, with values exceeding 0.90 signifying a favorable fit. The TLI of 0.745 is below the threshold, indicating that the model may not attain an optimal fit and may require enhancement. The Comparative Fit Index (CFI) is a prevalent fit index, where values exceeding 0.90 generally signify a satisfactory fit. The CFI of 0.804 is just below the threshold, suggesting that the model fits relatively well but might be enhanced to better correspond with the observed data.

The Akaike Information Criterion (AIC) and Bayesian Information Criterion (BIC) facilitate the comparison of the relative fit of several models, where lower values signify superior fit. The AIC is 127.503, and the BIC is 208.263. These values are chiefly beneficial for model comparison, enabling researchers to evaluate various models when applicable.

The model exhibits a generally satisfactory fit according to numerous critical indicators, including the chi-square test, RMSEA, GFI, and AGFI. Nevertheless, some indices, including SRMR, NFI, TLI, and CFI, are below optimal thresholds, indicating potential for enhancement. The low values of NFI, TLI, and CFI may suggest that the model inadequately represents the observed data, maybe due to absent pathways or unaccounted interactions. Notwithstanding these constraints, the robust performance on metrics such as RMSEA and the chi-square/df ratio indicates that the model offers a satisfactory match. Improving the model to target locations indicated by lower indices could augment its overall fit and explanatory capacity.

Discussion

The study's findings offer significant insights into the disruptive impacts of Artificial Intelligence (AI) on business models and workforce dynamics in India. The data indicates that AI significantly enhances corporate efficiency and fosters creativity, both of which are crucial for sustaining a competitive advantage in today's technological environment. Organizations that implement AI technologies provide enhancements in operational efficiency, as indicated by metrics such as work automation and process optimization. This corresponds with global trends where AI-driven organizations utilize technology to optimize operations, decrease operational expenses, and ultimately enhance productivity. This increase in efficiency necessitates intentional modifications within the workforce.

The structural equation model (SEM) analysis indicates that although AI enhances corporate efficiency, it concurrently poses issues related to employment dynamics. The substantial route coefficient connecting AI to job dynamics signifies that AI adoption affects alterations in job roles, job transformation, and the necessity for reskilling. Employees may experience displacement in positions that are being automated, while new roles arise necessitating specialized abilities to manage and collaborate with AI systems. Thus, worker adaptation is essential, and the imperative of reskilling emerges as a pivotal aspect in overseeing this transformation. Organizations, policymakers, and educational institutions must work to establish skill development programs that align with the requirements of an AI-driven economy. These programs should emphasize both technological competencies, such as artificial intelligence and data analysis, and interpersonal abilities, like adaptability and problem-solving, to guarantee that people can excel in emerging and evolving job roles.

Moreover, the model suggests a complex link between AI and innovation. Although AI positively influences innovation by facilitating the adoption of new practices, personalizing services, and forecasting market trends, the findings also indicate a possible drawback. The adverse path coefficient from AI to innovation indicates that the implementation of AI may occasionally stifle specific types of invention, potentially due to an excessive dependence on technology, which could constrain human creativity. In environments where AI automates repetitive jobs, there exists a risk that organizations may prioritize efficiency excessively, thereby inhibiting creativity and innovation. This underscores the necessity for organizations to equilibrate technological integration with avenues for human innovation, guaranteeing that AI serves as an enabler rather than a replacement for original thought.

The examination of model fit indices corroborates the validity of the findings, while specific indices like SRMR, NFI, TLI, and CFI indicate potential areas for enhancement. The results indicate that although the SEM framework successfully delineates the primary linkages among AI, company efficiency, employment dynamics, and innovation, the model might be enhanced to encompass extra complications. Industry-specific implications and regional variations may subtly affect the linkages between components, highlighting the necessity for future study to investigate these aspects.

This study highlights the dual influence of AI on Indian enterprises. Although AI improves operational efficiency and stimulates innovation to some degree, it also causes workforce disruptions that necessitate careful management. The results advocate for a hybrid strategy in workforce development, wherein AI is strategically integrated with human capabilities to optimize the advantages of technology implementation. This equilibrium will enhance production while safeguarding the imaginative and adaptive capacities of human personnel.

The findings indicate that AI is crucial in transforming business models and the workforce in India. The significant impact of AI on operational efficiency and creativity suggests that companies utilising AI are more likely to thrive in a competitive environment (Kaplan & Haenlein, 2019). As artificial intelligence advances, businesses must prioritise the integration of AI technology into their core processes to sustain agility and responsiveness to market demands (Ransbotham et al., 2020).

The results highlight the imperative of workforce reskilling to accommodate AI-driven changes in employment. While AI can replace routine tasks, it creates new opportunities for employees to engage in more complex, strategic positions (Brynjolfsson & McAfee, 2014). This requires a cooperative effort between enterprises and educational institutions to equip individuals with the essential skills for the AI-driven future of work (Huang et al., 2019).

The lack of a significant moderating effect of gender and experience suggests that AI's impact on business models and labour dynamics is consistent across different demographic groups (Jarrahi, 2018). This result aligns with McKnight & Kacmar (2006), who asserted that the adoption of technology and its benefits are predominantly universal, irrespective of personal characteristics. The swift advancement of AI necessitates ongoing learning and adaptation across all sectors (Wilson & Daugherty, 2018).

India, being an emerging country, is especially vulnerable to these fluctuations. The incorporation of AI into industries like manufacturing and services results in substantial productivity improvements (Bughin et al., 2018). Organisations must confront the socio-economic ramifications of employment displacements induced by AI (West, 2018). Policymakers must provide explicit frameworks that facilitate both innovation and the development of human capital (Chui et al., 2018).

CONCLUSION

Artificial intelligence is transforming business paradigms and the future of employment in India. The use of AI in company operations results in improved efficiency, innovation, and job reorganisation (Agrawal et al., 2018). Nonetheless, the transformation necessitates that organisations invest in reskilling their personnel and reevaluating their strategy methodologies to optimise AI's potential (Tegmark, 2017). The results of this study offer significant insights for policymakers and corporate leaders in India, assisting them in managing the intricacies of AI implementation (Manyika et al., 2017). Future study may investigate the enduring impacts of AI on employment displacement and the function of governmental measures in facilitating AI-induced transitions.

This study illustrates that Artificial Intelligence is transforming business models and employment frameworks in India. Artificial intelligence significantly enhances operational efficiency, granting organizations a competitive advantage through process optimization and data-informed decision-making. AI fosters innovation by providing organizations with tools to analyze and forecast market trends, customize client interactions, and develop novel business models. Nevertheless, these advantages are accompanied with obstacles, especially in workforce management, as AI-driven automation results in job displacement in specific sectors while generating a demand for new competencies in others.

The shift to an AI-integrated business landscape requires substantial expenditures in personnel retraining. Corporate leaders and policymakers must acknowledge the necessity of equipping the workforce for AI-driven positions. This encompasses both technical training in AI-related competencies and the cultivation of an environment that promotes adaptation and lifelong learning. Educational institutions are essential in this endeavor by connecting their curricula with industry requirements and offering skill development programs that ensure individuals remain pertinent in an AI-enhanced work environment.

Future study should investigate the long-term effects of AI on employment, emphasizing governmental initiatives that could enable seamless transitions in the labor market. Policymakers must develop frameworks that foster workforce resilience, allowing employees to adjust to new jobs generated by AI developments. Such policies may encompass subsidies for reskilling initiatives, collaborations between educational institutions and enterprises, and incentives for corporations who invest in worker development. By cultivating a supporting ecosystem, India can guarantee that AI-driven growth results in sustainable development, benefiting both enterprises and employees.

This research enhances the broader discussion on AI adoption in emerging economies by elucidating the opportunities and difficulties related to AI integration in India. It underscores the necessity for a balanced strategy that utilizes AI's potential to improve efficiency and innovation while considering the workforce consequences of technological disruption. As artificial intelligence advances, Indian enterprises and policymakers must collaborate to leverage its potential, maximizing its advantages while alleviating its effects on employment. This equitable strategy will augment India's competitiveness in the global marketplace while cultivating a resilient, talented, and adaptable workforce capable of navigating the intricacies of an AI-driven future.

REFERENCES

Abu-Rumman, A., Al Kurdi, B., Al Shraah, A., Alshurideh, M. T., Alzoubi, H. M., & AlHamad, A. (2024). *Impact of blockchain strategy and information sharing on digital operations: Empirical evidence from the UAE banking industry. Cyber Security Impact on Digitalization and Business Intelligence*. Springer International Publishing. DOI: 10.1007/978-3-031-14169-0_22

Agrawal, A., Gans, J. S., & Goldfarb, A. (2018). *Prediction machines: The simple economics of artificial intelligence*. Harvard Business Review Press.

Al Kurdi, B., & Alshurideh, M. T. (2023). The effect of social media influencer traits on consumer purchasing decisions for keto products. *Journal of Marketing Communications*, 1–22. Advance online publication. DOI: 10.1080/13527266.2023.2246043

Alhammadi, S., & Alshurideh, M. (2024). Factors influencing customers' attitude to adopt e-government mobile applications. *International Journal of Data and Network Science*, 8(2), 1129–1140. DOI: 10.5267/j.ijdns.2023.11.021

Andersson, A., Kreegimäe, E., & Niiranen, N. (2019). What makes your message credible? *International Journal of Business and Social Science Research*, 5(3), 211–228. DOI: 10.5267/j.ijbssr.2019.2.014

Brynjolfsson, E., & McAfee, A. (2014). *The second machine age: Work, progress, and prosperity in a time of brilliant technologies*. W. W. Norton & Company.

Bughin, J., Hazan, E., Ramaswamy, S., Chui, M., Allas, T., Dahlström, P., . . . Trench, M. (2018). Artificial intelligence: The next digital frontier? McKinsey Global Institute. https://www.mckinsey.com/business-functions/mckinsey-digital/our-insights/how-artificial-intelligence-and-data-add-value

Chui, M., Manyika, J., & Miremadi, M. (2018). What AI can and can't do (yet) for your business. McKinsey Quarterly. https://www.mckinsey.com/business-functions/mckinsey-digital/our-insights/what-ai-can-and-cant-do-yet-for-your-business

Fanoberova, A., & Kuczkowska, H. (2016). Effects of source credibility and information quality on attitudes and purchase intentions of apparel products. *Journal of Retailing and Consumer Services*, 30, 23–34. DOI: 10.1016/j.jretconser.2016.06.003

Huang, M. H., Rust, R. T., & Maksimovic, V. (2019). The AI dilemma: AI takes over human jobs but can't take over human touch. *Journal of Service Research*, 22(2), 158–166. DOI: 10.1177/1094670519827370

Jarrahi, M. H. (2018). Artificial intelligence and the future of work: Human-AI symbiosis in organizational decision making. *Business Horizons*, 61(4), 577–586. DOI: 10.1016/j.bushor.2018.03.007

Kaplan, A., & Haenlein, M. (2019). Siri, Siri, in my hand: Who's the fairest in the land? On the interpretations, illustrations, and implications of artificial intelligence. *Business Horizons*, 62(1), 15–25. DOI: 10.1016/j.bushor.2018.08.004

Li, R., & Suh, A. (2015). Factors influencing information credibility on social media platforms. *Procedia Computer Science*, 72, 314–328. DOI: 10.1016/j.procs.2015.12.146

Manyika, J., Lund, S., Chui, M., Bughin, J., Woetzel, J., Batra, P., & Sanghvi, S. (2017). What the future of work will mean for jobs, skills, and wages. McKinsey Global Institute. https://www.mckinsey.com/featured-insights/future-of-work/what-the-future-of-work-will-mean-for-jobs-skills-and-wages

McKnight, D. H., & Kacmar, C. J. (2006). Factors and effects of information technology on trust in the workplace. *Information & Management*, 43(8), 901–910. DOI: 10.1016/j.im.2006.08.003

Mcknight, H., & Kacmar, C. (2006). Factors of information credibility for an internet advice site. *Journal of Business Research*, 59(3), 249–256. DOI: 10.1016/j.jbusres.2005.10.005

Ransbotham, S., Kiron, D., Gerbert, P., & Reeves, M. (2020). Artificial intelligence in business gets real. MIT Sloan Management Review. https://sloanreview.mit.edu/article/artificial-intelligence-in-business-gets-real/

Tegmark, M. (2017). *Life 3.0: Being human in the age of artificial intelligence*. Knopf.

West, D. M. (2018). *The future of work: Robots, AI, and automation*. Brookings Institution Press.

Wilson, H. J., & Daugherty, P. R. (2018). Collaborative intelligence: Humans and AI are joining forces. Harvard Business Review. https://hbr.org/2018/07/collaborative-intelligence-humans-and-ai-are-joining-forces

Compilation of References

Aagaard, A. (2019). *Digital business models—Driving transformation and innovation*. Palgrave Macmillan. DOI: 10.1007/978-3-319-96902-2

Aagaard, A., & Tucci, C. (2024). AI-Driven Business Model Innovation: Pioneering New Frontiers in Value Creation. *Business Model Innovation: Game Changers and Contemporary Issues* (pp. 295–328). Springer International Publishing. DOI: 10.1007/978-3-031-57511-2_10

Aayog, N. I. T. I. (2018), *National strategy for artificial intelligence #AIFORALL*. niti.gov.in/ writereaddata/files/document_publication/NationalStrategy-for-AI-Discussion-Paper.pdf

Abbas Khan, M., Khan, H., Omer, M. F., Ullah, I., & Yasir, M. (2024). Impact of Artificial Intelligence on the Global Economy and Technology Advancements. *Artificial General Intelligence (AGI) Security: Smart Applications and Sustainable Technologies* (pp. 147–180). Springer Nature Singapore.

Abbas, J., Zhang, Q., Hussain, I., Akram, S., Afaq, A., & Shad, M. A. (2020). Sustainable innovation in small medium enterprises: The impact of knowledge management on organizational innovation through a mediation analysis by using SEM approach. *Sustainability (Basel)*, 12(6), 2407. DOI: 10.3390/su12062407

Abijith, A., & Wamba, S. F. (2012). Business value of RFID-enabled healthcare transformation projects. *Business Process Management Journal*, 19(1), 1–28.

Abou-Foul, M., Ruiz-Alba, J. L., & López-Tenorio, P. J. (2023). The impact of artificial intelligence capabilities on servitization: The moderating role of absorptive capacity—A dynamic capabilities perspective. *Journal of Business Research*, 157, 113609. DOI: 10.1016/j.jbusres.2022.113609

Abu-Rumman, A., Al Kurdi, B., Al Shraah, A., Alshurideh, M. T., Alzoubi, H. M., & AlHamad, A. (2024). *Impact of blockchain strategy and information sharing on digital operations: Empirical evidence from the UAE banking industry. Cyber Security Impact on Digitalization and Business Intelligence*. Springer International Publishing. DOI: 10.1007/978-3-031-14169-0_22

Act, E. U. A. I. (2023). https://digital-strategy.ec.europa.eu/en/policies/regulatory-framework-ai

Adeniyi, S., Joseph, S. B., Daniel, S., & Godwin, G. (2023). *The impact of augmented reality on social interaction: bridging the digital and physical worlds*. https://www.researchgate.net/publication/376642894_The_Impact_of_Augmented_Reality_on_Social_Interaction_Bridging_the_Digital_and_Physical_Worlds

Adula, M., Birbirsa, Z. A., & Kant, S. (2023). The effect of interpersonal, problem solving and technical training skills on performance of Ethiopia textile industry: Continuance, normative and affective commitment as mediators. *Cogent Business & Management*, 10(3), 2286672. Advance online publication. DOI: 10.1080/23311975.2023.2286672

Afeltra, G., Alerasoul, S. A., & Strozzi, F. (2023). The evolution of sustainable innovation: From the past to the future. *European Journal of Innovation Management*, 26(2), 386–421. DOI: 10.1108/EJIM-02-2021-0113

Agarwal, A., Singhal, C., & Thomas, R. (2021). *AI-powered decision making for the bank of the future*. McKinsey & Company.

Aggarwal, M., & Madhukar, M. (2017). IBM's Watson analytics for health care: A miracle made true. *Cloud Computing Systems and Applications in Healthcare* (pp. 117-134). IGI Global.

Agrawal, A., Gans, J. S., & Goldfarb, A. (2018). *Prediction machines: The simple economics of artificial intelligence*. Harvard Business Review Press.

Agrawal, A., Gans, J., & Goldfarb, A. (2018). Prediction, judgment, and complexity: A theory of decision-making and artificial intelligence. In *The economics of artificial intelligence: An agenda* (pp. 89–110). University of Chicago Press.

Aguilar-Fernández, M. E., & Otegi-Olaso, J. R. (2018). Firm size and the business model for sustainable innovation. *Sustainability (Basel)*, 10(12), 4785. DOI: 10.3390/su10124785

Ahmad Salleh, K., & Janczewski, L. (2018), *An implementation of Sec-TOE framework: identifying security determinants of big data solutions adoption an implementation of Sec-TOE framework: identifying security determinants of big data. PACIS 2018 Proceedings*, 211.

Akhtar, N., & Lin, M. (2023). Technological Disruption And Its Effects On Competitive Dynamics. *Competitive Research Journal Archive*, 1(02), 100–108.

Akindele, A. T., Arulogun, O. T., Taye, G. T., Amare, S. Y., Van Reisen, M., Berhe, K. F., & Gusite, B. (2022). The impact of COVID-19 and FAIR data innovation on distance education in Africa. *Data Intelligence*, 4(4), 1013–1032. DOI: 10.1162/dint_a_00184

Akter, S., Hossain, M. A., Sajib, S., Sultana, S., Rahman, M., Vrontis, D., & McCarthy, G. (2023). A framework for AI-powered service innovation capability: Review and agenda for future research. *Technovation*, 125, 102768. DOI: 10.1016/j.technovation.2023.102768

Al Kurdi, B., & Alshurideh, M. T. (2023). The effect of social media influencer traits on consumer purchasing decisions for keto products. *Journal of Marketing Communications*, 1–22. Advance online publication. DOI: 10.1080/13527266.2023.2246043

Alam, M. G. R., Masum, A. K. M., Beh, L. S., & Hong, C. S. (2016). Critical factors influencing decision to adopt human resource information system (HRIS) in hospitals. *PLoS One*, 11(8), 1–22. DOI: 10.1371/journal.pone.0160366 PMID: 27494334

Al-Ansi, A. M., Jaboob, M., Garad, A., & Al-Ansi, A. (2023). Analyzing augmented reality (AR) and virtual reality (VR) recent development in education. *Social Sciences & Humanities Open*, 8(1), 100532. DOI: 10.1016/j.ssaho.2023.100532

Albert, M. (2019). Sustainable frugal innovation-The connection between frugal innovation and sustainability. *Journal of Cleaner Production*, 237, 117747. DOI: 10.1016/j.jclepro.2019.117747

Al-Dmour, R. H. (2014). *An Integration Model for Identifying the Determinants of the Adoption and Implementation Level of HRIS Applications and Its Effectiveness in Business Organisations*. Brunel University.

Aldoseri, A., Al-Khalifa, K. N., & Hamouda, A. M. (2024). AI-Powered Innovation in Digital Transformation: Key Pillars and Industry Impact. *Sustainability (Basel)*, 16(5), 1790. DOI: 10.3390/su16051790

Alhammadi, S., & Alshurideh, M. (2024). Factors influencing customers' attitude to adopt e-government mobile applications. *International Journal of Data and Network Science*, 8(2), 1129–1140. DOI: 10.5267/j.ijdns.2023.11.021

Aljarboa, S. (2024). Factors influencing the adoption of artificial intelligence in e-commerce by small and medium-sized enterprises. *International Journal of Information Management Data Insights*, 4(2), 100285. DOI: 10.1016/j.jjimei.2024.100285

Alleyne, M. C. (2002). *The Construction and Representation of Race and Ethnicity in the Caribbean and the World*. University of the West Indies Press.

Alnuaimi, S. (2022). *New generation of innovation management: an integrated framework for the digital era* (Doctoral dissertation, Sheffield Hallam University).

Andersson, A., Kreegimäe, E., & Niiranen, N. (2019). What makes your message credible? *International Journal of Business and Social Science Research*, 5(3), 211–228. DOI: 10.5267/j.ijbssr.2019.2.014

Ardito, L., Petruzzelli, A. M., Panniello, U., & Garavelli, A. C. (2022). Towards Industry 4.0: Mapping digital technologies for supply chain management-marketing integration. *Business Process Management Journal*, 28(3), 561–583. DOI: 10.1108/BPMJ-05-2021-0274

Arena, F., Collotta, M., Pau, G., & Termine, F. (2022). An overview of augmented reality. *Computers*, 11(2), 28. DOI: 10.3390/computers11020028

Arias-Pérez, J., & Vélez-Jaramillo, J. (2022). Ignoring the three-way interaction of digital orientation, Not-invented-here syndrome and employee's artificial intelligence awareness in digital innovation performance: A recipe for failure. *Technological Forecasting and Social Change*, 174, 121305. DOI: 10.1016/j.techfore.2021.121305

Arsawan, I. W. E., Koval, V., Rajiani, I., Rustiarini, N. W., Supartha, W. G., & Suryantini, N. P. S. (2022). Leveraging knowledge sharing and innovation culture into SMEs sustainable competitive advantage. *International Journal of Productivity and Performance Management*, 71(2), 405–428. DOI: 10.1108/IJPPM-04-2020-0192

Arslan, A., Tarba, S., & Zheng, C. (2021). Human resource management in Industry 4.0: Emerging themes and research avenues. *Human Resource Management Review*, 31(3), 100778. DOI: 10.1016/j.hrmr.2020.100778

Arthanat, S., Vroman, K. G., Lysack, C., & Grizzetti, J. (2019). Multimodal training of AI systems for assistive technologies: A person-centered approach. *Assistive Technology Journal*, 31(2), 89–100. DOI: 10.1080/10400435.2019.1578254

Arthur, K. K., Bannor, R. K., Masih, J., Oppong-Kyeremeh, H., & Appiahene, P. (2024). Digital innovations: Implications for african agribusinesses. *Smart Agricultural Technology*, 7, 100407. DOI: 10.1016/j.atech.2024.100407

Artificial Intelligence-Enabled Business Model Innovation: Competencies and Roles of Top Management. (2024). *IEEE Transactions on Engineering Management*, 71. DOI: 10.1109/TEM.2023.3275643

Asefa, K., & Debela, K. L. (2023). Effect of Transformational Leadership on Organizational Performance: The Mediating Role of Employee Commitment and Expert Systems (AI) Inclusion in Ethiopia, *2023 International Conference on Communication, Security and Artificial Intelligence (ICCSAI)*, 305-310, DOI: 10.1109/ICCSAI59793.2023.10421269

Ashgan, E., Moubarki, N., Saif, M., & El-Shorbagy, A. (2023). Virtual Reality in architecture. *Civil Engineering and Architecture*, 11(1), 498-506. https://www.hrpub.org/download/20221230/CEA38-14892091.pdf

Ashok, M., Madan, R., Joha, A., & Sivarajah, U. (2022). Ethical framework for Artificial Intelligence and Digital technologies. *International Journal of Information Management*, 62, 102433. DOI: 10.1016/j.ijinfomgt.2021.102433

Asif, R., & Hassan, S. R. (2023). Exploring the confluence of IoT and Metaverse: Future opportunities and challenges. *IoT*, 4(3), 412-429. DOI: 10.3390/iot4030018

Åström, J., Reim, W., & Parida, V. (2022). Value creation and value capture for AI business model innovation: A three-phase process framework. *Review of Managerial Science*, 16(7), 2111–2133. DOI: 10.1007/s11846-022-00521-z

atragadda, V. (2023). Automating Customer Support: A Study on The Efficacy of Machine Learning-Driven Chatbots and Virtual Assistants. *Iconic Research and Engineering Journals*, 7(1), 600–601.

Attaran, M., Attaran, S., & Celik, B. G. (2023). The impact of digital twins on the evolution of intelligent manufacturing and Industry 4.0. *Advances in Computational Intelligence*, 3(3), 11. DOI: 10.1007/s43674-023-00058-y PMID: 37305021

Awa, H. O., Ukoha, O., & Emecheta, B. C. (2016). Using T-O-E theoretical framework to study the adoption of ERP solution. *Cogent Business & Management*, 3(1), 1196571. DOI: 10.1080/23311975.2016.1196571

Awa, H., Ojiabo, O., & Emecheta, B. (2015). Integrating TAM, TPB and TOE frameworks and expanding their characteristic constructs for e-commerce adoption by SMEs. *Journal of Science & Technology Policy Management*, 6(1), 76–94. DOI: 10.1108/JSTPM-04-2014-0012

Babaei, A. (2023, November 19). *The evolution of reality: Exploring the realm of AR, VR, and XR*. Medium. https://medium.com/@dr.arya.design/the-evolution-of-reality-exploring-the-realm-of-ar-vr-and-xr-f4c14178df73

Babatunde, S. O., Odejide, O. A., Edunjobi, T. E., & Ogundipe, D. O.Sodiq Odetunde BabatundeOpeyemi Abayomi OdejideTolulope Esther EdunjobiDamilola Oluwaseun Ogundipe. (2024). The role of AI in marketing personalization: A theoretical exploration of consumer engagement strategies. *International Journal of Management & Entrepreneurship Research*, 6(3), 936–949. DOI: 10.51594/ijmer.v6i3.964

Babic, B., Cohen, I. G., Evgeniou, T., & Gerke, S. (2021). *When Machine Learning Goes Off the Rails.Harvard Business Review*. January-February.

Bahoo, S., Cucculelli, M., & Qamar, D. (2023). Artificial intelligence and corporate innovation: A review and research agenda. *Technological Forecasting and Social Change*, 188, 122264. DOI: 10.1016/j.techfore.2022.122264

Balaji, K. (2024). Harnessing AI for Financial Innovations: Pioneering the Future of Financial Services. *Modern Management Science Practices in the Age of AI* (pp. 91-122). IGI Global.

Baldassarre, B., Keskin, D., Diehl, J. C., Bocken, N., & Calabretta, G. (2020). Implementing sustainable design theory in business practice: A call to action. *Journal of Cleaner Production*, 273, 123113. DOI: 10.1016/j.jclepro.2020.123113

Balsmeier, B., & Woerter, M. (2019). Is this time different? How digitalization influences job creation and destruction. *Research Policy*, 48(8), 103765. DOI: 10.1016/j.respol.2019.03.010

Bankins, S., Ocampo, A. C., Marrone, M., Restubog, S. L. D., & Woo, S. E. (2023). A multilevel review of artificial intelligence in organizations: Implications for organizational behavior research and practice. *Journal of Organizational Behavior*, 45(2), 159–182. DOI: 10.1002/job.2735

Bashir, M. F., Ma, B., Komal, B., Bashir, M. A., Tan, D., & Bashir, M. (2020). Correlation between climate indicators and COVID-19 pandemic in New York, USA. *The Science of the Total Environment*, 728, 138835. Retrieved October 3, 2024, from. DOI: 10.1016/j.scitotenv.2020.138835 PMID: 32334162

Baytar, F., Chung, T., & Shin, E. (2020). Evaluating garments in augmented reality when shopping online. *Journal of Fashion Marketing and Management*, 24(4), 667–683. DOI: 10.1108/JFMM-05-2018-0077

Benbya, H., Davenport, T. H., & Pachidi, S. (2020). Artificial intelligence in organizations: Current state and future opportunities. *MIS Quarterly Executive*, 19(4).

Benner, M. J., & Waldfogel, J. (2023). Changing the channel: Digitization and the rise of "middle tail" strategies. *Strategic Management Journal*, 44(1), 264–287. DOI: 10.1002/smj.3130

Berman, T., Schallmo, D., & Williams, C. A. (2021). Business model transformation through artificial intelligence in the Israeli InsurTech. In *ISPIM Conference Proceedings* (pp. 1-42). The International Society for Professional Innovation Management (ISPIM).

Bersin, J. (2018), *Talent trends technology disruptions for 2018*. www.isaconnection .org/ assets/documents/2018BersinHRTechDisruptionsReport.pdf

Bhuiyan, M. S. (2024). The role of AI-Enhanced personalization in customer experiences. *Journal of Computer Science and Technology Studies*, 6(1), 162–169. DOI: 10.32996/jcsts.2024.6.1.17

Birhane, M., Amentie, C., Borji, B., & Kant, S. (n.d.). Are Ethiopian Coffee Farmers Proficient to Predict Capital Structure with Mediation of AI Based Knowledge Systems and Asset Liquidity? In *AI in Agriculture for Sustainable and Economic Management* (pp. 199-215). CRC Press. DOI: 10.1201/9781003451648-15

Bitkina, O. V., Kim, H., & Park, J. (2020). Human factors in organizational digital transformation: Readiness and resistance. *Human Factors Journal*, 62(3), 456–470. DOI: 10.1177/0018720819873103

Bjørn, A., Owsianiak, M., Molin, C., & Hauschild, M. Z. (2018). LCA history. *Life cycle assessment: theory and practice*, 17-30.

Black, S., Samson, D., & Ellis, A. (2024). Moving beyond 'proof points': Factors underpinning AI-enabled business model transformation. *International Journal of Information Management*, 77, 102796. DOI: 10.1016/j.ijinfomgt.2024.102796

Blum, J. R., Greencorn, D. G., & Cooperstock, J. R. (2013). Smartphone sensor reliability for Augmented Reality applications. In: Zheng, K., Li, M., Jiang, H. (eds) *Mobile and Ubiquitous Systems: Computing, Networking, and Services*. MobiQuitous 2012. DOI: 10.1007/978-3-642-40238-8_11

Bocken, N. M., & Geradts, T. H. (2020). Barriers and drivers to sustainable business model innovation: Organization design and dynamic capabilities. *Long Range Planning*, 53(4), 101950. DOI: 10.1016/j.lrp.2019.101950

Bondarouk, T., Parry, E., & Furtmueller, E. (2017). Electronic HRM: Four decades of research on adoption and consequences. *International Journal of Human Resource Management*, 28(1), 98–131. DOI: 10.1080/09585192.2016.1245672

Boret Cordoba, D., & Veshagh, A. (2013). Managing eco design and sustainable manufacturing. In *Re-engineering Manufacturing for Sustainability:Proceedings of the 20th CIRP International Conference on Life Cycle Engineering,* Singapore 17-19 April, 2013 (pp. 59-67). Springer Singapore.

Bortola, G. W., Kero, C. A., & Bali, N. (2024). The Mediating Effect of Competitive Advantage between Innovation Capability and Firm's Competitiveness. *Horn of African Journal of Business and Economics*, 7(1), 75–96.

Bossuwé, E. (2023). *AI-Driven Business Models Aimed at Promoting A Circular Economy* (Doctoral dissertation, Ghent University).

Brandon, B. (2023, December 14). *Immersive reality: Unleash augmented, virtual, and mixed reality*. New York: The Learning Guild. https://www.learningguild.com/articles/immersive-reality-unleash-augmented-virtual--and-mixed-reality-/

Broderick, A. J. (1998). Role theory, role management and service performance. *Journal of Services Marketing*, 12(5), 348–361. DOI: 10.1108/08876049810235379

Brooks, L. A., & Saveri, A. (2017). Expanding imagined affordance with future-types: Challenging algorithmic power with collective 2040 imagination. *Proceedings of the 50th Hawaii International Conference on System Sciences (HICCS)*. DOI: 10.24251/HICSS.2017.215

Brynjolfsson, E. (2022). *The servitization economy: Understanding new paradigms in labor division*. MIT Press.

Brynjolfsson, E., & McAfee, A. (2014). *The second machine age: Work, progress, and prosperity in a time of brilliant technologies*. W. W. Norton & Company.

Bryson, J. J. (2018). Patiency is not a virtue: The design of intelligent systems and systems of ethics. *Ethics and Information Technology*, 20(1), 15–26. DOI: 10.1007/s10676-018-9448-6

Bughin, J., Hazan, E., Ramaswamy, S., Chui, M., Allas, T., Dahlström, P., . . . Trench, M. (2018). Artificial intelligence: The next digital frontier? McKinsey Global Institute. https://www.mckinsey.com/business-functions/mckinsey-digital/our-insights/how-artificial-intelligence-and-data-add-value

Bughin, J., Seong, J., Manyika, J., Chui, M., & Joshi, R. (2018, September). *Notes from the AI frontier: Modeling the impact of AI on the world economy*. McKinsey Global Institute. https://www.mckinsey.com/featured-insights/artificial-intelligence/notes-from-the-ai-frontier-modeling-the-impact-of-ai-on-the-world-economy

Bughin, J., Hazan, E., Ramaswamy, S., Chui, M., Allas, T., Dahlstro¨, M. P., Henke, N., & Trench, M. (2017). *Artificial Intelligence: The Next Digital Frontier? McKinsey Global Institute*. McKinsey & Company.

Bu, L., Chen, C. H., Zhang, G., Liu, B., Dong, G., & Yuan, X. (2020). A hybrid intelligence approach for sustainable service innovation of smart and connected product: A case study. *Advanced Engineering Informatics*, 46, 101163. DOI: 10.1016/j.aei.2020.101163

Burström, T., Parida, V., Lahti, T., & Wincent, J. (2021). AI-enabled business-model innovation and transformation in industrial ecosystems: A framework, model and outline for further research. *Journal of Business Research*, 127, 85–95. DOI: 10.1016/j.jbusres.2021.01.016

Buttle, F., & Maklan, S. (2019). *Customer relationship management: concepts and technologies*. Routledge. DOI: 10.4324/9781351016551

Calzarossa, M. C., De Lotto, I., & Rogerson, S. (2010). Ethics and information systems - guest editors introduction. *Information Systems Frontiers*, 12(4), 357–359. DOI: 10.1007/s10796-009-9198-4

Candelon, F., & Reeves, M. (Eds.). (2022). *The Rise of AI-Powered Companies*. Walter de Gruyter GmbH & Co KG. DOI: 10.1515/9783110775112

Cappa, F., Del Sette, F., Hayes, D., & Rosso, F. (2016). How to deliver open sustainable innovation: An integrated approach for a sustainable marketable product. *Sustainability (Basel)*, 8(12), 1341. DOI: 10.3390/su8121341

Carayannis, E. G., & Morawska-Jancelewicz, J. (2022). The futures of Europe: Society 5.0 and Industry 5.0 as driving forces of future universities. *Journal of the Knowledge Economy*, 13(4), 3445–3471. DOI: 10.1007/s13132-021-00854-2

Cennamo, C., Dagnino, G. B., Di Minin, A., & Lanzolla, G. (2020). Managing digital transformation: Scope of transformation and modalities of value co-generation and delivery. *California Management Review*, 62(4), 5–16. DOI: 10.1177/0008125620942136

Chang, I. C., Hwang, H. G., Hung, M. C., Lin, M. H., & Yen, D. C. (2007). Factors affecting the adoption of electronic signature: Executives' perspective of hospital information department. *Decision Support Systems*, 44(1), 350–359. DOI: 10.1016/j.dss.2007.04.006 PMID: 32287564

Charlier, R., & Kloppenburg, S. (2017), *Artificial intelligence in HR: a no-brainer*. www. pwc.nl

Chase, C. W.Jr. (2014). Innovations in Business Forecasting: Predictive Analytics. *Journal of Business Forecasting*, 33(2).

Chatterjee, S., Sarker, S., & Valacich, J. S. (2015). The behavioral roots of information systems security: Exploring key factors related to unethical IT use. *Journal of Management Information Systems*, 31(4), 49–87. DOI: 10.1080/07421222.2014.1001257

Chaudhuri, R., Chatterjee, S., Ghosh, A., Vrontis, D., & Thrassou, A. (2022). Sustainable innovation for shared mobility: Contextual and consumer factors of an Indian car subscription business model. *International Journal of Entrepreneurial Behaviour & Research*. Advance online publication. DOI: 10.1108/IJEBR-01-2022-0090

Chen, M., Tworek, J., Jun, H., Yuan, Q., Pinto, H. P. de O., Kaplan, J., Edwards, H., Burda, Y., Joseph, N., Brockman, G., Ray, A., Puri, R., Krueger, G., Petrov, M., Khlaaf, H., Sastry, G., Mishkin, P., Chan, B., Gray, S., & Zaremba, W. (2021). Evaluating large language models trained on code. *arXiv*. https://arxiv.org/abs/2107.03374

Chen, S. H. (2016). The influencing factors of enterprise sustainable innovation: An empirical study. *Sustainability (Basel)*, 8(5), 425. DOI: 10.3390/su8050425

Chen, S., Kharrazi, A., Liang, S., Fath, B. D., Lenzen, M., & Yan, J. (2020). Advanced approaches and applications of energy footprints toward the promotion of global sustainability. *Applied Energy*, 261, 114415. DOI: 10.1016/j.apenergy.2019.114415

Chen, Y., Jensen, S., Albert, L. J., Gupta, S., & Lee, T. (2023). Artificial Intelligence (AI) student assistants in the Classroom: Designing Chatbots to Support Student Success. *Information Systems Frontiers*, 25(1), 161–182. Advance online publication. DOI: 10.1007/s10796-022-10291-4

Chesbrough, H. W., & Tucci, C. L. (2020). The interplay between open innovation and lean startup, or, why large companies are not large versions of startups. *Strategic Management Review*, 1(2), 277–303. DOI: 10.1561/111.00000013

Chiarini, A. (2021). Industry 4.0 technologies in lean production systems: A methodological approach. *Production Planning and Control*, 32(13), 1106–1118. DOI: 10.1080/09537287.2020.1817603

Chiasson, M., Davidson, E., & Winter, J. (2018). Philosophical foundations for informing the future (S) through IS research. *European Journal of Information Systems*, 27(3), 367–379. DOI: 10.1080/0960085X.2018.1435232

Chui, M., Manyika, J., & Miremadi, M. (2018). What AI can and can't do (yet) for your business. McKinsey Quarterly. https://www.mckinsey.com/business-functions/mckinsey-digital/our-insights/what-ai-can-and-cant-do-yet-for-your-business

Chukwu, N., Yufenyuy, S., Ejiofor, E., Ekweli, D., Ogunleye, O., Clement, T., Obunadike, C., Adeniji, S., Elom, E., & Obunadike, C. (2024). Resilient Chain: AI-Enhanced Supply Chain Security and Efficiency Integration. *Int. J. Sci. Manag. Res*, 7(03), 46–65. DOI: 10.37502/IJSMR.2024.7306

Ciasullo, M. V., Troisi, O., Grimaldi, M., & Leone, D. (2020). Multi-level governance for sustainable innovation in smart communities: An ecosystems approach. *The International Entrepreneurship and Management Journal*, 16(4), 1167–1195. DOI: 10.1007/s11365-020-00641-6

Cicconi, P. (2020). Eco-design and Eco-materials: An interactive and collaborative approach. *Sustainable Materials and Technologies*, 23, e00135. DOI: 10.1016/j.susmat.2019.e00135

Cillo, P., Priem, R. L., Verona, G., & Zanella, P. (2021). Consumer-CEO interaction as catalyst for business model innovation in established firms. *Journal of Business Research*, 131, 241–253. DOI: 10.1016/j.jbusres.2021.04.001

Cillo, V., Petruzzelli, A. M., Ardito, L., & Del Giudice, M. (2019). Understanding sustainable innovation: A systematic literature review. *Corporate Social Responsibility and Environmental Management*, 26(5), 1012–1025. DOI: 10.1002/csr.1783

Clemons, E. K., & Row, M. C. (1991). Sustaining IT advantage: The role of structural differences. *Management Information Systems Quarterly*, 15(3), 275–292. DOI: 10.2307/249639

Combs, J., Liu, Y., Hall, A., & Ketchen, D. (2006). How much do high-performance work practices matter? A meta-analysis of their effects on organizational performance. *Personnel Psychology*, 59(3), 501–528. DOI: 10.1111/j.1744-6570.2006.00045.x

Cooke, F. L., Dickmann, M., & Parry, E. (2020). IJHRM after 30 years: Taking stock in times of COVID-19 and looking towards the future of HR research. *International Journal of Human Resource Management*, 32(1), 1–23. DOI: 10.1080/09585192.2020.1833070

Cooke, P. (2020). Gigafactory logistics in space and time: Tesla's fourth gigafactory and its rivals. *Sustainability (Basel)*, 12(5), 2044. DOI: 10.3390/su12052044

Coombs, C., Stacey, P., Kawalek, P., Simeonova, B., Becker, J., Bergener, K., & Trautmann, H. (2021). What is it about humanity that we can't give away to intelligent machines? A european perspective. *International Journal of Information Management*, 58, 102311. DOI: 10.1016/j.ijinfomgt.2021.102311

Costa, J., & Matias, J. C. (2020). Open innovation 4.0 as an enhancer of sustainable innovation ecosystems. *Sustainability (Basel)*, 12(19), 8112. DOI: 10.3390/su12198112

Coupe, T. (2019). Automation and labor substitution in a smart factory era. *Technological Forecasting and Social Change*, 141, 312–320. DOI: 10.1016/j.techfore.2018.09.022

Cubric, M. (2020). Drivers, barriers and social considerations for AI adoption in business and management: A tertiary study. *Technology in Society*, 62, 101257. DOI: 10.1016/j.techsoc.2020.101257

Dai, Z. (2024). An In-depth Analysis of JP Morgan Chase & Co. Highlights in Business. *Economics and Management*, 24, 2265–2272.

Dattathrani, S., & De, R. (2023). The Concept of Agency in the era of Artificial Intelligence: Dimensions and degrees. *Information Systems Frontiers*, 25(1), 29–54. Advance online publication. DOI: 10.1007/s10796-022-10336-8

Davenport, T. H., & Kirby, J. (2016). *Only humans need apply: Winners and losers in the age of smart machines*. Harper Business.

Davenport, T. H., & Miller, S. M. (2022). *Working with AI: real stories of human-machine collaboration*. MIT Press. DOI: 10.7551/mitpress/14453.001.0001

Davenport, T. H., & Ronanki, R. (2018). Artificial intelligence for the real world. *Harvard Business Review*, 96(1), 108–116.

de Almeida, P. G. R., dos Santos, C. D., & Farias, J. S. (2021). Artificial intelligence regulation: A framework for governance. *Ethics and Information Technology*, 23(3), 505–525. DOI: 10.1007/s10676-021-09593-z

De, D., Chowdhury, S., Dey, P. K., & Ghosh, S. K. (2020). Impact of lean and sustainability oriented innovation on sustainability performance of small and medium sized enterprises: A data envelopment analysis-based framework. *International Journal of Production Economics*, 219, 416–430. DOI: 10.1016/j.ijpe.2018.07.003

Deguchi, A., Hirano, T., Matsuoka, F., & Nakano, Y. (2020). *Society 5.0: A people-centric super-smart society*. Springer. DOI: 10.1007/978-981-15-2989-4_1

Del Giudice, M. (2016). Discovering the human role in IoT-driven environments: A dynamic capabilities approach. *Technological Forecasting and Social Change*, 125, 42–49. DOI: 10.1016/j.techfore.2017.07.021

Del Giudice, M., Scuotto, V., Orlando, B., & Pagani, M. (2023). AI-enabled workforce transformation: Implications for organizational change and human resource management. *Journal of Business Research*, 148, 122–134. DOI: 10.1016/j.jbusres.2022.12.001

Demir, K., Wang, C., & Turner, T. (2020). Ethical issues and decision biases in AI implementation. *Journal of Business Ethics*, 162(1), 129–145. DOI: 10.1007/s10551-020-04348-x

Deng, Z., Xiang, N., & Pan, J. (2023). State of the art in immersive interactive technologies for surgery simulation: A review and prospective. *Bioengineering (Basel, Switzerland)*, 10(12), 1346. DOI: 10.3390/bioengineering10121346 PMID: 38135937

Dereso, C. W., Kant, S., Muthuraman, M., & Tufa, G. (2023). Effect of Point of Service on Health Department Student's Creativity in Comprehensive Universities of Ethiopia: Moderating Role of Public-Private Partnership and Mediating Role of Work Place Learning. In: Jain, S., Groppe, S., Mihindukulasooriya, N. (eds) *Proceedings of the International Health Informatics Conference. Lecture Notes in Electrical Engineering*, vol 990. Springer, Singapore. DOI: 10.1007/978-981-19-9090-8_13

Devezas, T. C., & Sarygulov, A. I. (2017). *Industry 4.0: Entrepreneurship and structural change in the new digital landscape*. Springer. DOI: 10.1007/978-3-319-49604-7

Dhamija, P., & Bag, S. (2020). Role of artificial intelligence in operations environment: A review and bibliometric analysis. *The TQM Journal*, 32(4), 869–986. DOI: 10.1108/TQM-10-2019-0243

Dhar, P., Rocks, T., Samarasinghe, R. M., Stephenson, G., & Smith, C. (2021). Augmented reality in medical education: Students' experiences and learning outcomes. *Medical Education Online*, 26(1), 1953953. DOI: 10.1080/10872981.2021.1953953 PMID: 34259122

Dhiman, B. (2023). A paradigm shift in the entertainment industry in the digital age: A critical Review. https://nbnresolving.org/urn:nbn:de:0168-ssoar-86963-8

Di Vaio, A., Palladino, R., Hassan, R., & Escobar, O. (2020). Artificial intelligence and business models in the sustainable development goals perspective: A systematic literature review. *Journal of Business Research*, 121, 283–314. DOI: 10.1016/j.jbusres.2020.08.019

Didier, T. (2021, January 29). *1990 - First mention of the term "Augmented Reality"*. Atomic. https://atomicdigital.design/blog-post/1990-first-mention-of-the-term-augmented-reality

Driskell, J. E., Salas, E., & Driskell, T. (2018). Foundations of teamwork and collaboration. *The American Psychologist*, 73(4), 334–348. DOI: 10.1037/amp0000241 PMID: 29792452

Duan, Y., Edwards, J. S., & Dwivedi, Y. K. (2019). Artificial intelligence for decision making in the era of Big Data–evolution, challenges and research agenda. *International Journal of Information Management*, 48, 63–71. DOI: 10.1016/j.ijinfomgt.2019.01.021

Dubey, R., Gunasekaran, A., Childe, S. J., Bryde, D. J., Giannakis, M., Foropon, C., Roubaud, D., & Hazen, B. T. (2020). Big data analytics and artificial intelligence pathway to operational performance under the effects of entrepreneurial orientation and environmental dynamism: A study of manufacturing organisations. *International Journal of Production Economics*, 226, 107599. DOI: 10.1016/j.ijpe.2019.107599

Durga, P., Godavarthi, D., Kant, S., & Basa, S. S. (2024). Aspect-based drug review classification through a hybrid model with ant colony optimization using deep learning. *Discov Computing*, 27(1), 19. DOI: 10.1007/s10791-024-09441-w

Dwivedi, , Hughes, L., Baabdullah, A. M., Ribeiro-Navarrete, S., Giannakis, M., Al-Debei, M. M., Dennehy, D., Metri, B., Buhalis, D., Cheung, C. M. K., Conboy, K., Doyle, R., Dubey, R., Dutot, V., Felix, R., Goyal, D. P., Gustafsson, A., Hinsch, C., Jebabli, I., & Wamba, S. F. (2022). Metaverse beyond the hype: Multidisciplinary perspectives on emerging challenges, opportunities, and agenda for research, practice and policy. *International Journal of Information Management*, 66, 102542. DOI: 10.1016/j.ijinfomgt.2022.102542

Dwivedi, Y. K., Hughes, L., Ismagilova, E., Aarts, G., Coombs, C., Crick, T., Duan, Y., Dwivedi, R., Edwards, J., Eirug, A., Galanos, V., Ilavarasan, P. V., Janssen, M., Jones, P., Kar, A. K., Kizgin, H., Kronemann, B., Lal, B., Lucini, B., & Williams, M. D. (2021). Artificial Intelligence (AI): Multidisciplinary perspectives on emerging challenges, opportunities, and agenda for research, practice and policy. *International Journal of Information Management*, 57, 101994. DOI: 10.1016/j.ijinfomgt.2019.08.002

ElBaih, M. (2023). The role of privacy regulations in AI development (A Discussion of the Ways in Which Privacy Regulations Can Shape the Development of AI). *SSRN* 4589207. DOI: 10.2139/ssrn.4589207

Elbanna, A., Dwivedi, Y., Bunker, D., & Wastell, D. (2020). The search for smartness in working, living and organising: Beyond the 'Technomagic.'. *Information Systems Frontiers*, 22(2), 275–280. DOI: 10.1007/s10796-020-10013-8

Enholm, I. M., Papagiannidis, E., Mikalef, P., & Krogstie, J. (2022). Artificial intelligence and business value: A literature review. *Information Systems Frontiers*, 24(5), 1709–1734. DOI: 10.1007/s10796-021-10186-w

Eubanks, S. (2022). Trust and integrity in AI-human interactions. *Journal of Organizational Psychology*, 35(1), 72–88. DOI: 10.1007/s11575-022-00799-0

Evjemo, L. D., Gjerstad, T., Grøtli, E. I., & Sziebig, G. (2020). Trends in smart manufacturing: Role of humans and industrial robots in smart factories. *Current Robotics Reports*, 1(2), 35–41. DOI: 10.1007/s43154-020-00006-5

Fanoberova, A., & Kuczkowska, H. (2016). Effects of source credibility and information quality on attitudes and purchase intentions of apparel products. *Journal of Retailing and Consumer Services*, 30, 23–34. DOI: 10.1016/j.jretconser.2016.06.003

Farayola, O. A., Abdul, A. A., Irabor, B. O., & Okeleke, E. C. (2023). Innovative business models driven by ai technologies: A review. *Computer Science & IT Research Journal*, 4(2), 85–110. DOI: 10.51594/csitrj.v4i2.608

Ferrario, M., Loi, M., & Viganò, E. (2020). Luddite anxiety and AI adoption in organizations. *Ethics and Information Technology*, 22(4), 423–437. DOI: 10.1007/s10676-020-09534-4

Ferràs-Hernández, X., Nylund, P. A., & Brem, A. (2023). The emergence of dominant designs in artificial intelligence. *California Management Review*, 65(3). DOI: 10.1177/00081256231164362

Figueroa-Armijos, M., Clark, B. B., & da Motta Veiga, S. P. (2023). Ethical perceptions of AI in hiring and organizational trust: The role of performance expectancy and social influence. *Journal of Business Ethics*, 186(1), 179–197. DOI: 10.1007/s10551-022-05166-2

Forbes. (2023, July 24). The difference between generative AI and traditional AI: An easy explanation by Bernard Marr. https://www.forbes.com/sites/bernardmarr/2023/07/24/the-difference-between-generative-ai-and-traditional-ai-an-easy-explanation-for-anyone/?sh=1260f473508a

Franco, M., Minatogawa, V., Duran, O., Battocchio, A., & Quadros, R. (2021). Opening the Dynamic Capability Black Box: An Approach to Business Model Innovation Management in the Digital Era. *IEEE Access : Practical Innovations, Open Solutions*, 9, 69189–69209. DOI: 10.1109/access.2021.3077849

Frank, M., Roehrig, P., & Pring, B. (2017). *What to do when machines do everything: How to get ahead in a world of ai, algorithms, bots, and big data*. John Wiley & Sons.

Frey, M. (2021). *Netflix recommends: algorithms, film choice, and the history of taste*. Univ of California Press.

Gama, F., & Magistretti, S. (2023). Artificial intelligence in innovation management: A review of innovation capabilities and a taxonomy of AI applications. *Journal of Product Innovation Management*, 1–16. DOI: 10.1111/jpim.12698

Gams, M., Gu, I. Y. H., Härmä, A., Muñoz, A., & Tam, V. (2019). Artificial intelligence and ambient intelligence. *Journal of Ambient Intelligence and Smart Environments*, 11(1), 71–86. DOI: 10.3233/AIS-180508

Gao, Y., & Liu, H. (2023). Artificial intelligence-enabled personalization in interactive marketing: A customer journey perspective. *Journal of Research in Interactive Marketing*, 17(5), 663–680. DOI: 10.1108/JRIM-01-2022-0023

Garbuio, M., & Lin, N. (2019). Artificial intelligence as a growth engine for health care startups: Emerging business models. *California Management Review*, 61(2), 59–83. DOI: 10.1177/0008125618811931

Garlinska, M., Osial, M., Proniewska, K., & Pregowska, A. (2023). The Influence of Emerging Technologies on Distance Education. *Electronics (Basel)*, 12(7), 1550. DOI: 10.3390/electronics12071550

Gartner. (n.d.). Beyond ChatGPT: The future of generative AI for enterprises. Retrieved February 28, 2024, from https://www.gartner.com/en/articles/beyond-chatgpt-the-future-of-generative-ai-for-enterprises

Gaur, L., Afaq, A., Singh, G., & Dwivedi, Y. K. (2021). Role of artificial intelligence and robotics to foster the touchless travel during a pandemic: A review and research agenda. *International Journal of Contemporary Hospitality Management*, 33(11), 4079–4098. DOI: 10.1108/IJCHM-11-2020-1246

Gaw, F. (2022). Algorithmic logics and the construction of cultural taste of the Netflix Recommender System. *Media Culture & Society*, 44(4), 706–725. DOI: 10.1177/01634437211053767

Gillath, O., Ai, T., & Fink, J. (2021). Human-AI communication and its ethical implications. *Computers in Human Behavior*, 124, 106918. DOI: 10.1016/j.chb.2021.106918

Giuggioli, G., & Pellegrini, M. M. (2023). Artificial intelligence as an enabler for entrepreneurs: A systematic literature review and an agenda for future research. *International Journal of Entrepreneurial Behaviour & Research*, 29(4), 816–837. DOI: 10.1108/IJEBR-05-2021-0426

Glickson, E., & Woolley, A. W. (2020). Human-AI collaboration: Challenges and solutions. *Journal of Management Studies*, 57(7), 1173–1197. DOI: 10.1111/joms.12520

Godavarthi, B., Narisetty, N., Gudikandhula, K., Muthukumaran, R., Kapila, D., & Ramesh, J. (2023). Cloud computing enabled business model innovation. *The Journal of High Technology Management Research*, 34(2), 100469. DOI: 10.1016/j.hitech.2023.100469

Gordon, W., & Langmaid, R. (2022). *Qualitative market research: a practitioner's and buyer's guide*. Routledge. DOI: 10.4324/9781315245553

Greenhalgh, T., Robert, G., Macfarlane, F., Bate, P., & Kyriakidou, O. (2004). Diffusion of innovations in service organizations: Systematic review and recommendations. *The Milbank Quarterly*, 82(4), 581–629. DOI: 10.1111/j.0887-378X.2004.00325.x PMID: 15595944

Green, M., Tariq, R., & Green, P. (2016). Improving patient safety through simulation training in anesthesiology: Where are we? *Anesthesiology Research and Practice*, 4237523, 1–12. Advance online publication. DOI: 10.1155/2016/4237523 PMID: 26949389

Gregersen, M. F., Trischler, J., & Li-Ying, J. (2022). Digital business model innovation: Toward construct clarity and future research directions. *Review of Managerial Science*, 17, 3–32. DOI: 10.1007/s11846-021-00508-2

Guenole, N. and Feinzig, S. (2018), *The business case for AI in HR: with insights and tips on getting started.* IBM Smarter Workforce Institute, IBM.

Guyo, D. M., Kero, C. A., & Kant, S. (2025). Is Marketing Intermediaries' Mediation Required for Livestock and Products Marketing to Improve the Economic Status of Pastoralist Communities in Ethiopia? In *AI in Agriculture for Sustainable and Economic Management* (pp. 216-234). CRC Press.

Guyo, K., & Kero, C. A. (2023). Mediation of Marketing Intermediaries and AI Adoption Between Livestock Products Marketing and Economic Status of Pastoralist in Ethiopia. *2023 International Conference on Communication, Security and Artificial Intelligence (ICCSAI)*, 311-316, DOI: 10.1109/ICCSAI59793.2023.10421261

Haamer, R. E., Mikhailava, N., Podliesnova, V., Saremat, R., Lusmägi, T., Petrinec, A., & Anbarjafari, G. (2024). Motion sickness in mixed-reality situational awareness system. *Applied Sciences (Basel, Switzerland)*, 14(6), 2231. DOI: 10.3390/app14062231

Haas, L., & Tussey, J. (Eds.). (2021). *Connecting Disciplinary Literacy and Digital Storytelling in K-12 Education*. IGI Global., DOI: 10.4018/978-1-7998-5770-9

Habbal, A., Ali, M. K., & Abuzaraida, M. A. (2024). Artificial Intelligence Trust, risk and security management (AI trism): Frameworks, applications, challenges and future research directions. *Expert Systems with Applications*, 240, 122442. DOI: 10.1016/j.eswa.2023.122442

Haefner, N., Wincent, J., Parida, V., & Gassmann, O. (2021). Artificial intelligence and innovation management: A review, framework, and research agenda. *Technological Forecasting and Social Change*, 162, 120392. DOI: 10.1016/j.techfore.2020.120392

Haenlein, M., & Kaplan, A. (2019). A brief history of artificial intelligence: On the past, present, and future of artificial intelligence. *California Management Review*, 61(4), 5–14. DOI: 10.1177/0008125619864925

Hagl, R., & Duane, A. (2018). *Exploring the impact of augmented reality and virtual reality technologies on business model innovation in technology companies in Germany*. In: Australasian Conference on Information Systems, (ed.), Australasian Conference on Information Systems 2018. Sydney: UTS ePRESS. DOI: DOI: 10.5130/acis2018.ao

Haleem, A., Javaid, M., Qadri, M. A., & Suman, R. (2022). Understanding the role of digital technologies in education: A review. *Sustainable Operations and Computers*, 3, 275–285. DOI: 10.1016/j.susoc.2022.05.004

Halper, F. (2014). Predictive analytics for business advantage. *TDWI Research*, 1-32.

Hamad, A., & Jia, B. (2022). How Virtual Reality Technology Has Changed Our Lives: An Overview of the Current and Potential Applications and Limitations. *International Journal of Environmental Research and Public Health*, 19(18), 11278. DOI: 10.3390/ijerph191811278 PMID: 36141551

Hanaysha, J. R., Al-Shaikh, M. E., Joghee, S., & Alzoubi, H. M. (2022). Impact of innovation capabilities on business sustainability in small and medium enterprises. *FIIB Business Review*, 11(1), 67–78. DOI: 10.1177/23197145211042232

Harris, D. J., Arthur, T., Kearse, J., Olonilua, M., Hassan, E. K., De Burgh, T. C., Wilson, M. R., & Vine, S. J. (2023). Exploring the role of virtual reality in military decision training. *Frontiers in Virtual Reality*, 4, 1165030. Advance online publication. DOI: 10.3389/frvir.2023.1165030

Hechler, E., Oberhofer, M., & Schaeck, T. (2020). *Deploying AI in the Enterprise. IT Approaches for Design, DevOps, Governance, Change Management, Blockchain, and Quantum Computing*. Apress.

Heilig, M. (1962). *US Patent #3,050,870*. https://patentimages.storage.googleapis.com/90/34/2f/24615bb97ad68e/US3050870.pdf

Herrmann, S., & Pfeiffer, S. (2023). Collaborative intelligence in Industry 4.0: Designing socio-technical systems. *Technology Innovation Management Review*, 13(2), 5–15. DOI: 10.22215/timreview/1618

Holm, J. R., & Lorenz, E. (2022). Task restructuring and work fragmentation: Impacts of Industry 4.0. *Industrial Relations Journal*, 53(4), 289–307. DOI: 10.1111/irj.12362

Hoyer, W. D., Kroschke, M., Schmitt, B., Kraume, K., & Shankar, V. (2020). Transforming the customer experience through new technologies. *Journal of Interactive Marketing*, 51(1), 57–71. DOI: 10.1016/j.intmar.2020.04.001

Huang, M. H., Rust, R. T., & Maksimovic, V. (2019). The AI dilemma: AI takes over human jobs but can't take over human touch. *Journal of Service Research*, 22(2), 158–166. DOI: 10.1177/1094670519827370

Huang, Q., Lin, J., Han, R., Peng, C., & Huang, A. (2022). Using Virtual Reality exposure therapy in pain management: A systematic review and meta-analysis of randomized controlled trials. *Value in Health*, 25(2), 288–301. DOI: 10.1016/j.jval.2021.04.1285 PMID: 35094802

Huotari, P., & Ritala, P. (2021). When to switch between subscription-based and ad-sponsored business models: Strategic implications of decreasing content novelty. *Journal of Business Research*, 129, 14–28. DOI: 10.1016/j.jbusres.2021.02.037

Hutson, J. (2023). Shared cinematic experience and emerging technologies: Integrating mixed-reality components for the future of cinema. *Faculty Scholarship*. 504. https://digitalcommons.lindenwood.edu/faculty-research-papers/504

Huynh-The, T., Gadekallu, T. R., Wang, W., Yenduri, G., Ranaweera, P., Pham, Q., Costa, D. B., & Liyanage, M. (2023). Blockchain for the metaverse: A Review. *Future Generation Computer Systems*, 143, 401–419. DOI: 10.1016/j.future.2023.02.008

Hysa, X., & Themeli, A. (2022). Interorganizational coworking: attenuating complexity, enhancing resilience and fostering open innovation and knowledge cocreation. *Transforming Government: People. Process and Policy*, 16(2), 244–257.

Iaia, L., Isidori, D., Vitale, G., & Leone, D. (2023). Cognitive automation in Industry 4.0: Human-centered approaches. *Journal of Manufacturing Systems*, 69, 309–320. DOI: 10.1016/j.jmsy.2022.07.003

Iansiti, M., & Lakhani, K. (2020a, January–February). Competing in the age of artificial intelligence. Harvard Business Press.

Iansiti, M., & Lakhani, K. R. (2020b). Competing in the age of AI: How machine intelligence changes the rules of business. *Harvard Business Review*, 98(1), 60–67.

Idonije, P. I., Dangana, E. A., Ameh, A. A., & Okafor, G. O. (2022). Entrepreneurial Orientation and Sustainable Job Creation: A Study of Small and Medium Enterprises in South-South, Nigeria. *Journal of Business Management. Innovation and Creativity*, 1(1), 254–277.

Impact of Crisis on Sustainable Business Model Innovation—The Role of Technology Innovation. (2022). *Sustainability*, 14, 11596. DOI: 10.3390/su141811596

Ismanov, I., Qayumov, N., Mukhamadjonova, D., & Akhmadaliyev, B. (2024, April). AI and Cost Management: Strategies for Reducing Expenses and Improving Profit Margins in Business. In *2024 International Conference on Knowledge Engineering and Communication Systems (ICKECS)* (Vol. 1, pp. 1-7). IEEE. DOI: 10.1109/ICKECS61492.2024.10616761

Ivanov, S., & Webster, C. (2019). Perceived appropriateness and intention to use service robots in tourism. In *Information and Communication Technologies in Tourism 2019:Proceedings of the International Conference in Nicosia, Cyprus, January 30–February 1, 2019* (pp. 237-248). Springer International Publishing. DOI: 10.1007/978-3-030-05940-8_19

Jabo, B., & Kant, S. (2024). Impact of Technical CRM on Ethiopia Bank Human-Computer Interface and Competitive Advantage as Mediators of Performance. *2024 IEEE International Conference on Computing, Power and Communication Technologies (IC2PCT)*, 679-682, DOI: 10.1109/IC2PCT60090.2024.10486237

Jacobides, M. G., Cennamo, C., & Gawer, A. (2018). Towards a theory of ecosystems. *Strategic Management Journal*, 39(8), 2255–2276. DOI: 10.1002/smj.2904

Janssen, M., Brous, P., Estevez, E., Barbosa, L. S., & Janowski, T. (2020). Data governance: Organizing data for trustworthy Artificial Intelligence. *Government Information Quarterly*, 37(3), 101493. DOI: 10.1016/j.giq.2020.101493

Jarrahi, M. H. (2018). Artificial intelligence and the future of work: Human-AI symbiosis in organizational decision-making. *Business Horizons*, 61(4), 577–586. DOI: 10.1016/j.bushor.2018.03.007

Jia, N., Luo, X., Fang, Z., & Liao, C. (2024). When and how artificial intelligence augments employee creativity. *Academy of Management Journal*, 67(1), 5–32. DOI: 10.5465/amj.2022.0426

Jin, M., Tang, R., Ji, Y., Liu, F., Gao, L., & Huisingh, D. (2017). Impact of advanced manufacturing on sustainability: An overview of the special volume on advanced manufacturing for sustainability and low fossil carbon emissions. *Journal of Cleaner Production*, 161, 69–74. DOI: 10.1016/j.jclepro.2017.05.101

Jo¨hnk, J., Weißert, M., & Wyrtki, K. (2021). Ready or not, AI comes – an interview study of organizational AI readiness factors. *Business & Information Systems Engineering*, 63(1), 5–20. DOI: 10.1007/s12599-020-00676-7

Jones, P., Osborne, T., Sullivan-Drage, C., Keen, N., & Gadsby, E. (2022). ONE: What is VR and why use it in research? In *Virtual Reality Methods*. Bristol, UK: Policy Press. DOI: 10.51952/9781447360773.ch001

Jorna, R. (Ed.). (2017). *Sustainable innovation: The organisational, human and knowledge dimension*. Routledge. DOI: 10.4324/9781351280365

Jorzik, P., Klein, S. P., Kanbach, D. K., & Kraus, S. (2024). AI-driven business model innovation: A systematic review and research agenda. *Journal of Business Research*, 182, 114764. DOI: 10.1016/j.jbusres.2024.114764

Kant, S., & Adula, M. (2024). AI Learning and Work Attitude Mediation Between Reward and Organizational Support in Ethiopia. In Gomathi Sankar, J., & David, A. (Eds.), *Generative AI for Transformational Management* (pp. 109–136). IGI Global., DOI: 10.4018/979-8-3693-5578-7.ch005

Kant, S., & Adula, M. (2024). Human-Machine Interaction in the Metaverse in the Context of Ethiopia. In *Impact and Potential of Machine Learning in the Metaverse* (pp. 196–212). IGI Global., DOI: 10.4018/979-8-3693-5762-0.ch008

Kaplan, A., & Haenlein, M. (2019). Siri, Siri, in my hand: Who's the fairest in the land? On the interpretations, illustrations, and implications of artificial intelligence. *Business Horizons*, 62(1), 15–25. DOI: 10.1016/j.bushor.2018.08.004

Kato, H., & Billinghurst, M. (2004). *Developing AR applications with ARToolKit*. Conference: 3rd IEEE and ACM International Symposium on Mixed and Augmented Reality (ISMAR 2004), 2-5 November 2004, Arlington, VA, USA. https://www.researchgate.net/publication/221221056_Developing_AR_Applications_with_ARToolKit

Kautish, P., & Khare, A. (2022). Investigating the moderating role of AI-enabled services on flow and awe experience. *International Journal of Information Management*, 66, 102519. DOI: 10.1016/j.ijinfomgt.2022.102519

Keegan, B. J., Dennehy, D., & Naudé, P. (2022). Implementing artificial intelligence in traditional B2B marketing practices: An activity theory perspective. *Information Systems Frontiers*. Advance online publication. DOI: 10.1007/s10796-022-10294-1 PMID: 35637917

Kent, L., Snider, C., Gopsill, J., & Hicks, B. (2021). Mixed reality in design prototyping: A systematic review. *Design Studies*, 77, 101046. DOI: 10.1016/j.destud.2021.101046

Khemthong, S., & Roberts, L. (2006). Adoption of internet and web technology for hotel marketing: A study of hotels in Thailand. *Journal of Business Systems, Governance, and Ethics*, 1(2), 47–60. DOI: 10.15209/jbsge.v1i2.74

Khogali, H. O., & Mekid, S. (2023). The blended future of automation and AI: Examining some long-term societal and ethical impact features. *Technology in Society*, 73, 102232. DOI: 10.1016/j.techsoc.2023.102232

Kim, G., Shin, B., Kim, K. K., & Lee, H. G. (2011). IT capabilities, process-oriented dynamic capabilities, and firm financial performance. *Journal of the Association for Information Systems*, 12(7), 487–517. DOI: 10.17705/1jais.00270

Kim, J. (2020). The influence of perceived costs and perceived benefits on AI-driven interactive recommendation agent value. *Journal of Global Scholars of Marketing Science*, 30(3), 319–333. DOI: 10.1080/21639159.2020.1775491

Kohli, R., & Melville, N. P. (2019). Digital innovation: A review and synthesis. *Information Systems Journal*, 29(1), 200–223. DOI: 10.1111/isj.12193

Kohtamäki, M., Parida, V., Patel, P. C., & Gebauer, H. (2020). The relationship between digitalization and servitization: The role of servitization in capturing the financial potential of digitalization. *Technological Forecasting and Social Change*, 151, 119804. DOI: 10.1016/j.techfore.2019.119804

Koumpouros, Y. (2024). Revealing the true potential and prospects of augmented reality in education. *Smart Learning Environments*, 11(2), 2. Advance online publication. DOI: 10.1186/s40561-023-00288-0

Krakowski, S., Luger, J., & Raisch, S. (2023). Artificial intelligence and the changing sources of competitive advantage. *Strategic Management Journal*, 44(6), 1425–1452. DOI: 10.1002/smj.3387

Krasonikolakis, I., Vrechopoulos, A., Pouloudi, A., & Dimitriadis, S. (2018). Store layout effects on consumer behavior in 3D online stores. *European Journal of Marketing*, 52(5/6), 1223–1256. DOI: 10.1108/EJM-03-2015-0183

Kraus, S., Kanback, D. K., Krysta, P. M., Steinhoff, M. M., & Tomini, N. (2022). Facebook and the creation of the metaverse: Radical business model innovation or incremental transformation? *International Journal of Entrepreneurial Behaviour & Research*, 28(9), 52–77. DOI: 10.1108/IJEBR-12-2021-0984

Kuhn, A. W., Yu, J. K., Gerull, K. M., Silverman, R. M., & Aleem, A. W. (2024). Virtual Reality and surgical simulation training for orthopaedic surgery residents: A qualitative assessment of trainee perspectives. *JBJS: Open Access*, 9(1), e23.00142. https://journals.lww.com/jbjsoa/fulltext/2024/03000/virtual_reality_and_surgical_simulation_training.17.aspx

Kumari, B., Kaur, J., & Swami, S. (2021). System dynamics approach for adoption of artificial intelligence in finance. In *Advances in Systems Engineering: Select Proceedings of NSC 2019* (pp. 555-575). Springer Singapore. DOI: 10.1007/978-981-15-8025-3_54

Kumari, D., & Bhat, S. (2021). Application of artificial intelligence technology in tesla-a case study. *International Journal of Applied Engineering and Management Letters*, 5(2), 205–218. DOI: 10.47992/IJAEML.2581.7000.0113

Kusiak, A. (2018). Smart manufacturing. *International Journal of Production Research*, 56(1-2), 508–517. DOI: 10.1080/00207543.2017.1351644

Kuzma, E., Padilha, L. S., Sehnem, S., Julkovski, D. J., & Roman, D. J. (2020). The relationship between innovation and sustainability: A meta-analytic study. *Journal of Cleaner Production*, 259, 120745. DOI: 10.1016/j.jclepro.2020.120745

Lal, R. (2024). *AR In E-commerce for virtual shopping experience*. Idea Usher. https://ideausher.com/blog/ar-in-e-commerce/

Lampropoulos, G., & Kinshuk, . (2024). Virtual reality and gamification in education: A systematic review. *Educational Technology Research and Development*, 72(3), 1691–1785. Advance online publication. DOI: 10.1007/s11423-024-10351-3

Lamssarbi, B., & Bouaziz, S. M. (2023, April). The Impact of Digitalization and Managerial Innovation on Resilience in the Face of the COVID-19 Crisis: The Case of SMEs in the Greater Agadir Region. In *International Conference on Current Business Issues in African Countries* (pp. 155-174). Cham: Springer Nature Switzerland.

Laurens-Arredondo, L. A., & Laurens, L. (2023). Metaversity: Beyond emerging educational technology. *Sustainability (Basel)*, 15(22), 15844. DOI: 10.3390/su152215844

Lauterbach, A., & Bonime-Blanc, A. (2018). *The artificial intelligence imperative: A practical roadmap for business*. Bloomsbury Publishing USA. DOI: 10.5040/9798400614835

Lee, J., Suh, T., Roy, D., & Baucus, M. (2019). Emerging technology and business model innovation: The case of artificial intelligence. *Journal of Open Innovation*, 5(3), 44. DOI: 10.3390/joitmc5030044

Lengnick-Hall, C. A., Beck, T. E., & Lengnick-Hall, M. L. (2011). Developing a capacity for organizational resilience through strategic human resource management. *Human Resource Management Review*, 21(3), 243–255. DOI: 10.1016/j.hrmr.2010.07.001

Leone, D., Vitale, G., & Zucchella, A. (2020). Value co-creation in Industry 4.0 ecosystems. *Strategic Change*, 29(5), 515–525. DOI: 10.1002/jsc.2384

Leroy, K. (2023, June 21). Revolutionizing reality: The current uses and future of AR. *Forbes Business Council*.https://www.forbes.com/sites/forbesbusinesscouncil/2023/06/21/revolutionizing-reality-the-current-uses-and-future-of-ar/?sh=6f3097428836

Liao, Y. C. (2024). Innovative interaction mode in VR games. In: Hung, J.C., Yen, N., Chang, JW. (eds) *Frontier Computing on Industrial Applications,* Volume 4. FC 2023. Lecture Notes in Electrical Engineering, 1134. Springer, Singapore. DOI: 10.1007/978-981-99-9342-0_9

Liao, T., & Humphreys, L. (2015). Layar-ed places: Using mobile augmented reality to tactically reengage, reproduce, and reappropriate public space. *New Media & Society*, 17(9), 1418–1435. DOI: 10.1177/1461444814527734

Li, F. (2020). The digital transformation of business models in the creative industries: A holistic framework and emerging trends. *Technovation*, 92, 102012. DOI: 10.1016/j.technovation.2017.12.004

Lindecrantz, E., Gi, M. T. P., & Zerbi, S. (2020). *Personalizing the customer experience: Driving differentiation in retail.*

Lindgren, P. (2020). Multi Business Model Innovation in a World of Smart Cities with Future Wireless Technologies. *Wireless Personal Communications*, 113(3), 1423–1435. DOI: 10.1007/s11277-020-07314-1

Lins, S., Pandl, K. D., Teigeler, H., Thiebes, S., Bayer, C., & Sunyaev, A. (2021). Artificial intelligence as a service: Classification and research directions. *Business & Information Systems Engineering*, 63(4), 441–456. DOI: 10.1007/s12599-021-00708-w

Li, R., & Suh, A. (2015). Factors influencing information credibility on social media platforms. *Procedia Computer Science*, 72, 314–328. DOI: 10.1016/j.procs.2015.12.146

Liu, D., Gong, Y., Zhou, J., & Huang, J. (2017). Human resource systems, employee creativity, and firm innovation: The moderating role of firm ownership. *Academy of Management Journal*, 60(3), 1164–1188. DOI: 10.5465/amj.2015.0230

Lowood, H. E. (2024). Virtual Reality. *Encyclopedia Britannica*. https://www.britannica.com/technology/virtual-reality

Lu, B. (2022). Analysis on Innovation Path of Business Administration Based on Artificial Intelligence. *Mathematical Problems in Engineering*, 2022, 1–7. DOI: 10.1155/2022/6790836

Lüdeke-Freund, F. (2020). Sustainable entrepreneurship, innovation, and business models: Integrative framework and propositions for future research. *Business Strategy and the Environment*, 29(2), 665–681. DOI: 10.1002/bse.2396

Lu, Y. (2017). Industry 4.0: A review on technologies, applications, and open research issues. *Journal of Industrial Information Integration*, 6, 1–10. DOI: 10.1016/j.jii.2017.04.005

Lu, Y. (2019). Artificial intelligence: A survey on evolution, models, applications and future trends. *Journal of Management Analytics*, 6(1), 1–29. DOI: 10.1080/23270012.2019.1570365

Lysyakov, M., & Viswanathan, S. (2023). Threatened by AI: Analyzing users' responses to the introduction of AI in a crowd-sourcing platform. *Information Systems Research*, 34(3), 1191–1210. DOI: 10.1287/isre.2022.1184

Magistretti, S., Dell'Era, C., & Petruzzelli, A. M. (2019). How intelligent is Watson? Enabling digital transformation through artificial intelligence. *Business Horizons*, 62(6), 819–829. DOI: 10.1016/j.bushor.2019.08.004

Mahadev Madgule, N. (2023). Mechanical properties and microstructure of activated TIG welded similar joints of Inconel alloys by desirability approaches. *Materials Today: Proceedings*, 77, 528–533. DOI: 10.1016/j.matpr.2022.12.250

Malik, A., Pereira, V., & Budhwar, P. (2020). HRM in the global information technology (IT) industry: Towards multivergent configurations in strategic business partnerships. *Human Resource Management Review*, 31(3), 100743. DOI: 10.1016/j.hrmr.2020.100743

Manley, D., & Williams, J. (2022). Socio-technical symbiosis in Industry 4.0: Toward a framework for human-machine collaboration. *Systems Research and Behavioral Science*, 39(5), 1238–1254. DOI: 10.1002/sres.2845

Manyika, J., Lund, S., Chui, M., Bughin, J., Woetzel, J., Batra, P., & Sanghvi, S. (2017). What the future of work will mean for jobs, skills, and wages. McKinsey Global Institute. https://www.mckinsey.com/featured-insights/future-of-work/what-the-future-of-work-will-mean-for-jobs-skills-and-wages

Maresova, P., Soukal, I., & Kuca, K. (2018). Technological trends in Industry 4.0 and their impact on business models. *Economic Research-Ekonomska Istraživanja*, 31(1), 1843–1857. DOI: 10.1080/1331677X.2018.1519691

Mariani, M., & Dwivedi, Y. K. (2024). Generative artificial intelligence in innovation management: A preview of future research developments. *Journal of Business Research*, 175, 114542. DOI: 10.1016/j.jbusres.2024.114542

Marr, B. (2021). The important difference between Virtual Reality, Augmented Reality and Mixed Reality. *Bernerd Marr & Company.* https://bernardmarr.com/the-important-difference-between-virtual-reality-augmented-reality-and-mixed-reality/

Marwaha, K. (2017). Corporate governance and whistle blowing in India: Promises or reality? *International Journal of Law and Management*, 59(3), 430–441. DOI: 10.1108/IJLMA-12-2015-0064

Mathew, P. S., & Pillai, A. S. (2020). Role of Immersive (XR) Technologies in Improving Healthcare Competencies: A Review. In Guazzaroni, G., & Pillai, A. (Eds.), *Virtual and Augmented Reality in Education, Art, and Museums* (pp. 23–46). IGI Global., DOI: 10.4018/978-1-7998-1796-3.ch002

Mattan, M. (2024, March 19). Unlocking the mystery: How does augmented reality transform our world? *BrandXR.* https://www.brandxr.io/unlocking-the-mystery-how-does-augmented-reality-transform-our-world

McKnight, D. H., & Kacmar, C. J. (2006). Factors and effects of information technology on trust in the workplace. *Information & Management*, 43(8), 901–910. DOI: 10.1016/j.im.2006.08.003

Mcknight, H., & Kacmar, C. (2006). Factors of information credibility for an internet advice site. *Journal of Business Research*, 59(3), 249–256. DOI: 10.1016/j.jbusres.2005.10.005

Metaxiotis, K., Zafeiropoulos, I., & Askounis, D. (2005). Dynamic risk management system for the modeling, optimal adaptation and implementation of an ERP system. *Information Management & Computer Security*, 13(3), 212–234. DOI: 10.1108/09685220510602031

Metelskaia, I., Ignatyeva, O., Denef, S., & Samsonowa, T. (2018, June). A business model template for AI solutions. In *Proceedings of the international conference on intelligent science and technology* (pp. 35-41). DOI: 10.1145/3233740.3233750

Mikalef, P., & Gupta, M. (2021). Artificial intelligence capability: Conceptualization, measurement calibration, and empirical study on its impact on organizational creativity and firm performance. *Information & Management*, 58(3), 103434. DOI: 10.1016/j.im.2021.103434

Mistry, H. K., Mavani, C., Goswami, A., & Patel, R. (2024). The Impact Of Cloud Computing And Ai On Industry Dynamics And Competition. *Educational Administration: Theory and Practice*, 30(7), 797–804.

Modgil, S., Gupta, S., Stekelorum, R., & Laguir, I. (2022). AI technologies and their impact on supply chain resilience during COVID-19. *International Journal of Physical Distribution & Logistics Management*, 52(2), 130–149. DOI: 10.1108/IJPDLM-12-2020-0434

Modgil, S., Singh, R. K., & Hannibal, C. (2021). Artificial intelligence for supply chain resilience: Learning from covid-19. *International Journal of Logistics Management*. Advance online publication. DOI: 10.1108/IJLM-02-2021-0094

Mooney, J. G., Gurbaxani, V., & Kraemer, K. L. (1996). A process oriented framework for assessing the business value of information technology. *The Data Base for Advances in Information Systems*, 27(2), 68–81. DOI: 10.1145/243350.243363

Moore, G. C., & Benbasat, I. (1991). Development of an instrument to measure the perceptions of adopting an information technology innovation. *Information Systems Research*, 2(3), 192–222. DOI: 10.1287/isre.2.3.192

Mostafa, M. (2020). *Artificial intelligence applications in supply chain management and analysis in Turkey* (Master's thesis, İstanbul Sabahattin Zaim Üniversitesi, Lisansüstü Eğitim Enstitüsü, İşletme Anabilim Dalı).

Mourtzis, D. (2020). Simulation and virtual commissioning of Industry 4.0 technologies in lean manufacturing systems. *CIRP Annals*, 69(1), 7–20. DOI: 10.1016/j.cirp.2020.04.121

Muduli, A., & Trivedi, J. J. (2020). Recruitment methods, recruitment outcomes and information credibility and sufficiency. *Benchmarking*, 27(4), 1615–1631. DOI: 10.1108/BIJ-07-2019-0312

Mukherjee, A., & Chang, H. (2023). Managing the Creative frontier of generative AI: The novelty-usefulness tradeoff. *California Management Review*.

Murshed, N. A., & Ugurlu, E. (2023). Navigating the Digital Marketplace: A Holistic Model Integrating Social Media Engagement and Consumer Behavior Factors to Enhance Online Shopping Adoption. *Jurnal Manajemen Teori dan Terapan, 16*(3).

Musawa, M., & Wahab, E. (2012). The adoption of EDI technology by Nigerian SMEs: A conceptual framework. *Journal of Business Management and Economics*, 3(2), 55–68.

Mustak, M., Salminen, J., Plé, L., & Wirtz, J. (2021). Artificial intelligence in marketing: Topic modeling, scientometric analysis, and research agenda. *Journal of Business Research*, 124, 389–404. DOI: 10.1016/j.jbusres.2020.10.044

Nair, P. (2017), *The rise of the AI recruiter: is HR tech the next to challenge human intuition*. www.growthbusiness.co.uk/rise-ai-recruiter-hr-tech-next-challenge-human -intuition-2550350

Nambisan, S., Wright, M., & Feldman, M. (2019). The digital transformation of innovation and entrepreneurship: Progress, challenges and key themes. *Research Policy*, 48(8), 103773. DOI: 10.1016/j.respol.2019.03.018

Nayak, A., Patnaik, A., Satpathy, I., Khang, A., & Patnaik, B. C. M. (2023). Applications of the Internet of Things (IoT) in Smart Cities: A Step toward Innovation. In *Smart Cities* (pp. 57–77). CRC Press. DOI: 10.1201/9781003376064-4

Neuhüttler, J., Kett, H., Frings, S., Falkner, J., Ganz, W., & Urmetzer, F. (2020a). Artificial Intelligence as Driver for Business Model Innovation in Smart Service Systems. In Advances in Intelligent Systems and Computing (pp. 212–219). DOI: 10.1007/978-3-030-51057-2_30

Niederman, F. (2021). Project management: Openings for disruption from AI and advanced analytics. *Information Technology & People*, 34(6), 15701599. DOI: 10.1108/ITP-09-2020-0639

Nielsen, C. (2023). Business Model Innovation in the Era of Digital Technologies and Societal Challenges. *Journal of Business Models*, 11(3), 2–12.

Niessen, L., Bocken, N. M., & Dijk, M. (2023). The impact of business sufficiency strategies on consumer practices: The case of bicycle subscription. *Sustainable Production and Consumption*, 35, 576–591. DOI: 10.1016/j.spc.2022.12.007

Nitzberg, M., & Zysman, J. (2022). Algorithms, data, and platforms: The diverse challenges of governing AI. *Journal of European Public Policy*, 29(11), 1753–1778. DOI: 10.1080/13501763.2022.2096668

Niyitunga, E. B. (2024). The Role of Artificial Intelligence in Promoting Digital Public Participation for Successful Peacebuilding in Africa. *African Journal of Peace and Conflict Studies (formerly Ubuntu: Journal of Conflict and Social Transformation), 13*(1), 25-49.

Novak, S., & Wisdom, J. (2018). Addressing anxiety in workplace AI integration. *The Journal of Applied Psychology*, 103(7), 895–912. DOI: 10.1037/apl0000314

Nyoach, T. D., Lemi, K., Debela, T., & Kant, S. (2024). Does Organizational Commitment Mediate the Relationship between Employee Relationship Management and Bank Performance? The Case of Banks in Ethiopia. *International Journal of Organizational Leadership*, 13(2), 355–376. DOI: 10.33844/ijol.2024.60419

O'Meara, J., & Szita, K. (2021). AR cinema: Visual storytelling and embodied experiences with Augmented Reality filters and backgrounds. *Presence (Cambridge, Mass.)*, 30, 99–123. DOI: 10.1162/pres_a_00376

Oesterreich, T. D., & Teuteberg, F. (2016). Understanding the implications of Industry 4.0: A review of the research agenda. *Computers in Industry*, 83, 121–137. DOI: 10.1016/j.compind.2016.09.006

Okumus, F., Ali, F., & Bilgihan, A. (2017). Workplace technology adoption: Perceptions of AI and robotics. *International Journal of Contemporary Hospitality Management*, 29(5), 1388–1410. DOI: 10.1108/IJCHM-02-2016-0066

Omrani, N., Rejeb, N., Maalaoui, A., Dabić, M., & Kraus, S. (2022). Drivers of digital transformation in SMEs. *IEEE Transactions on Engineering Management*.

Onu, P., Pradhan, A., & Mbohwa, C. (2023). Potential to use metaverse for future teaching and learning. *Education and Information Technologies*. Advance online publication. DOI: 10.1007/s10639-023-12167-9

Oscherwitz, T., & Löffler, C. (2024). A conceptual framework for AI-driven innovation: Shaping the business model of the future. *Journal of Business Research*, 182, 114767.

Oskam, I., Bossink, B., & de Man, A. P. (2021). Valuing value in innovation ecosystems: How cross-sector actors overcome tensions in collaborative sustainable business model development. *Business & Society*, 60(5), 1059–1091. DOI: 10.1177/0007650320907145

Ostmeier, E., & Strobel, M. (2022). Addressing fears of AI in the workplace: Strategies for human-centered AI integration. *AI & Society*, 37(1), 45–57. DOI: 10.1007/s00146-020-01068-1

Oufqir, Z., Abderrahmani, A., & Satori, K. (2020). ARKit and ARCore in serve to augmented reality, 2020 *International Conference on Intelligent Systems and Computer Vision* (ISCV), Fez, Morocco, 2020, pp. 1-7. DOI: 10.1109/ISCV49265.2020.9204243

Palumbo, A. (2022). Microsoft HoloLens 2 in medical and healthcare context: State of the art and future prospects. *Sensors (Basel)*, 22(20), 7709. DOI: 10.3390/s22207709 PMID: 36298059

Panigrahi, A., Pati, A., Sahu, B., Das, M. N., Nayak, D. S. K., Sahoo, G., & Kant, S. (2023). En-MinWhale: An ensemble approach based on MRMR and Whale optimization for Cancer diagnosis. *IEEE Access : Practical Innovations, Open Solutions*, 11, 113526–113542. DOI: 10.1109/ACCESS.2023.3318261

Pan, Y., Froese, F., Liu, N., Hu, Y., & Ye, M. (2021). The adoption of artificial intelligence in employee recruitment: The influence of contextual factors. *International Journal of Human Resource Management*, 1–23. DOI: 10.1080/09585192.2021.1879206

Pappas, I. O., & Giannakos, M. N. (2021, April). Rethinking learning design in IT education during a pandemic. *Frontiers in Education*, 6, 652856. DOI: 10.3389/feduc.2021.652856

Partarakis, N., & Zabulis, X. (2024). A Review of Immersive Technologies, Knowledge Representation, and AI for Human-Centered Digital Experiences. *Electronics (Basel)*, 13(2), 269. DOI: 10.3390/electronics13020269

Patell, H., & Jha, D. (2023). Evolution and trends in artificial intelligence applications in supply chain management: A comprehensive review. *International Journal of Operations & Production Management*, 43(5), 1079–1109.

Petiwala, F. F., Shukla, V. K., & Vyas, S. (2021). IBM watson: redefining artificial intelligence through cognitive computing. In *Proceedings of International Conference on Machine Intelligence and Data Science Applications: MIDAS 2020* (pp. 173-185). Springer Singapore. DOI: 10.1007/978-981-33-4087-9_15

Pieroni, M. P., McAloone, T. C., & Pigosso, D. C. (2019). Business model innovation for circular economy and sustainability: A review of approaches. *Journal of Cleaner Production*, 215, 198–216. DOI: 10.1016/j.jclepro.2019.01.036

Pillai, R., & Sivathanu, B. (2020). Adoption of artificial intelligence (AI) for talent acquisition in IT/ITeS organizations. *Benchmarking*, 27(9), 2599–2629. DOI: 10.1108/BIJ-04-2020-0186

Pinski, M., Hofmann, T., & Benlian, A. (2024). AI Literacy for the top management: An upper echelons perspective on corporate AI orientation and implementation ability. *Electronic Markets*, 34(1), 24. DOI: 10.1007/s12525-024-00707-1

Plantinga, P. (2024). Digital discretion and public administration in Africa: Implications for the use of artificial intelligence. *Information Development*, 40(2), 332–352. DOI: 10.1177/02666669221117526

Pompa, D. (2015). Prepared Statement.

Pranciulyte-Bagdziūniene, A., & Petraite, M. (2019). Developing Industry 4.0 skills in the workforce: Insights from Lithuanian case studies. *Management of Sustainable Development*, 11(1), 17–22. DOI: 10.2478/msd-2019-0003

Prifti, L., Knigge, M., Kienegger, H., & Krcmar, H. (2017). A competency model for "Industrie 4.0" employees. *Business & Information Systems Engineering*, 59(4), 219–229. DOI: 10.1007/s12599-017-0484-6

Priya, E. (2023). The impact of technology on cinematic storytelling. *Global Media Journal*, 21, 66. https://www.globalmediajournal.com/open-access/the-impact-of-technology-on-cinematic-storytelling.php?aid=94036

Provén, C., & Skoglund, N. (2023). *The Role Of Value Creation In Sustainable Product Service System Implementation: A Case Study On Lynk & Co's Subscription Model.*

Pucci, T., Casprini, E., Galati, A., & Zanni, L. (2020). The virtuous cycle of stakeholder engagement in developing a sustainability culture: Salcheto winery. *Journal of Business Research*, 119, 364–376. DOI: 10.1016/j.jbusres.2018.11.009

Qu, S., Shi, H., Zhao, H., Yu, L., & Yu, Y. (2021). Research on enterprise business model and technology innovation based on artificial intelligence. EURASIP Journal on Wireless Communications and Networking, 2021(1). DOI: 10.1186/s13638-021-02025-y

Rakova, B., Yang, J., Cramer, H., & Chowdhury, R. (2021). Where responsible AI meets reality: Practitioner perspectives on enablers for shifting organizational practices. Proceedings of the ACM on Human-Computer Interaction, 5(CSCW1), 1–23.

Ramakrishnan, T., Mohan Gift, M. D., Chitradevi, S., Jegan, R., & Subha Hency Jose, P. (2022). Study of Numerous Resins Used in Polymer Matrix Composite Materials. Advances in Materials Science and Engineering. DOI: 10.1155/2022/1088926

Ramírez, J. G. C. (2023). Incorporating Information Architecture (IA), Enterprise Engineering (EE) and Artificial Intelligence (AI) to Improve Business Plans for Small Businesses in the United States. *Journal of Knowledge Learning and Science Technology* ISSN: 2959-6386 (online), 2(1), 115-127.

Ramsbotham, G. (2024). Artificial Intelligence Global Executive Study and Research Report.

Rana, N., & Sharma, P. (2019). Assessing HR challenges in Industry 4.0: Workforce transformations. *Asia Pacific Journal of Human Resources*, 57(2), 138–154. DOI: 10.1111/1744-7941.12226

Rane, N., Choudhary, S., & Rane, J. (2023). Metaverse marketing strategies: Enhancing customer experience and analysing consumer behaviour through leading-edge metaverse technologies, platforms, and models. *SSRN*. DOI: 10.2139/ssrn.4624199

Ransbotham, S., Kiron, D., Gerbert, P., & Reeves, M. (2020). Artificial intelligence in business gets real. MIT Sloan Management Review. https://sloanreview.mit.edu/article/artificial-intelligence-in-business-gets-real/

Ransbotham, S., Kiron, D., Gerbert, P., & Reeves, M. (2017). Reshaping business with artificial intelligence: Closing the gap between ambition and action. *MIT Sloan Management Review*, 59(1), 1–17.

Rao, D. A. S., & Verweij, G. (2017). *Sizing the Prize: What's the Real Value of AI for Your Business and How Can You Capitalise?* PwC Publication.

Rathnayake, D. M., & Roca, T. (2022). The emergence of technopreneurship for sustainable and ethical economic growth: Theory, research and practice. In *Integrated business models in the digital age: Principles and practices of technology empowered strategies* (pp. 467–535). Springer International Publishing. DOI: 10.1007/978-3-030-97877-8_13

Rauschnabel, P. A., Felix, R., Hinsch, C., Shahab, H., & Alt, F. (2022). What is XR? Towards a framework for Augmented and Virtual reality. *Computers in Human Behavior*, 133, 107289. DOI: 10.1016/j.chb.2022.107289

Reer, F., Wehden, L., Janzik, R., Tang, W. Y., & Quandt, T. (2022). Virtual reality technology and game enjoyment: The contributions of natural mapping and need satisfaction. *Computers in Human Behavior*, 132, 107242. DOI: 10.1016/j.chb.2022.107242

Reficco, E., Gutiérrez, R., Jaén, M. H., & Auletta, N. (2018). Collaboration mechanisms for sustainable innovation. *Journal of Cleaner Production*, 203, 1170–1186. DOI: 10.1016/j.jclepro.2018.08.043

Reim, W., Åström, J., & Eriksson, O. (2020). Implementation of artificial intelligence (AI): A roadmap for business model innovation. *AI*, 1(2), 11. DOI: 10.3390/ai1020011

Reis, I. F., Gonçalves, I., Lopes, M. A., & Antunes, C. H. (2021). Business models for energy communities: A review of key issues and trends. *Renewable & Sustainable Energy Reviews*, 144, 111013. DOI: 10.1016/j.rser.2021.111013

Repo, P., & Matschoss, K. (2019). Social innovation for sustainability challenges. *Sustainability (Basel)*, 12(1), 319. DOI: 10.3390/su12010319

Rock, D. (2019). Engineering value: The returns to technological talent and investments in artificial intelligence. *SSRN* 3427412. DOI: 10.2139/ssrn.3427412

Rogers, E.M. (2003), *The Diffusion of Innovations* (5th ed.) Free Press.

Rogers, E. M. (1995). *Diffusion of Innovations* (4th ed.). The Free Press.

Rosenberg, L. B. (2022). Augmented reality: Reflections at thirty years. In: Arai, K. (eds) *Proceedings of the Future Technologies Conference* (FTC) 2021, Volume 1. FTC 2021. Lecture Notes in Networks and Systems, 358. Springer, Cham. DOI: 10.1007/978-3-030-89906-6_1

Ross, J. W., Beath, C. M., & Goodhue, D. L. (1996). Develop long-term competitiveness through IT assets. *Sloan Management Review*, 38(1), 31–42.

Russell, S. J., & Norvig, P. (2016). *Artificial Intelligence: A Modern Approach.* Pearson Education.

Sala, N. (2021). Virtual Reality, Augmented Reality, and Mixed Reality in Education: A Brief Overview. In Choi, D., Dailey-Hebert, A., & Estes, J. (Eds.), *Current and Prospective Applications of Virtual Reality in Higher Education* (pp. 48–73). IGI Global. DOI: 10.4018/978-1-7998-4960-5.ch003

Sampson, G., Wills, M., & Brown, A. (2020). Clarifying expectations and training for AI integration. *Human Resource Development Quarterly*, 31(2), 151–165. DOI: 10.1002/hrdq.21385

Sanchez-Planelles, J., Segarra-Oña, M., & Peiro-Signes, A. (2022). Identifying different sustainable practices to help companies to contribute to the sustainable development: Holistic sustainability, sustainable business and operations models. *Corporate Social Responsibility and Environmental Management*, 29(4), 904–917. DOI: 10.1002/csr.2243

Sanders, D. H. (1997). Virtual worlds for archaeological research and education. *Archaeology in the Age of the Internet: Proceedings of the 25th Anniversary Conference of CAA*, Birmingham, April 1997. https://publikationen.uni-tuebingen.de/xmlui/bitstream/handle/10900/62120/CD31_Sanders_CAA_1997.pdf?isAllowed=y&sequence=2

Sarakatsanos, O., Papazoglou-Chalikias, A., Boikou, M., Chatzilari, E., Jauk, M., Hafliger, V., Nikolopoulos, S., & Kompatsiaris, I. C. (2024). VR designer: Enhancing fashion showcases through immersive virtual garment fitting. *Virtual Reality (Waltham Cross)*, 28(2), 70. DOI: 10.1007/s10055-024-00945-w

Schuh, G., Frank, J., Jussen, P., Rix, C., & Harland, T. (2019, June). Monetizing industry 4.0: Design principles for subscription business in the manufacturing industry. In *2019 IEEE international conference on engineering, technology and innovation (ICE/ITMC)* (pp. 1-9). IEEE.

Shakeel, J., Mardani, A., Chofreh, A. G., Goni, F. A., & Klemeš, J. J. (2020). Anatomy of sustainable business model innovation. *Journal of Cleaner Production*, 261, 121201. DOI: 10.1016/j.jclepro.2020.121201

Sharma, M., & Biros, D. (2021). AI and its implications for organisations. In Lee, Z. W. Y., Chan, T. K. H., & Cheung, C. M. K. (Eds.), *Information Technology in Organisations and Societies: Multidisciplinary Perspectives from AI to Technostress* (pp. 1–24). Emerald Publishing.

Sheikh, S. (Ed.). (2020). *Understanding the role of artificial intelligence and its future social impact*. IGI Global.

Shen, A. (2014). Recommendations as personalized marketing: Insights from customer experiences. *Journal of Services Marketing*, 28(5), 414–427. DOI: 10.1108/JSM-04-2013-0083

Shinde, Y. (2024, March 7). Immersive media market to achieve staggering USD 178.7 Bn by 2032. *Asia-Pacific Market News*. https://scoop.market.us/immersive-media-market-news/

Shokeen, J., & Rana, C. (2020). A study on features of social recommender systems. *Artificial Intelligence Review*, 53(2), 965–988. DOI: 10.1007/s10462-019-09684-w

Sicart, M. (2017). Reality has always been augmented: Play and the promises of Pokémon GO. *Mobile Media & Communication*, 5(1), 30–33. DOI: 10.1177/2050157916677863

Siddiquee, M. S. A. (2024). Augmented Reality (AR) and Virtual Reality (VR): Transforming gaming, education, and enterprise. *Medium.*https://medium.com/@msa.sid/augmented-reality-ar-and-virtual-reality-vr-transforming-gaming-education-and-enterprise-28888ced035c

Sivathanu, B., & Pillai, R. (2018). Smart manufacturing and Industry 4.0: Implications for older workers. *Ageing International*, 43(3), 391–405. DOI: 10.1007/s12126-018-9323-2

Sjödin, D., Parida, V., & Kohtamäki, M. (2023). Artificial intelligence enabling circular business model innovation in digital servitization: Conceptualizing dynamic capabilities, AI capacities, business models and effects. *Technological Forecasting and Social Change*, 197, 122903. DOI: 10.1016/j.techfore.2023.122903

Sodiya, E. O., Umoga, U. J., Amoo, O. O., & Atadoga, A. (2024). AI-driven warehouse automation: A comprehensive review of systems. *GSC Advanced Research and Reviews*, 18(2), 272–282. DOI: 10.30574/gscarr.2024.18.2.0063

Soliman, M. M., Ahmed, E., Darwish, A., & Hassanien, A. E. (2024). Artificial intelligence powered Metaverse: Analysis, challenges and future perspectives. *Artificial Intelligence Review*, 57(2), 36. DOI: 10.1007/s10462-023-10641-x

Soni, N., Sharma, E. K., Singh, N., & Kapoor, A. (2019). *Impact of artificial intelligence on businesses: from research, innovation, market deployment to future shifts in business models.* arXiv preprint arXiv:1905.02092.

Sorko, M., Nguyen, T., & Fung, C. (2016). Augmented workforce dynamics in Industry 4.0: Leveraging AI for human augmentation. *Journal of Organizational Computing and Electronic Commerce*, 26(2), 171–192. DOI: 10.1080/10919392.2016.1157543

Spence, C. (2022). The human factor in automation and augmentation: A future skills perspective. *Technovation*, 120, 102544. DOI: 10.1016/j.technovation.2021.102544

Sreenivasulu, A., & Manimozhi, T. (2022). The Model of Smart Sensing Device For Sensitive Nanoclusters Modification in Sensing Properties. 2022 2nd International Conference on Advance Computing and Innovative Technologies in Engineering (ICACITE), 1043-1047. DOI: 10.1109/ICACITE53722.2022.9823846

Steck, H., Baltrunas, L., Elahi, E., Liang, D., Raimond, Y., & Basilico, J. (2021). Deep learning for recommender systems: A Netflix case study. *AI Magazine*, 42(3), 7–18. DOI: 10.1609/aimag.v42i3.18140

Steffen, J. H., Gaskin, J. E., Meservy, T. O., Jenkins, J. L., & Wolman, I. (2019). Framework of affordances for Virtual Reality and Augmented Reality. *Journal of Management Information Systems*, 36(3), 683–729. DOI: 10.1080/07421222.2019.1628877

Sugumaran, K. M. D., Pandiyarajan V., Y. B S, Selvakumar, P., & M. S, (2024). Analysis of Electromyography Signals for Control of Mechanical Prosthesis using Machine Learning Techniques. 2024 2nd International Conference on Intelligent Data Communication Technologies and Internet of Things (IDCIoT), 1059-1067. DOI: 10.1109/IDCIoT59759.2024.10467707

Sullivan, Y., & Wamba, S. F. (2024). Artificial intelligence and adaptive response to market changes: A strategy to enhance firm performance and innovation. *Journal of Business Research*, 174, 114500. DOI: 10.1016/j.jbusres.2024.114500

Sundaresan, S., & Zhang, X. (2022). Understanding the human factors in human-AI collaboration: A meta-analytic approach. *Computers in Human Behavior*, 133, 107266. DOI: 10.1016/j.chb.2022.107266

Suresh, N. V., Selvakumar, A., Sridhar, G., & Catherine, S. (2024). Operational Efficiency and Cost Reduction: The Role of AI in Healthcare Administration. In *Revolutionizing the Healthcare Sector with AI* (pp. 262-272). IGI Global.

Szabo-Szentgróti, G., Fekete, P., & Bányai, T. (2021). Labor transformation in AI-driven organizations: A European perspective. *European Management Review*, 18(4), 585–602. DOI: 10.1111/emre.12429

Tambe, P., Cappelli, P., & Yakubovich, V. (2019). Artificial intelligence in human resources management: Challenges and a path forward. *California Management Review*, 61(4), 15–42. DOI: 10.1177/0008125619867910

Tang, X., Li, X., Ding, Y., Song, M., & Bu, Y. (2020). The pace of artificial intelligence innovations: Speed, talent, and trial-and-error. *Journal of Informetrics*, 14(4), 101094. DOI: 10.1016/j.joi.2020.101094

Tang, Y. M., Chau, K. Y., Kwok, A. P. K., Zhu, T., & Ma, X. (2022). A systematic review of immersive technology applications for medical practice and education - Trends, application areas, recipients, teaching contents, evaluation methods, and performance. *Educational Research Review*, 35, 100429. DOI: 10.1016/j.edurev.2021.100429

Tang, Y., Au, K., & Leung, Y. (2018). Comprehending products with mixed reality: Geometric relationships and creativity. *International Journal of Engineering Business Management*, 10, 1847979018809599. Advance online publication. DOI: 10.1177/1847979018809599

Tan, Y.-C., Chandukala, S. R., & Reddy, S. K. (2022). Augmented reality in retail and its impact on sales. *Journal of Marketing*, 86(1), 48–66. DOI: 10.1177/0022242921995449

Tata consultancy services (2017), *TCS global trend study on artificial intelligence reveals industry wide investment by 2020*. www.tcs.com/global-trend-study-artificial-intelligence-revealsindustry-wide-investment-2020

Tavoletti, E., Kazemargi, N., Cerruti, C., Grieco, C., & Appolloni, A. (2022). Business model innovation and digital transformation in global management consulting firms. *European Journal of Innovation Management*, 25(6), 612–636. DOI: 10.1108/EJIM-11-2020-0443

Teece, D. J. (2018). Profiting from innovation in the digital economy: Standards, complementary assets, and business models in the wireless world. *Research Policy*, 47, 1367–1387. DOI: 10.1016/j.respol.2017.01.015

Teece, D. J. (2023). Big tech and strategic management: How management scholars can inform competition policy. *The Academy of Management Perspectives*, 37(1), 1–15. DOI: 10.5465/amp.2022.0013

Tegmark, M. (2017). *Life 3.0: Being human in the age of artificial intelligence*. Knopf.

Teo, T., Lawrence, L., Lee, G. A., Billinghurst, M., & Adcock, M. (2019). Mixed Reality remote collaboration combining 360 video and 3D reconstruction. *CHI '19:Proceedings of the 2019 CHI Conference on Human Factors in Computing Systems*, 1–14. DOI: 10.1145/3290605.3300431

Thaichon, P., Quach, S., Barari, M., & Nguyen, M. (2023). Exploring the role of omnichannel retailing technologies: Future research directions. *Australasian Marketing Journal*, 0(0). Advance online publication. DOI: 10.1177/14413582231167664

Thies, C. G., & Wehner, L. E. (2019). The role of role theory in international political economy. *Cambridge Review of International Affairs*, 32(6), 712–733. DOI: 10.1080/09557571.2019.1609415

Tidy, J. (2020, April 24). Fortnite's Travis Scott virtual concert watched by millions. *BBC News*. https://www.bbc.com/news/technology-52410647

Tisler, M. (2024). *The fascinating evolution of virtual reality history*. https://myriamtisler.com/virtual-reality-history

Tubis, A. A., Jodejko-Pietruczuk, A., & Nowakowski, T. (2024). Use of Augmented Reality as a tool to support cargo handling operations at the CARGO air terminal. *Sensors (Basel)*, 24(4), 1099. DOI: 10.3390/s24041099 PMID: 38400257

Turner, J. (2022). Myron Krueger live. *Ctheory.Net: Journal of Theory, Technology and Culture*. https://journals.uvic.ca/index.php/ctheory/article/view/14583/5428

Usman, F. O., Eyo-Udo, N. L., Etukudoh, E. A., Odonkor, B., Ibeh, C. V., & Adegbola, A. (2024). A critical review of ai-driven strategies for entrepreneurial success. *International Journal of Management & Entrepreneurship Research*, 6(1), 200–215. DOI: 10.51594/ijmer.v6i1.748

Ustundag, A., & Cevikcan, E. (2018). *Industry 4.0: Managing the digital transformation*. Springer. DOI: 10.1007/978-3-319-57870-5

Valter, P., Lindgren, P., & Prasad, R. (2018). Advanced Business Model Innovation Supported by Artificial Intelligence and Deep Learning. *Wireless Personal Communications*, 100(1), 97–111. DOI: 10.1007/s11277-018-5612-x

van-Esch, P., Black, J. S., & Ferolie, J. (2019). Marketing AI recruitment: The next phase in job application and selection. *Computers in Human Behavior*, 90(1), 215–222. DOI: 10.1016/j.chb.2018.09.009

Varadarajan, R. (2017). Innovating for sustainability: A framework for sustainable innovations and a model of sustainable innovations orientation. *Journal of the Academy of Marketing Science*, 45(1), 14–36. DOI: 10.1007/s11747-015-0461-6

Vassilakopoulou, P., Haug, A., Salvesen, L. M., & Pappas, O. I. (2022). Developing human/AI interactions for chat-based customer services: Lessons learned from the norwegian government. *European Journal of Information Systems*, 1–13. DOI: 10.1080/0960085X.2022.2096490

Venkatesan, M., Mohan, H., Ryan, J. R., Schürch, C. M., Nolan, G. P., Frakes, D. H., & Coskun, A. F. (2021). Virtual and augmented reality for biomedical applications. *Cell Reports Medicine*, 2(7), 100348. DOI: 10.1016/j.xcrm.2021.100348 PMID: 34337564

Verganti, R., Vendraminelli, L., & Iansiti, M. (2020). Innovation and design in the age of artificial intelligence. *Journal of Product Innovation Management*, 37(3), 212–227. DOI: 10.1111/jpim.12523

Veza, I., Mladineo, M., & Potočan, V. (2015). Digital transformation of production systems in value chains. *Management*, 20(2), 25–40.

Vijayakumar, G., Rajkumar, M., Rajiv Chandar, N., Selvakumar, P., & Duraisamy, R. (2024). Environmentally friendly TDS removal from waste water by electrochemical ion exchange batch-type recirculation (EIR) technique. *Environmental Science. Water Research & Technology*, 10(4), 826–835. DOI: 10.1039/D3EW00793F

Villarroel, J. A., Taylor, J. E., & Tucci, C. L. (2013). Innovation and learning performance implications of free revealing and knowledge brokering in competing communities: Insights from the Netflix Prize challenge. *Computational & Mathematical Organization Theory*, 19(1), 42–77. DOI: 10.1007/s10588-012-9137-7

Villegas-Ch, W., Amores-Falconi, R., & Coronel-Silva, E. (2023). Design proposal for a virtual shopping assistant for people with vision problems applying Artificial Intelligence techniques. *Big Data and Cognitive Computing*, 7(2), 96. DOI: 10.3390/bdcc7020096

Vinolo, G. M., Gonzalez-Medina, G., Lucena-Anton, D., Perez-Cabezas, V., Ruiz-Molinero, M. D. C., & Martín-Valero, R. (2021). Augmented Reality in physical therapy: Systematic review and meta-analysis. *JMIR Serious Games*, 9(4), e30985. DOI: 10.2196/30985 PMID: 34914611

Vocke, C., Constantinescu, C., & Popescu, D. (2019). Application potentials of artificial intelligence for the design of innovation processes. *Procedia CIRP*, 84, 810–813. DOI: 10.1016/j.procir.2019.04.230

Vrontis, D., Bresciani, S., & Giacosa, E. (2022). Transforming business models through Industry 4.0 technologies. *Journal of Business Research*, 140, 88–99. DOI: 10.1016/j.jbusres.2022.07.031

Vyas, V., Sharma, A., Goyal, S., & Kothari, N. (2021). Infrared vein visualization devices for ease of intravenous access in children: Hope versus hype. *Anaesthesiology Intensive Therapy*, 53(1), 69–78. DOI: 10.5114/ait.2021.103515 PMID: 33586417

Wakweya, D. K., Kero, C. A., & Bali, N. (2024). Market Orientation and Manufacturing Firm's Performance. [HAJBE]. *Horn of African Journal of Business and Economics*, 7(1), 97–120.

Wamba, S. F., Bawack, R. E., Guthrie, C., Queiroz, M. M., & Carillo, K. D. A. (2021). Are we preparing for a good AI society? A bibliometric review and research agenda. *Technological Forecasting and Social Change*, 164, 120482. DOI: 10.1016/j.techfore.2020.120482

Wamba, S. F., Gunasekaran, A., Akter, S., Ren, S. J. F., Dubey, R., & Childe, S. J. (2017). Big data analytics and firm performance: Effects of dynamic capabilities. *Journal of Business Research*, 70(1), 356–365. DOI: 10.1016/j.jbusres.2016.08.009

Wamba-Taguimdje, S. L., Fosso Wamba, S., Kala Kamdjoug, J. R., & Tchatchouang Wanko, C. E. (2020). Influence of artificial intelligence (AI) on firm performance: The business value of AI-based transformation projects. *Business Process Management Journal*, 26(7), 1893–1924. DOI: 10.1108/BPMJ-10-2019-0411

Wang, S., Li, Q., & Khaskheli, M. B. (2024). Management Economic Systems and Governance to Reduce Potential Risks in Digital Silk Road Investments: Legal Cooperation between Hainan Free Trade Port and Ethiopia. *Systems*, 12(8), 305. DOI: 10.3390/systems12080305

Weber, R. (2016). Automation and digital transformation: The paradox of the fourth industrial revolution. *Journal of Manufacturing Systems*, 39, 229–238. DOI: 10.1016/j.jmsy.2016.08.011

West, D. M. (2018). *The future of work: Robots, AI, and automation*. Brookings Institution Press.

Wheeler, A. R., & Buckley, M. R. (2021). The current and future states of automation, artificial intelligence, and machine learning. In *HR without People? (The Future of Work)* (pp. 29–44). Emerald Publishing. DOI: 10.1108/978-1-80117-037-620211003

Widayanti, R., & Meria, L. (2023). Business Modeling Innovation Using Artificial Intelligence Technology. *International Transactions on Education Technology*, 2, 95–104.

Williams, R. M., Alikhademi, K., Drobina, E., Gilbert, J. E., & Sutor, T. (2019). Augmented Reality for rehabilitative therapy: Patient experiences and practitioner perspectives. *Proceedings of the Human Factors and Ergonomics Society Annual Meeting*, 63(1), 748–752. DOI: 10.1177/1071181319631140

Wilson, H. J., & Daugherty, P. R. (2018). Collaborative intelligence: Humans and AI are joining forces. Harvard Business Review. https://hbr.org/2018/07/collaborative-intelligence-humans-and-ai-are-joining-forces

Wilson, H. J., & Daugherty, P. R. (2018). Collaborative intelligence: Humans and AI are joining forces. *Harvard Business Review*, 96(4), 114–123.

Winter, J. (2021a). Digital Business Model Innovation: Empirical insights into the drivers and value of Artificial Intelligence. *International Journal of Computers and Technology*, 21, 63–75. DOI: 10.24297/ijct.v21i.9035

Woodcock, J., & Johnson, M. R. (2019). Live streamers on Twitch.tv as social media influencers: Chances and challenges for strategic communication. *International Journal of Strategic Communication*, 13(4), 321–335. DOI: 10.1080/1553118X.2019.1630412

Wörsdörfer, M. (2023). The EU's artificial intelligence act: An ordoliberal assessment. *AI and Ethics*, 1–16.

Yanamala, A. K. Y., & Suryadevara, S. (2023). Advances in Data Protection and Artificial Intelligence: Trends and Challenges. *International Journal of Advanced Engineering Technologies and Innovations*, 1(01), 294–319.

Yáñez-Valdés, C., Guerrero, M., Barros-Celume, S., & Ibáñez, M. J. (2023). Winds of change due to global lockdowns: Refreshing digital social entrepreneurship research paradigm. *Technological Forecasting and Social Change*, 190, 122454. DOI: 10.1016/j.techfore.2023.122454

Yang, Z., Kankanhalli, A., Ng, B. Y., & Lim, J. T. Y. (2013). Analyzing the enabling factors for the organizational decision to adopt healthcare information systems. *Decision Support Systems*, 55(3), 764–776. DOI: 10.1016/j.dss.2013.03.002

Yaseen, A. (2022). Accelerating The Soc: Achieve Greater Efficiency With Ai-Driven Automation. *International Journal of Responsible Artificial Intelligence*, 12(1), 1–19.

Yates, B. T., & Marra, M. (2017). Social Return On Investment (SROI): Problems, solutions… and is SROI a good investment? *Evaluation and Program Planning*, 64, 136–144. DOI: 10.1016/j.evalprogplan.2016.11.009 PMID: 27979379

Yathiraju, N. (2022). Investigating the use of an artificial intelligence model in an ERP cloud-based system. International Journal of Electrical. *Electronics and Computers*, 7(2), 1–26.

Yu, C. (2023). AI Revolution: Reshaping Global Value Chains for the Future. *Center for Open Science*.https://osf. io/n6hb2/download

Yun, J. J., Zhao, X., Jung, K., & Yigitcanlar, T. (2020). The culture for open innovation dynamics. *Sustainability (Basel)*, 12(12), 5076. DOI: 10.3390/su12125076

Zamani, E. D., & Pouloudi, N. (2020). Generative mechanisms of Workarounds, Discontinuance and Reframing: A study of negative disconfirmation with consumerised IT. *Information Systems Journal*, 31(3), 384–428. DOI: 10.1111/isj.12315

Zhang, W., Shi, J., Wang, X., & Wynn, H. (2023). AI-powered decision-making in facilitating insurance claim dispute resolution. *Annals of Operations Research*, 1–30. DOI: 10.1007/s10479-023-05631-9 PMID: 37361057

Zhang, X., Guo, X., Yue, W. T., & Yu, Y. (2022). Servitization for the environment? The impact of data-centric product-service models. *Journal of Management Information Systems*, 39(4), 1146–1183. DOI: 10.1080/07421222.2022.2127454

Zhu, K., Kraemer, K., Xu, S., & Dedrick, J. (2004). Information technology payoffs in e-business environment: An international perspective on value creation of e-business in the financial services industry. *Journal of Management Information Systems*, 21(1), 17–54. DOI: 10.1080/07421222.2004.11045797

Zollmann, S., Langlotz, T., Loos, M., Lo, W. H., & Baker, L. (2019). AR spectator: Exploring Augmented Reality for sport events. *SIGGRAPH Asia 2019 Technical Briefs (SA '19)* (pp. 75–78). Association for Computing Machinery. DOI: 10.1145/3355088.3365162

About the Contributors

Maryam Khokhar is a dynamic researcher, academic, and innovator dedicated to advancing knowledge and solving real-world problems with a strong background in Management Science & Economics of Supply chain, Corporate Social Responsibility, & marketing. Maryam Khokhar has consistently demonstrated a passion for interdisciplinary collaboration and a commitment to excellence in research. They were born and raised in Sindh, Pakistan. Maryam Khokhar exhibited an early curiosity for Management Science & Economics. This passion led them to pursue higher education in Management Science & Economics. They earned their PhD from Yanshan University, China. Presently, Dr. Maryam Khokhar is a postdoctoral researcher at the School of Economics and Management, Tongji University, Shanghai, China. She has also worked as a Senior Assistant Professor at Bahria University Karachi, Pakistan, Assistant Professor at the Sir Syed University of Engineering and Technology. She has also worked with ranked universities in Pakistan, such as the University of Sindh Jamshoro, as Assistant Professor and Federal Urdu University of Arts, Science & Technology.

* * *

Sudhanshu Chandra is Assistant Professor (Academic Coordinator) at Manuu Law School, Maulana Azad National Urdu University Hyderabad A Central University Established by an Act of Parliament in 1988, Accredited with Grade A+ by NACC, (Hyderabad Telangana) -500032. He Completed his B.A.LLB (Hons)-Dr. Ram Manohar Lohiya National Law University Lucknow (U.P) LLM-National Law University Jodhpur (Rajasthan), Cleared UGC-NET, Ph.D. in Law from Gautam Buddha University Greater Noida (U.P.).

Parihar Suresh Dahake is working as an Assistant Professor at School of Management, Ramdeobaba University, Nagpur. He received his BTech, MBA, and

Ph.D. from the Rashtrasant Tukdoji Maharaj Nagpur University and PGDIBO, M.Com from Indira Gandhi National Open University (IGNOU). Dr. Parihar Dahake has Qualified SET(Commerce) and SET (Management). He has 14 Years of Teaching Experience and 13 years of Research Experience. His areas of expertise are Consumer behavior, Organizational Behaviour, Marketing Management, and IMC.

Vishal Jain is presently working as Professor at the Department of Computer Science and Engineering, School of Engineering and Technology, Sharda University, Greater Noida, India. Before that, he worked for several years as an Associate Professor at Bharati Vidyapeeth's Institute of Computer Applications and Management (BVICAM), New Delhi. He has more than 18 years of experience in the academics. He has earned degrees: Ph.D (CSE), M.Tech (CSE), MBA (HR), MCA, MCP, and CCNA. He has more than 2200 research citations with Google Scholar (h-index score 24 and i-10 index 55) and has authored more than 150 research papers in professional journals and conferences. He has authored and edited more than 60 books (most of them are indexed at the Scopus) with various reputed publishers, including Elsevier, Springer, IET, Apple Academic Press, CRC, Taylor and Francis Group, Scrivener, Wiley, Emerald, NOVA Science, River Publishers, IGI-Global and Bentham Science. He has more than 200 Scopus publications. His research areas include machine learning, information retrieval, semantic web, ontology engineering, data mining, ad hoc networks, sensor networks and network security.

Manjit Kour is working as Professor at University Business School at Chandigarh University. She holds a PhD in Business Management from IK Gujral Punjab Technical University, India. She has a good research record with several research papers published in reputed journals. She is an editorial board member and reviewer of many reputed journals including Scopus and ABDC-indexed journals. Her areas of interest include sustainability, green practices, Fintech, online marketing trends and business ethics.

Shanthi M. is an experienced academician in the Department of Economics at Avinashilingam Institute for Home Science and Higher Education for Women, Coimbatore, Tamil Nadu. With over 10 years of teaching and research experience, Dr. Shanthi specializes in Development Economics. Her research and academic contributions focus on the economic aspects of development, particularly how economic policies and strategies can foster growth and improve living standards. Driven by a passion for advancing knowledge in the field, she continues to make valuable contributions to both the academic community and society at large.

T. C. Manjunath is a distinguished professor in the Department of Computer Science & Engineering at Rajarajeswari College of Engineering, Bangalore, specializing in IoT Cybersecurity and Blockchain Technology. He serves as the Dean of Research (R&D) at the college, leading initiatives in technological innovation and academic research. With extensive expertise in cutting-edge technologies, Dr. Manjunath plays a crucial role in advancing the college's research agenda and fostering an academic excellence. His contributions to the field and the institution have made him a key figure in the academic and research community at Rajarajeswari College of Engineering.

Mohit is a research scholar at the Institute of Management Studies and Research, Maharshi Dayanand University, Rohtak, Haryana, India. His research focuses on the dynamic relationship between brand image and purchase intentions, particularly in the context of brand extensions within the FMCG sector. Mohit actively engages in bibliometric research, analyzing publication trends and identifying research gaps in his area of interest. He has co-authored several scholarly works and continues to contribute to the academic community.

Tunde Toyese Oyedokun is the Ag. University Librarian at Thomas Adewumi University in Oko-Irese, Kwara State, Nigeria. He is an academic researcher and writer, focusing on the intersection of emerging technologies and library services. His work spans topics such as AI integration in small businesses within Industry 5.0, immersive technologies in education, and the future of academic libraries. Oyedokun is committed to exploring the transformative potential of technologies like AI and mixed reality to foster inclusive learning environments and advance digital libraries.

Selvakumar P. is currently an Associate Professor in the Department of Science and Humanities at Nehru Institute of Technology, Coimbatore, Tamil Nadu, India. Since 2023, he has served as the Department IQAC Coordinator at the institute. Prior to joining Nehru Institute of Technology, he held positions as an Assistant Professor in the Department of Science and Humanities various engineering colleges in Coimbatore, Tamil Nadu, India, spanning from 2011 to 2023. Dr.P. Selvakumar's academic and research interests lie primarily in the field of phytochemistry. He has made significant contributions to his field, with an impressive record that includes 30 journal publications, 12 patents, and 20 conference papers. Additionally, he has organized 5 seminars and conferences, further demonstrating his commitment to academic and scientific exchange. Throughout his career, Dr. P.Selvakumar has been recognized for his dedication and excellence in teaching, having been honored with several awards, including the Best Teacher Awards. He holds a prominent position in the academic community, contributing actively to research.

Repudi Pitchiah is a dedicated professional in the Department of Computer Science and Engineering at Koneru Lakshmaiah Education Foundation, Vijayawada,

Andhra Pradesh. With a strong commitment to advancing knowledge and innovation in the field of computer science, he actively contributes to the academic environment at the institution. His expertise and contributions support the growth and development of students and the department. Koneru Lakshmaiah Education Foundation, located in Vijayawada, serves as a hub for technological education and research in the region.

Nandhini R. is the Deputy Director of the Centre for Distance and Online Education (CDOE) at AMET Deemed to be University, located in Chennai, Tamil Nadu. She is a dedicated academic professional with a strong background in higher education and distance learning. Dr. Nandhini plays a pivotal role in overseeing the operations and strategic direction of the CDOE, contributing significantly to the university's mission to provide quality education through flexible learning methods. Based in Chennai, Tamil Nadu, her work focuses on enhancing educational accessibility and promoting academic excellence in the field of distance education.

Prateek Srivastava is an assistant professor at the Department of Information Technology, School of Engineering and Technology (UIET), CSJM University, Kanpur, India. He is pursuing his PhD degree in information technology from AIIT, Amity University Uttar Pradesh, Lucknow Campus, India. He has more than ten years of vast teaching and learning experience. His area of research includes software engineering, cloud computing, machine learning, and computer programming.

Richa Tiwari is currently working as Assistant Professor in Centre for Management Studies, Jain Deemed-to-be University, Bengaluru (IN). Her research areas include work culture, organizational productivity, and employee engagement. Prior to the role, she worked as Academic Associate at the Indian Institute of Management, Ahmedabad in the Human Resource Area and alongwith a rich corporate experience in diverse roles of assistant manager human resources, public relations and editorials. She is an FDP alumnus of Indian Institute of Management, Ahmedabad and MBA from Devi Ahilya University, Indore. She holds certification in Industrial Relations and Personnel Management and other certifications in management areas from institutes like Academy of Management, USA, IIM Ahmedabad, IIM Indore, NIIT, INDAM to name a few. Her research work has appeared in multiple international ABDC indexed & Peer-reviewed journals. She also presented her work in conferences across the management world for events of IITs, IIMs, EDII, INDAM, AOM and others. Dr. Richa has also been invited for a series of lectures on transformational leadership, Research Analytics and others.

Index

A

B

C

D

E

F

I

www.ingramcontent.com/pod-product-compliance
Lightning Source LLC
LaVergne TN
LVHW081336300926
849161LV00008B/1987